FORTRESS

A Two-Volume
Beginner's Guide to Lawful
Avoidance of and Protection from
State and Federal Income Taxation

MP, LLC, Ed.

Order this book online at www.trafford.com
or email orders@trafford.com

Most Trafford titles are also available at major online book retailers.

Printed in the United States of America.

ISBN: 978-1-4669-5176-1 (sc)
ISBN: 978-1-4669-5175-4 (e)

Trafford rev. 09/25/2012

www.trafford.com

North America & international
toll-free: 1 888 232 4444 (USA & Canada)
phone: 250 383 6864 ♦ fax: 812 355 4082

Notice

TAX AVOIDANCE AND TAX EVASION

A fine line exists between legal tax planning and illegal tax planning—tax avoidance versus tax evasion. Tax avoidance is merely tax minimization through legal techniques. In this sense, tax avoidance becomes the proper objective of all tax planning. Though eliminating or reducing taxes is also a goal of tax evasion, the term implies the use of subterfuge and fraud as a means to this end. Perhaps because common goals are involved, popular usage has blurred the distinction between the two concepts. Consequently, the association of tax avoidance with tax evasion has kept some taxpayers from properly taking advantage of planning possibilities. The now-classic words of Judge Learned Hand in *Commissioner v. Newman* reflect the true values a taxpayer should have:

> Over and over again courts have said that there is nothing sinister in so arranging one's affairs as to keep taxes as low as possible. Everybody does so, rich or poor; and all do right, for nobody owes any public duty to pay more than the law demands: taxes are enforced extractions, not voluntary contributions. To demand more in the name of morals is mere cant.—47-1 USTC ¶9175, 35 AFTR 857, 159 F.2d 848 (CA-2, 1947).

[West Federal Taxation Corporations, Partnerships, Estates & Trusts, 2001 Edition by Hoffman, Raabe, Smith, Maloney, © 2001 by South-Western College Publishing]

Written for the non-professional (as well as the professional who is still willing to learn), this brief-yet-comprehensive twin volume contains the basics of both state and federal income tax statutes. The first volume, **Strategic Tax Planning: Auditing the State Statutes: The Truth About State Income Tax: How to Obey the Law and Not Get Caught (and Generate Tax-Free-Interest-Bearing Wealth and Income),** contains explication of applicable tax law for each of the fifty States. As the Appendix to the state volume, the second volume, **Strategic Tax Planning: Auditing the Federal Statutes (and Other Sources of Authority): The Truth About Federal Income Tax: How to Obey the Law and Escape the Unlawful Activities of Others** (originally self-published in 2005), contains explication of the US Constitution, applicable federal tax law and regulations, Dept. of the Treasury - IRS instructions, and Internal Revenue Manual directives. With the aid of this straightforward and easy-to-read-and-apply reference guide, any taxpayer may become quickly and sufficiently informed and empowered lawfully to reduce his or her state and federal income tax burden, generate permanently-tax-free-interest-bearing retirement savings, and contribute to the health of both personal and national economy.

Disclaimer

The author of this book is neither an attorney nor a lawyer. Neither the information contained in this book nor references to various tax codes constitutes either legal advice or an inducement to violate any statutes of law. This book has been prepared for educational, entertainment, and informational purposes and is intended for "nontaxpayers." The author has taken great care to make plain, easily understandable statements that are completely true and neither self-contradictory nor misleading. However, so as to prevent any misunderstanding, it is recommended that readers vigorously scrutinize, research, challenge, and prove the information contained in this book by inquiry into the original sources of authority—namely, the various tax codes—cited throughout this book.

> "The [federal] revenue laws are a code or system in regulation of tax assessment and collection. They relate to taxpayers, and not to nontaxpayers. The latter are without their scope. No procedure is prescribed for nontaxpayers, and no attempt is made to annul any of their rights and remedies in due course of law. With them [nontaxpayers] Congress does not assume to deal, and they are neither of the subject nor of the object of the revenue laws." Economy Plumbing and Heating Co. v. United States, 470 F. 2d 585 (1972) [Moreover,] "The laws of Congress in respect to those matters [federal income taxation] do not extend into the territorial limits of the states, but have force only in the District of Columbia, and other places that are within the exclusive jurisdiction of the national government." Caha v. United States, 152 U.S. 211, 215, 14 S. Ct. 513 (1894)

If the reader is a "taxpayer" defined at IRC § 7701(a)(14) or in one or more of the various state statutes, information can be obtained at http://www.irs.gov or on one or more of the various state web sites.

None of this book is intended to interfere with the proper administration or enforcement of the tax laws of the federal government or any state government; nor can there be found any false, deceptive, or misleading commercial statement regarding the excludability of income known to be false or fraudulent in relation to any material matter or any information pertaining to the organizing or selling of an abusive tax shelter, plan, or arrangement that might incite taxpayers to attempt to violate the tax laws, to unlawfully evade the assessment or collection of their federal or state tax liabilities, or to unlawfully claim improper tax refunds.

It is the intent of this book and its author to motivate one and all to adhere to and obey federal and state income tax law carefully and dutifully. This intent is based on the author's firm opinion that it is possible to observe both the spirit and the letter of the law and, at the same time, enjoy all of the rights and privileges the law provides, particularly, in the words of the US Dept. of the Treasury - IRS, to pay "no more" than "only the correct amount of tax due under the law" [Dept. of the Treasury - IRS Publication 1] and thereby effect general economic benefits.

The reader is encouraged to gain accurate knowledge of the actual requirements of applicable tax law, to obey diligently all requirements of such law, and to exercise fully all rights and privileges afforded by such law. The author assumes no responsibility for the success or failure of this information to produce the effects desired by the reader. The method and utilization of the information in this book is strictly the choice of the reader.

After completing this "basic training" in lawful tax avoidance, the reader is invited to contact the editor for "advance training" in lawful exercise of rights and privileges and lawful asset protection: mpllc@ymail.com, Attn: Advance Training.

Contents

NOTE: To utilize this book fully, one must have a connection to the World Wide Web (preferably, a high-speed connection) and Adobe Acrobat Reader software.

STP State

Appendix: STP Federal

Foreword to STP State

It is entirely up to the reader to agree or disagree with the conclusions presented herein. The intent of this book and the audit of the state statutes it contains is not merely to help the reader identify what the various laws say or do not say regarding the requirement to pay income taxes but to help the reader understand the simple, easy steps to verify for himself or herself the same facts, to reach the same conclusions, to stay up to date from year to year with any legislative changes, and even to implement a lawful strategy to reduce the reader's cost of state (and federal) income taxes. In other words, one of the goals of this book is to help the reader equip himself or herself to be aware of the facts of income tax law and to stay abreast of the infrequent changes or updates to income tax law in his or her respective state. Although this book highlights basic language present in or absent from state statutes, it is the reader's sole responsibility to determine exhaustively whether or not lawful obligation for the payment of income tax exists in the state statutes.

For best results, it is recommended that this book is read twice, both the text and the Appendix. Reasonably, text on states that are not of interest may be skipped, but the reader should be familiar with both the federal Internal Revenue Code (IRC) and the laws of his or her particular state(s) of residency. Many state revenue or tax laws are based on the federal IRC, which makes it essential that residents of such states understand the basic facts of the IRC presented in the Appendix as well as the basic facts of the applicable state statutes.

The reader is cautioned not to hurry to reach any conclusion. For example, the fact that a state revenue code is entitled "Taxation" does not automatically indicate that the code requires the payment of income tax—in fact, like the IRC, many state codes contain statutes that expressly indicate that titles and headings are not law and have no force and effect in and of themselves. The code doubtless contains various rates and specific exceptions, and may contain no specific language at all regarding income tax. Such characterizations must be considered carefully to determine accurately and correctly whether or not the code specifically and expressly requires the payment of income tax. This book provides guidance for such proper determination, but it is the reader's sole responsibility to determine exhaustively whether or not lawful obligation for the payment of income tax exists in the state statutes.

Is This Book for You?

If you prefer just to "go with the flow," "be like everyone else," and let someone else take responsibility for your tax matters rather than make your own decisions, take responsibility for your own actions, and exercise your rights, privileges and freedoms under the law, this book may not be for you. If you prefer to waive your rights to privacy—by *default* rather than by *choice*—rather than avoid intrusions by taxpayer investigators, this book may not be for you. If you prefer to be issued a tax refund rather than keep your weekly, monthly, and quarterly tax payments to a minimum or even reduce them further—that is, if you prefer each year to give a sizeable loan to the government that the government pays back to you with no—*zero*—interest rather than *increase* your weekly "take-home pay" and even earn some interest, this book may not be for you. Frankly, if you *prefer* not to be in control of your tax matters, if you *prefer* to remain uninformed of the facts of the law, if you *prefer* to be *told* how much income tax you have to pay, if you *prefer* not to know how *little* income tax the law actually requires of you, and if you *prefer* blaming your income tax preparer and the government for your income tax costs instead of exercising control, verifying for yourself just how little income tax the law actually requires of you, and legally and lawfully *preventing* uninformed withholding agents and tax collectors from seizing your money, this book may not be for you.

Nevertheless, even if this book is not for you, after reading it you may realize that you truly *do* prefer to make your own decisions, take responsibility for your own actions, exercise your rights, privileges and freedoms under the law, avoid intrusions by taxpayer investigators, keep your weekly, monthly, and quarterly tax payments to a minimum or even reduce them further, and *increase* your weekly "take-home pay" and even earn some interest and that you truly *do* like exercising control and legally and lawfully *preventing* uninformed withholding agents and tax collectors from seizing your money. At the very least, this book and its Appendix (and the Appendix to its Appendix) will enlighten you (or, at the very least, *entertain* you).

If you wish to argue any of the conclusions presented in this book (whether you are a taxpayer, a tax legislator, or a tax administrator), you are encouraged first to verify the language of the statutes quoted and cited in this book. If you are unable—or unwilling—to read and follow the suggestions in this book to verify the language of the statutes, you most likely will find it impossible to prove from the language of the statutes that the conclusions presented in this book are incorrect.

Enjoy the book!

Foreword to STP Federal

United States Supreme Court: "Anyone may so arrange his affairs so that his taxes shall be as low as possible. He is not bound to choose that pattern which best pays the treasury. There is not even a patriotic duty to increase one's taxes."—60 Federal 2nd 809, United States Supreme Court Justice Learned Hand (1872-1961).

"What does retirement mean to you?" "A funeral," said one individual. Sadly, that's actually true for far too many of us. Statistics show that about a third of us are *dead* before we reach age 65, another third of us are *dead broke,* and another third of us are *still working* to survive. In fact, some are saying that we should begin expecting to work well into our *seventies* before retiring—it's no wonder, since 95% of Americans don't have even $10,000 in savings when they reach age 65! Worse yet, since unfunded obligations total more than $4 trillion over the next 75 years, Social Security Administration trustees recently admitted that the trust fund will go broke in 2041. (One projected solution would be to reduce benefits by 22%—the current maximum monthly retirement benefit with no disability is only $255.00.) Medicare likewise faces insolvency in 2020—as if 95% of us being in dire straits isn't bad enough!

The 2004 IRS Data Book* reports that **in 1970**, 68,683 IRS employees collected $195,722,096 income and profits taxes for both individuals and corporations, resulting in **a tax per capita of merely $955.31**, from a US population of some 204,878,000 people, and efficiency was measured at a cost to the government of $0.45 per $100 of tax collected. **In 2004**, 98,735 IRS employees—nearly half again as many as in 1970—collected $2,018,502,103 in taxes—more than ten times the amount collected in 1970—resulting in **a tax per capita of $6,848.87**—more than seven times as much as the 1970 figure—from a US population of some 294,721,000 people, at a cost of $0.48 per $100 of tax collected.

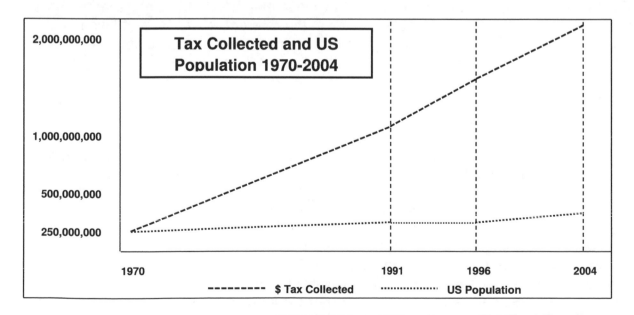

*See the Information Please® Database, © 2005 Pearson Education, Inc., Internal Revenue Service Statistics at http://www.infoplease.com/ipa/A0005923.html.

The goal of this book is to help the reader, in very little time, understand enough of the federal and state tax codes to act lawfully, discretely, and confidently in saving as much federal income, capital gains, social security, Medicare, and self-employment and state income tax costs as desired and in turning some or all of the savings into permanently-tax-free-interest-earning retirement savings while preventing IRS agents from seizing any property or bringing any other harm to the reader. If the reader is already enduring the scrutiny of an IRS agent or the threat of seizure or other harm or *actual* seizure or other harm, properly implementing the recommendations in this book will bring about relief.

There are, then, two main purposes of this book: to educate the reader briefly yet sufficiently in the statutes of the Internal Revenue Code and to help the reader prevent and defend against unlawful and fraudulent activity on the part of IRS employees without ever going to court. There are many things that one can do without cost by simply being fully aware of one's Constitutional rights and lawful freedoms and living by them. However, most people unwittingly create evidence, or at least an appearance, that they have liability for (requirement to pay) federal income and other taxes even though, lawfully, they actually have no such liability. For some, correcting matters can be extremely costly, but the benefits greatly and lastingly outweigh the effort and any costs—particularly when *foregone* costs far exceed correctional costs.

The information contained in this book is by no means absolutely exhaustive, but the facts presented and the references cited will help the reader both to verify the facts and conclusions presented and to arrive at the reader's own conclusions of fact and law. Actually, the information contained in this book is designed to give the reader a thorough overview rather than an exhaustive explanation of every point—which would be nearly impossible in a single, even very large volume. However, the appendices of this book add to the weight of the text by providing sufficiently detailed support for the points made in the text. Since it is easy to become overwhelmed with all of the information, the reader must take care to pay close attention to the simple statements in the text and carefully verify such statements in the referenced sections of law and regulations. While it is not necessary to study the book as if preparing for a rigorous, written examination, a cursory approach to the book will undoubtedly lead to poor understanding. It is easy to notice apparent contradictions between the book and the law as well as within the law itself, but these apparent contradictions must be carefully examined for clarity and reconciled for accurate application.

The appendices can be used to verify and cross-reference the information presented and are particularly helpful when meeting with and/or making a defense before IRS agents or employees (although the recommendation of this book is to prevent the need to appear before any IRS agents or employees by employing administrative procedure). Appendix D on the Internal Revenue Code (IRC) uses brief language to explain the purpose of the particular sections of the Code contained in the text. Conversely, since sections of the Code of Federal Regulations (CFR) explain statutes in the Internal Revenue Code, Appendix E on the Code of Federal Regulations uses no language to introduce the particular sections of the Code or explain the reasons they are contained in the text. In these two appendices, marginal notes indicate related information in other appendices in this order: section number(s), source(s), and page or item number(s). As of this edition, only twenty-one pertinent court cases are contained in Appendix F on the Courts. The language in this appendix shouts for itself and needs no explanation.

The text of this book highlights the lack of contradiction within the law and even within the publications of the IRS and the contradictions that do exist between (a) popular belief and the actual requirements of the sections of the Internal Revenue Code, (b) behavior of IRS employees and the actual requirements of the sections of the Internal Revenue Code, and (c) pronouncements of IRS employees and pronouncements of the courts. Thus, this book conveys authoritative language with the purpose of demonstrating both *lack of **internal** contradiction* and *existence of **inter-authority** contradiction*. In other words, while internal harmony exists within each body of authoritative language, there are key areas of *disharmony* among such bodies.

Making oral and written statements that are true, correct, accurate, complete, and reliable is of utmost importance to the author. However, given the complexity of federal tax laws, numerous IRS publications, countless number of taxpayers, and equally countless number of taxpayer situations, what may be true for one or two taxpayers may be anywhere from less than true to completely false for all other taxpayers. Anyone who wants to argue or disprove any of the conclusions presented herein will, no doubt, enjoy unending rewards conducting research to support one's views—such research is strongly recommended anyway. On the other hand, it is recommended that anyone who wants to argue or disprove any of the conclusions presented in letters from IRS agents stay out of court if at all possible—whether or not assisted by an attorney—and e-mail mpllc@ymail.com, Attn: Advance Training, for effective administrative argument for preventing such IRS agents from proceeding further. One might agree that it is wiser to act prudently, live privately, stay out of trouble, and stay out of court. Arguing administratively is prerequisite to filing suit and is also safer, more effective, less expensive, and possibly better documented than battling in the courtroom.

A veteran of the accounting and tax industry since 1983, the author has provided bookkeeping and tax return preparation services as a staff member of several accounting firms and numerous small companies, accounting and tax services as a private contractor since 1991, and financial services as an independent agent since 2003. The author possesses a Bachelor of Science in Business Administration degree in accounting from The University of West Florida as well as a Florida Life, Health and Annuities license for retirement planning purposes. In addition to providing local and nationwide accounting, consulting, training, and corporate income tax return preparation services, the author also assists clients in their individual efforts to comply with the laws of the state and federal governments and save as much money for retirement as possible by lawfully reducing their voluntary contributions for federal income, capital gains, social security, Medicare, and self-employment taxes, and state income taxes, keeping the savings for retirement, and earning interest on the savings without *ever* paying any of these taxes on the savings or the interest (see illustration below). The author also assists clients in their efforts lawfully to restructure their businesses to prevent even the *appearance* of a tax liability where none has ever actually lawfully existed. Such restructuring provides lawful freedom from income *and* estate taxes.

As mentioned earlier, few taxpayers can afford to save any money for retirement. As illustrated in Appendix X, **Strategic Tax Planning** provides responsible persons the lawful opportunity to convert federal income, capital gains, social security, Medicare, and self-employment tax costs, as well as state income tax costs, to permanently-tax-free-interest-bearing retirement savings to provide tax-free retirement income. The following simplified illustration compares "nontaxpayers" who lawfully convert internal revenue taxes to permanently-tax-free-interest-bearing retirement savings and "taxpayers" who pay statutorily baseless internal revenue taxes and are barely—if at all—able to save anything for retirement:

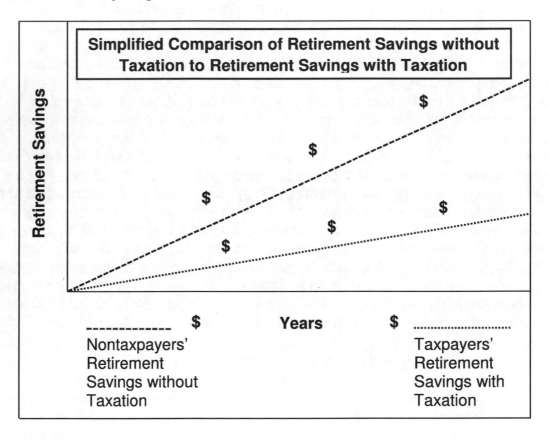

Notice to IRS Agents (STP Federal)
(Principles Also Apply to State Agents)

Imagine being in a crowd of people, innocently strolling along and minding your own business. Suddenly, you find yourself surrounded by armed police officers. Without preamble, they force you to the ground and cuff your hands behind your back. As they haul you to your feet, one of them tells you that you are under arrest and explains that you have committed a crime and the powers that be want to make an example out of you as a deterrent for others who might consider committing the same crime.

You would not want one of these police officers who doesn't know the law to violate your rights, presume you're guilty, and execute you then and there even though you're unarmed and cooperative (and in hand-cuffed custody). Police officers have *licenses* to *kill* people they believe are endangering the lives of other people, but you would not want one of these police officers to kill you based on a *presumption* that you are armed, dangerous, and committing criminal acts that endanger the lives of other people. Not certain that all police officers are aware of and abide by all of their responsibilities and obligations under the law, you might choose to become fully knowledgeable of your own responsibilities and obligations under the law (as well as at least some of theirs) so as to avoid any possibility that an armed officer of the law might misconstrue your location and behavior as indicative of criminal activity and possibly take away your life.

Accordingly, before becoming offended at the references to IRS agents and their occupational routines, keep in mind that even though you may have been given an amount of training and education in the law you do not automatically know *everything* about the law, especially if your duties constrain you to activities under only a small portion of the law. If you were a prison guard, you would carry out your duties under the small portion of the law regarding prisons and penitentiaries (Title 28 Judicial Administration or possibly just Chapter V Bureau of Prisons, Department of Justice or possibly just Part 552 Custody). Without knowing *everything* about the criminal justice system, you would normally assume that all inmates have fully enjoyed and exhausted their rights of due process. Similarly, as an IRS agent you carry out your duties under your particular, small portion of the law (Title 26 Internal Revenue Code or possibly just Subtitle A Income Taxes or possibly just Sections 61 Gross Income Defined and 63 Taxable Income Defined). Without knowing *everything* about tax law, you would normally assume that every case file that reaches your desk *belongs* there (just as a convicted criminal belongs in a prison). If your particular duties involve the collection of internal revenue taxes and someone hands you a file and says, "This person has a tax liability," assuming that the person handing you the file has already determined that a tax liability in fact lawfully exists, you would proceed to try to collect the amount of the tax liability from the taxpayer. As a prison guard, assuming that all inmates were properly convicted in courts of law, you would proceed to keep the inmates imprisoned. Remember, however, that every taxpayer has the right to determine for himself or herself the correct amount of tax due under the law and the responsibility to pay no more and no less than what the law requires (IRS Publication 1, Taxpayer Right #V). People in general are aware that they have due process rights (US Constitution, Fifth

Amendment) yet unaware that these rights encompass determinations and procedures under the Internal Revenue Code along with the other forty-nine titles of the United States Code. Remember also that "Avoidance of taxes is not a criminal offence. Any attempt to reduce, avoid, minimize, or alleviate taxes by legitimate means is permissible" [Department of the Treasury, IRS Handbook for Special Agents, p. 412 on Tax Avoidance Distinguished from Evasion].

As a tax specialist, you may be aware that property tax is often assessed based on the average appraised value of homes in each respective neighborhood, not on the *specific* appraised value of *each* home in the neighborhood. If a homeowner believes his property taxes are too high, it is up to that homeowner to demonstrate that his home has an appraised value *lower* than the *average* appraised value for lower *ad valorem taxes*. In the same way, it is up to each individual taxpayer to determine her own liability for *internal revenue taxes*. The taxpayer is not bound simply to rely on the presumption of others that she owes taxes based on averages or generalities.

The purpose of this book is to help responsible individuals carry out their obligations of law responsibly by helping them recognize what the law actually states regarding their obligation to pay internal revenue taxes, not to induce them deliberately to violate the nation's tax laws. As illustrated in the first chapter, people tend to do things a certain way just because "everybody else does it" that way or "that's just the way it is," even committing unlawful acts out of ignorance of the law (i.e., passing on the right and crossing the solid white line on the side of the roadway—unlawful in some jurisdictions). So the purpose of this book is also to help responsible individuals prevent their own (former) ignorance of the law from allowing others to act against them unlawfully, whether or not these others commit such unlawful acts out of ignorance of the law.

Helping others learn what the law says does not make the author an attorney or a lawyer, nor does the author's study of the law qualify the author to practice law, but it does help the author exercise due diligence as an accountant to help clients and others know and fulfill their obligations of law. This book challenges professionals and non-professionals alike not simply to believe hearsay generalizations and evasions but to *read all* of the statutes of law relating to internal revenue taxes and to determine what the sum total of these statutes indicates as to the intent of Congress when legislating these statutes.

Some IRS agents have exercised commendable diligence in ascertaining such intent and in carrying out their obligations of law responsibly. Upon discovering the same truths highlighted in this book, they likewise have taught others what the law actually says (i.e., Joseph R. Banister, CPA; Sherry Jackson, CPA, CFE).

The author is neither a tax protester nor a tax resister. The author pays all taxes the author is lawfully obligated to pay and recommends others do the same. The author is in subjection to the US government (as well as that of any State in which the author conducts business) and bears no animosity toward the US government or the Department of the Treasury or the Internal Revenue Service or IRS agents (or any State agents). The author has no feelings of superiority over or contempt for IRS (or State) agents or other individuals who are not well versed in the letter and the spirit of the Codes, although the Internal Revenue Manual states that all IRS employees have a "*commitment* to observe both the spirit as well as the letter of all legal requirements" (emphasis added—see Appendix IV, **TAXPAYER RIGHTS**). Instead, the author considers it a personal and professional obligation to help others in their efforts to read and comply with all applicable laws.

Definitions* for STP Federal
(Also Applicable to STP State)

1. Citizen:
26 CFR 1.1-1(c) Who is a citizen.
Every person born or naturalized in the United States and subject to its [exclusive] jurisdiction is a citizen.

2. Extort:
"To obtain by force or improper pressure <~ a bribe> — **extortion**" [The New Merriam-Webster Dictionary].

3. Fraud:
"The intentional perversion of the truth for the purpose of inducing another in reliance to part with some valuable thing belonging to him or to surrender a legal right."

"A false representation of a matter of fact, whether by words or by conduct, by false or misleading allegations, or by concealment of that which should have been disclosed, which deceives and is intended to deceive another so that he shall act upon it to his legal injury."

"Anything calculated to deceive, whether by a single act or combination or by suppression of truth, or suggestion of what is false, whether it be by direct falsehood or innuendo, by speech or silence, word of mouth, or look or gesture." [Black's Law Dictionary]

4. Include:
"When 'INCLUDE' or 'INCLUDING' is used it expands to take in all of the items stipulated or listed, but is then limited to them."

"'Including' within statute is interpreted as a word of enlargement or of illustrative application as well as a word of limitation." [Black's Law Dictionary]

5. Nonresident: "... One who is not a dweller within the jurisdiction in question; not an inhabitant of the state of the forum."
Alien: "In the United States, one born out of the jurisdiction of the United States." [Black's Law Dictionary]

6. US Jurisdiction:
"The laws of Congress in respect to those matters do not extend into the territorial limits of the states, but have force only in the District of Columbia, and other places that are within the exclusive jurisdiction of the national government." Caha v. United States, 152 U.S. 211, 215, 14 S. Ct. 513 (1894)

*One might find it beneficial, if enlightening, to skip forward to Appendix F and read the courts' definitions of law, as well.

Strategic Tax Planning:
Auditing the State Statutes:
The Truth About State Income Tax:
How to Obey the Law and Not Get Caught
(and Generate Tax-Free-Interest-Bearing Wealth and Income)

I: Brief Steps for Learning the Basic Facts of Tax Law

Considering the Appropriate Perspective

How does it feel to be overcharged? Is it of no consequence at all, "no big deal," to pay too much at a drive-through restaurant or at a convenience store? How about when the bottom line is more than just a few cents, such as at a grocery store? Is it wrong to request a refund if overcharged when making a larger purchase, such as in the electronics section or in the lawn and garden section or in the appliance section of a home and business supplier? Is it not objectionable to pay too much to own a vehicle or a home? Is it truly acceptable to pay too much *each and every week for life* just to earn a living?

Typically, people say that they "don't really pay that much in income taxes" and are accordingly unconcerned about the matter. In many cases, however, people are simply unaware of how much in income taxes they really *do* pay—each one tends to focus only on the amounts due or refundable with his or her annual income tax returns rather than on the total taxes paid over the course of each year. How much, though, is too much to be overcharged for income tax? A thousand dollars a year? Two thousand? Five? Ten? Probably nobody *wants* to pay more in income taxes than actually required, but most people *do* without even realizing it, and, due to the typical lack of concern just mentioned, many do not even notice.

This is not to suggest that anyone should not pay what taxes the law requires but to recommend that everyone *pay attention* to the menu right above the cash register, the price on the item or the display shelf, the details on the finance documents, the *actual requirements* of income tax law, and *especially* any coupons, discounts, rebates, and *lack* of lawful obligation, *and not get overcharged.* The cumulative cost of being overcharged in each of these areas—and particularly in state and federal income taxation—is staggering. In fact, as the Appendix demonstrates, a person could literally *retire* on income tax savings alone!

Being overcharged just $1.00 *occasionally* at a drive-through restaurant (and not noticing until it's too late) is only just irritating. Being overcharged just $1.00 *each and every hour, year-round* for income tax (and not noticing until it's too late) is only just *$2,000.00* (five to ten car payments, depending on whether the car is a Toyota or a Lexus—at forty hours a week, a person typically works about 2,000 hours a year (40 hours x 50 weeks = 2,000 hours)). Being overcharged just *$2.50* each and every hour, year-round for income tax (*$5,000.00*) is enough to generate a retirement income of nearly *$7,500.00 a month for life!* (Refer to the chart in Chapter IV, page 163, and Appendix X for further discussion.)

How can one get overcharged (and not refunded) for income taxes? This happens when one is not aware of one's statutory limits (because of not paying attention to the *actual requirements* of income tax law and *lack* of lawful obligation). There are, basically, two types of taxation: that which is required by law and that which is not, but there are at least a few similarities between the two. That which is required by law is usually collected as a matter of course. Like sales taxes, fuel taxes are collected from the consumer as part of the purchase—from the consumer's perspective, the tax is inseparably linked to the price of the product being purchased, and, typically, the consumer is not even aware of the rate of tax. Since the kind of taxation that is **not** required by law is also often collected as a matter of course, most people accordingly **presume** that such taxation **is** required by law (refer to Chapter IV, page 164). Like sales and fuel taxes, payroll taxes are collected from the worker (typically called "employee") as deductions from earnings (typically called "gross pay"). Payroll taxes **mimic** sales and fuel taxes in that, from the worker's perspective, they **appear** to be inseparably linked to the earnings being taxed, and, typically, the worker is not even aware of the rate of tax.

Understanding the Federal Model

The US Congress has legislated taxation of certain activities by establishing both **imposition** of the taxes and **liability** for the taxes imposed (the statutes thus enacted have been matriculated into the federal Internal Revenue Code (IRC)):

IRC § 4401
Imposition of tax.
(a) Wagers.
(1) State authorized wagers.
There shall be imposed on any wager authorized under the law of the State ….
…
(c) Persons liable for tax.
Each person who is engaged in the business of accepting wagers shall be liable for and shall pay the tax under this subchapter …
[http://codes.lp.findlaw.com/uscode/26/D/35/A/4401].

IRC § 5701
Rate of tax.
(a) Cigars.
On cigars, … there shall be imposed the following taxes ….
…
(b) Cigarettes.
On cigarettes, … there shall be imposed the following
taxes … [http://codes.lp.findlaw.com/uscode/26/E/52/A/5701].

IRC § 5703
Liability for tax and method of payment.
(a) Liability for tax.
(1) The manufacturer or importer of tobacco products and cigarette papers and tubes shall be liable for the taxes imposed thereon by Section 5701 ….
…

(b) Method of payment of tax.
(1) The taxes imposed by section 5701 shall be determined . . . [and] paid on the
basis of return [http://codes.lp.findlaw.com/uscode/26/E/52/A/5703].

IRC § 5001
Imposition, rate, and attachment of tax.
(a) Rate of tax.
(1) There is hereby imposed on all distilled spirits ... a tax
[http://codes.lp.findlaw.com/uscode/26/E/51/A/I/A/5001].

IRC § 5005
Persons liable for tax.
(a) General.
The distiller or importer of distilled spirits shall be liable for the tax imposed
thereon by section 5001(a)(1)
[http://codes.lp.findlaw.com/uscode/26/E/51/A/I/A/5005].

However, while the US Congress has enacted statutes that establish *imposition* of
income tax, it has *not* enacted *even one* statute to establish *liability* on the part of the
individual for income tax and other federal payroll taxes that companies customarily
withhold from earnings of workers. Nevertheless, perhaps on the possibility that at
some point in the future it *will* enact such a statute, it *has* enacted countless statutes
related to such an as-yet-to-be-enacted liability statute, so that *IF* such an as-yet-to-be-
enacted liability statute is actually ever enacted by Congress, the *related* statutes will
actually apply, as well. The result of the fact that Congress *has* enacted so many
statutes *related* to the as-yet-to-be-enacted liability statute is that most people
(university doctors, certified public accountants, and the general public) believe that the
liability statute itself "must exist in there somewhere" (that is, somewhere in the law).

Understanding Payroll Tax Withholding

The liability statute *does not* exist in there somewhere, but people are almost invariably
misled by such *related* statutes as the following:

IRC § 1461
Liability for withheld tax.
Every person required to deduct and withhold any tax under this chapter is
hereby made liable for such tax and is hereby indemnified against the claims and
demands of any person for the amount of any payments made in a accordance
with the provisions of this chapter
[http://codes.lp.findlaw.com/uscode/26/A/3/B/1461].

A curiosity about this statute, Internal Revenue Code (IRC) Section 1461, is that it
establishes *liability* for income taxes that are *withheld* according to any requirement to
withhold that is established by statute in the same chapter of statutes but *does not*
establish the original requirement to withhold itself (the language clearly indicates that

any such requirement would be established elsewhere in the chapter—the statute does not say, "Every person *is* required to deduct and withhold"). (Although IRC Section 3101 establishes *imposition* of social security ("Old-age, survivors, and disability insurance") and Medicare ("Hospital insurance") taxes, Section 3102(a) and (b) establish a requirement to collect such taxes and *liability* for such taxes collected, Section 3402* establishes a requirement to withhold taxes according to [income tax] tables or computational procedures from the Secretary of the US Treasury, and Section 3403 establishes *liability* for such taxes withheld (this is the second section that establishes *liability* for income taxes that are *withheld*), the US Congress has not enacted any statute(s) establishing *liability* for income or social security ("Old-age, survivors, and disability insurance") or Medicare ("Hospital insurance") taxes for individuals.) Another curiosity about IRC Section 1461 is that it is the first statute containing the word "liable" in the entire Internal Revenue Code—naturally, since no statute(s) state(s) that anyone is "liable" (or required to pay) for federal income tax or other federal payroll taxes.

Noteworthy, however, is the fact that, by its use of the words "made liable for such tax," IRC 1461 establishes the requirement to *remit* any taxes withheld (regardless of the statutory basis—or lack thereof—for the withholding). Here, again, payroll taxes *mimic* sales taxes in that they must be remitted to the taxing authority, the applicable government. In simple language, if one collects taxes for the government, then one is required by law to remit to the government any and all taxes collected for the government, and if an employer withholds taxes for the government, then the employer is required by law to remit to the government any and all taxes withheld for the government—*whether or not* the employees of the employer are required by law to *pay* the taxes withheld by the employer. In other words, even if the employees of an employer are not required by law to pay income tax and other federal payroll taxes, once the employer has withheld income taxes and other federal payroll taxes from the employees, the *employer* is required by law to pay the income tax and other federal payroll taxes withheld.

Whereas the US Congress is actually prohibited by the US Constitution from enacting statutory liability for federal income tax, it is not prohibited by the US Constitution from enacting statutes that require employers—or, due to the great number, length and complexity of such statutes, make employers *believe* they are required—to withhold federal income tax from employees. By labeling federal income tax as a "pay as you go" tax in its various publications, the Dept. of the Treasury - IRS has incited employers to withhold federal income tax from individual employees' earnings in spite of the fact that the US Congress—in technical compliance with the express prohibitions of the US

---

*Although IRC Section 3402(n) expressly relieves an employer of the obligation to withhold any tax from wages in the case of an employee who has submitted a withholding exemption certificate (IRS Form W-4) certifying that the employee incurred no liability for income tax for the previous tax year and that the employee anticipates incurring no liability for income tax for the current tax year, the IRS requires employers immediately to submit such certifications for review (and the IRS typically demands that such employers begin withholding taxes from wages without regard to such submitted certifications—refer to Chapter IV, page 164, and Appendix III, pages 177-181).

Brief Steps for Learning the Basic Facts of Tax Law

Constitution—has not enacted any statutory liability for federal income tax for individuals. In a climate of ignorance and the practice of withholding federal income tax without regard for federal statutes, employers withhold state income tax with no regard for whether or not state income tax liability or withholding requirements are established by state statutes. (Refer to Appendix II and Appendix D for further discussion. State statutes relative to payroll tax withholding are beyond the scope of this book.)

There are no further similarities between sales and payroll taxes, for at least a few reasons. First, sales taxes are generally required by statute, and, second, such statutes are generally legislated by individual states or state legislatures rather than by the US Congress. A third reason relates to the practical ability of the individual to avoid the tax: whereas one can simply choose not to purchase something that is sales taxed and thereby not incur any obligation to pay the tax, it is practically impossible for an employee to avoid federal payroll taxes (even if the employee is not required by statute to pay such payroll taxes) since, in practice, payroll taxes are, at least *apparently,* inseparably linked to the earnings being taxed. Any company whose officers—either due to being simply uninformed or due to being deliberately ignorant of the law—are in fear of the US government withholds and remits federal income tax and other federal payroll taxes, and the employees are left with only a fraction of their actual earnings. (Anyone with basic math skills can easily calculate the resulting enormous cost to the economy.)

Understanding Basic Terms and the Facts of Sovereignty

Understanding the definition of each of a few basic terms used in the various tax codes is essential to living in both compliance with such law and freedom from restrictive slavery and economic poverty resulting from *gross ignorance and misrepresentation* of such law. In the federal tax code of laws (statutes), chief of all terms are "liable" and "liability," which refer to legal or lawful obligation. The oft-cited federal Internal Revenue Code (Title 26 of the United States Code, or 26 USC, or 26 IRC, or just IRC) does not define either of these terms and does not use them to establish a statutory liability for income taxes—without statutory liability (requirement created by law), no legal or lawful obligation exists. A *state* code of tax statutes that specifically establishes *imposition* of income taxes but does not specifically establish *liability* for the taxes imposed and yet establishes one or more rates of tax effectively does establish liability for the taxes imposed. The *federal* code of tax statutes specifically establishes *imposition* of income taxes but does not specifically establish *liability* for the taxes imposed and yet establishes that liability *must* be established before any income taxes can be required to be paid, so that it is necessary to establish *both imposition and liability* to create a lawful obligation to pay federal income taxes. (The US Supreme Court has repeatedly affirmed that liability *must* be established before any federal income taxes can be required to be paid. The book *Strategic Tax Planning: The Truth About Federal Income Tax: How to Obey the Law and Escape the Unlawful Activities of Others* is a concise discussion of federal income tax—liability for which is not established by federal statutes but is, in fact, categorically *prohibited* by the US Constitution—and comprises the Appendix to this book and the Appendix to the Appendix.) Finally, any code of tax statutes—state or federal—that specifically establishes the *definition* of income that is taxable specifies what is to be taxed. When attempting to verify the statutory requirement to pay income tax, it is necessary to verify the *imposition* of income tax, *liability* for the tax imposed, and the *definition* of what is taxable.

Each sovereign government possesses its own ability to legislate taxation—to enact statutes of law to define terms and to require the payment of taxes. Hence, all the individual must do is read such statutes—and pay attention to some details, namely, the definitions and requirements the statutes contain—in order to comply with them and also enjoy the rights and privileges they afford. It is not necessary to possess particular skill or credentials to do so. In fact, ignorance of the law being no excuse for failing to obey it, one should be motivated to make the effort to read and understand the law— especially wherever it is to one's great benefit—rather than continue to ignore it.

An audit of the state statutes is necessary in order to determine whether or not each state has exercised, through its legislature, its sovereign ability—authority and power— to require the payment of income tax by enacting statutes that clearly, unambiguously, and actually establish a lawful obligation to pay income tax. Of the fifty States, there are nine *known* "no-income-tax" states, so called since, as it is commonly known, the legislatures of these states—namely, Alaska, Florida, Nevada, New Hampshire, South Dakota, Tennessee, Texas, Washington, and Wyoming—have not enacted (or have *repealed*) statutes requiring the payment of income taxes by individuals. There remain forty-one *known* "income-tax" states, so called since laws requiring the payment of income taxes by individuals exist in these states—at least, as it is *commonly understood* (or *guessed* or *imagined*) by educated and uneducated professionals and non-professionals who remain uninformed of the few basic terms used in the tax codes—certainly, these states *collect* income taxes from individuals. Each state government has sovereign, unlimited authority and power to tax, whether or not—or by whatever means—its legislature chooses to act on such authority and power. (By contrast, the *federal* government has been given *only limited* authority and power to tax—see Appendix II for discussion of limits imposed on the federal government by the US Constitution.)

With the goal of both complying with the requirements of tax law and enjoying the freedoms it affords, it is appropriate to *verify* or *audit* the requirements of tax law by considering its simple language. Areas of key interest should be the definition of basic terms used in a particular tax code and the statutes, if any, that actually establish a requirement to pay income tax.

Finding Basic Terms (Two Steps)

Consider, for example, the simple language of the tax statutes of Alabama (alphabetically, state #1), a *known* so-called "income-tax state." Although the Alabama Legislature has neither used the terms "liable" or "liability" to establish statutory liability (responsibility created by law, or lawful obligation) for the payment of state income tax nor relied on the federal Internal Revenue Code (IRC) for this purpose, it has enacted statutes of law establishing a requirement to pay individual state income tax. Notice how this can be determined in just two steps.

First, a simple internet search for "Alabama Code" or "Alabama revenue statutes" or "Alabama state statutes" or "Alabama tax code" or "Alabama tax statutes" will result in a link to, among others, "Code of Alabama" or "Alabama Code." (FindLaw provides links to official state codes for all fifty States: http://law.findlaw.com/state-laws/state-codes.html, http://tax.findlaw.com/tax-laws-forms/state-tax-codes.html.) The reader should pursue a link to the actual code itself rather than links to government agencies and companies providing fee-based assistance and services or even free access to databases of information that do not contain the actual statutes related to taxation. A visual scan within the state code will reveal the state revenue or tax code.

Initially, looking at a law code online is much like looking at a directory or outline, with each major item representing a specific subject or a general category of laws or statutes. When searching for a particular law, it is necessary to start with the major outline item or category with which the law is most likely associated or where it is most likely to appear. (This search began, for example, by looking in the online directory for State Code or State Revenue Statutes or State Statutes or State Tax Code or State Tax Statutes, as opposed to State Banking Statutes or State Labor Laws or State Transportation Code.) Usually, each major item or category is comprised of a number of minor or subsidiary categories, and these are further comprised of successively subsidiary categories and laws (statutes). It is typical to see a law code broken down by titles, subtitles, parts, subparts, chapters, subchapters, and, finally, the actual statutes of law, often called sections, comprising the entire code itself. Paragraphs within each statute or section of law are often referred to as subsections.

Unlike a typical directory or outline, however, the digitized law codes viewable on the Internet typically are not indented—a code outline itself may be indented, but the sections, subsections, and lists within sections of law (the part one wants to *read*) typically are not further indented according to respective subsidiary level of importance. Especially if the language of a particular section of law is lengthy, maintaining a sense of position within the section can be challenging, which at the very least necessitates counting the number of lettered and numbered paragraphs within the section.

To illustrate, the following outline presentation of successively subsidiary categories within sections of law may be preferred (but only a few state codes appear this way online):

29.82.5 (the name or number of the section)
    (a) (the first subsection)
    (b) (the second subsection)
        (1) (the first sub-subsection)
        (2) (the second sub-subsection)
            (A) (the first sub-sub-subsection)
            (B) (the second sub-sub-subsection)

           (C) (the third sub-sub-subsection)
      (c) (the third subsection)
      (d) (the fourth subsection)
        (1) (the first sub-subsection)
        (2) (the second sub-subsection)
          (A) (the first sub-sub-subsection)
          (B) (the second sub-sub-subsection)

However, the following outline presentation of successively subsidiary categories within sections of law is typical (most state codes appear *this* way online):

29.82.5 (the name or number of the section)
(a) (the first subsection)
(b) (1) (the second subsection and the first sub-subsection)
(2) (the second sub-subsection)
(A) (the first sub-sub-subsection)
(B) (the second sub-sub-subsection)
(C) (the third sub-sub-subsection)
(c) (the third subsection)
(d) (1) (the fourth subsection and the first sub-subsection)
(2) (A) (the second sub-subsection the first sub-sub-subsection)
(B) (the second sub-sub-subsection)

This may appear intimidating, but it is possible to master navigating through such outline presentations with even only a little practice. (Refer to Appendix C for further discussion.)

Second, upon locating the revenue or tax code within the state code, a visual scan within the revenue or tax code will reveal the subcategory(ies) containing the pertinent statutes. (For example, visually scanning for "Income Tax" may very well reveal "Income Taxation" or "Taxation of Income," but visually scanning for "General Provisions" or "Calculation" or "Computation" or "Determination" or some other subcategory(ies) may also be necessary to reveal the pertinent statutes.) Visually scanning the subcategories of revenue or tax codes often reveals important areas for consideration, such as property and sales taxation or excise and gross receipts taxation in addition to or instead of income taxation.

A quick visual scan of the **Code of Alabama** will reveal **Title 40, Revenue and Taxation.** Another quick visual scan within **Title 40** will reveal **Chapter 1, General Provisions.** Yet another quick visual scan within this chapter will reveal **Section 40-1-1, Definitions,** which contains important terms used to establish the requirement of law (or statutory obligation) to pay Alabama state income tax. Often, a particular code's use of terms not contained in the definitions section(s) of the code establishes the meaning of the terms and the obligation to pay income tax and supports governmental income tax collection activity. However, it is *vitally important* to note that a code's use of terms that are *not* specifically defined in the definitions section(s) of the code does not automatically establish the meaning of the terms, the obligation to pay income tax, and legitimacy of income tax collection activity by government agents. In other words, *Caveat emptor!* (This is Latin for "*Let the buyer [or the taxpayer] beware!*") Pertinent examples of this are the federal IRC's use of the undefined terms "liable" and "liability" and such statements as 'any unpaid tax liability shall be collected' when *nothing* in the IRC actually establishes *any* liability (obligation) for income tax.

Still another quick visual scan within **Title 40** will reveal **Chapter 18 Income Taxes.** A final quick visual scan within this chapter will reveal **Sections 40-18-2 Levied; persons and subjects taxable generally, 40-18-5 Tax on individuals, 40-18-14 Adjusted gross income of individuals,** and **40-18-15.1 Net income taxable income defined - Generally,** which contain other important terms used to establish the requirement of law (statutory obligation) to pay Alabama state income tax.

Understanding Statutory Liability (or Lack Thereof)

This book contains a brief consideration of the laws of each state (as well as, for comparison, the District of Columbia) and of what they do and do not establish regarding any requirement for the payment of income tax. Each state is identified by (a) whether or not its legislature has based its requirement for the payment of individual state income tax on either the federal IRC or (b) its own statutes and (c) whether or not it thereby actually has established a requirement for the payment of individual state income tax. Each state is also identified by whether or not it defines in its own state statute(s) the terms "liable" and "liability." Each consideration discusses, from the perspective of the statutes enacted by the state legislature, the definitions of liable and liability, if any, as well as gross income, adjusted gross income, net income, taxable income, and other terms as necessary for clear, concise explanation of each state's actual statutory requirements. Each consideration also discusses the statutory basis, if any, for any requirement to pay corporate state income tax. Again, this is a brief consideration, rather than an exhaustive discussion, of the applicable laws of each of the fifty States. Nevertheless, sufficient information is provided for the reader to recognize and verify the simple facts of law and their net effect relative to state income tax. (It is the reader's sole responsibility to determine exhaustively whether or not lawful obligation for the payment of state income tax exists in the statutes of any state.)

In order to draw reliable conclusions while reading the information on any state, it is appropriate for the reader to ask two initial questions. **First,** if the state is a *known* income-tax state, does the state code establish *imposition* of and *liability* for income tax as well as the *definition(s)* of income that is taxable, or does it simply refer to the federal IRC for definitions and determination of income tax liability? **Second,** if the state code refers to the IRC, does it *rely* on the IRC for imposition of or liability for income tax or the definition(s) of income that is taxable or for two or all three of these?

As the federal model demonstrates, to establish lawful obligation (statutory liability) to pay for federal taxes, the US Congress typically establishes *both* an *imposition* of tax *and* a *liability* for the tax imposed as well as the *definition* of what is taxable. Since it lacks power and authority from the US Constitution to do so, the US Congress has carefully **refrained** from enacting any statute(s) establishing **liability** for federal **income** tax (see Appendix III and Appendix D). Accordingly, failing to exercise their power and authority to establish liability for **state** income tax, state legislatures that enact laws that do not establish liability for income tax but refer to or rely on the IRC for this purpose do not create liability for state income tax (since the IRC does not establish liability for income tax). The US Congress has also carefully **refrained** from enacting any statute(s) specifically establishing the **definition** of income that is taxable for nearly all types of domestic income (particularly what is by far the most common type of domestic income: wages—except in the case of nonresident aliens—see Appendix III and Appendix D). Accordingly, failing to exercise their power and authority to establish the definition of income that is taxable, state legislatures that enact laws that do not establish the definition of income that is taxable but refer to or rely on the IRC for this purpose do not establish any income as taxable (since the IRC does not establish any income as taxable).

Some state codes contain specific statutes that indicate legislative **intent** to require the payment of state income tax, and some of these even indicate that such intent is exercised by relying partly or entirely on the IRC—usually by stating that provisions of the IRC are applicable to state income tax—or by mimicking the language of the IRC without specifically relying on it. However, **legislative intent** does not create **statutory obligation** unless the legislature follows through and actually enacts the statutes necessary for creating such an obligation.

In the case of each legislative body, this begs the question: has the legislature enacted the statutes necessary for creating an obligation to pay income tax? If it lacks power and authority, it cannot enact such statutes, but any such statutes it does enact are effectively null and void. However, if it possesses the power and authority to enact the statutes necessary for creating an obligation to pay income tax but has not exercised its power and authority, why has it not exercised its power and authority? In many cases, for whatever reason, state legislatures have simply mimicked the US Congress and mimicked the language of the IRC. The questions, then, are, is the particular state legislature simply **unaware** that the US Congress is prohibited by the US Constitution to require the payment of income tax, is it simply **unaware** that the US Congress has enacted statutes that are, prohibitions of the US Constitution notwithstanding, without force and effect, given that they neither establish liability for the tax imposed or the definition of what is taxable nor otherwise create any obligation to pay income tax, or **is** the particular state legislature **aware** of these facts but mimicking the language of the IRC regardless simply because "**it works**" (since the greater number of the people prefer to remain uninformed of the facts and just keep paying federal income tax in spite of lack of statutory obligation to pay federal income tax and in spite of their IRS-published right to pay "no more" than "only the correct amount of tax due under the law" [Dept. of the Treasury - IRS Pub. 1])?

Consider this typical scenario. A state legislature enacts a statute that indicates the legislature's intent to require the payment of state income tax (and, perhaps, to apply the provisions of the IRC for this purpose). The legislature also enacts a statute that says that an income tax is imposed at five percent of income that is taxable. The legislature also enacts a statute of definitions that either defines various terms relative to income tax without specifically defining income that is taxable or refers to the IRC for this purpose.

It is accordingly appropriate for the reader to ask two additional questions. **Third,** if the state legislature has enacted a specific statute that indicates *intent* to require the payment of state income tax, has it also enacted the statutes necessary for creating such an obligation, or, if not, why has it specifically *refrained* from enacting such statutes and, perhaps, applied the provisions of the IRC for this purpose? **Fourth,** if it has enacted a statute of definitions that either defines various terms relative to income tax without specifically defining income that is taxable or refers to the IRC for this purpose, why has it specifically *refrained* from establishing the definition of income that is taxable?

In other words, does the state tax code clearly establish a statutory liability to pay state income tax, or does it make liability for state income tax *contingent* or *conditional* on the *federal* tax code, for example, does the state code establish *imposition* of income tax but then refer to the IRC to establish *liability* for the tax imposed or for the *definition* of income that is taxable?

By now, the reader should recognize that, whether based on the federal model or the state model, *the essential statutory formula for income tax is comprised of three elements: imposition of tax, liability for the tax imposed, and the definition of income that is taxable.* (Mathematically, this would appear as (Imposition + Liability) x Definition = Tax.) The US Congress has established this formula in the case of federal taxation other than income tax, the US Supreme Court has repeatedly enforced this formula in the case of federal income tax, and several state legislatures have established this formula for state income tax. Alternately, unless a particular state legislature requires both imposition and liability, one or the other is also acceptable (since each state has sovereign authority and power), that is, a state legislature may only impose a tax on taxable income or it may only create a liability for tax on taxable income—federal income tax statutes require both imposition and liability. If the statutes of a particular state neither require liability nor expressly define liable or liability, this book treats the tax rate(s) applied to taxable income as established liability for that state only.

This book presents only the essential language of applicable state laws relative to income or income-based taxes. Accordingly, any portion of a statute that is, for the purposes of this book, extraneous is not presented but is instead represented by an ellipsis ("…"). (Text that is thus replaced, while important, is nevertheless unnecessary for the purposes of this book. The reader should review entire statutes wherever any clarification is necessary.) For each state code considered, the terms and definitions that comprise what this book calls the *essential statutory formula for income tax* are presented in their briefest possible form. Typically, the language of each code is presented to the extent that it establishes specific imposition of and/or specific liability for tax and the specific definition(s) of income that is taxable and to the extent that any element of the essential statutory formula is contingent on any other definition(s) in the state code or in the federal code.

#1 Alabama, a *Known* Income-Tax State

Federal statute based: No
State statute based: Yes
Actual liability: Yes

"Liable" defined by state statute: No
"Liability" defined by state statute: No

For general state income tax purposes, the Alabama Legislature relies on both **The Code of Alabama 1975** and the federal **Internal Revenue Code.**

The Code of Alabama 1975 does not define liable or liability for income tax purposes (reference **Title 40 Revenue and Taxation, Chapter 18 Income Taxes, Article 1 General Provisions, Section 40-18-1 Definitions**).

Title 40 Revenue and Taxation, Chapter 18 Income Taxes, Article 1 General Provisions, Section 40-18-2 Levied; persons and subjects taxable generally establishes by specific language *imposition* of tax and states:

Section 40-18-2
Levied; persons and subjects taxable generally.
(a) In addition to all other taxes now imposed by law, there is hereby levied and imposed a tax on the taxable income, as defined in this chapter, which tax shall be assessed, collected, and paid annually at the rate specified herein and for each taxable year as hereinafter provided. Persons and subjects taxable under this chapter are:
(1) Every individual residing in Alabama.
(2) Every corporation domiciled in Alabama or licensed or qualified to transact business in Alabama.
(3) Every corporation doing business in Alabama or deriving income from sources within Alabama, including income from property located in Alabama.
… [http://alisondb.legislature.state.al.us/acas/CodeofAlabama/1975/coatoc.htm].

For individuals, Article 1 General Provisions, Section 40-18-5 Tax on individuals establishes by specific rates *liability* for the tax imposed and states:

Section 40-18-5
Tax on individuals.
The tax levied and imposed by Section 40-18-2 shall be computed as follows:
… [http://alisondb.legislature.state.al.us/acas/CodeofAlabama/1975/coatoc.htm].

Article 1 General Provisions also establishes the ***definitions*** of income that is taxable and states:

Section 40-18-14
Adjusted gross income of individuals.
The term "gross income" as used herein:
(1) Includes gains, profits and income derived from salaries, wages, or compensation for personal services of whatever kind, or in whatever form paid …
[http://alisondb.legislature.state.al.us/acas/CodeofAlabama/1975/coatoc.htm].

Section 40-18-15.1
Net income taxable income defined - Generally.
For purposes of this chapter, the term "taxable income" or "net income" shall mean "gross income," as defined in Section 40-18-14, less the deductions allowed to individuals by this chapter
[http://alisondb.legislature.state.al.us/acas/CodeofAlabama/1975/coatoc.htm].

So, the Code establishes imposition of individual income tax and liability for the tax imposed as well as the definition of income that is taxable.

For corporations, **Section 40-18-31 Corporate income tax - Generally** establishes by a specific rate *liability* for the tax imposed and states:

Section 40-18-31
Corporate income tax - Generally.
(a) A corporation subject to the tax imposed by Section 40-18-2 shall pay a tax equal to six and one-half percent of the taxable income of the corporation, as defined in this chapter
… [http://alisondb.legislature.state.al.us/acas/CodeofAlabama/1975/coatoc.htm].

However, **Section 40-18-33 Corporate income tax - Taxable income** refers to the federal IRC for the *definition* of income that is taxable and states:

Section 40-18-33
Corporate income tax - Taxable income.
In the case of a corporation subject to the tax imposed by Section 40-18-31, the term "taxable income" means federal taxable income without the benefit of federal net operating losses plus the additions prescribed and less the deductions and adjustments allowed by this chapter and as allocated and apportioned to Alabama
[http://alisondb.legislature.state.al.us/acas/CodeofAlabama/1975/coatoc.htm].

So while the Code establishes imposition of corporate income tax and liability for the tax imposed, its definition of what is taxable is based on the IRC. In other words, the state legislature has established imposition and liability without also establishing anything on which to impose the liability. (Anything multiplied by nothing is nothing, that is, a percentage of nothing is nothing. Refer to Appendix III and Appendix D for further discussion.)

The Alabama Legislature statutorily requires the payment of individual state income tax. Without any reference to or reliance on the IRC, it has established ***all three elements of the essential statutory formula for income tax: imposition of tax, liability for the tax imposed, and the definition of income that is taxable.*** However, it does not statutorily require the payment of corporate state income tax.

#2 Alaska, a *Known* No-Income-Tax State

Federal statute based: No
State statute based: No
Actual liability: No

"Liable" defined by state statute: No
"Liability" defined by state statute: No

For general state income tax purposes, the Alaska State Legislature relies on both the **Alaska Statutes** and the federal **Internal Revenue Code.**

It is commonly understood—***known***—that Alaska is a no-income-tax state, that is, The Alaska State Legislature has not enacted *or has repealed* any statutes of law that require the payment of individual state income tax. **Title 43** of the **Alaska Statutes** contains various statutes concerning **Revenue and Taxation** but does not establish imposition of tax, liability for tax, or the definition of income that is taxable for individual income taxes.

Interestingly, this title contains a valuable statement for educational purposes under **Chapter 10 Enforcement and Collection of Taxes, Section 80 Definition of Taxes,** which states: "'[T]axes' includes (1) tax and license assessments *lawfully made* ..." [emphasis added—
http://www.touchngo.com/lglcntr/akstats/Statutes/Title43/Chapter10/Section080.htm].
This is interesting and valuable, of course, because, reasonably, *all* tax and license assessments, whether state or federal, should be *lawfully made.*

For individuals, it is worth noting that **Chapter 20 Alaska Net Income Tax Act, Section 10 Tax On Individuals, Fiduciaries, and Corporations** is noted as "Repealed, Sec. 13 Ch 70 SLA 1975"
[http://www.touchngo.com/lglcntr/akstats/Statutes/Title43/Chapter20/Section010.htm].
Likewise, **Section 50 Taxpayer Liable** is noted as "Repealed, Sec. 13 Ch 70 SLA 1975"
[http://www.touchngo.com/lglcntr/akstats/Statutes/Title43/Chapter20/Section050.htm].

For corporations, it is also worth noting that **Chapter 20, Section 11 Tax On Corporations** establishes by specific language *imposition* of tax and by specific rates *liability* for the tax imposed:

...
    (e) There is imposed for each taxable year upon the entire taxable income of every corporation derived from sources within the state a tax computed as follows:
...
[http://www.touchngo.com/lglcntr/akstats/Statutes/Title43/Chapter20/Section011.htm].

However, **Section 340 Definitions** provides no ***definition*** of "taxable income"; **Section 150 Definitions** is noted as "Repealed, Sec. 45 Ch 113 SLA 1980" [http://www.touchngo.com/lglcntr/akstats/Statutes/Title43/Chapter20/Section150.htm]; and **Section 21 Internal Revenue Code Adopted By Reference** and **Section 300 References to Internal Revenue Code** explain the state legislature's reliance on the IRC to calculate corporate income tax. So the state legislature has established imposition and liability without also establishing anything on which to impose the liability. (Anything multiplied by nothing is nothing, that is, a percentage of nothing is nothing. Refer to Appendix III and Appendix D for further discussion.)

The Alaska State Legislature does not statutorily require the payment of either individual or corporate state income tax.

#3 Arizona, a *Known* Income-Tax State

Federal statute based: Yes
State statute based: Yes
Actual liability: No

"Liable" defined by state statute: No
"Liability" defined by state statute: No

For general state income tax purposes, the Arizona State Legislature relies on both the **The Arizona Revised Statutes** and the federal **Internal Revenue Code.**

The Arizona Revised Statutes do not define liable or liability for income tax purposes (reference **Title 43, Taxation of Income, Chapter 1 Definitions and General Provisions, Article 1 General Provisions, Section 43-104 Definitions**).

For individuals, **Title 43 Taxation of Income, Chapter 5 Payment and Collection of Tax, Article 5 Collections, Section 43-562 Husband and wife, liability for tax** instead establishes by specific language *liability* for tax and states:

43-562. Husband and wife, liability for tax
The spouse who controls the disposition of or who receives or spends community income as well as the spouse who is taxable on such income is liable for the payment of the taxes imposed by this title on such income. If a joint return is filed, the liability for the tax on the aggregate income is joint and several [http://www.azleg.state.az.us/FormatDocument.asp?inDoc=/ars/43/00562.htm&Title=43&DocType=ARS].

However, **Chapter 10 Individuals, Article 1 Definitions, Section 43-1001 Definitions** refers to the federal IRC for the ***definitions*** of income that is taxable and states:

43-1001. Definitions
In this chapter, unless the context otherwise requires:
1. "Arizona adjusted gross income" of a resident individual means the individual's Arizona gross income subject to modifications specified in sections 43-1021 and 43-1022.
2. "Arizona gross income" of a resident individual means the individual's federal adjusted gross income for the taxable year, computed pursuant to the internal revenue code.
...
4. "Federal adjusted gross income" of a resident individual means the individual's adjusted gross income computed pursuant to the internal revenue code.
...
7. "Net income" means taxable income.
...

11. "Taxable income" of a resident individual shall be Arizona adjusted gross income less the exemptions and deductions allowed in article 4 of this chapter.
…
[http://www.azleg.state.az.us/FormatDocument.asp?inDoc=/ars/43/01001.htm&Title=43&DocType=ARS].

So while the Code establishes liability for individual income tax, its definitions of what is taxable are based on the IRC. In other words, the state legislature has established liability without also establishing anything on which to impose the liability. (Anything multiplied by nothing is nothing, that is, a percentage of nothing is nothing. Refer to Appendix III and Appendix D for further discussion.)

For corporations, **Chapter 11 Corporations, Article 2 Taxes and Rates, Section 43-1111 Tax rates for corporations** establishes by specific language *imposition* of tax and by specific rates *liability* for the tax imposed and states:

43-1111. Tax rates for corporations
There shall be levied, collected and paid for each taxable year upon the entire Arizona taxable income of every corporation, unless exempt under section 43-1126 or 43-1201 or as otherwise provided in this title or by law, taxes in an amount of the greater of fifty dollars or:
1. For taxable years beginning through December 31, 2013, 6.968 per cent of net income.
…
[http://www.azleg.state.az.us/FormatDocument.asp?inDoc=/ars/43/01111.htm&Title=43&DocType=ARS].

However, **Chapter 11 Corporations, Article 1 Definitions, Section 43-1101 Definitions** also refers to the IRC for the *definitions* of income that is taxable and states:

43-1101. Definitions
In this chapter, unless the context otherwise requires:
1. "Arizona gross income" of a corporation means its federal taxable income for the taxable year.
2. "Arizona taxable income" of a corporation means its Arizona gross income adjusted by the modifications specified in article 3 of this chapter.
…
4. "Federal taxable income" means the taxable income of a corporation computed pursuant to the internal revenue code.
…
6. "Net income" means Arizona taxable income.
7. "Person" and "taxpayer" means a corporation
[http://www.azleg.state.az.us/FormatDocument.asp?inDoc=/ars/43/01101.htm&Title=43&DocType=ARS].

So while the Code establishes imposition of corporate income tax and liability for the tax imposed, its definitions of what is taxable are based on the IRC. In other words, the state legislature has established imposition and liability without also establishing anything on which to impose the liability. (Anything multiplied by nothing is nothing, that is, a percentage of nothing is nothing.)

The Arizona State Legislature has not enacted its own statutes for the definition of income that is taxable for either individual or corporate state income tax. While it has enacted certain statutes that establish liability for individual state income tax as well as imposition of and liability for corporate state income tax, it has relied on the IRC for the definitions of what is taxable. So while Arizona is a **known** income-tax state, its legislature does not statutorily require the payment of state income tax.

#4 Arkansas, a *Known* Income-Tax State

Federal statute based: No
State statute based: Yes
Actual liability: Yes

"Liable" defined by state statute: No
"Liability" defined by state statute: No

For general state income tax purposes, the Arkansas State Legislature relies solely on **The Arkansas Code of 1987.**

The Arkansas Code of 1987 does not define liable or liability for income tax purposes (reference **Title 26 Taxation, Subtitle 1 General Provisions, Chapter 1 General Provisions, Section 26-1-101 Definitions** and **Subtitle 5 State Taxes, Chapter 51 Income Taxes, Subchapter 1 General Provisions, Section 26-51-102 Definitions**).

For individuals, **Subtitle 1 General Provisions, Chapter 51 Income Taxes, Subchapter 2 Imposition of Tax, Section 26-51-201 Individuals, trusts, and estates** instead establishes by specific language *imposition* of tax and by specific rates *liability* for the tax imposed and states:

26-51-201. Individuals, trusts, and estates.

(a) A tax is imposed upon, and with respect to, the entire income of every resident, individual, trust, or estate. The tax shall be levied, collected, and paid annually upon the entire net income as defined and computed in this chapter at the following rates, giving effect to the tax credits provided hereafter, in the manner set forth:
… [http://www.lexisnexis.com/hottopics/arcode/Default.asp].

Chapter 51 Income Taxes, Subchapter 4 Computation of Tax Liability, Section 26-51-403 Income generally and **Section 26-51-404 Gross income generally** establish the *definitions* of income that is taxable and state:

26-51-403. Income generally.

(a) The term "net income" means the adjusted gross income of a taxpayer less the deductions allowed by the Income Tax Act of 1929, § 26-51-101 et seq.

(b) "Adjusted gross income" means, in the case of an individual, gross income minus the following deductions:

… [http://www.lexisnexis.com/hottopics/arcode/Default.asp].

26-51-404. Gross income generally.

(a) (1) "Gross income" includes:

(A) Gains, profits, and income derived from salaries, wages, or compensation for personal service of whatever kind and in whatever form paid;

(B) Gains, profits, and income derived from professions, vocations, trades, business, commerce, or sales;

(C) Gains, profits, and income derived from dealings in property, whether real or personal, growing out of the ownership of, use of, or interest in the property;

(D) Gains, profits, and income derived from interest, rent, royalties, dividends, annuities, securities, or the transaction of any business carried on for gain or profit;

(E) Gains or profits and income derived from any source whatever; and

(F) Any payments of alimony and separate maintenance received pursuant to a court order.

(2) The amount of all such items shall be included in the gross income of the taxable year in which received by the taxpayer.

… [http://www.lexisnexis.com/hottopics/arcode/Default.asp].

So, the Code establishes imposition of individual income tax and liability for the tax imposed as well as the definition of income that is taxable.

For corporations, **Subchapter 2 Imposition of Tax, Section 26-51-205 Corporations -- Work Force 2000 Development Fund** also establishes by specific language ***imposition*** of tax and by specific rates ***liability*** for the tax imposed and states:

26-51-205. Corporations -- Work Force 2000 Development Fund.

(a) Every corporation organized under the laws of this state shall pay annually an income tax with respect to carrying on or doing business on the entire net income of the corporation, as now defined by the laws of the State of Arkansas, received by such corporation during the income year, on the following basis:
… [http://www.lexisnexis.com/hottopics/arcode/Default.asp].

However, although this section specifically states that "net income" is "defined by the laws of the State of Arkansas," the Code does not actually establish any ***definition*** of net income that is taxable, although neither does it refer to the IRC for such definition.

Arkansas

By enacting this statute, the state legislature has established imposition of and liability for corporate income tax without also establishing anything on which to impose the liability. (Anything multiplied by nothing is nothing, that is, a percentage of nothing is nothing. Refer to Appendix III and Appendix D for further discussion.)

The Arkansas General Assembly statutorily requires the payment of individual state income tax. Without any reference to or reliance on the IRC, it has established *all three elements of the essential statutory formula for income tax: imposition of tax, liability for the tax imposed, and the definition of income that is taxable.* However, it does not statutorily require the payment of corporate state income tax.

#5 California, a *Known* Income-Tax State

Federal statute based: Yes
State statute based: Yes
Actual liability: No

"Liable" defined by state statute: No
"Liability" defined by state statute: No

For general state income tax purposes, the California State Legislature relies on both the **California Code** and the federal **Internal Revenue Code.**

The **California Code** does not define liable or liability for income tax purposes (reference **Division 2 Other Taxes, Part 10 Personal Income Tax, Chapter 1 General Provisions and Definitions, Sections 17001-17039.2**).

For individuals, **Division 2 Other Taxes, Part 10 Personal Income Tax, Chapter 2 Imposition of Tax, Section 17041** instead establishes by specific language *imposition* of tax and by specific rates *liability* for the tax imposed and states:

> **17041. (a) (1)** There shall be imposed for each taxable year upon the entire taxable income of every resident of this state who is not a part-year resident, except the head of a household as defined in Section 17042, taxes in the following amounts and at the following rates upon the amount of taxable income computed for the taxable year as if the resident were a resident of this state for the entire taxable year and for all prior taxable years for any carryover items, deferred income, suspended losses, or suspended deductions:
> … [http://www.leginfo.ca.gov/cgi-bin/displaycode?section=rtc&group=17001-18000&file=17041-17061].

However, **Part 10 Personal Income Tax, Chapter 3 Computation of Taxable Income, Article 1 Definition of Gross Income, Adjusted Gross Income, Taxable Income, etc., Sections 17071-17078** refer to the IRC for the *definitions* of what is taxable and state:

> **17071.** Section 61 of the Internal Revenue Code, relating to gross income defined, shall apply, except as otherwise provided.

> **17072.** (a) Section 62 of the Internal Revenue Code, relating to adjusted gross income defined, shall apply, except as otherwise provided.
> …

> **17073.** (a) Section 63 of the Internal Revenue Code, relating to taxable income defined, shall apply, except as otherwise provided.
> …

17074. Section 64 of the Internal Revenue Code, relating to ordinary income defined, shall apply, except as otherwise provided [http://www.leginfo.ca.gov/cgi-bin/displaycode?section=rtc&group=17001-18000&file=17071-17078].

So while the Code establishes imposition of individual income tax and liability for the tax imposed, its definitions of what is taxable are based on the IRC. In other words, the state legislature has established imposition and liability without also establishing anything on which to impose the liability. (Anything multiplied by nothing is nothing, that is, a percentage of nothing is nothing. Refer to Appendix III and Appendix D for further discussion.)

For corporations, **Part 11 Corporation Tax law, Chapter 3 The Corporation Income Tax, Article 1 Imposition of Tax, Section 23501** also establishes by specific language *imposition* of tax and by specific rates *liability* for the tax imposed and states:

23501. (a) There shall be imposed upon every corporation, other than a bank, for each taxable year, a tax at the rate of 7.6 percent upon its net income derived from sources within this state on or after January 1, 1937, other than income for any period for which the corporation is subject to taxation under Chapter 2 (commencing with Section 23101), according to or measured by its net income.
   (b) For calendar or fiscal years ending after June 30, 1973, the rate of tax shall be 9 percent instead of 7.6 percent as provided by subdivision (a).
   (c) For calendar or fiscal years ending after December 31, 1979, the rate of tax shall be the rate specified for those years by Section 23151 [http://www.leginfo.ca.gov/cgi-bin/displaycode?section=rtc&group=23001-24000&file=23501-23504].

However, the Code does not establish any *definition* of income that is taxable, although, with the exception of **Section 23049.1** regarding any gain from the sale or exchange of property which is neither a capital asset nor 1231(b) property, neither does it refer to the IRC for such definition. In other words, the state legislature has established imposition of and liability for corporate income tax without also establishing anything on which to impose the liability. (Anything multiplied by nothing is nothing, that is, a percentage of nothing is nothing.)

The California State Legislature has not enacted its own statutes for the definition of income that is taxable for either individual or corporate state income tax. While it has enacted certain statutes that establish imposition of state income tax and liability for the tax imposed, it has relied on the IRC for the definitions of what is taxable for individuals but not established any definition of income that is taxable for corporations. So while California is a *known* income-tax state, its legislature does not statutorily require the payment of state income tax.

#6 Colorado, a *Known* Income-Tax State

Federal statute based: Yes
State statute based: Yes
Actual liability: No

"Liable" defined by state statute: No
"Liability" defined by state statute: No

For general state income tax purposes, the Colorado General Assembly relies on both the **Colorado Revised Statutes** and the federal **Internal Revenue Code.**

The **Colorado Revised Statutes** do not define liable or liability for income tax purposes (reference **Title 39 Taxation, Article 22 Income Tax, Part 1 General, Section 39-22-103 Definitions – construction of terms**).

For individuals, **Article 22 Income Tax, Part 1 General, Section 39-22-104 Income tax imposed on individuals, estates, and trusts - single rate - definitions - repeal** instead establishes by specific language *imposition* of tax and by a specific percentage *liability* for the tax imposed and states:

39-22-104. Income tax imposed on individuals, estates, and trusts - single rate - definitions - repeal.

...

(1.7) Except as otherwise provided in section 39-22-627, subject to subsection (2) of this section, with respect to taxable years commencing on or after January 1, 2000, a tax of four and sixty-three one hundredths percent is imposed on the federal taxable income, as determined pursuant to section 63 of the internal revenue code, of every individual, estate, and trust.

... [http://www.michie.com/colorado/lpext.dll?f=templates&fn=main-h.htm&cp=].

However, this section also refers to the federal IRC for the ***definition*** of what is taxable, actually stating that tax is imposed on ***federal*** taxable income (rather than ***Colorado*** taxable income). By enacting this statute, the state legislature has established imposition of and liability for individual income tax without also establishing anything on which to impose the liability. (Anything multiplied by nothing is nothing, that is, a percentage of nothing is nothing. Refer to Appendix III and Appendix D for further discussion.)

For corporations, **Part 3 Corporations, Subpart 1 C Corporations, Section 39-22-301 Corporate tax imposed** also establishes by specific language *imposition* of tax and by specific rates *liability* for the tax imposed as well as the *definition* of income that is taxable and states:

39-22-301. Corporate tax imposed.

(1) …

…

(d) (I) A tax is imposed upon each domestic C corporation and foreign C corporation doing business in Colorado annually in an amount of the net income of such C corporation during the year derived from sources within Colorado as set forth in the following schedule of rates:

…

(H) For income tax years commencing on or after January 1, 1999, but prior to January 1, 2000, four and three-quarters percent of the Colorado net income;

(I) Except as otherwise provided in section 39-22-627, for income tax years commencing on or after January 1, 2000, four and sixty-three one hundredths percent of the Colorado net income.

(II) For purposes of this paragraph (d), income from sources within Colorado shall be determined in accordance with the provisions of this part 3 and includes income from tangible or intangible property located or having a situs in this state and income from any activities carried on in this state, regardless of whether carried on in intrastate, interstate, or foreign commerce….

… [http://www.michie.com/colorado/lpext.dll?f=templates&fn=main-h.htm&cp=].

So, the Code establishes imposition of corporate income tax and liability for the tax imposed as well as the definition of income that is taxable.

The Colorado General Assembly has not enacted its own statutes for the definition of income that is taxable for individual state income tax. While it has enacted a certain statute that establishes imposition of individual state income tax and liability for the tax imposed, it has relied on the IRC for the definition of what is taxable. So while Colorado is a *known* income-tax state, its legislature does not statutorily require the payment of individual state income tax. However, it does statutorily require the payment of corporate state income tax, having—without any reference to or reliance on the IRC— established *all three elements of the essential statutory formula for income tax: imposition of tax, liability for the tax imposed, and the definition of income that is taxable.*

#7 Connecticut, a *Known* Income-Tax State

Federal statute based: No
State statute based: Yes
Actual liability: Yes

"Liable" defined by state statute: No
"Liability" defined by state statute: No

For general state income tax purposes, the Connecticut General Assembly relies on both the **General Statutes of Connecticut** and the federal **Internal Revenue Code.**

The **General Statutes of Connecticut** do not define liable or liability for income tax purposes (reference **Volume 4, Title 12 Taxation, Chapter 229 Income Tax, Section 12-701 Definitions, Regulations** and **Chapter 208 Corporation Business Tax, Part I Imposition and Payment of Tax, Section 12-213 Definitions**).

For individuals, **Title 12 Taxation, Chapter 229 Income Tax, Section 12-700 Imposition of tax on income, rate** instead establishes by specific language *imposition* of tax and by specific rates *liability* for the tax imposed and states:

Sec. 12-700. Imposition of tax on income. Rate. (a) There is hereby imposed on the Connecticut taxable income of each resident of this state a tax:

...

(7) For taxable years commencing on or after January 1, 2009, in accordance with the following schedule:

... [http://www.cga.ct.gov/current/pub/chap229.htm#Sec12-700.htm].

Interestingly, this section contains as a footnote a valuable statement for educational purposes. The legislature points out that it is autonomous, that is, it does not rely on federal statutes to determine its own authority to impose any tax, and states:

State has power to tax separate from that of federal government and therefore it cannot be limited by federal statutes or regulations. 49 CS 38 [http://www.cga.ct.gov/current/pub/chap229.htm].

Indeed, the Code establishes its own *definitions* of income that is taxable and states:

Sec. 12-701. Definitions. Regulations. (a) For purposes of this chapter:

...

(8) "Connecticut taxable income of a resident" means the Connecticut adjusted gross income of a natural person with respect to any taxable year reduced by the amount of the exemption provided in section 12-702.

…

(20) "Connecticut adjusted gross income" means adjusted gross income, with the following modifications:

…

[http://www.cga.ct.gov/current/pub/chap229.htm#Sec12-701.htm].

So, the Code establishes imposition of individual income tax and liability for the tax imposed as well as the definition of income that is taxable.

For corporations, **Chapter 208 Corporation Business Tax, Part I Imposition and Payment of Tax, Section 12-214 Imposition of tax, surcharge** establishes by specific language *imposition* of tax and by a specific percentage *liability* for the tax imposed and states:

Sec. 12-214. Imposition of tax. Surcharge. (a)(1) Every mutual savings bank, savings and loan association and every company engaged in the business of carrying passengers for hire over the highways of this state in common carrier motor vehicles doing business in this state, and every other company carrying on, or having the right to carry on, business in this state, including a dissolved corporation which continues to conduct business, except those companies described in subdivision (2) of this subsection, shall pay, annually, a tax or excise upon its franchise for the privilege of carrying on or doing business, owning or leasing property within the state in a corporate capacity or as an unincorporated association taxable as a corporation for federal income tax purposes or maintaining an office within the state, such tax to be measured by the entire net income as herein defined received by such corporation or association from business transacted within the state during the income year and to be assessed for each income year commencing prior to January 1, 1995, at the rate of eleven and one-half per cent, for income years commencing on or after January 1, 1995, and prior to January 1, 1996, at the rate of eleven and one-quarter per cent, for income years commencing on or after January 1, 1996, and prior to January 1, 1997, at the rate of ten and three-fourths per cent, for income years commencing on or after January 1, 1997, and prior to January 1, 1998, at the rate of ten and one-half per cent, for income years commencing on or after January 1, 1998, and prior to January 1, 1999, at the rate of nine and one-half per cent, for income years commencing on or after January 1, 1999, and prior to January 1, 2000, at the rate of eight and one-half per cent, and for income years commencing on or after January 1, 2000, at the rate of seven and one-half per cent. The exemption of companies described in subparagraphs (G) and (H) of subdivision (2) of this

subsection shall not be allowed with respect to any income year of any such company commencing on or after January 1, 1998, and any such company claiming such exemption for any income years commencing on or after January 1, 1985, but prior to January 1, 1998, shall be required to file a corporation business tax return in accordance with section 12-222 for each such income year.
… [http://www.cga.ct.gov/current/pub/chap208.htm#Sec12-214.htm].

However, **Section 12-213 Definitions** refers to the federal IRC for the *definitions* of income that is taxable and states:

Sec. 12-213. Definitions. (a) When used in this part, unless the context otherwise requires:

…

(9) (A) "Gross income" means gross income, as defined in the Internal Revenue Code …

…

(10) "Net income" means net earnings received during the income year and available for contributors of capital, whether they are creditors or stockholders, computed by subtracting from gross income the deductions allowed by the terms of section 12-217 …

… [http://www.cga.ct.gov/current/pub/chap208.htm#Sec12-213.htm].

So while the Code establishes imposition of corporate income tax and liability for the tax imposed, its definitions of what is taxable are based on the IRC. In other words, the state legislature has established imposition and liability without also establishing anything on which to impose the liability. (Anything multiplied by nothing is nothing, that is, a percentage of nothing is nothing. Refer to Appendix III and Appendix D for further discussion.)

The Connecticut General Assembly statutorily requires the payment of individual state income tax. Without any reference to or reliance on the IRC, it has established *all three elements of the essential statutory formula for income tax: imposition of tax, liability for the tax imposed, and the definition of income that is taxable.* However, it does not statutorily require the payment of corporate state income tax.

#8 Delaware, a *Known* Income-Tax State

Federal statute based: Yes
State statute based: Yes
Actual liability: No

"Liable" defined by state statute: No
"Liability" defined by state statute: No

For general state income tax purposes, the Delaware General Assembly relies on both the **Delaware Code** and the federal **Internal Revenue Code.**

The **Delaware Code** does not define liable or liability for income tax purposes (reference **Title 30 State Taxes, Chapter 1 General Provisions, Section 101 Definitions**).

For individuals, **Title 30 State Taxes, Chapter 11 Personal Income Tax, Subchapter 1 General Provisions, Section 1102 Imposition and rate of tax; separate tax on lump-sum distributions,** although it does not actually establish by specific language *imposition* of tax as its name suggests, instead establishes by specific rates *liability* for tax and states:

> **§ 1102. Imposition and rate of tax; separate tax on lump-sum distributions.**
> (a) ...
> ...
> (13) For taxable years beginning after December 31, 2011, and before January 1, 2014, the amount of tax shall be determined as follows:
> ... [http://delcode.delaware.gov/title30/c011/sc01/index.shtml].

However, **Chapter 11 Personal Income Tax, Subchapter 2 Resident Individuals, Section 1105 Taxable income** refers to the federal IRC for the *definition* of income that is taxable and states:

> **§ 1105. Taxable income.**
> The entire taxable income of a resident of this State shall be the federal adjusted gross income as defined in the laws of the United States as the same are or shall become effective for any taxable year with the modifications and less the deductions and personal exemptions provided in this subchapter [http://delcode.delaware.gov/title30/c011/sc02/index.shtml].

So while the Code establishes liability for individual income tax, its definition of what is taxable is based on the IRC. In other words, the state legislature has established liability without also establishing anything on which to impose the liability. (Anything multiplied by nothing is nothing, that is, a percentage of nothing is nothing. Refer to Appendix III and Appendix D for further discussion.)

For corporations, **Chapter 19 Corporation Income Tax, Section 1902 Imposition of tax on corporations; exemptions** establishes by specific language *imposition* of tax and by a specific rate *liability* for the tax imposed and states:

> **§ 1902. Imposition of tax on corporations; exemptions.**
> (a) Every domestic or foreign corporation that is not exempt under subsection (b) of this section shall annually pay a tax of 8.7 percent on its taxable income, computed in accordance with § 1903 of this title, which shall be deemed to be its net income derived from business activities carried on and property located within the State during the income year....
> ... [http://delcode.delaware.gov/title30/c019/index.shtml].

However, **Section 1903 Computation of taxable income** refers to the IRC for the *definition* of income that is taxable and states:

> **§ 1903. Computation of taxable income.**
> (a) The "entire net income" of a corporation for any income year means the amount of its federal taxable income for such year as computed for purposes of the federal income tax increased by:
> ... [http://delcode.delaware.gov/title30/c019/index.shtml].

So while the Code establishes imposition of corporate income tax and liability for the tax imposed, its definition of what is taxable is based on the IRC. In other words, the state legislature has established imposition and liability without also establishing anything on which to impose the liability. (Anything multiplied by nothing is nothing, that is, a percentage of nothing is nothing.)

The Delaware General Assembly has not enacted its own statutes for the definition of income that is taxable for either individual or corporate state income tax. While it has enacted certain statutes that establish liability for individual state income tax as well as imposition of corporate state income tax and liability for the tax imposed, it has relied on the IRC for the definitions of what is taxable. So while Delaware is a *known* income-tax state, its legislature does not statutorily require the payment of state income tax.

#9 Florida, a *Known* No-Income-Tax State

Federal statute based: No
State statute based: Yes
Actual liability: No

"Liable" defined by state statute: No
"Liability" defined by state statute: No

For general state income tax purposes, the Florida State Legislature relies on both the **Florida Statutes** and the federal **Internal Revenue Code.**

It is commonly understood—***known***—that Florida is a no-income-tax state, that is, the Florida State Legislature has not enacted any statutes of law that require the payment of individual state income tax. **Title XIV** of the **Florida Statutes** contains various statutes concerning **Taxation and Finance** but does not establish imposition, liability, or the definition of income that is taxable for individual income taxes.

For individuals, it is worth noting that **Title XIV Taxation and Finance, Chapter 220 - Income Tax Code, Part I Title; Legislative Intent; Definitions, Section 220.02 Legislative intent** specifically declares the legislature's intent to exempt individuals from state income tax and states:

220.02   Legislative intent.—
(1) … This code is not intended to tax, and shall not be construed so as to tax, any natural person who engages in a trade, business, or profession in this state under his or her own or any fictitious name, whether individually as a proprietorship or in partnership with others, or as a member or a manager of a limited liability company classified as a partnership for federal income tax purposes; any estate of a decedent or incompetent; or any testamentary trust….
… [http://www.flsenate.gov/Laws/Statutes/2011/220.02].

It is also worth noting that this section also references "the mandate in s. 5, Art. VII of the State Constitution that no income tax be levied upon natural persons who are residents and citizens of this state"
[http://www.flsenate.gov/Laws/Statutes/2011/220.02].

For corporations, **Chapter 220 - Income Tax Code, Part II, Tax Imposed; Apportionment, Section 220.11 Tax imposed** establishes by specific language ***imposition*** of tax and by a specific rate ***liability*** for the tax imposed and states:

220.11   Tax imposed.—
(1)   A tax measured by net income is hereby imposed on every taxpayer for each taxable year commencing on or after January 1, 1972, ...
(2)   The tax imposed by this section shall be an amount equal to 51/2 percent of the taxpayer's net income for the taxable year.
... [http://www.flsenate.gov/Laws/Statutes/2011/220.11].

However, **Chapter 220 - Income Tax Code** refers to the federal IRC for the *definitions* of income that is taxable, actually stating that net income shall be its adjusted *federal* income (rather than adjusted *Florida* income), adjusted federal income means taxable income, and taxable income means taxable income as defined in the IRC, and states:

220.12   "Net income" defined.—For purposes of this code, a taxpayer's net income for a taxable year shall be its adjusted federal income, or that share of its adjusted federal income for such year which is apportioned to this state under s. 220.15, plus nonbusiness income allocated to this state pursuant to s. 220.16, less the exemption allowed by s. 220.14
[http://www.flsenate.gov/Laws/Statutes/2011/220.12].

220.13   "Adjusted federal income" defined.—
(1)   The term "adjusted federal income" means an amount equal to the taxpayer's taxable income as defined in subsection (2), or such taxable income of more than one taxpayer as provided in s. 220.131, for the taxable year, adjusted as follows:
...
(2)   For purposes of this section, a taxpayer's taxable income for the taxable year means taxable income as defined in s. 63 of the Internal Revenue Code and properly reportable for federal income tax purposes for the taxable year ...
... [http://www.flsenate.gov/Laws/Statutes/2011/220.13].

So while the Code establishes imposition of corporate income tax and liability for the tax imposed, its definitions of what is taxable are based on the IRC. In other words, the state legislature has established imposition and liability without also establishing anything on which to impose the liability. (Anything multiplied by nothing is nothing, that is, a percentage of nothing is nothing. Refer to Appendix III and Appendix D for further discussion.)

The Florida State Legislature does not statutorily require the payment of either individual or corporate state income tax.

#10 Georgia, a *Known* Income-Tax State

Federal statute based: Yes
State statute based: Yes
Actual liability: No

"Liable" defined by state statute: No
"Liability" defined by state statute: No

For general state income tax purposes, the Georgia General Assembly relies on both the **Official Code of Georgia Annotated** and the federal **Internal Revenue Code.**

The **Official Code of Georgia Annotated** does not define liable or liability for income tax purposes (reference **Title 48 Revenue and Taxation, Chapter 1 General Provisions, Section 48-1-2 Definitions** and **Chapter 7 Income Taxes, Article 1 General Provisions, Section 48-7-1 Definitions**).

For individuals, **Title 48 Revenue and Taxation, Chapter 7 Income Taxes, Article 2 Imposition, Rate, and Computation; Exemptions, Section 48-7-20 Individual tax rate; tax table; credit for withholding and other payments; applicability to estates and trusts** instead establishes by specific language *imposition* of tax and by specific rates *liability* for the tax imposed and states:

48-7-20. Individual tax rate; tax table; credit for withholding and other payments; applicability to estates and trusts

(a) A tax is imposed upon every resident of this state with respect to the Georgia taxable net income of the taxpayer as defined in Code Section 48-7-27....
Except as otherwise provided in this chapter, the tax imposed by this subsection shall be levied, collected, and paid annually.
(b)(1) The tax imposed pursuant to subsection (a) of this Code section shall be computed in accordance with the following tables:
… [http://law.justia.com/codes/georgia/2010/title-48/chapter-7/article-2/48-7-20/].

However, **Section 48-7-27 Computation of taxable net income** refers to the federal IRC for the *definition* of income that is taxable:

48-7-27. Computation of taxable net income

(a) Georgia taxable net income of an individual shall be the taxpayer's federal adjusted gross income, as defined in the United States Internal Revenue Code of 1986 …
… [http://law.justia.com/codes/georgia/2010/title-48/chapter-7/article-2/48-7-27/].

So while the Code establishes imposition of individual income tax and liability for the tax imposed, its definition of what is taxable is based on the IRC. In other words, the state legislature has established imposition and liability without also establishing anything on which to impose the liability. (Anything multiplied by nothing is nothing, that is, a percentage of nothing is nothing. Refer to Appendix III and Appendix D for further discussion.)

For corporations, Article 2 Imposition, Rate, and Computation; Exemptions, Section 48-7-21 Taxation of corporations also establishes by specific language *imposition* of tax and by a specific rate *liability* for the tax imposed and states:

48-7-21. Taxation of corporations

(a) Every domestic corporation and every foreign corporation shall pay annually an income tax equivalent to 6 percent of its Georgia taxable net income. Georgia taxable net income of a corporation shall be the corporation's taxable income from property owned or from business done in this state. A corporation's taxable income from property owned or from business done in this state shall consist of the corporation's taxable income as defined in the Internal Revenue Code of 1986 ....
... [http://law.justia.com/codes/georgia/2010/title-48/chapter-7/article-2/48-7-21/].

However, this section also refers to the IRC for the *definition* of what is taxable, actually stating that taxable income shall consist of taxable income as defined in the IRC.

Interestingly, moreover, this title contains a valuable statement for educational purposes under **Section 48-7-31 Taxation of corporations; allocation and apportionment of income; formula for apportionment,** which also refers to the US Constitution for the *definition* of income that is taxable, namely, the extent to which income is taxable, and states:

48-7-31. Taxation of corporations; allocation and apportionment of income; formula for apportionment

(a) The tax imposed by this chapter shall apply to the entire net income, as defined in this article, received by every foreign or domestic corporation owning property within this state, doing business within this state, or deriving income from sources within this state to the extent permitted by the United States Constitution....
... [http://law.justia.com/codes/georgia/2010/title-48/chapter-7/article-2/48-7-31/].

This is interesting and valuable because the US Constitution expressly prohibits tax that is not proportional to the census, and the IRC accordingly does not establish liability for federal income tax, so that any corporation is exempt from federal income tax, specific exemption from federal income tax or lack thereof notwithstanding. (To eliminate any doubt about the intent of this section, it does not refer to an exemption or exclusion of income the taxation of which is prohibited by the US Constitution—see Appendix II for discussion of limits imposed on the federal government by the US Constitution.)

So while the Code establishes imposition of corporate income tax and liability for the tax imposed, its definitions of what is taxable are based on both the IRC and the US Constitution. By enacting these statutes, the state legislature has established imposition and liability without also establishing anything on which to impose the liability. (Anything multiplied by nothing is nothing, that is, a percentage of nothing is nothing.)

The Georgia General Assembly has not enacted its own statutes for the definition of income that is taxable for either individual or corporate state income tax. While it has enacted certain statutes that establish imposition of state income tax and liability for the tax imposed, it has relied on both the IRC and the US Constitution for the definitions of what is taxable. So while Georgia is a **known** income-tax state, its legislature does not statutorily require the payment of state income tax.

#11 Hawaii, a *Known* Income-Tax State

Federal statute based: Yes
State statute based: Yes
Actual liability: No

"Liable" defined by state statute: No
"Liability" defined by state statute: No

For general state income tax purposes, the Hawaii State Legislature relies on both the **Hawaii Revised Statutes** and the federal **Internal Revenue Code.**

The **Hawaii Revised Statutes** do not define liable or liability for income tax purposes (reference **Division 1 Government, Title 14 Taxation, Chapter 235 Income Tax Law, Part I General Provisions, Section 235-1 Definitions** and **Part II Uniform Division of Income for Tax Purposes, Section 235-21 Definitions**).

For individuals, **Chapter 235 Income Tax Law, Part III Individual Income Tax, Section 235-51 Tax imposed on individuals; rates** establishes by specific language *imposition* of tax and by specific rates *liability* for the tax imposed and states:

> **§235-51 Tax imposed on individuals; rates.** (a) *[Repeal and reenactment on December 31, 2015. L 2009, c 60, §6(3); L 2011, c 97, §4.]* There is hereby imposed on the taxable income ... a tax determined in accordance with the following table:
> ... [http://www.capitol.hawaii.gov/hrscurrent/Vol04_Ch0201-0257/HRS0235/HRS_0235-0051.htm].

This statute, which apparently has been repealed but becomes effective again in 2015, also contains this note: "The 2009 amendment applies to taxable years beginning after December 31, 2008" [http://www.capitol.hawaii.gov/hrscurrent/Vol04_Ch0201-0257/HRS0235/HRS_0235-0051.htm].

However, **Part I General Provisions, Section 235-1 Definitions** refers to the federal IRC for the *definition* of income that is taxable and states:

> "Gross income", "adjusted gross income", "ordinary income", "ordinary loss", and "taxable income" respectively mean the same as gross income, adjusted gross income, ordinary income, ordinary loss, and taxable income as defined and determined under the Internal Revenue Code, except as otherwise provided in this chapter [http://www.capitol.hawaii.gov/hrscurrent/Vol04_Ch0201-0257/HRS0235/HRS_0235-0001.htm].

Nevertheless, **Section 235-4 Income taxes by the State; residents, nonresidents, corporations, estates, and trusts** also establishes the *definition* of income that is taxable and states:

§235-4 Income taxes by the State; residents, nonresidents, corporations, estates, and trusts. (a) Residents. The tax imposed by this chapter applies to the entire income of a resident, computed without regard to source in the State [http://www.capitol.hawaii.gov/hrscurrent/Vol04_Ch0201-0257/HRS0235/HRS_0235-0004.htm].

Interestingly, notwithstanding that the Code does not define entire income, this title contains a valuable statement for educational purposes under **Section 235-7 Other provisions as to gross income, adjusted gross income, and taxable income,** which also refers to both the US Constitution and the IRC for another *definition* of income that is taxable, namely, income that is excluded from taxable income, and states:

§235-7 Other provisions as to gross income, adjusted gross income, and taxable income. (a) *[Repeal and reenactment on January 1, 2013. L 2007, c 166, §3.]* There shall be excluded from gross income, adjusted gross income, and taxable income:
(1) Income not subject to taxation by the State under the Constitution and laws of the United States; … [http://www.capitol.hawaii.gov/hrscurrent/Vol04_Ch0201-0257/HRS0235/HRS_0235-0007.htm].

This is interesting and valuable because the US Constitution expressly prohibits tax that is not proportional to the census, and the IRC accordingly does not establish liability for federal income tax, so that any person is exempt from federal income taxation, specific exemption from federal income taxation or lack thereof notwithstanding. (To eliminate any doubt about the intent of this section, it does not refer to an exemption or exclusion of income the taxation of which by the State is prohibited by the US Constitution or US statutes—see Appendix II for discussion of limits imposed on the federal government by the US Constitution.)

By enacting this statute, which apparently has been repealed but becomes effective again in 2013, the state legislature has established that income not subject to taxation pursuant to the US Constitution and US laws is also not subject to taxation pursuant to Hawaii laws, actually stating that such income is specifically excluded from gross income, adjusted gross income, and taxable income. (When effective, this section supersedes any other definition of income that is taxable. This section also contains this note: "The 2007 amendment applies to taxable years beginning after December 31, 2007 and ending prior to January 1, 2013." To eliminate any doubt about the intent of this section, it does not refer to an exclusion of income the taxation of which by the State is prohibited by the US Constitution or US laws.)

So while the Code establishes imposition of individual income tax and liability for the tax imposed, its definitions of what is taxable are based on both the IRC and the US Constitution. In other words, the state legislature has established imposition and liability without also establishing anything on which to impose the liability. (Anything multiplied by nothing is nothing, that is, a percentage of nothing is nothing. Refer to Appendix III and Appendix D for further discussion.)

For corporations, **Section 235-4 Income taxes by the State; residents, nonresidents, corporations, estates, and trusts** establishes by specific language *imposition* of tax and also the *definition* of income that is taxable and states:

> **§235-4 Income taxes by the State; residents, nonresidents, corporations, estates, and trusts.**
> …
> (d) A corporation, foreign or domestic, is taxable upon the income received or derived from property owned, trade or business carried on, and any and every other source in the State….
> … [http://www.capitol.hawaii.gov/hrscurrent/Vol04_Ch0201-0257/HRS0235/HRS_0235-0004.htm].

Part IV Corporation Income Tax, Section 235-71 Tax on corporations; rates; credit of shareholder of regulated investment company establishes by specific rates *liability* for the tax imposed and states:

> **§235-71 Tax on corporations; rates; credit of shareholder of regulated investment company.** (a) A tax at the rates herein provided shall be assessed, levied, collected, and paid for each taxable year on the taxable income of every corporation, including a corporation carrying on business in partnership, except that in the case of a regulated investment company the tax is as provided by subsection (b) and further that in the case of a real estate investment trust as defined in section 856 of the Internal Revenue Code of 1954 the tax is as provided in subsection (d). "Corporation" includes any professional corporation incorporated pursuant to chapter 415A.
> The tax on all taxable income shall be at the rate of 4.4 per cent if the taxable income is not over $25,000, 5.4 per cent if over $25,000 but not over $100,000, and on all over $100,000, 6.4 per cent.
> … [http://www.capitol.hawaii.gov/hrscurrent/Vol04_Ch0201-0257/HRS0235/HRS_0235-0071.htm].

So, the Code establishes imposition of corporate income tax and liability for the tax imposed as well as the definition of income that is taxable.

The Hawaii State Legislature has not enacted its own statutes for the definition of income that is taxable for individual state income tax. While it has enacted a certain statute that establishes imposition of individual state income tax and liability for the tax imposed, it has relied on the IRC and the US Constitution for the definitions of what is taxable. So while Hawaii is a *known* income-tax state, its legislature does not statutorily require the payment of individual state income tax. However, it does statutorily require the payment of corporate state income tax, having—without any reference to or reliance on the IRC—established *all three elements of the essential statutory formula for income tax: imposition of tax, liability for the tax imposed, and the definition of income that is taxable.*

#12 Idaho, a *Known* Income-Tax State

Federal statute based: Yes
State statute based: Yes
Actual liability: No

"Liable" defined by state statute: No
"Liability" defined by state statute: No

For general state income tax purposes, the Idaho Legislature relies on both the **Idaho Statutes** and the federal **Internal Revenue Code.**

The **Idaho Statutes** do not define liable or liability for income tax purposes (reference **Title 63 Revenue and Taxation, Chapter 2 Definitions -- General Provisions, Section 63-201 Definitions** and **Chapter 30 Income Tax, Section 63-3003 Definitions**).

For individuals, **Title 63 Revenue and Taxation, Chapter 30 Income Tax, Section 63-3024 Individuals' tax and tax on estates and trusts** instead establishes by specific language *imposition* of tax and by specific rates *liability* for the tax imposed and states:

63-3024. Individuals' tax and tax on estates and trusts. For taxable year 2001, and each taxable year thereafter, a tax measured by Idaho taxable income as defined in this chapter is hereby imposed upon every individual, trust, or estate required by this chapter to file a return.
(a) The tax imposed upon individuals, trusts and estates shall be computed at the following rates:
… [http://www.legislature.idaho.gov/idstat/Title63/T63CH30SECT63-3024.htm].

However, **Chapter 30 Income Tax** refers to the federal IRC for the *definitions* of income that is taxable and states:

63-3011. Gross income. The term "gross income" means gross income as defined in section 61(a) of the Internal Revenue Code [http://www.legislature.idaho.gov/idstat/Title63/T63CH30SECT63-3011.htm].

63-3011A. Adjusted gross income. The term "adjusted gross income" means adjusted gross income as defined in section 62 of the Internal Revenue Code [http://www.legislature.idaho.gov/idstat/Title63/T63CH30SECT63-3011A.htm].

63-3011B. Taxable income. The term "taxable income" means federal taxable income as determined under the Internal Revenue Code [http://www.legislature.idaho.gov/idstat/Title63/T63CH30SECT63-3011B.htm].

63-3011C. Idaho taxable income. The term "Idaho taxable income" means taxable income as modified pursuant to the Idaho adjustments specifically provided in this chapter [http://www.legislature.idaho.gov/idstat/Title63/T63CH30SECT63-3011C.htm].

That is, gross income means gross income as defined in the IRC, adjusted gross income means adjusted gross income as defined in the IRC, and Idaho taxable income means taxable income, which means taxable income as determined under the IRC.

So while the Code establishes imposition of individual income tax and liability for the tax imposed, its definitions of what is taxable are based on the IRC. In other words, the state legislature has established imposition and liability without also establishing anything on which to impose the liability. (Anything multiplied by nothing is nothing, that is, a percentage of nothing is nothing. Refer to Appendix III and Appendix D for further discussion.)

For corporations, **Section 63-3025 Tax on corporate income** also establishes by specific language *imposition* of tax and by a specific rate *liability* for the tax imposed and states:

63-3025. Tax on corporate income. (1) For taxable years commencing on and after January 1, 2001, a tax is hereby imposed on the Idaho taxable income of a corporation, other than an S corporation, which transacts or is authorized to transact business in this state or which has income attributable to this state. The tax shall be equal to seven and six-tenths percent (7.6%) of Idaho taxable income.

However, **Chapter 30 Income Tax** also refers to the federal IRC for the *definitions* of income that is taxable and states:

63-3011B. Taxable income. The term "taxable income" means federal taxable income as determined under the Internal Revenue Code [http://www.legislature.idaho.gov/idstat/Title63/T63CH30SECT63-3011B.htm].

63-3011C. Idaho taxable income. The term "Idaho taxable income" means taxable income as modified pursuant to the Idaho adjustments specifically provided in this chapter [http://www.legislature.idaho.gov/idstat/Title63/T63CH30SECT63-3011C.htm].

That is, Idaho taxable income means taxable income, which means taxable income as determined under the IRC.

So while the Code establishes imposition of corporate income tax and liability for the tax imposed, its definition of what is taxable is based on the IRC. In other words, the state legislature has established imposition and liability without also establishing anything on which to impose the liability. (Anything multiplied by nothing is nothing, that is, a percentage of nothing is nothing.)

The Idaho Legislature has not enacted its own statutes for the definition of income that is taxable for either individual or corporate state income tax. While it has enacted certain statutes that establish imposition of state income tax and liability for the tax imposed, it has relied on the IRC for the definitions of what is taxable. So while Idaho is a *known* income-tax state, its legislature does not statutorily require the payment of state income tax.

#13 Illinois, a *Known* Income-Tax State

Federal statute based: Yes
State statute based: Yes
Actual liability: No

"Liable" defined by state statute: No
"Liability" defined by state statute: No

For general state income tax purposes, the Illinois General Assembly relies on both the **Illinois Compiled Statutes** and the federal **Internal Revenue Code.**

The **Illinois Compiled Statutes** do not define liable or liability for income tax purposes (reference **Chapter 35 Revenue, 35 ILCS 5/ Illinois Income Tax Act, Article 15 Definitions and Rules of Interpretation, Section 1501 Definitions**).

Instead, **Chapter 35 Revenue, 35 ILCS 5/ Illinois Income Tax Act, Article 2 Tax Imposed, Section 201 Tax Imposed** establishes by specific language *imposition* of tax and by specific rates *liability* for the tax imposed and states:

Sec. 201. Tax Imposed.
(a) In general. A tax measured by net income is hereby imposed on every individual, corporation, trust and estate for each taxable year ending after July 31, 1969 on the privilege of earning or receiving income in or as a resident of this State. Such tax shall be in addition to all other occupation or privilege taxes imposed by this State or by any municipal corporation or political subdivision thereof.
(b) Rates. The tax imposed by subsection (a) of this Section shall be determined as follows, except as adjusted by subsection (d-1):
...
[http://www.ilga.gov/legislation/ilcs/ilcs4.asp?DocName=003500050HArt%2E+2&ActID=577&ChapterID=8&SeqStart=600000&SeqEnd=3100000].

For individuals, **Chapter 35 Revenue** refers to the federal IRC for the *definitions* of income that is taxable, actually stating that adjusted gross income shall mean adjusted gross income reportable for *federal* income tax purposes (rather than *Illinois* income tax purposes) under the provisions of the IRC, and states:

Sec. 202. Net Income Defined. In general. For purposes of this Act, a taxpayer's net income for a taxable year shall be that portion of his base income for such year which is allocable to this State under the provisions of Article 3, less the standard exemption allowed by Section 204 and the deduction allowed by Section 207....
[http://www.ilga.gov/legislation/ilcs/ilcs4.asp?DocName=003500050HArt%2E+2&ActID=577&ChapterID=8&SeqStart=600000&SeqEnd=3100000]

Sec. 203. Base income defined.

(a) Individuals.

(1) In general. In the case of an individual, base income means an amount equal to the taxpayer's adjusted gross income for the taxable year as modified by paragraph (2).

...

(e) Gross income; adjusted gross income; taxable income.

(1) In general. Subject to the provisions of paragraph (2) and subsection (b) (3), for purposes of this Section and Section 803(e), a taxpayer's gross income, adjusted gross income, or taxable income for the taxable year shall mean the amount of gross income, adjusted gross income or taxable income properly reportable for federal income tax purposes for the taxable year under the provisions of the Internal Revenue Code....

...

[http://www.ilga.gov/legislation/ilcs/ilcs4.asp?DocName=003500050HArt%2E+2& ActID=577&ChapterID=8&SeqStart=600000&SeqEnd=3100000].

That is, net income is base income, which is adjusted gross income, which is adjusted gross income under the IRC.

So while the Code establishes imposition of individual income tax and liability for the tax imposed, its definitions of what is taxable are based on the IRC. In other words, the state legislature has established imposition and liability without also establishing anything on which to impose the liability. (Anything multiplied by nothing is nothing, that is, a percentage of nothing is nothing. Refer to Appendix III and Appendix D for further discussion.)

For corporations, Chapter 35 Revenue refers to the federal IRC for the *definitions* of income that is taxable, actually stating that taxable income shall mean taxable income reportable for *federal* income tax purposes (rather than *Illinois* income tax purposes) under the provisions of the IRC, and states:

Sec. 202. Net Income Defined. In general. For purposes of this Act, a taxpayer's net income for a taxable year shall be that portion of his base income for such year which is allocable to this State under the provisions of Article 3, less the standard exemption allowed by Section 204 and the deduction allowed by Section 207....

[http://www.ilga.gov/legislation/ilcs/ilcs4.asp?DocName=003500050HArt%2E+2& ActID=577&ChapterID=8&SeqStart=600000&SeqEnd=3100000]

Sec. 203. Base income defined.

...

(b) Corporations.

(1) In general. In the case of a corporation, base income means an amount equal to the taxpayer's taxable income for the taxable year as modified by paragraph (2).

(2) Modifications. The taxable income referred to in paragraph (1) shall be modified by adding thereto the sum of the following amounts:

…

(e) Gross income; adjusted gross income; taxable income.
(1) In general. Subject to the provisions of paragraph (2) and subsection (b) (3), for purposes of this Section and Section 803(e), a taxpayer's gross income, adjusted gross income, or taxable income for the taxable year shall mean the amount of gross income, adjusted gross income or taxable income properly reportable for federal income tax purposes for the taxable year under the provisions of the Internal Revenue Code….

…

[http://www.ilga.gov/legislation/ilcs/ilcs4.asp?DocName=003500050HArt%2E+2&ActID=577&ChapterID=8&SeqStart=600000&SeqEnd=3100000].

That is, net income is base income, which is taxable income, which is taxable income under the IRC.

So while the Code establishes imposition of corporate income tax and liability for the tax imposed, its definitions of what is taxable are based on the IRC. In other words, the state legislature has established imposition and liability without also establishing anything on which to impose the liability. (Anything multiplied by nothing is nothing, that is, a percentage of nothing is nothing.)

The Illinois General Assembly has not enacted its own statutes for the definition of income that is taxable for either individual or corporate state income tax. While it has enacted a certain statute that establishes imposition of state income tax and liability for the tax imposed, it has relied on the IRC for the definition of what is taxable. So while Illinois is a **known** income-tax state, its legislature does not statutorily require the payment of state income tax.

#14 Indiana, a *Known* Income-Tax State

Federal statute based: Yes
State statute based: Yes
Actual liability: No

"Liable" defined by state statute: No
"Liability" defined by state statute: No

For general state income tax purposes, the Indiana General Assembly relies on both the **Indiana Code** and the federal **Internal Revenue Code.**

The **Indiana Code** does not define liable or liability for income tax purposes (reference **Title 6 Taxation, Article 3 Other State Income Taxes, Chapter 1 Definitions**).

Instead, **Title 6 Taxation, Article 3 Other State Income Taxes, Chapter 2 Imposition of Tax and Deductions, Section 1** establishes by specific language *imposition* of tax and by specific rates *liability* for the tax imposed and states:

IC 6-3-2-1
Tax rate
Sec. 1. (a) Each taxable year, a tax at the rate of three and four-tenths percent (3.4%) of adjusted gross income is imposed upon the adjusted gross income of every resident person, and on that part of the adjusted gross income derived from sources within Indiana of every nonresident person.
(b) Except as provided in section 1.5 of this chapter, each taxable year, a tax at the following rate of adjusted gross income is imposed on that part of the adjusted gross income derived from sources within Indiana of every corporation: … [http://www.in.gov/legislative/ic/code/title6/ar3/ch2.html].

For individuals, **Chapter 1 Definitions, Section 3.5 Version c "Adjusted gross income"** refers to the federal IRC for the *definition* of adjusted gross income and states:

IC 6-3-1-3.5 Version c
"Adjusted gross income"
Note: This version of section amended by P.L.172-2011, SEC.53, effective 1-1-2012. See also preceding version of this section amended by P.L.229-2011, SEC.83, effective until 1-1-2012, and preceding version of this section amended by P.L.171-2011, SEC.4, effective 7-1-2011.
Sec. 3.5. When used in this article, the term "adjusted gross income" shall mean the following:
(a) In the case of all individuals, "adjusted gross income" (as defined in Section 62 of the Internal Revenue Code), modified as follows:

(1) Subtract income that is exempt from taxation under this article by the Constitution and statutes of the United States.
… [http://www.in.gov/legislative/ic/code/title6/ar3/ch1.html].

Interestingly, moreover, this subsection contains a valuable statement for educational purposes, as it also states that income that is exempt from taxation by the US Constitution and US statutes is subtracted from adjusted gross income. This is interesting and valuable because the US Constitution expressly prohibits tax that is not proportional to the census, and the IRC accordingly does not establish liability for federal income tax, so that any individual is exempt from federal income taxation, specific exemption from federal income taxation or lack thereof notwithstanding. (To eliminate any doubt about the intent of this section, it does not refer to an exemption or exclusion of income the taxation of which is prohibited by the US Constitution or US statutes—see Appendix II for discussion of limits imposed on the federal government by the US Constitution.)

For corporations, **Chapter 1 Definitions, Section 3.5 Version c "Adjusted gross income"** also refers to the IRC for the *definition* of taxable income and states:

IC 6-3-1-3.5 Version c
"Adjusted gross income"
Note: This version of section amended by P.L.172-2011, SEC.53, effective 1-1-2012. See also preceding version of this section amended by P.L.229-2011, SEC.83, effective until 1-1-2012, and preceding version of this section amended by P.L.171-2011, SEC.4, effective 7-1-2011.
Sec. 3.5. When used in this article, the term "adjusted gross income" shall mean the following:
…
(b) In the case of corporations, the same as "taxable income" (as defined in Section 63 of the Internal Revenue Code) adjusted as follows:
(1) Subtract income that is exempt from taxation under this article by the Constitution and statutes of the United States.
… [http://www.in.gov/legislative/ic/code/title6/ar3/ch1.html].

Moreover, this subsection also states that income that is exempt from taxation by the US Constitution and US statutes is subtracted from taxable income. The US Constitution expressly prohibits tax that is not proportional to the census, and the IRC accordingly does not establish liability for federal income tax, so that any corporation is exempt from federal income taxation, specific exemption from federal income taxation or lack thereof notwithstanding. (To eliminate any doubt about the intent of this section, it does not refer to an exemption or exclusion of income the taxation of which is prohibited by the US Constitution or US statutes—see Appendix II for discussion of limits imposed on the federal government by the US Constitution.)

So while the Code establishes imposition of corporate income tax and liability for the tax imposed, its definitions of what is taxable are based on both the IRC and the US

Constitution. In other words, the state legislature has established imposition and liability without also establishing anything on which to impose the liability. (Anything multiplied by nothing is nothing, that is, a percentage of nothing is nothing. Refer to Appendix III and Appendix D for further discussion.)

The Indiana General Assembly has not enacted its own statutes for the definition of income that is taxable for either individual or corporate state income tax. While it has enacted a certain statute that establishes imposition of state income tax and liability for the tax imposed, it has relied on both the IRC and the US Constitution for the definitions of what is taxable. So while Indiana is a *known* income-tax state, its legislature does not statutorily require the payment of state income tax.

#15 Iowa, a *Known* Income-Tax State

Federal statute based: Yes
State statute based: Yes
Actual liability: No

"Liable" defined by state statute: No
"Liability" defined by state statute: No

For general state income tax purposes, The Iowa Legislature relies on both the **Iowa Code** and the federal **Internal Revenue Code.**

The **Iowa Code** does not define liable or liability for income tax purposes (reference **Title X Financial Resources, Subtitle 1 Revenues and Financial Management, Chapter 422 Individual Income, Corporate, and Franchise Taxes, Sections 422.3 Definitions controlling chapter, 422.4 Definitions controlling division,** and **422.32 Definitions**).

For individuals, **Title X Financial Resources, Subtitle 1 Revenues and Financial Management, Chapter 422 Individual Income, Corporate, and Franchise Taxes, Section 422.5 Tax imposed — exclusions — alternative minimum tax** instead establishes by specific language *imposition* of tax and by specific rates *liability* for the tax imposed and states:

422.5 Tax imposed — exclusions — alternative minimum tax.
1. A tax is imposed upon every resident and nonresident of the state which tax shall be levied, collected, and paid annually upon and with respect to the entire taxable income as defined in this division at rates as follows:
... [http://search.legis.state.ia.us/nxt/gateway.dll/ic?f=templates&fn=default.htm].

However, **Title X Financial Resources** refers to the federal IRC for the *definitions* of income that is taxable, actually stating that taxable income means net income and net income means adjusted gross income for *federal* income tax purposes (rather than *Iowa* income tax purposes) under the IRC, and states:

422.4 Definitions controlling division.
For the purpose of this division and unless otherwise required by the context:
...
16. The words *"taxable income"* mean the net income as defined in section 422.7 minus the deductions allowed by section 422.9, in the case of individuals ....
... [http://search.legis.state.ia.us/nxt/gateway.dll/ic?f=templates&fn=default.htm].

422.7 "Net income" — how computed.
The term *"net income"* means the adjusted gross income before the net operating loss deduction as properly computed for federal income tax purposes under the Internal Revenue Code ...
... [http://search.legis.state.ia.us/nxt/gateway.dll/ic?f=templates&fn=default.htm].

So while the Code establishes imposition of individual income tax and liability for the tax imposed, its definition of what is taxable is based on the IRC. In other words, the state legislature has established imposition and liability without also establishing anything on which to impose the liability. (Anything multiplied by nothing is nothing, that is, a percentage of nothing is nothing. Refer to Appendix III and Appendix D for further discussion.)

For corporations, Section 422.33 Corporate tax imposed — credit also establishes by specific language *imposition* of tax and by specific rates *liability* for the tax imposed and states:

422.33 Corporate tax imposed — credit.
1. A tax is imposed annually upon each corporation doing business in this state, or deriving income from sources within this state, in an amount computed by applying the following rates of taxation to the net income received by the corporation during the income year:
... [http://search.legis.state.ia.us/nxt/gateway.dll/ic?f=templates&fn=default.htm].

However, the Code does not establish any *definition* of income that is taxable, although neither does it refer to the IRC for such definition. In other words, the state legislature has established imposition of and liability for corporate income tax without also establishing anything on which to impose the liability. (Anything multiplied by nothing is nothing, that is, a percentage of nothing is nothing.)

The Iowa General Assembly has not enacted its own statutes for the definition of income that is taxable for either individual or corporate state income tax. While it has enacted certain statutes that establish imposition of state income tax and liability for the tax imposed, it has relied on the IRC for the definition of what is taxable for individuals but not established any definition of income that is taxable for corporations. So while Iowa is a *known* income-tax state, its legislature does not statutorily require the payment of state income tax.

#16 Kansas, a *Known* Income-Tax State

Federal statute based: Yes
State statute based: Yes
Actual liability: No

"Liable" defined by state statute: No
"Liability" defined by state statute: No

For general state income tax purposes, the Kansas Legislature relies on both the **Kansas Statutes Annotated** and the federal **Internal Revenue Code.**

The **Kansas Statutes Annotated** do not define liable or liability for income tax purposes (reference **Chapter 79 Taxation, Article 32 Income Tax, Sections 79-32,109 Definitions** and **79-3271 Apportionment of net income; definitions**).

For individuals, **Chapter 79 Taxation, Article 32 Income Tax, Section 79-32,110 Tax imposed; classes of taxpayers; rates** instead establishes by specific language *imposition* of tax and by specific rates *liability* for the tax imposed and states:

> **79-32,110.   Tax imposed; classes of taxpayers; rates.** (a) *Resident Individuals.* Except as otherwise provided by subsection (a) of K.S.A. 79-3220, and amendments thereto, a tax is hereby imposed upon the Kansas taxable income of every resident individual, which tax shall be computed in accordance with the following tax schedules:
> ... [http://kansasstatutes.lesterama.org/Chapter_79/Article_32/#79-32,110].

However, **Article 32 Income Tax** refers to the federal IRC for the *definitions* of Kansas taxable income, actually stating that Kansas adjusted gross income means *federal* adjusted gross income, and states:

> **79-32,116.   Kansas taxable income of an individual.** The Kansas taxable income of an individual shall be his or her Kansas adjusted gross income less his or her Kansas deductions and Kansas personal exemptions [http://kansasstatutes.lesterama.org/Chapter_79/Article_32/#79-32,116].

> **79-32,117.   Kansas adjusted gross income of an individual.** (a) The Kansas adjusted gross income of an individual means such individual's federal adjusted gross income for the taxable year, with the modifications specified in this section. ... [http://kansasstatutes.lesterama.org/Chapter_79/Article_32/#79-32,117].

That is, Kansas taxable income is Kansas adjusted gross income, which is *federal* adjusted gross income.

So while the Code establishes imposition of individual income tax and liability for the tax imposed, its definitions of what is taxable are based on the IRC. In other words, the state legislature has established imposition and liability without also establishing anything on which to impose the liability. (Anything multiplied by nothing is nothing, that is, a percentage of nothing is nothing. Refer to Appendix III and Appendix D for further discussion.)

For corporations, Section 79-32,110 Tax imposed; classes of taxpayers; rates also establishes by specific language *imposition* of tax and by specific rates *liability* for the tax imposed and states:

> **79-32,110.   Tax imposed; classes of taxpayers; rates.**
> …
> (c)   *Corporations.* A tax is hereby imposed upon the Kansas taxable income of every corporation doing business within this state or deriving income from sources within this state. Such tax shall consist of a normal tax and a surtax and shall be computed as follows:
> … [http://kansasstatutes.lesterama.org/Chapter_79/Article_32/#79-32,110].

However, **Section 79-32,138 Kansas taxable income of corporations** refers to the IRC for the *definition* of income that is taxable, actually stating that Kansas taxable income shall be *federal* taxable income, and states:

> **79-32,138.   Kansas taxable income of corporations.** (a) Kansas taxable income of a corporation taxable under this act shall be the corporation's federal taxable income for the taxable year with the modifications specified in this section.
> … [http://kansasstatutes.lesterama.org/Chapter_79/Article_32/#79-32,138].

So while the Code establishes imposition of corporate income tax and liability for the tax imposed, its definition of what is taxable is based on the IRC. In other words, the state legislature has established imposition and liability without also establishing anything on which to impose the liability. (Anything multiplied by nothing is nothing, that is, a percentage of nothing is nothing.)

Interestingly, moreover, this chapter contains a valuable statement for educational purposes under **Section 79-32,113 Exempted organizations,** which also refers to IRC for the *definition* of income that is taxable, namely, income that is exempt from federal income taxation under the IRC, and states:

> **79-32,113.   Exempted organizations.** (a) A person or organization exempt from federal income taxation under the provisions of the federal internal revenue code shall also be exempt from the tax imposed by this act in each year in which such person or organization satisfies the requirements of the federal internal revenue code for exemption from federal income taxation….
> … [http://kansasstatutes.lesterama.org/Chapter_79/Article_32/#79-32,113].

This is interesting and valuable because the IRC does not establish liability for federal income tax, so that any person or organization is exempt from federal income taxation, specific exemption from federal income taxation or lack thereof notwithstanding.

The Kansas Legislature has not enacted its own statutes for the definition of income that is taxable for either individual or corporate state income tax. While it has enacted a certain statute that establishes imposition of state income tax and liability for the tax imposed, it has relied on the IRC for the definitions of what is taxable. So while Kansas is a *known* income-tax state, its legislature does not statutorily require the payment of state income tax.

#17 Kentucky, a *Known* Income-Tax State

Federal statute based: Yes
State statute based: Yes
Actual liability: No

"Liable" defined by state statute: No
"Liability" defined by state statute: No

For general state income tax purposes, the Kentucky Legislature relies on both the **Kentucky Revised Statutes** and the federal **Internal Revenue Code.**

The **Kentucky Revised Statutes** do not define liable or liability for income tax purposes (reference **Title XI - Revenue and Taxation, Chapter 141 Income Taxes, Section 141.010 Definitions for chapter**).

For individuals, **Section 141.020 Levy of income tax on individuals -- Rate of normal tax -- Tax credits -- Income of nonresidents subject to tax -- Election to pay tax imposed by KRS 141.023** instead establishes by specific language *imposition* of tax and by specific rates *liability* for the tax imposed and states:

> **141.020 Levy of income tax on individuals -- Rate of normal tax -- Tax credits -- Income of nonresidents subject to tax -- Election to pay tax imposed by KRS 141.023.**
> (1) An annual tax shall be paid for each taxable year by every resident individual of this state upon his entire net income as defined in this chapter. The tax shall be determined by applying the rates in subsection (2) of this section to net income and subtracting allowable tax credits provided in subsection (3) of this section.
> ... [http://lrc.ky.gov/KRS/141-00/020.PDF].

However, **Section 141.010 Definitions for chapter** refers to the IRC for the *definitions* of income that is taxable and states:

> **141.010 Definitions for chapter.**
> As used in this chapter, unless the context requires otherwise:
> ...
> (9) "Gross income," in the case of taxpayers other than corporations, means "gross income" as defined in Section 61 of the Internal Revenue Code;
> (10) "Adjusted gross income," in the case of taxpayers other than corporations, means gross income as defined in subsection (9) of this section minus the deductions allowed individuals by Section 62 of the Internal Revenue Code and as modified by KRS 141.0101 and adjusted as follows, except that deductions shall be limited to amounts allocable to income subject to taxation under the provisions of this chapter, and except that nothing in this chapter shall be construed to permit the same item to be deducted more than once:

...
(11) "Net income," in the case of taxpayers other than corporations, means adjusted gross income as defined in subsection (10) of this section, minus:
... [http://lrc.ky.gov/KRS/141-00/010.PDF].

So while the Code establishes imposition of individual income tax and liability for the tax imposed, its definitions of what is taxable are based on the IRC. In other words, the state legislature has established imposition and liability without also establishing anything on which to impose the liability. (Anything multiplied by nothing is nothing, that is, a percentage of nothing is nothing. Refer to Appendix III and Appendix D for further discussion.)

For corporations, Section 141.040 Corporation income tax -- Exemption -- Rate also establishes by specific language *imposition* of tax and by specific rates *liability* for the tax imposed and states:

141.040 Corporation income tax -- Exemption -- Rate.
(1) Every corporation doing business in this state, except those corporations listed in paragraphs (a) to (i) of this subsection, shall pay for each taxable year a tax to be computed by the taxpayer on taxable net income or the alternative minimum calculation computed under this section at the rates specified in this section:
... [http://lrc.ky.gov/KRS/141-00/040.PDF].

However, **Section 141.010 Definitions for chapter** refers to the IRC for the *definitions* of income that is taxable and states:

141.010 Definitions for chapter.
As used in this chapter, unless the context requires otherwise:
...
(12) "Gross income," in the case of corporations, means "gross income" as defined in Section 61 of the Internal Revenue Code and as modified by KRS 141.0101 and adjusted as follows:
...
(13) "Net income," in the case of corporations, means "gross income" as defined in subsection (12) of this section ....
...
(14) (a) "Taxable net income," in the case of corporations that are taxable in this state, means "net income" as defined in subsection (13) of this section;
... [http://lrc.ky.gov/KRS/141-00/010.PDF].

So while the Code establishes imposition of corporate income tax and liability for the tax imposed, its definitions of what is taxable are based on the IRC. In other words, the state legislature has established imposition and liability without also establishing anything on which to impose the liability. (Anything multiplied by nothing is nothing, that is, a percentage of nothing is nothing.)

The Kentucky General Assembly has not enacted its own statutes for the definition of income that is taxable for either individual or corporate state income tax. While it has enacted certain statutes that establish imposition of state income tax and liability for the tax imposed, it has relied on the IRC for the definitions of what is taxable. So while Kentucky is a *known* income-tax state, its legislature does not statutorily require the payment of state income tax.

#18 Louisiana, a *Known* Income-Tax State

Federal statute based: No
State statute based: Yes
Actual liability: Yes

"Liable" defined by state statute: No
"Liability" defined by state statute: No

For general state income tax purposes, the Louisiana State Legislature relies on both the **Louisiana Administrative Code** and the federal **Internal Revenue Code.**

The **Louisiana Administrative Code** does not define liable or liability for income tax purposes (reference **Title 47 Revenue and Taxation, Sections 47:2 General definitions** and **47:6 Definitions**).

For individuals, **Title 47 Revenue and Taxation** instead establishes by specific language *imposition* of tax and by specific rates *liability* for the tax imposed as well as the *definitions* of income that is taxable and states:

SUBPART B. TAX LEVY; RATES OF TAX
§31. Individuals, corporations and trusts subject to tax
There shall be levied, collected, and paid for each taxable year a tax upon the net income of residents and nonresidents, estates, trusts and corporations, as hereinafter provided.
(1) Resident individuals. Every person residing within the state, or the personal representative in the event of death, shall pay a tax on net income from whatever source derived, except as hereinafter exempted.
… [http://law.justia.com/codes/louisiana/2011/rs/title47/rs47-31/].

§32. Rates of tax
A. On individuals. The tax to be assessed, levied, collected and paid upon the taxable income of an individual shall be computed at the following rates:
… [http://law.justia.com/codes/louisiana/2011/rs/title47/rs47-32/].

SUBPART C. COMPUTATION OF NET INCOME
§41. Net income
"Net income" means the gross income computed under R.S. 47:42 through 47:53, less the deductions allowed by R.S. 47:54 through 47:77
[http://law.justia.com/codes/louisiana/2011/rs/title47/rs47-41/].

§42. Gross income defined
A. General definition. "Gross income" includes gains, profits, and income derived from salaries, wages, or compensation for personal service, of whatever kind and in whatever form paid, or from professions, vocations, trades, businesses, commerce, or sales, or dealing in property, whether real or personal, growing out

of the ownership or use of or interest in such property; also from interest, rent, dividends, securities, or the transaction of any business carried on for gain or profit, or gains or profits and income derived from any source whatever.
… [http://law.justia.com/codes/louisiana/2011/rs/title47/rs47-42/].

So, the Code establishes imposition of individual income tax and liability for the tax imposed as well as the definition of income that is taxable.

For corporations, **Title 47 Revenue and Taxation** also establishes by specific language *imposition* of tax and by specific rates *liability* for the tax imposed and states:

SUBPART B. TAX LEVY; RATES OF TAX
§31. Individuals, corporations and trusts subject to tax
There shall be levied, collected, and paid for each taxable year a tax upon the net income of residents and nonresidents, estates, trusts and corporations, as hereinafter provided.
…

(3) Corporations. Corporations shall be taxed on net income from sources within the state, as hereinafter set out.
… [http://law.justia.com/codes/louisiana/2011/rs/title47/rs47-31/].

§287.11. Tax imposed
A. There shall be levied, collected, and paid for each taxable year a tax upon the Louisiana taxable income of corporations and other entities taxed as corporations for federal income tax purposes, which entities shall be considered to be corporations for the purposes of this Chapter only, other than insurance companies as hereinafter provided.
B. Corporations shall be taxed on their Louisiana taxable income, except as otherwise exempted.
… [http://law.justia.com/codes/louisiana/2011/rs/title47/rs47-287-11/].

§32. Rates of tax
…
C. On corporations. The tax to be assessed, levied, collected, and paid upon the net income of every corporation shall be computed at the rate of:
… [http://law.justia.com/codes/louisiana/2011/rs/title47/rs47-32/].

§287.12. Rates of tax
The tax to be assessed, levied, collected, and paid upon the Louisiana taxable income of every corporation shall be computed at the rate of:
… [http://law.justia.com/codes/louisiana/2011/rs/title47/rs47-287-12/].

However, **Title 47 Revenue and Taxation** refers to the federal IRC for the *definitions* of income that is taxable, actually stating that net income means the taxable income computed in accordance with *federal* law (rather than *Louisiana* law), and states:

SUBPART F. NONRESIDENT INDIVIDUALS AND CORPORATIONS
§241. Net income subject to tax
The net income of a nonresident individual or a corporation subject to the tax imposed by this Chapter shall be the sum of the net allocable income earned within or derived from sources within this state, as defined in R.S. 47:243, and the net apportionable income derived from sources in this state, as defined in R.S. 47:244, … [http://law.justia.com/codes/louisiana/2011/rs/title47/rs47-241/].

§287.65. Net income defined
"Net income" of a corporation for a taxable year means the taxable income of the corporation computed in accordance with federal law for the same accounting period and under the same method of accounting, including statutorily required accounting adjustments, subject to the modifications specified in this Part [http://law.justia.com/codes/louisiana/2011/rs/title47/rs47-287-65/].

§287.67. Louisiana net income defined
"Louisiana net income" means net income which is earned within or derived from sources within the state of Louisiana [http://law.justia.com/codes/louisiana/2011/rs/title47/rs47-287-67/].

§287.69. Louisiana taxable income defined
"Louisiana taxable income" means Louisiana net income, after adjustments, less the federal income tax deduction allowed by R.S. 47:287.85. "After adjustments" means after the application of the net operating loss adjustment allowed by R.S. 47:287.86 [http://law.justia.com/codes/louisiana/2011/rs/title47/rs47-287-69/].

So while the Code establishes imposition of corporate income tax and liability for the tax imposed, its definitions of what is taxable are based on the IRC. In other words, the state legislature has established imposition and liability without also establishing anything on which to impose the liability. (Anything multiplied by nothing is nothing, that is, a percentage of nothing is nothing. Refer to Appendix III and Appendix D for further discussion.)

The Louisiana State Legislature statutorily requires the payment of individual state income tax. Without any reference to or reliance on the IRC, it has established **all three elements of the essential statutory formula for income tax: imposition of tax, liability for the tax imposed, and the definition of income that is taxable.** However, it does not statutorily require the payment of corporate state income tax.

#19 Maine, a *Known* Income-Tax State

Federal statute based: Yes
State statute based: Yes
Actual liability: No

"Liable" defined by state statute: No
"Liability" defined by state statute: No

For general state income tax purposes, the Maine State Legislature relies on both the **Maine Revised Statutes** and the federal **Internal Revenue Code.**

The **Maine Revised Statures** do not define liable or liability for income tax purposes (reference **Title 36 Taxation, Part 8 Income Taxes, Chapter 801 Definitions, Section 5102 Definitions**).

For individuals, **Part 8 Income Taxes, Chapter 803 Imposition of Tax on Individuals, Section 5111 Imposition and rate of tax** instead establishes by specific language *imposition* of tax and by specific rates *liability* for the tax imposed and states:

§5111. Imposition and rate of tax
A tax is imposed for each taxable year beginning on or after January 1, 2000, on the Maine taxable income of every resident individual of this State. The amount of the tax is determined as provided in this section.
… [http://www.mainelegislature.org/legis/statutes/36/title36sec5111.html].

However, **Chapter 805 Computation of Taxable Income of Resident Individuals, Section 5121 Maine taxable income** refers to the federal IRC for the *definition* of income that is taxable, actually stating that Maine taxable income is equal to *federal* adjusted gross income (rather than *Maine* adjusted gross income), and states:

§5121. Maine taxable income
The Maine taxable income of a resident individual is equal to the individual's federal adjusted gross income as defined by the Code with the modifications and less the deductions and personal exemptions provided in this chapter [http://www.mainelegislature.org/legis/statutes/36/title36sec5121.html].

So while the Code establishes imposition of individual income tax and liability for the tax imposed, its definition of what is taxable is based on the IRC. In other words, the state legislature has established imposition and liability without also establishing anything on which to impose the liability. (Anything multiplied by nothing is nothing, that is, a percentage of nothing is nothing. Refer to Appendix III and Appendix D for further discussion.)

For corporations, **Chapter 817 Imposition of Tax on Corporations, Section 5200. Imposition and rate of tax** establishes by specific language *imposition* of tax and by specific rates *liability* for the tax imposed and states:

> **§5200. Imposition and rate of tax**
> **1. Imposition and rate of tax.** A tax is imposed for each taxable year at the following rates on each taxable corporation and on each group of corporations that derives income from a unitary business carried on by 2 or more members of an affiliated group:
> …
> **5. Net income.** For purposes of this section, "net income" means, for any taxable year, the taxable income of the taxpayer for that taxable year under the laws of the United States as modified by section 5200-A.
> … [http://www.mainelegislature.org/legis/statutes/36/title36sec5200.html].

However, this section also refers to the IRC for the definition of income that is taxable , actually stating that net income means taxable income under the laws of the *US* (rather than under the laws of *Maine*).

Moreover, **Chapter 801 Definitions, Section 5102 Definitions** also refers to the IRC for the *definitions* of income that is taxable, actually stating that Maine net income means taxable income under the laws of the *US* (rather than under the laws of *Maine*), and states:

> **§5102. Definitions**
> The following definitions shall apply throughout this Part, except as the context may otherwise require:
> …
> **8. Maine net income.** "Maine net income" means, for any taxable year for any corporate taxpayer, the taxable income of that taxpayer for that taxable year under the laws of the United States ….
> …
> **10. Taxable corporation.** "Taxable corporation" means, for any taxable year, a corporation that, at any time during that taxable year, realized Maine net income….
> … [http://www.mainelegislature.org/legis/statutes/36/title36sec5102.html]

So while the Code establishes imposition of corporate income tax and liability for the tax imposed, its definitions of what is taxable are based on the IRC. In other words, the state legislature has established imposition and liability without also establishing anything on which to impose the liability. (Anything multiplied by nothing is nothing, that is, a percentage of nothing is nothing.)

The Maine State Legislature has not enacted its own statutes for the definition of income that is taxable for either individual or corporate state income tax. While it has enacted certain statutes that establish imposition of state income tax and liability for the tax imposed, it has relied on the IRC for the definitions of what is taxable. So while Maine is a **known** income-tax state, its legislature does not statutorily require the payment of state income tax.

#20 Maryland, a *Known* Income-Tax State

Federal statute based: Yes
State statute based: Yes
Actual liability: No

"Liable" defined by state statute: No
"Liability" defined by state statute: No

For general state income tax purposes, the Maryland General Assembly relies on both the **Maryland Code** and the federal **Internal Revenue Code.**

The **Maryland Code** does not define liable or liability for income tax purposes (reference **Tax - General, Title 1 Definitions; General Provisions, Subtitle 1 Definitions, Section 1-101 Definitions** and **Title 10 Income Tax, Subtitle 1 Definitions; General Provisions, Section 10-101 Definitions**).

Instead, **Title 10 Income Tax, Subtitle 1 Definitions; General Provisions** establishes by specific language *imposition* of tax and by specific rates *liability* for the tax imposed as well as the *definition* of Maryland taxable income and states:

§ 10-102. Imposition of tax - In general.
Except as provided in § 10-104 of this subtitle, a tax is imposed on the Maryland taxable income of each individual and of each corporation [http://law.justia.com/codes/maryland/2010/tax-general/title-10/subtitle-1/10-102/].

§ 10-105. State income tax rates.
(a) Individual.-
(1) Except as provided in paragraph (3) of this subsection, for an individual other than an individual described in paragraph (2) of this subsection, the State income tax rate is:
…
(b) Corporation.- The State income tax rate for a corporation is 8.25% of Maryland taxable income.
… [http://law.justia.com/codes/maryland/2010/tax-general/title-10/subtitle-1/10-105/].

§ 10-101. Definitions.
(a) In general.- In this title the following words have the meanings indicated.
…
(i) Maryland taxable income.- "Maryland taxable income" means:
(1) for an individual, Maryland adjusted gross income, less the exemptions and deductions allowed under this title; and
 (2) for a corporation, Maryland modified income as allocated under this title.
… [http://law.justia.com/codes/maryland/2010/tax-general/title-10/subtitle-1/10-101/].

For individuals, however, **Subtitle 2 Maryland Taxable Income Calculations for Individual** also refers to the federal IRC for the ***definitions*** of income that is taxable, actually stating that Maryland adjusted gross income is ***federal*** adjusted gross income, and states:

Part I. Maryland Taxable Income for Individual.
§ 10-201. In general.
An individual shall calculate Maryland taxable income by subtracting from the individual's Maryland adjusted gross income calculated under Part II of this subtitle an amount that equals:
(1) the exemptions allowed under Part III of this subtitle; and
(2) the deductions allowed under Part IV of this subtitle
[http://law.justia.com/codes/maryland/2010/tax-general/title-10/subtitle-2/10-201/].

Part II. Maryland Adjusted Gross Income.
§ 10-203. In general.
Except as provided in Subtitle 4 of this title, the Maryland adjusted gross income of an individual is the individual's federal adjusted gross income for the taxable year as adjusted under this Part II of this subtitle
[http://law.justia.com/codes/maryland/2010/tax-general/title-10/subtitle-2/10-203/].

So while the Code establishes imposition of individual income tax and liability for the tax imposed, its definitions of what is taxable are based on the IRC. In other words, the state legislature has established imposition and liability without also establishing anything on which to impose the liability. (Anything multiplied by nothing is nothing, that is, a percentage of nothing is nothing. Refer to Appendix III and Appendix D for further discussion.)

For corporations, **Subtitle 3 Maryland Taxable Income Calculations for Corporation** also refers to the IRC for the ***definitions*** of income that is taxable, actually stating that Maryland modified income is ***federal*** taxable income, and states:

Part I. Maryland Taxable Income for Corporation.
§ 10-301. In general.
The Maryland taxable income of a corporation is its Maryland modified income as allocated to the State under Subtitle 4 of this title
[http://law.justia.com/codes/maryland/2010/tax-general/title-10/subtitle-3/10-301/].

Part II. Maryland Modified Income.
§ 10-304. In general.
Except as provided in Subtitle 4 of this title, the Maryland modified income of a corporation, including a real estate investment trust or regulated investment company, is:

(1) the corporation's federal taxable income for the taxable year as determined under the Internal Revenue Code and as adjusted under this Part II of this subtitle;
… [http://law.justia.com/codes/maryland/2010/tax-general/title-10/subtitle-3/10-304/].

So while the Code establishes imposition of corporate income tax and liability for the tax imposed, its definitions of what is taxable are based on the IRC. In other words, the state legislature has established imposition and liability without also establishing anything on which to impose the liability. (Anything multiplied by nothing is nothing, that is, a percentage of nothing is nothing.)

The Maryland General Assembly has not enacted its own statutes for the definition of income that is taxable for either individual or corporate state income tax. While it has enacted certain statutes that establish imposition of state income tax and liability for the tax imposed, it has relied on the IRC for the definitions of what is taxable. So while Maryland is a *known* income-tax state, its legislature does not statutorily require the payment of state income tax.

#21 Massachusetts, a *Known* Income-Tax State

Federal statute based: Yes
State statute based: Yes
Actual liability: No

"Liable" defined by state statute: No
"Liability" defined by state statute: No

For general state income tax purposes, the Massachusetts General Court relies on both the **Massachusetts Code** and the federal **Internal Revenue Code.**

The **Massachusetts Code** does not define liable or liability for income tax purposes (reference **Part I Administration of the Government, Title IX Taxation, Chapter 62 Taxation of Incomes, Section 1 Definitions** and **Chapter 63 Taxation of Corporations, Section 1 Definitions**).

For individuals, **Title IX Taxation, Chapter 62 Taxation of Incomes, Section 4 Rates of tax for residents, non-residents and corporate trusts** instead establishes by specific language *imposition* of tax and by specific rates *liability* for the tax imposed and states:

> **Section 4.** Residents shall be taxed on their taxable income, and non-residents shall be taxed to the extent specified in section 5A on their taxable income, as follows:
>
> ...
>
> [http://law.justia.com/codes/massachusetts/2010/parti/titleix/chapter62/section4/].

However, **Title IX Taxation** refers to the federal IRC for the *definitions* of income that is taxable, actually stating that Massachusetts gross income means *federal* gross income, and states:

> **Section 3 Taxable income: adjusted gross income less deductions and exemptions**
> **Section 3.** A. In determining the Part A taxable income, the Part A adjusted gross income shall be reduced by the following deductions and exemptions.
>
> ...
>
> B. In determining the Part B taxable income, the Part B adjusted gross income shall be reduced by the following deductions and exemptions:
>
> ...
>
> C. In determining the Part C taxable income, the Part C adjusted gross income shall be reduced by the following deductions and exemptions:
>
> ...
>
> [http://law.justia.com/codes/massachusetts/2010/parti/titleix/chapter62/section3/].

Section 2 Gross income, adjusted gross income and taxable income defined; classes
Section 2. (a) Massachusetts gross income shall mean the federal gross income, modified as required by section six F, with the following further modifications:--

…

(b) Massachusetts gross income shall be divided into three Parts:

…

(i) Massachusetts adjusted gross income shall be the sum of Part A adjusted gross income, Part B adjusted gross income and Part C adjusted gross income.

…

[http://law.justia.com/codes/massachusetts/2010/parti/titleix/chapter62/section2/].

That is, taxable income, which is divided into three parts, is determined by subtracting deductions and exemptions from adjusted gross income, which is divided into three parts, the sum of which comprises Massachusetts adjusted gross income, which is derived from Massachusetts gross income, which is also divided into three parts, which means *federal* gross income.

So while the Code establishes imposition of individual income tax and liability for the tax imposed, its definitions of what is taxable are based on the IRC. In other words, the state legislature has established imposition and liability without also establishing anything on which to impose the liability. (Anything multiplied by nothing is nothing, that is, a percentage of nothing is nothing. Refer to Appendix III and Appendix D for further discussion.)

For corporations, **Title IX Taxation, Chapter 63 Taxation of Corporations, Section 39 Tax rate** also establishes by specific language *imposition* of tax and by specific rates *liability* for the tax imposed and states:

Section 39. Except as otherwise provided in this section, every business corporation, organized under the laws of the commonwealth, or exercising its charter or other means of legal authority, or qualified to do business or actually doing business in the commonwealth, or owning or using any part or all of its capital, plant or any other property in the commonwealth, shall pay, on account of each taxable year, the excise provided in subsection (a) or (b), whichever is greater, except that an insurance mutual holding company established under chapter 175 or under the equivalent law of another state shall pay, on account of each taxable year, only the excise provided in clause (2) of subsection (a) or subsection (b), whichever is greater.

…

[http://law.justia.com/codes/massachusetts/2010/parti/titleix/chapter63/section39/].

However, **Title IX Taxation** refers to the IRC for the *definitions* of income that is taxable, actually stating that gross income is gross income as defined, and net income is gross income, under the provisions of the federal IRC, and states:

Section 30 Definitions; value of tangible property; net worth
Section 30. When used in this section and in sections 31 to 52, inclusive, the following terms shall have the following meanings, and the terms "business corporation," "disregarded entity," and "partnership," defined in paragraphs 1, 2 and 16 of this section, shall, unless otherwise provided, also have the following meanings and effect for purposes of all sections of this chapter:--.

...

3. "Gross income", gross income as defined under the provisions of the Federal Internal Revenue Code, ...

4. "Net income", gross income less the deductions, but not credits, allowable under the provisions of the Federal Internal Revenue Code, ...

...

[http://law.justia.com/codes/massachusetts/2010/parti/titleix/chapter63/section30/].

Section 38 Determination of net income derived from business carried on within commonwealth
Section 38. The commissioner shall determine the part of the net income of a business corporation derived from business carried on within the commonwealth as follows:

(a) Net income as defined in section thirty of this chapter adjusted as follows shall constitute taxable net income:

...

[http://law.justia.com/codes/massachusetts/2010/parti/titleix/chapter63/section38/].

Section 38A Taxable net income
Section 38A. The taxable net income of a business corporation allocated or apportioned to this commonwealth under the provisions of section thirty-eight shall be its net income subject to tax under this chapter
[http://law.justia.com/codes/massachusetts/2010/parti/titleix/chapter63/section38a/].

That is, gross income is gross income as defined under the IRC, net income is gross income less the deductions allowable under the IRC, which constitutes taxable income, and taxable income is net income subject to tax.

So while the Code establishes imposition of corporate income tax and liability for the tax imposed, its definitions of what is taxable are based on the IRC. In other words, the state legislature has established imposition and liability without also establishing anything on which to impose the liability. (Anything multiplied by nothing is nothing, that is, a percentage of nothing is nothing.)

The Massachusetts General Court has not enacted its own statutes for the definition of income that is taxable for either individual or corporate state income tax. While it has enacted certain statutes that establish imposition of state income tax and liability for the tax imposed, it has relied on the IRC for the definitions of what is taxable. So while Massachusetts is a *known* income-tax state, its legislature does not statutorily require the payment of state income tax.

#22 Michigan, a *Known* Income-Tax State

Federal statute based: Yes
State statute based: Yes
Actual liability: No

"Liable" defined by state statute: No
"Liability" defined by state statute: No

For general state income tax purposes, the Michigan Legislature relies on both the **Michigan Compiled Laws** and the federal **Internal Revenue Code.**

The **Michigan Compiled Laws** do not define liable or liability for income tax purposes (reference **Chapter 206 Income Tax Act of 1967, Act 281 of 1967, Part 1, Chapter 1, Section 206.12 Definitions**).

For individuals, **Chapter 206 Income Tax Act of 1967, Act 281 of 1967, Part I, Chapter 2, Section 206.51** instead establishes by specific language *imposition* of tax and by specific rates *liability* for the tax imposed and states:

> **206.51 Tax rate on taxable income of person other than corporation; percentages of revenues deposited in state school aid fund; imposition of annualized rates; computation of taxable income of nonresident; resident beneficiary of trust; tax credit; including items of income and deductions from trust in taxable income; intent of section; "person other than a corporation" and "taxable income" defined.**
> **Sec. 51.**
> (1) For receiving, earning, or otherwise acquiring income from any source whatsoever, there is levied and imposed under this part upon the taxable income of every person other than a corporation a tax at the following rates in the following circumstances:
> ...
> (8) As used in this section:
> ...
> (b) "Taxable income" means taxable income as defined in this part subject to the applicable source and attribution rules contained in this part [http://www.legislature.mi.gov/(S(4stn3v45ob1rx5rqf4xmghuu))/mileg.aspx?page=getObject&objectName=mcl-206-51].

However, **Chapter 206 Income Tax Act of 1967** refers to the federal IRC for the *definitions* of income that is taxable, actually stating that gross income means gross income as defined in the IRC, taxable income means adjusted gross income as defined in the IRC, and income means *federal* adjusted gross income as defined in the IRC, and states:

Chapter 1, 206.12 Definitions.
Sec. 12.

…

(2) "Gross income" means gross income as defined in the internal revenue code.

…

[http://www.legislature.mi.gov/(S(4stn3v45ob1rx5rqf4xmghuu))/mileg.aspx?page
=getObject&objectName=mcl-206-12].

**Chapter 1, 206.30 "Taxable income" defined; personal exemption; single
additional exemption; deduction not considered allowable federal
exemption for purposes of subsection (2); allowable exemption or
deduction for nonresident or part-year resident; subtraction of prizes under
MCL 432.1 to 432.47 from adjusted gross income prohibited; adjusted
personal exemption; "retirement or pension benefits" defined; limitations
and restrictions; "oil and gas" and "total household resources" defined.**
Sec. 30.

(1) "Taxable income" means, for a person other than a corporation, estate, or
trust, adjusted gross income as defined in the internal revenue code subject to
the following adjustments under this section:

…

[http://www.legislature.mi.gov/(S(4stn3v45ob1rx5rqf4xmghuu))/mileg.aspx?page
=getObject&objectName=mcl-206-30].

**Chapter 1, 206.31a Taxable income; determination; deduction; eligibility;
filing annual return; withholding form; filing claim to which not entitled;
penalty and interest; taxable income derived from illegal activity;
calculation of net operating loss deduction; change in status; definitions.**
Sec. 31a.

(1) Notwithstanding any other provision of this act and for the 2012 tax year and
each tax year after 2012, "taxable income" means taxable income as determined
under section 30 and, except as otherwise provided, subsequently adjusted
under this section.

…

[http://www.legislature.mi.gov/(S(4stn3v45ob1rx5rqf4xmghuu))/mileg.aspx?page
=getObject&objectName=mcl-206-31a].

Chapter 9, 206.510 "Income" and "owner" defined.
Sec. 510.

(1) "Income" means the sum of federal adjusted gross income as defined in the
internal revenue code plus all income specifically excluded or exempt from the
computations of the federal adjusted gross income.

Interestingly, moreover, this part contains a valuable statement for educational
purposes under **Chapter 4, Section 206.201 Exemption of persons exempt from
federal income tax; exceptions,** which also refers to the IRC for the *definition* of

income that is taxable, namely, income of a person who is exempt from federal income tax under the IRC, and states:

206.201 Exemption of persons exempt from federal income tax; exceptions. Sec. 201.
(1) A person who is exempt from federal income tax pursuant to the provisions of the internal revenue code shall be exempt from the tax imposed by this part ....
...
[http://www.legislature.mi.gov/(S(4stn3v45ob1rx5rqf4xmghuu))/mileg.aspx?page =getObject&objectName=mcl-206-201].

This is interesting and valuable because the IRC does not establish liability for federal income tax, so that any person is exempt from federal income tax, specific exemption from federal income tax or lack thereof notwithstanding. (To eliminate any doubt about the intent of this section, it does not refer to an exemption or exclusion of income the taxation of which is prohibited by federal statutes.)

So while the Code establishes imposition of individual income tax and liability for the tax imposed, its definitions of what is taxable are based on the IRC. In other words, the state legislature has established imposition and liability without also establishing anything on which to impose the liability. (Anything multiplied by nothing is nothing, that is, a percentage of nothing is nothing. Refer to Appendix III and Appendix D for further discussion.)

For corporations, **Part 2, Chapter 11, 206.623 Corporate income tax; levy and imposition; base; adjustments; business income of unitary business group; "business loss" and "oil and gas" defined** establishes by specific language *imposition* of tax and by a specific rate *liability* for the tax imposed and states:

Sec. 623.
(1) Except as otherwise provided in this part, there is levied and imposed a corporate income tax on every taxpayer with business activity within this state or ownership interest or beneficial interest in a flow-through entity that has business activity in this state unless prohibited by 15 USC 381 to 384. The corporate income tax is imposed on the corporate income tax base, after allocation or apportionment to this state, at the rate of 6.0%.
(2) The corporate income tax base means a taxpayer's business income subject to the following adjustments, before allocation or apportionment, and the adjustment in subsection (4) after allocation or apportionment:
...
[http://www.legislature.mi.gov/(S(o5wukmux5ynvst45tkbpw255))/mileg.aspx?pag e=getObject&objectName=mcl-206-623].

However, **Part 2, Chapter 10, Section 206.603 Definitions; B** refers to the IRC for the *definitions* of income that is taxable, actually stating that business income means *federal* taxable income (rather than *Michigan* taxable income), and states:

Sec. 603.

(1) "Business activity" means a transfer of legal or equitable title to or rental of property, whether real, personal, or mixed, tangible or intangible, or the performance of services, or a combination thereof, made or engaged in, or caused to be made or engaged in, whether in intrastate, interstate, or foreign commerce, with the object of gain, benefit, or advantage, whether direct or indirect, to the taxpayer or to others, but does not include the services rendered by an employee to his or her employer or services as a director of a corporation. Although an activity of a taxpayer may be incidental to another or to others of his or her business activities, each activity shall be considered to be business engaged in within the meaning of this part.

(2) "Business income" means federal taxable income. For a tax-exempt taxpayer, business income means only that part of federal taxable income derived from unrelated business activity [http://www.legislature.mi.gov/(S(ivuk4355mwcxsi55avtksh55))/mileg.aspx?page =getObject&objectName=mcl-206-603].

Interestingly, moreover, this part contains a valuable statement for educational purposes under **Chapter 11, 206.625 Exemptions; corporate income tax base of foreign person; sales factor; "business income," "domiciled," and "foreign person" defined,** which also refers to the IRC for the *definition* of income that is taxable, namely, income of a person who is exempt from federal income tax under the IRC, and states:

Sec. 625.

(1) Except as otherwise provided in this section, the following are exempt from the tax imposed by this part:

…

(b) A person who is exempt from federal income tax under the internal revenue code except the following:

…

[http://www.legislature.mi.gov/(S(o5wukmux5ynvst45tkbpw255))/mileg.aspx?pag e=getObject&objectName=mcl-206-625].

Chapter 10, 206.609 Definitions; P to S.
Sec. 609.

(1) "Person" means an individual, bank, financial institution, insurance company, association, corporation, flow-through entity, receiver, estate, trust, or any other group or combination of groups acting as a unit.

…

[http://www.legislature.mi.gov/(S(o5wukmux5ynvst45tkbpw255))/mileg.aspx?pag e=getObject&objectName=mcl-206-609].

This is interesting and valuable because the IRC does not establish liability for federal income tax, so that any corporation is exempt from federal income tax, specific exemption from federal income tax or lack thereof notwithstanding. (To eliminate any doubt about the intent of this section, it does not refer to an exemption or exclusion of income the taxation of which is prohibited by federal statutes.)

So while the Code establishes imposition of corporate income tax and liability for the tax imposed, its definitions of what is taxable are based on the IRC. In other words, the state legislature has established imposition and liability without also establishing anything on which to impose the liability. (Anything multiplied by nothing is nothing, that is, a percentage of nothing is nothing.)

The Michigan Legislature has not enacted its own statutes for the definition of income that is taxable for either individual or corporate state income tax. While it has enacted certain statutes that establish imposition of state income tax and liability for the tax imposed, it has relied on the IRC for the definitions of what is taxable. So while Michigan is a *known* income-tax state, its legislature does not statutorily require the payment of state income tax.

#23 Minnesota, a *Known* Income-Tax State

Federal statute based: Yes
State statute based: Yes
Actual liability: No

"Liable" defined by state statute: No
"Liability" defined by state statute: No

For general state income tax purposes, the Minnesota State Legislature relies on both the **Minnesota Statutes** and the federal **Internal Revenue Code.**

The **Minnesota Statutes** do not define liable or liability for income tax purposes (reference **Various State Taxes and Programs, Chapter 290 Income and Franchise Taxes, Section 290.01 Definitions**).

Instead, **Various State Taxes and Programs, Chapter 290 Income and Franchise Taxes** establishes by specific language and rates *liability* for tax imposed and states:

> **290.04 Liability for Tax.**
> Subdivision 1.**Accrual.**
> The liability for the tax imposed by section 290.02 shall arise upon the first day of the taxable year upon which a domestic corporation exercises any of the privileges specified in section 290.02 or exists as a corporation, or on which a foreign corporation is possessed of the privilege for the grant to it of the privilege of transacting or for the actual transaction by it of any local business within this state during any part of its taxable year, in corporate or organized form. The liability for the tax imposed by section 290.03 shall arise concurrently with the receipt or accrual of income during the taxable year....
> ... [https://www.revisor.mn.gov/statutes/?id=290.04].
>
> **290.06 Rates of Tax; Credits.**
> Subdivision 1. **Computation, corporations.** The franchise tax imposed upon corporations shall be computed by applying to their taxable income the rate of 9.8 percent.
> ...
> Subd. 2c. **Schedules of rates for individuals, estates, and trusts.** (a) The income taxes imposed by this chapter ... must be computed by applying to their taxable net income the following schedule of rates:
> ... [https://www.revisor.mn.gov/statutes/?id=290.06].

For individuals, **Section 290.03 Income Tax; Imposition, Classes of Taxpayers** establishes by specific language *imposition* of tax and states:

290.03 INCOME TAX; IMPOSITION, CLASSES OF TAXPAYERS.
An annual tax for each taxable year, computed in the manner and at the rates hereinafter provided, is hereby imposed upon the taxable income for such year of the following classes of taxpayers:
(1) Resident and nonresident individuals;
(2) Estates of decedents, dying domiciled within or without this state;
(3) Trusts (except those taxable as corporations) however created by residents or nonresidents or by domestic or foreign corporations [https://www.revisor.mn.gov/statutes/?id=290.03].

However, **Section 290.01 Definitions** refers to the IRC for the ***definitions*** of income that is taxable, actually stating that net income means ***federal*** taxable income (rather than ***Minnesota*** taxable income) as defined in the IRC, and states:

290.01 DEFINITIONS.

...
Subd. 19.**Net income.**
The term "net income" means the federal taxable income, as defined in section 63 of the Internal Revenue Code of 1986, ...
...
Subd. 22.**Taxable net income.**
For tax years beginning after December 31, 1986, the term "taxable net income" means:
(1) for resident individuals the same as net income;
...
Subd. 29.**Taxable income.**
The term "taxable income" means:
(1) for individuals, estates, and trusts, the same as taxable net income;
... [https://www.revisor.mn.gov/statutes/?id=290.01].

That is, taxable income means taxable net income, which means net income, which means ***federal*** taxable income.

So while the Code establishes imposition of individual income tax and liability for the tax imposed, its definitions of what is taxable are based on the IRC. In other words, the state legislature has established imposition and liability without also establishing anything on which to impose the liability. (Anything multiplied by nothing is nothing, that is, a percentage of nothing is nothing. Refer to Appendix III and Appendix D for further discussion.)

For corporations, **Section 290.02 Franchise Tax on Corporations Measured by Net Income** also establishes by specific language ***imposition*** of tax and states:

290.02 FRANCHISE TAX ON CORPORATIONS MEASURED BY NET INCOME.

An annual franchise tax on the exercise of the corporate franchise to engage in contacts with this state that produce gross income attributable to sources within this state is imposed upon every corporation that so exercises its franchise during the taxable year.

...

The tax so imposed is measured by the corporations' taxable income and alternative minimum taxable income for the taxable year for which the tax is imposed, and computed in the manner and at the rates provided in this chapter [https://www.revisor.mn.gov/statutes/?id=290.02].

However, **Section 290.01 Definitions** refers to the IRC for the **definitions** of income that is taxable, actually stating that net income means **federal** taxable income (rather than **Minnesota** taxable income) as defined in the IRC, and states:

290.01 DEFINITIONS.

...

Subd. 19.**Net income.**
The term "net income" means the federal taxable income, as defined in section 63 of the Internal Revenue Code of 1986, ...

...

Subd. 22.**Taxable net income.**
For tax years beginning after December 31, 1986, the term "taxable net income" means:
(1) for resident individuals the same as net income;
(2) for individuals who were not residents of Minnesota for the entire year, the same as net income except that the tax is imposed only on the Minnesota apportioned share of that income as determined pursuant to section 290.06, subdivision 2c, paragraph (e);
(3) for all other taxpayers, the part of net income that is allocable to Minnesota by assignment or apportionment under one or more of sections 290.17, 290.191, 290.20, and 290.36.

...

Subd. 29.**Taxable income.**
The term "taxable income" means:

...

(2) for corporations, the taxable net income less
... [https://www.revisor.mn.gov/statutes/?id=290.01].

That is, taxable income means taxable net income, which means net income, which means **federal** taxable income.

So while the Code establishes imposition of corporate franchise tax and liability for the tax imposed, its definitions of what is taxable are based on the IRC. In other words, the state legislature has established imposition and liability without also establishing anything on which to impose the liability. (Anything multiplied by nothing is nothing, that is, a percentage of nothing is nothing.)

The Minnesota State Legislature has not enacted its own statutes for the definition of income that is taxable for either individual state income or corporate state franchise tax. While it has enacted certain statutes that establish imposition of state income and franchise taxes and liability for the taxes imposed, it has relied on the IRC for the definitions of what is taxable. So while Minnesota is a *known* income-tax state, its legislature does not statutorily require the payment of either state income or state franchise tax.

#24 Mississippi, a *Known* Income-Tax State

Federal statute based: No
State statute based: Yes
Actual liability: Yes

"Liable" defined by state statute: No
"Liability" defined by state statute: No

For general state income tax purposes, the Mississippi State Legislature relies solely on the **Mississippi Code.**

The **Mississippi Code** does not define liable or liability for income tax purposes (reference **Title 27 - Taxation and Finance, Chapter 7 Income Tax and Withholding, Section 27-7-3 Definitions**).

Instead, **Title 27 - Taxation and Finance, Chapter 7 Income Tax and Withholding, Section 27-7-5 Imposition of the tax** establishes by specific language *imposition* of tax and by specific rates *liability* for the tax imposed and states:

§ 27-7-5. Imposition of the tax.
(1) There is hereby assessed and levied, to be collected and paid as hereinafter provided, for the calendar year 1983 and fiscal years ending during the calendar year 1983 and all taxable years thereafter, upon the entire net income of every resident individual, corporation, association, trust or estate, in excess of the credits provided, a tax at the following rates:
… [http://law.justia.com/codes/mississippi/2010/title-27/7/27-7-5/].

Chapter 7 Income Tax and Withholding also establishes the *definitions* of income that is taxable and states:

§ 27-7-13. Net income defined.
(1) The term "net income" means the gross income as defined hereunder, less allowable business expenses and expenses incurred in the taxpayer's regular trade or profession.
… [http://law.justia.com/codes/mississippi/2010/title-27/7/27-7-13/].

§ 27-7-15. Gross income defined.
(1) For the purposes of this article, except as otherwise provided, the term "gross income" means and includes the income of a taxpayer derived from salaries, wages, fees or compensation for service, of whatever kind and in whatever form paid, including income from governmental agencies and subdivisions thereof; or from professions, vocations, trades, businesses, commerce or sales, or renting or dealing in property, or reacquired property; also from annuities, interest, rents, dividends, securities, insurance premiums, reinsurance premiums, considerations for supplemental insurance contracts, or the transaction of any

business carried on for gain or profit, or gains, or profits, and income derived from any source whatever and in whatever form paid. The amount of all such items of income shall be included in the gross income for the taxable year in which received by the taxpayer. The amount by which an eligible employee's salary is reduced pursuant to a salary reduction agreement authorized under Section 25-17-5 shall be excluded from the term "gross income" within the meaning of this article [http://law.justia.com/codes/mississippi/2010/title-27/7/27-7-15/].

The Mississippi State Legislature statutorily requires the payment of both individual and corporate state income tax. Without any reference to or reliance on the IRC, it has established *all three elements of the essential statutory formula for income tax: imposition of tax, liability for the tax imposed, and the definition of income that is taxable.*

#25 Missouri, a *Known* Income-Tax State

Federal statute based: Yes
State statute based: Yes
Actual liability: No

"Liable" defined by state statute: No
"Liability" defined by state statute: No

For general state income tax purposes, the Missouri General Assembly relies on both the **Missouri Revised Statutes** and the federal **Internal Revenue Code.**

The **Missouri Revised Statutes** do not define liable or liability for income tax purposes (reference **Title X Taxation and Revenue, Chapter 143 Income Tax, Section 143.101 Definitions**).

For individuals, **Title X Taxation and Revenue, Chapter 143 Income Tax, Section 143.011 Resident individuals--tax rates** instead establishes by specific language *imposition* of tax and by specific rates *liability* for the tax imposed and states:

Resident individuals--tax rates.
143.011. A tax is hereby imposed for every taxable year on the Missouri taxable income of every resident. The tax shall be determined by applying the tax table or the rate provided in section 143.021, which is based upon the following rates:
....
... [http://www.moga.mo.gov/statutes/C100-199/1430000011.HTM].

However, **Chapter 143 Income Tax** refers to the federal IRC for the *definitions* of income that is taxable, actually stating that Missouri taxable income shall be Missouri adjusted gross income and Missouri adjusted gross income shall be *federal* adjusted gross income, and states:

Missouri taxable income.
143.111. The Missouri taxable income of a resident shall be such resident's Missouri adjusted gross income less:
(1) Either the Missouri standard deduction or the Missouri itemized deduction;
(2) The Missouri deduction for personal exemptions;
(3) The Missouri deduction for dependency exemptions;
(4) The deduction for federal income taxes provided in section 143.171; and
(5) The deduction for a self-employed individual's health insurance costs provided in section 143.113
[http://www.moga.mo.gov/statutes/C100-199/1430000111.HTM].

Missouri adjusted gross income.
143.121. 1. The Missouri adjusted gross income of a resident individual shall be the taxpayer's federal adjusted gross income subject to the modifications in this section.
… [http://www.moga.mo.gov/statutes/C100-199/1430000121.HTM].

So while the Code establishes imposition of individual income tax and liability for the tax imposed, its definitions of what is taxable are based on the IRC. In other words, the state legislature has established imposition and liability without also establishing anything on which to impose the liability. (Anything multiplied by nothing is nothing, that is, a percentage of nothing is nothing. Refer to Appendix III and Appendix D for further discussion.)

For corporations, **Chapter 143 Income Tax** also establishes by specific language *imposition* of tax and by specific rates *liability* for the tax imposed and states:

Corporations.
143.071. ….
2. For all tax years beginning on or after September 1, 1993, a tax is hereby imposed upon the Missouri taxable income of corporations in an amount equal to six and one-fourth percent of Missouri taxable income
[http://www.moga.mo.gov/statutes/C100-199/1430000071.HTM].

Corporations.
143.105. Notwithstanding the provisions of section 143.071, to the contrary, a tax is hereby imposed upon the Missouri taxable income of corporations in an amount equal to five percent of Missouri taxable income
[http://www.moga.mo.gov/statutes/C100-199/1430000105.HTM].

However, **Section 143.431 Missouri taxable income and tax** refers to the IRC for the *definition* of income that is taxable, actually stating that Missouri taxable income shall be *federal* taxable income, and states:

Missouri taxable income and tax.
143.431. 1. The Missouri taxable income of a corporation taxable under sections 143.011 to 143.996 shall be so much of its federal taxable income for the taxable year, with the modifications specified in subsections 2 to 4 of this section, as is derived from sources within Missouri as provided in section 143.451. The tax of a corporation shall be computed on its Missouri taxable income at the rates provided in section 143.071.
… [http://www.moga.mo.gov/statutes/C100-199/1430000431.HTM].

Interestingly, moreover, this title contains a valuable statement for educational purposes under **Section 143.441 Corporation defined--corporate tax inapplicable, when,** which also refers to the IRC for the *definition* of income that is taxable, namely, income of a corporation that is exempt from federal income tax, and states:

Corporation defined--corporate tax inapplicable, when.
143.441. ...
...
2. The tax on corporations provided in subsection 1 of section 143.431 and section 143.071 shall not apply to:
(1) A corporation which by reason of its purposes and activities is exempt from federal income tax. ...
[http://www.moga.mo.gov/statutes/C100-199/1430000441.HTM].

This is interesting and valuable because the IRC does not establish liability for federal income tax, so that any corporation is exempt from federal income tax, specific exemption from federal income taxation or lack thereof notwithstanding.

So while the Code establishes imposition of corporate income tax and liability for the tax imposed, its definition of what is taxable is based on the IRC. In other words, the state legislature has established imposition and liability without also establishing anything on which to impose the liability. (Anything multiplied by nothing is nothing, that is, a percentage of nothing is nothing.)

The Missouri General Assembly has not enacted its own statutes for the definition of income that is taxable for either individual or corporate state income tax. While it has enacted certain statutes that establish imposition of state income tax and liability for the tax imposed, it has relied on the IRC for the definitions of income that is taxable. So while Missouri is a *known* income-tax state, its legislature does not statutorily require the payment of state income tax.

#26 Montana, a *Known* Income-Tax State

Federal statute based: Yes
State statute based: Yes
Actual liability: No

"Liable" defined by state statute: No
"Liability" defined by state statute: No

For general state income tax purposes, the Montana Legislature relies on both the **Montana Code Annotated** and the federal **Internal Revenue Code.**

The **Montana Code Annotated** does not define liable or liability for income tax purposes (reference **Title 15 Taxation, Chapter 30 Individual Income Tax, Part 21 Rate and General Provisions, Section 15-30-2101 Definitions** and **Chapter 31 Corporation License or Income Tax**).

For individuals, **Title 15 Taxation, Chapter 30 Individual Income Tax, Part 21 Rate and General Provisions, Section 15-30-2103 Rate of tax** instead establishes by specific language *imposition* of tax and by specific rates *liability* for the tax imposed and states:

15-30-2103. Rate of tax. (1) There must be levied, collected, and paid for each tax year upon the taxable income of each taxpayer subject to this tax, after making allowance for exemptions and deductions as provided in this chapter, a tax on the brackets of taxable income as follows:
… [http://data.opi.mt.gov/bills/mca/15/30/15-30-2103.htm].

However, **Part 21 Rate and General Provisions** refers to the federal IRC for the *definitions* of income that is taxable, actually stating that taxable income means adjusted gross income and adjusted gross income is *federal* adjusted gross income as defined in the IRC, and states:

15-30-2101. Definitions. For the purpose of this chapter, unless otherwise required by the context, the following definitions apply:
…
(32) "Taxable income" means the adjusted gross income of a taxpayer less the deductions and exemptions provided for in this chapter.
… [http://data.opi.mt.gov/bills/mca/15/30/15-30-2101.htm].

15-30-2110. Adjusted gross income. (1) Subject to subsection (13), adjusted gross income is the taxpayer's federal adjusted gross income as defined in section 62 of the Internal Revenue Code, 26 U.S.C. 62, and in addition includes the following:
… [http://data.opi.mt.gov/bills/mca/15/30/15-30-2110.htm].

Interestingly, moreover, this title contains a valuable statement for educational purposes under **Section 15-30-2102 Construction of net income,** which also refers to both the US Constitution and the IRC for another *definition* of income that is taxable, namely, income that is excluded from taxable income, and states:

> **15-30-2102. Construction of net income.** For the purpose of raising revenue, the net income required to be shown on returns under this chapter and taken as the basis for determining the tax hereunder shall not be classified or held or construed to be property. All income except what has been expressly exempted under the provisions of this chapter and income not permitted to be taxed under the constitution of this state or the constitution or laws of the United States shall be included and considered in determining the net income of taxpayers within the provision of this chapter [http://data.opi.mt.gov/bills/mca/15/30/15-30-2102.htm].

This is interesting and valuable because the US Constitution expressly prohibits tax that is not proportional to the census, and the IRC accordingly does not establish liability for federal income tax, so that any individual is exempt from federal income taxation, specific exemption from federal income taxation or lack thereof notwithstanding. (To eliminate any doubt about the intent of this section, it does not refer to an exemption or exclusion of income the taxation of which by the State is prohibited by the US Constitution or US statutes—see Appendix II for discussion of limits imposed on the federal government by the US Constitution.)

So while the Code establishes imposition of individual income tax and liability for the tax imposed, its definitions of what is taxable are based on the IRC. In other words, the state legislature has established imposition and liability without also establishing anything on which to impose the liability. (Anything multiplied by nothing is nothing, that is, a percentage of nothing is nothing. Refer to Appendix III and Appendix D for further discussion.)

For corporations, **Chapter 31 Corporation License or Income Tax, Part 4 Corporation Income Tax** also establishes by specific language *imposition* of tax and by specific rates *liability* for the tax imposed and states:

> **15-31-403. Rate of tax imposed -- income from sources within state defined -- alternative tax.** (1) Except as provided in 15-31-401, there is hereby imposed upon every corporation for each taxable year an income tax at the rate specified in 15-31-121 and 15-31-122 upon its net income derived from sources within this state for taxable years beginning after December 31, 1970, other than income for any period for which the corporation is subject to taxation under part 1 of this chapter, according to or measured by its net income.
> ... [http://data.opi.mt.gov/bills/mca/15/31/15-31-403.htm].

However, **Part 1 Corporation License Tax Rate and Return** refers to the IRC for the *definitions* of income that is taxable, actually stating that net income is computed from gross income and gross income means gross income for *federal* income tax purposes, and states:

> **15-31-113. Gross income and net income.** (1) The term "gross income" means all income recognized in determining the corporation's gross income for federal income tax purposes and:
> … [http://data.opi.mt.gov/bills/mca/15/31/15-31-113.htm].

> **15-31-114. Deductions allowed in computing income.** (1) In computing the net income, the following deductions are allowed from the gross income received by the corporation within the year from all sources:
> … [http://data.opi.mt.gov/bills/mca/15/31/15-31-114.htm].

So while the Code establishes imposition of corporate income tax and liability for the tax imposed, its definitions of what is taxable are based on the IRC. In other words, the state legislature has established imposition and liability without also establishing anything on which to impose the liability. (Anything multiplied by nothing is nothing, that is, a percentage of nothing is nothing.)

The Montana Legislature has not enacted its own statutes for the definition of income that is taxable for either individual or corporate state income tax. While it has enacted certain statutes that establish imposition of state income tax and liability for the tax imposed, it has relied on the IRC for the definitions of what is taxable. So while Montana is a *known* income-tax state, its legislature does not statutorily require the payment of state income tax.

#27 Nebraska, a *Known* Income-Tax State

Federal statute based: Yes
State statute based: Yes
Actual liability: No

"Liable" defined by state statute: No
"Liability" defined by state statute: No

For general state income tax purposes, the Nebraska Legislature relies on both the **Nebraska Revised Statutes** and the federal **Internal Revenue Code.**

The **Nebraska Revised Statutes** do not define liable or liability for income tax purposes (reference **Chapter 77 Revenue and Taxation, Sections 77-101 Definition, where found, 77-381 Terms, defined,** and **77-2701.04 Definitions, where found**).

For individuals, **Chapter 77 Revenue and Taxation, Section 77-2715 Income tax; rate; credits; refund** instead establishes by specific language *imposition* of tax but also refers to the federal IRC, actually stating that the tax shall be a percentage of *federal* adjusted gross income (rather than *Nebraska* adjusted gross income), and states:

> **77-2715. Income tax; rate; credits; refund.**
> (1) A tax is hereby imposed for each taxable year on the entire income of every resident individual ….
> (2) The tax for each resident individual shall be a percentage of such individual's federal adjusted gross income ….
> … [http://uniweb.legislature.ne.gov/laws/statutes.php?statute=77-2715].

Section 77-2701.01. Income tax; rate establishes by specific rates *liability* for the tax imposed but also refers to the IRC, actually stating that for all taxable years, under the IRC, the tax rate shall be 3.07%, and states:

> **77-2701.01. Income tax; rate.**
> … Pursuant to section 77-2715.01, for all taxable years beginning or deemed to begin on or after January 1, 1991, under the Internal Revenue Code of 1986, as amended, the rate of the income tax levied pursuant to section 77-2715 shall be three and seventy-hundredths percent
> [http://uniweb.legislature.ne.gov/laws/statutes.php?statute=77-2701.01].

Moreover, **Section 77-2714.01 Terms, defined** refers to the IRC for the *definition* of income that is taxable and states:

> **77-2714.01. Terms, defined.**
> As used in sections 77-2714 to 77-27,123, unless the context otherwise requires:

(1) Nebraska adjusted gross income shall mean (a) for resident individuals, their federal adjusted gross income as modified in section 77-2716 and (b) for nonresident individuals and partial-year resident individuals, the portion of the federal adjusted gross income that is derived from or connected with sources within this state as provided in section 77-2715;
… [http://uniweb.legislature.ne.gov/laws/statutes.php?statute=77-2714.01].

So the Code's imposition of individual income tax and liability for the tax imposed as well as the definition of what is taxable are based on the IRC. In other words, the state legislature has not established imposition or liability or anything on which to impose such a liability. (Nothing multiplied by nothing is nothing, that is, a percentage of nothing of nothing is nothing. Refer to Appendix III and Appendix D for further discussion.)

For corporations, **Section 77-2734.02 Corporate taxpayer; income tax rate; how determined** establishes by specific language *imposition* of tax and by specific rates *liability* for the tax imposed and states:

77-2734.02. Corporate taxpayer; income tax rate; how determined.
(1) Except as provided in subsection (2) of this section, a tax is hereby imposed for each taxable year on the taxable income of every corporate taxpayer that is doing business in this state at a rate equal to one hundred fifty and eight-tenths percent of the primary rate imposed on individuals under section 77-2701.01 on the first one hundred thousand dollars of taxable income and at the rate of two hundred eleven percent of such rate on all taxable income in excess of one hundred thousand dollars. The resultant rates shall be rounded to the nearest one hundredth of one percent.
… [http://uniweb.legislature.ne.gov/laws/statutes.php?statute=77-2734.02].

However, **Section 77-2734.04. Income tax; terms, defined** refers to the IRC for the *definitions* of income that is taxable and states:

77-2734.04. Income tax; terms, defined.
As used in sections 77-2734.01 to 77-2734.15, unless the context otherwise requires:
…
(3) Corporate taxpayer shall mean any corporation that is not a part of a unitary business or the part of a unitary business, whether it is one or more corporations, that is doing business in this state. …;
(4) Corporation shall mean all corporations and all other entities that are taxed as corporations under the Internal Revenue Code;
…
(6) Federal taxable income shall mean the corporate taxpayer's federal taxable income as reported to the Internal Revenue Service or as subsequently changed or amended. Except as provided in subsection (5) or (6) of section 77-2716, no adjustment shall be allowed for a change from any election made or the method

used in computing federal taxable income. An election to file a federal consolidated return shall not require the inclusion in any unitary group of a corporation that is not a part of the unitary business;

...

(11) Taxable income shall mean federal taxable income as adjusted and, if appropriate, as apportioned;

... [http://uniweb.legislature.ne.gov/laws/statutes.php?statute=77-2734.04].

That is, the taxable income of every corporate taxpayer is *federal* taxable income, which is the corporate taxpayer's *federal* taxable income, which is the corporation's *federal* taxable income.

Interestingly, moreover, this chapter contains a valuable statement for educational purposes under **Section 77-2714 Terms; references; incorporation of federal law,** which also refers to the IRC for the *definition* of income that is taxable, namely, income of any organization that is exempt from income taxes under US law, and states:

77-2714. Terms; references; incorporation of federal law.
... Any organization to the extent that it is exempt from income taxes under the laws of the United States shall be exempt from income tax under the Nebraska Revenue Act of 1967
[http://uniweb.legislature.ne.gov/laws/statutes.php?statute=77-2714].

This is interesting and valuable because the IRC does not establish liability for federal income tax, so that any organization is exempt from federal income tax, specific exemption from federal income tax or lack thereof notwithstanding.

So while the Code establishes imposition of corporate income tax and liability for the tax imposed, its definitions of what is taxable are based on the IRC. In other words, the state legislature has established imposition and liability without also establishing anything on which to impose the liability. (Anything multiplied by nothing is nothing, that is, a percentage of nothing is nothing.)

The Nebraska Legislature has not enacted its own statutes for the definition of income that is taxable for either individual or corporate state income tax. While it has enacted a certain statute that establishes imposition of corporate state income tax and liability for the tax imposed, it has relied on the IRC to establish imposition of individual income tax and liability for the tax imposed and for the definitions of what is taxable. So while Nebraska is a *known* income-tax state, its legislature does not statutorily require the payment of state income tax.

#28 Nevada, a *Known* No-Income-Tax State

Federal statute based: No
State statute based: Yes
Actual liability: No

"Liable" defined by state statute: No
"Liability" defined by state statute: No

For general state income tax purposes, the Nevada Legislature relies solely on the **Nevada Revised Statutes.**

It is commonly understood—***known***—that Nevada is a no-income-tax state, that is, the Nevada Legislature has not enacted any statutes of law that require the payment of individual state income tax. **Title 32** of the **Nevada Revised Statutes** does not establish imposition of tax, liability for tax, or the definition of income that is taxable for either individual or corporate income taxes.

For corporations, it is worth noting that, while the legislature does not statutorily require the payment of corporate state income tax, **Title 32—Revenue and Taxation, Chapter 364 License Taxes, Taxes and Fees Measured by Income or Revenue of Private Enterprise, Section NRS 364-200 Statement required in ordinance imposing or increasing tax or fee; contents of agenda proposing ordinance; notice of proposal to change another tax or fee to tax or fee measured by income or revenue** places limitations on cities and counties intending to impose or increase taxes or fees on private enterprises that are measured by the income or revenue of the enterprises and states:

NRS 364-200 Statement required in ordinance imposing or increasing tax or fee; contents of agenda proposing ordinance; notice of proposal to change another tax or fee to tax or fee measured by income or revenue.
1. An ordinance adopted by a city or county after July 1, 1997, which imposes or increases a tax or fee on a private enterprise that is measured by the income or revenue of the enterprise, including, without limitation, any fee imposed for the regulation and licensing of a business or occupation, must include a statement of:
(a) The need for and purpose of the ordinance.
(b) The intended use for the revenue to be obtained pursuant to the ordinance.
2. An agenda that proposes such an ordinance must include a statement indicating whether the proposed ordinance establishes a new tax or fee, or increases an existing tax or fee.
3. If a city or county wishes to change a tax or fee on a private enterprise that is not a tax or fee that is measured by the income or revenue of the enterprise to a tax or fee that is measured by the income or revenue of the enterprise, the city or county must send a written notice, at least 14 days before the adoption of the ordinance that changes a tax or fee on a private enterprise to a tax or fee that is

measured by the income or revenue of the enterprise, to each enterprise to which the ordinance will apply.
[http://lrc.ky.gov/KRS/141-00/040.PDF].

The Nevada Legislature does not statutorily require the payment of either individual or corporate state income tax.

#29 New Hampshire, a *Known* No-Income-Tax State

Federal statute based: No
State statute based: Yes
Actual liability: No

"Liable" defined by state statute: No
"Liability" defined by state statute: No

For general state income tax purposes, The New Hampshire General Court relies on both the **New Hampshire Revised Statutes** and the federal **Internal Revenue Code.**

It is commonly understood—***known***—that New Hampshire is a no-income-tax state, that is, The New Hampshire General Court has not enacted any statutes of law that require the payment of individual state income tax. **Title V** of the **New Hampshire Revised Statutes** contains various statutes concerning **Taxation** but, with the only exception discussed next, does not establish imposition of tax, liability for tax, or the definition of income that is taxable for individual income taxes.

For individuals, it is worth noting that **Title V Taxation, Chapter 77 Taxation of Incomes, Section 77:1 Rate** establishes a five percent *liability* for tax on income, but **Sections 77:3 Who Taxable, 77:4 What Taxable,** and **77:4-b through 77:4-g** establish the ***definitions*** of who and what are taxable, namely, only individuals with certain interest and dividends exceeding $2,400.00 during the taxable period.

Quite interestingly, **Chapter 77 Taxation of Incomes** contains a valuable statement for educational purposes under **Section 77:2 Conformity to Laws,** which refers to both the US Constitution and the federal IRC for the ***definition*** of income that is taxable, namely, income that is exempt from taxation under the US Constitution and constitutional federal laws, and states:

> **77:2 Conformity to Laws. –** It is the intention of this chapter, and it shall be construed, anything contained herein to the contrary notwithstanding, not to impose any tax upon any income in violation of the Constitution of the United States or in violation of any constitutional federal laws, or in violation of the constitution of this state, or in violation of any contractual obligations of exemption from taxation established prior to May 4, 1923, by the state or any of its political subdivisions or by the United States, which may not be impaired lawfully hereby [http://www.gencourt.state.nh.us/rsa/html/V/77/77-2.htm].

This is quite interesting and valuable because the US Constitution expressly prohibits tax that is not proportional to the census, and the IRC accordingly does not establish liability for federal income tax. Although the US Constitution does not prohibit ***state*** legislatures from enacting income tax liability statutes, by enacting this statute, the state legislature has demonstrated both its awareness of the US Constitution's express prohibition of ***federal*** tax that is not proportional to the census and its general intent not to impose *state* tax on income (see Appendix II for discussion of limits imposed on the federal government by the US Constitution).

Also quite interestingly, moreover, **Title V Taxation** contains another valuable statement for educational purposes under **Chapter 72 Persons and Property Liable to Taxation, Resident Taxes, Section 72:1 Persons Liable,** which assesses on every inhabitant from 18 to 65 years of age a specific dollar amount of tax and states:

> **72:1 Persons Liable. –** On April 1 a tax of $10, to be known as the "resident tax," shall be assessed on every inhabitant of the state from 18 to 65 years of age … [http://www.gencourt.state.nh.us/rsa/html/V/72/72-1.htm].

This is also quite interesting and valuable because, by enacting this statute, the state legislature has exemplified, except for the age constraint, the style of a tax that is proportional to the census: a tax that is the *exact same dollar amount per person regardless of income or wealth.*

So the Code establishes liability for individual income tax as well as the definition of income that is taxable, that is, only certain taxable interest and dividends exceeding $2,400.00.

For corporations, it is also worth noting that **Chapter 77-A Business Profits Tax, Section 77-A:2 Imposition of Tax** establishes by specific language *imposition* of tax and by a specific rate *liability* for the tax imposed and states:

> **77-A:2 Imposition of Tax. –** A tax is imposed at the rate of 8.5 percent upon the taxable business profits of every business organization [http://www.gencourt.state.nh.us/rsa/html/V/77-A/77-A-2.htm].

However, **Section 77-A:1 Definitions** refers to the IRC for the *definitions* of income that is taxable and states:

> **77-A:1 Definitions. –** When appearing in this chapter:
> I. "Business organization" means any enterprise, whether corporation, partnership, limited liability company, proprietorship, association, business trust, real estate trust or other form of organization; organized for gain or profit, carrying on any business activity within the state, except such enterprises as are expressly made exempt from income taxation under the United States Internal Revenue Code as defined in RSA 77-A: 1, XX….
> …
> III. "Gross business profits" means:
> (a) In the case of a corporation, except "S" corporations, or any other business organization required to make and file a United States corporation income tax return, or in the case of a corporation which does not make and file a separate United States corporation income tax return for itself because it is a member of an affiliated group pursuant to the provisions of chapter 6 of the United States

Internal Revenue Code as defined in RSA 77-A:1, XX, the amount of taxable income as would be determinable under the provisions of the United States Internal Revenue Code ....

...

IV. "Taxable business profits" means gross business profits adjusted by the additions and deductions provided in RSA 77-A:4 and then adjusted by the method of apportionment provided in RSA 77-A:3.

...

VI. "Gross business income" means all income for federal income tax purposes from whatever source derived in the conduct of business activity, ...

... [http://www.gencourt.state.nh.us/rsa/html/V/77-A/77-A-1.htm].

That is, gross business income means all income for *federal* income tax purposes, and taxable business profits means gross business profits, which means corporate taxable income under the IRC.

Interestingly, moreover, Subsection I contains a valuable statement for educational purposes, as it states that any corporation expressly made exempt from income taxation under the IRC is not [treated as] a business organization with taxable business profits. This is interesting and valuable because the IRC does not establish liability for federal income tax, so that any corporation is exempt from federal income taxation, express exemption from federal income taxation or lack thereof notwithstanding.

So while the Code establishes imposition of business profits tax and liability for the tax imposed, its definitions of what is taxable are based on the IRC. In other words, the state legislature has established imposition and liability without also establishing anything on which to impose the liability. (Anything multiplied by nothing is nothing, that is, a percentage of nothing is nothing. Refer to Appendix III and Appendix D for further discussion.)

The New Hampshire General Court does not statutorily require the payment of either individual or corporate state income tax beyond that relative to certain individual interest and dividends exceeding $2,400.00.

#30 New Jersey, a *Known* Income-Tax State

Federal statute based: No
State statute based: Yes
Actual liability: Yes

"Liable" defined by state statute: No
"Liability" defined by state statute: No

For general state income tax purposes, the New Jersey Legislature relies on both the **New Jersey Permanent Statutes** and the federal **Internal Revenue Code.**

The **New Jersey Permanent Statutes** do not define liable or liability for income tax purposes (reference **Title 54A New Jersey Gross Income Tax Act, Section 54A:1-2 Definitions**).

For individuals, **Title 54A New Jersey Gross Income Tax Act** instead establishes by specific language *imposition* of tax and by specific rates *liability* for the tax imposed as well as the *definition* of income that is taxable and states:

54A:2-1. Imposition of tax.

54A:2-1. Imposition of tax. There is hereby imposed a tax for each taxable year (which shall be the same as the taxable year for federal income tax purposes) on the New Jersey gross income as herein defined of every individual, estate or trust (other than a charitable trust or a trust forming part of a pension or profit-sharing plan), subject to the deductions, limitations and modifications hereinafter provided, determined in accordance with the following tables with respect to taxpayers' taxable income:
... [http://law.onecle.com/new-jersey/54a-new-jersey-gross-income-tax-act/2-1.html].

54A:5-1. New Jersey gross income defined.

54A:5-1. New Jersey Gross Income Defined. New Jersey gross income shall consist of the following categories of income:

a. Salaries, wages, tips, fees, commissions, bonuses, and other remuneration received for services rendered whether in cash or in property, and amounts paid or distributed, or deemed paid or distributed, out of a medical savings account that are not excluded from gross income pursuant to section 5 of P.L.1997, c.414 (C.54A:6-27).

b. Net profits from business. The net income from the operation of a business, profession or other activity after provision for all costs and expenses incurred in the conduct thereof, determined either on a cash or accrual basis in accordance with the method of accounting allowed for federal income tax purposes but without deduction of the amount of:

… [http://law.onecle.com/new-jersey/54a-new-jersey-gross-income-tax-act/5-1.html].

So, the Code establishes imposition of individual income tax and liability for the tax imposed as well as the definition of income that is taxable.

For corporations, **Title 54 Taxation** also establishes by specific language *imposition* of tax and by specific rates *liability* for the tax imposed and states:

54:10A-2. Payment of annual franchise tax.

2. Every domestic or foreign corporation which is not hereinafter exempted shall pay an annual franchise tax for each year, ….

… [http://law.onecle.com/new-jersey/54-taxation/10a-2.html].

54:10A-5. Franchise tax.

5. The franchise tax to be annually assessed to and paid by each taxpayer shall be the greater of the amount computed pursuant to this section or the alternative minimum assessment computed pursuant to section 7 of P.L.2002, c.40 (C.54:10A-5a); ….

(c) (1) For a taxpayer that is not a New Jersey S corporation, 3 1/4% of its entire net income or such portion thereof as may be allocable to this State as provided in section 6 of P.L.1945, c.162 (C.54:10A-6) plus such portion thereof as is specifically assigned to this State as provided in section 5 of P.L.1993, c.173 (C.54:10A-6.1); provided, however, … that with respect to reports covering privilege periods or parts thereof ending after December 31, 1979, the rate shall be 9%; provided however, that for a taxpayer that has entire net income of $100,000 or less for a privilege period and is not a partnership the rate for that privilege period shall be 7 1/2% and provided further that for a taxpayer that has entire net income of $50,000 or less for a privilege period and is not a partnership the rate for that privilege period shall be 6 1/2%.

… [http://law.onecle.com/new-jersey/54-taxation/10a-5.html].

However, **Section 54:10A-4 Definitions** refers to the IRC for the *definition* of what is taxable, actually stating that entire net income shall be taxable income reported for *federal* income tax purposes, and states:

54:10A-4. Definitions.

4. For the purposes of this act, unless the context requires a different meaning:

…

(k) "Entire net income" shall mean total net income from all sources, ….

For the purpose of this act, the amount of a taxpayer's entire net income shall be deemed prima facie to be equal in amount to the taxable income, before net operating loss deduction and special deductions, which the taxpayer is required to report, or, if the taxpayer is classified as a partnership for federal tax purposes, would otherwise be required to report, to the United States Treasury Department for the purpose of computing its federal income tax, …

… [http://law.onecle.com/new-jersey/54-taxation/10a-4.html].

By enacting this statute, the state legislature has established imposition of corporate franchise tax and liability for the tax imposed without also establishing anything on which to impose the liability. (Anything multiplied by nothing is nothing, that is, a percentage of nothing is nothing. Refer to Appendix III and Appendix D for further discussion.)

The New Jersey Legislature statutorily requires the payment of individual state income tax. Without any reference to or reliance on the IRC, it has established *all three elements of the essential statutory formula for income tax: imposition of tax, liability for the tax imposed, and the definition of income that is taxable.* However, it does not statutorily require the payment of corporate state income or franchise tax.

#31 New Mexico, a *Known* Income-Tax State

Federal statute based: Yes
State statute based: Yes
Actual liability: No

"Liable" defined by state statute: No
"Liability" defined by state statute: No

For general state income tax purposes, the New Mexico Legislature relies on both the **New Mexico Statutes Annotated** and the federal **Internal Revenue Code.**

The **New Mexico Statutes Annotated** do not define liable or liability for income tax purposes (reference **Chapter 7 Taxation, Article 2 Income Tax General Provisions, Section 7-2-2 Definitions** and **Article 2A Corporate Income and Franchise Tax, Section 7-2A-2 Definitions**).

For individuals, **Chapter 7 Taxation, Article 2 Income Tax General Provisions** instead establishes by specific language *imposition* of tax and by specific rates *liability* for the tax imposed and states:

7-2-3. Imposition and levy of tax.

A tax is imposed at the rates specified in the Income Tax Act [7-2-1 NMSA 1978] upon the net income of every resident individual and upon the net income of every nonresident individual employed or engaged in the transaction of business in, into or from this state, or deriving any income from any property or employment within this state [http://www.conwaygreene.com/nmsu/lpext.dll?f=templates&fn=main-h.htm&2.0].

7-2-7. Individual income tax rates. (Effective January 1, 2008.)

The tax imposed by Section 7-2-3 NMSA 1978 shall be at the following rates for any taxable year beginning on or after January 1, 2008:
… [http://www.conwaygreene.com/nmsu/lpext.dll?f=templates&fn=main-h.htm&2.0].

However, **7-2-2. Definitions** refers to the IRC for the *definitions* of income that is taxable, actually stating that adjusted gross income means adjusted gross income as defined in the IRC, and states:

7-2-2. Definitions.

For the purpose of the Income Tax Act and unless the context requires otherwise:

A. "adjusted gross income" means adjusted gross income as defined in Section 62 of the Internal Revenue Code, as that section may be amended or renumbered;

...

X. "taxable income" means net income less any lump-sum amount;

... [http://www.conwaygreene.com/nmsu/lpext.dll?f=templates&fn=main-h.htm&2.0].

So while the Code establishes imposition of individual income tax and liability for the tax imposed, its definitions of what is taxable are based on the IRC. In other words, the state legislature has established imposition and liability without also establishing anything on which to impose the liability. (Anything multiplied by nothing is nothing, that is, a percentage of nothing is nothing. Refer to Appendix III and Appendix D for further discussion.)

For corporations, **Article 2A Corporate Income and Franchise Tax** also establishes by specific language *imposition* of tax and by specific rates *liability* for the tax imposed and states:

7-2A-3. Imposition and levy of taxes.

A. A tax to be known as the "corporate income tax" is imposed at the rate specified in the Corporate Income and Franchise Tax Act [7-2A-1 NMSA 1978] upon the net income of every domestic corporation and upon the net income of every foreign corporation employed or engaged in the transaction of business in, into or from this state or deriving any income from any property or employment within this state.

... [http://www.conwaygreene.com/nmsu/lpext.dll?f=templates&fn=main-h.htm&2.0].

7-2A-5. Corporate income tax rates.

The corporate income tax imposed on corporations by Section 7-2A-3 NMSA 1978 shall be at the rates specified in the following table:

... [http://www.conwaygreene.com/nmsu/lpext.dll?f=templates&fn=main-h.htm&2.0].

However, **Section 7-2A-2 Definitions** refers to the IRC for the *definitions* of income that is taxable and states:

7-2A-2. Definitions.

For the purpose of the Corporate Income and Franchise Tax Act [7-2A-1 NMSA 1978] and unless the context requires otherwise:

...

C. "base income" means that part of the taxpayer's income defined as taxable income and upon which the federal income tax is calculated in the Internal Revenue Code for income tax purposes ...

...

H. "net income" means base income ...

... [http://www.conwaygreene.com/nmsu/lpext.dll?f=templates&fn=main-h.htm&2.0].

That is, net income is base income, which means taxable income for *federal* income tax purposes.

So while the Code establishes imposition of corporate income tax and liability for the tax imposed, its definitions of what is taxable are based on the IRC. In other words, the state legislature has established imposition and liability without also establishing anything on which to impose the liability. (Anything multiplied by nothing is nothing, that is, a percentage of nothing is nothing.)

The New Mexico Legislature has not enacted its own statutes for the definition of income that is taxable for either individual or corporate state income tax. While it has enacted certain statutes that establish imposition of state income tax and liability for the tax imposed, it has relied on the IRC for the definitions of what is taxable. So while New Mexico is a *known* income-tax state, its legislature does not statutorily require the payment of state income tax.

#32 New York, a *Known* Income-Tax State

Federal statute based: Yes
State statute based: Yes
Actual liability: No

"Liable" defined by state statute: No
"Liability" defined by state statute: No

For general state income tax purposes, the New York State Legislature relies on both the **Laws of New York** and the federal **Internal Revenue Code.**

The **Laws of New York** do not define liable or liability for income tax purposes (reference **Tax, Article 1, Section 2 Definitions, Article 22 Personal Income Tax, Part 1 General, Section 607 Meaning of terms, Article 9 Corporation Tax,** and **Article 9-A Franchise Tax on Business Corporations, Section 208 Definitions**).

For individuals, **Tax, Article 22 Personal Income Tax** instead establishes by specific language *imposition* of tax and by specific rates *liability* for the tax imposed as well as the *definitions* of income that is taxable and states:

Part 1 General
§ 601. Imposition of tax. (a) ... There is hereby imposed for each taxable year on the New York taxable income of every resident ... a tax determined in accordance with the following tables:
...
[http://public.leginfo.state.ny.us/LAWSSEAF.cgi?QUERYTYPE=LAWS+&QUERY DATA=$$TAX601$$@TXTAX0601+&LIST=LAW+&BROWSER=EXPLORER+&T OKEN=07950948+&TARGET=VIEW].

Part 2 Residents
§ 611. New York taxable income of a resident individual. (a) General. The New York taxable income of a resident individual shall be his New York adjusted gross income less his New York deduction and New York exemptions, as determined under this part
[http://public.leginfo.state.ny.us/LAWSSEAF.cgi?QUERYTYPE=LAWS+&QUERY DATA=$$TAX611$$@TXTAX0611+&LIST=LAW+&BROWSER=EXPLORER+&T OKEN=07950948+&TARGET=VIEW].

§ 612. New York adjusted gross income of a resident individual. (a) General. The New York adjusted gross income of a resident individual means his federal adjusted gross income as defined in the laws of the United States for the taxable year, with the modifications specified in this section
[http://public.leginfo.state.ny.us/LAWSSEAF.cgi?QUERYTYPE=LAWS+&QUERY DATA=$$TAX612$$@TXTAX0612+&LIST=LAW+&BROWSER=EXPLORER+&T OKEN=07950948+&TARGET=VIEW].

However, **Section 612 New York adjusted gross income of a resident individual** also refers to the federal IRC for the ***definition*** of income that is taxable, actually stating that New York adjusted gross income means ***federal*** adjusted gross income as defined in the laws of the US.

So while the Code establishes imposition of individual income tax and liability for the tax imposed, its definitions of what is taxable are based on the IRC. In other words, the state legislature has established imposition and liability without also establishing anything on which to impose the liability. (Anything multiplied by nothing is nothing, that is, a percentage of nothing is nothing. Refer to Appendix III and Appendix D for further discussion.)

For corporations, **Tax, Article 9-A Franchise Tax on Business Corporations** also establishes by specific language ***imposition*** of tax and by specific rates ***liability*** for the tax imposed and states:

> **§ 209. Imposition of tax; exemptions.** 1. For the privilege of exercising its corporate franchise, or of doing business, or of employing capital, or of owning or leasing property in this state in a corporate or organized capacity, or of maintaining an office in this state, for all or any part of each of its fiscal or calendar years, every domestic or foreign corporation, except corporations specified in subdivision four of this section, shall annually pay a franchise tax, upon the basis of its entire net income base, …
> [http://public.leginfo.state.ny.us/LAWSSEAF.cgi?QUERYTYPE=LAWS+&QUERY DATA=$$TAX209$$@TXTAX0209+&LIST=LAW+&BROWSER=EXPLORER+&TOKEN=08173627+&TARGET=VIEW].

> **§ 210. Computation of tax.** 1. The tax imposed by subdivision one of section two hundred nine of this chapter shall be: (A) in the case of each taxpayer other than a New York S corporation or a qualified homeowners association, the sum of (1) the highest of the amounts prescribed in paragraphs (a), (b), (c) and (d) of this subdivision and (2) the amount prescribed in paragraph (e) of this subdivision, ….
> (a) Entire net income base. … For taxable years beginning on or after January first, two thousand seven, the amount prescribed by this paragraph shall be computed at the rate of seven and one-tenth percent of the taxpayer's entire net income base. The taxpayer's entire net income base shall mean the portion of the taxpayer's entire net income allocated within the state …
> [http://public.leginfo.state.ny.us/LAWSSEAF.cgi?QUERYTYPE=LAWS+&QUERY DATA=$$TAX210$$@TXTAX0210+&LIST=LAW+&BROWSER=EXPLORER+&TOKEN=08173627+&TARGET=VIEW].

However, **Article 9-A Franchise Tax on Business Corporations** does not establish the ***definition*** of income that is taxable, stating that entire net income means total net income but not defining total net income, and states:

§ 208. Definitions. As used in this article:

...

9. The term "entire net income" means total net income from all sources, which shall be presumably the same as the entire taxable income (but not alternative minimum taxable income),

(i) which the taxpayer is required to report to the United States treasury department, or

...

(iii) which the taxpayer, in the case of a corporation which is exempt from federal income tax (other than the tax on unrelated business taxable income imposed under section 511 of the internal revenue code) but which is subject to tax under this article, would have been required to report to the United States treasury department but for such exemption, except as hereinafter provided, and subject to any modification required by paragraphs (d) and (e) of subdivision three of section two hundred ten of this article.

...

[http://public.leginfo.state.ny.us/LAWSSEAF.cgi?QUERYTYPE=LAWS+&QUERY DATA=$$TAX208$$@TXTAX0208+&LIST=LAW+&BROWSER=EXPLORER+&T OKEN=08173627+&TARGET=VIEW].

Interestingly, this section contains two valuable statements for educational purposes. First, the definition of entire net income is interesting and valuable because the IRC does not establish liability for federal income tax, so that no corporation is required to report any income to the US Treasury. Second, the reference to a corporation which is exempt from federal income tax is interesting and valuable also because the IRC does not establish liability for federal income tax, so that any corporation is exempt from federal income tax, specific exemption from federal income tax or lack thereof notwithstanding.

So while the Code establishes imposition of corporate franchise tax and liability for the tax imposed, it does not establish the definition of income that is taxable, although neither does it refer to the IRC for such definition. In other words, the state legislature has established imposition and liability without also establishing anything on which to impose the liability. (Anything multiplied by nothing is nothing, that is, a percentage of nothing is nothing.)

The New York State Legislature has not enacted its own statutes for the definition of income that is taxable for either individual state income or corporate state franchise tax. While it has enacted certain statutes that establish imposition of state income and franchise taxes and liability for the taxes imposed, it has relied on the IRC for the definitions of what is taxable for individuals but not established the definition of income that is taxable for corporations. So while New York is a **known** income-tax state, its legislature does not statutorily require the payment of either state income or state franchise tax.

#33 North Carolina, a *Known* Income-Tax State

Federal statute based: Yes
State statute based: Yes
Actual liability: No

"Liable" defined by state statute: No
"Liability" defined by state statute: No

For general state income tax purposes, the North Carolina General Assembly relies on both the **North Carolina General Statutes** and the federal **Internal Revenue Code.**

The **North Carolina General Statutes** do not define liable or liability for income tax purposes (reference **Chapter 105 Taxation, Article 4 Income Tax, Sections 105-134.1 … Definitions** and **105-130.2 Definitions**).

For individuals, **Chapter 105 Taxation, Article 4 Income Tax, Section 105-134.2 Individual income tax imposed** instead establishes by specific language *imposition* of tax and by specific rates *liability* for the tax imposed and states:

§ 105-134.2. Individual income tax imposed.
(a) A tax is imposed upon the North Carolina taxable income of every individual. The tax shall be levied, collected, and paid annually and shall be computed at the following percentages of the taxpayer's North Carolina taxable income.
…
[http://www.ncga.state.nc.us/EnactedLegislation/Statutes/HTML/BySection/Chapter_105/GS_105-134.2.html].

However, **Article 4 Income Tax** refers to the federal IRC ("the Code") for the *definitions* of income that is taxable, actually stating that North Carolina taxable income means adjusted gross income and adjusted gross income is defined in the IRC, and states:

§ 105-134.1. (Effective for taxable years beginning on or after January 1, 2012) Definitions.
The following definitions apply in this Part:
(1) Adjusted gross income. – Defined in section 62 of the Code.
…
(5) Gross income. – Defined in section 61 of the Code.
…
(10) North Carolina taxable income. – Defined in G.S. 105-134.5.
…
[http://www.ncga.state.nc.us/EnactedLegislation/Statutes/HTML/BySection/Chapter_105/GS_105-134.1.html].

§ 105-134.5. (Effective for taxable years beginning on or after January 1, 2012) North Carolina taxable income defined.
(a) Residents. – For an individual who is a resident of this State, the term "North Carolina taxable income" means the taxpayer's adjusted gross income as modified in G.S. 105-134.6.
…

[http://www.ncga.state.nc.us/EnactedLegislation/Statutes/HTML/BySection/Chapter_105/GS_105-134.5.html].

That is, gross income is defined in the IRC and derives adjusted gross income, which is defined in the IRC and derives North Carolina taxable income.

So while the Code establishes imposition of individual income tax and liability for the tax imposed, its definitions of what is taxable are based on the IRC. In other words, the state legislature has established imposition and liability without also establishing anything on which to impose the liability. (Anything multiplied by nothing is nothing, that is, a percentage of nothing is nothing. Refer to Appendix III and Appendix D for further discussion.)

For corporations, Section 105-130.3 Corporations also establishes by specific language *imposition* of tax and by specific rates *liability* for the tax imposed and states:

§ 105-130.3. Corporations.
A tax is imposed on the State net income of every C Corporation doing business in this State. An S Corporation is not subject to the tax levied in this section. The tax is a percentage of the taxpayer's State net income computed as follows:
…

[http://www.ncga.state.nc.us/EnactedLegislation/Statutes/HTML/BySection/Chapter_105/GS_105-130.3.html].

However, **Section 105-130.2 Definitions** refers to the IRC ("the Code") for the *definition* of income that is taxable, actually stating that State net income is *federal* taxable income (rather than *North Carolina* taxable income), and states:

§ 105-130.2. Definitions.
The following definitions apply in this Part:
…

(5c) State net income. – The taxpayer's federal taxable income as determined under the Code, adjusted as provided in G.S. 105-130.5 and, in the case of a corporation that has income from business activity that is taxable both within and without this State, allocated and apportioned to this State as provided in G.S. 105-130.4.
…

[http://www.ncga.state.nc.us/EnactedLegislation/Statutes/HTML/BySection/Chapter_105/GS_105-130.2.html].

So while the Code establishes imposition of corporate income tax and liability for the tax imposed, its definition of what is taxable is based on the IRC. In other words, the state legislature has established imposition and liability without also establishing anything on which to impose the liability. (Anything multiplied by nothing is nothing, that is, a percentage of nothing is nothing.)

The North Carolina General Assembly has not enacted its own statutes for the definition of income that is taxable for either individual or corporate state income tax. While it has enacted certain statutes that establish imposition of state income tax and liability for the tax imposed, it has relied on the IRC for the definitions of what is taxable. So while North Carolina is a *known* income-tax state, its legislature does not statutorily require the payment of state income tax.

#34 North Dakota, a *Known* Income-Tax State

Federal statute based: Yes
State statute based: Yes
Actual liability: No

"Liable" defined by state statute: No
"Liability" defined by state statute: No

For general state income tax purposes, the North Dakota Legislative Assembly relies on both the **North Dakota Century Code** and the federal **Internal Revenue Code.**

The **North Dakota Century Code** does not define liable or liability for income tax purposes (reference **Title 57 Taxation, Chapter 57-38 Income Tax, Section 57-38-01 Definitions**).

For individuals, **Title 57 Taxation, Chapter 57-38 Income Tax, Section 57-38-30.3 Individual, estate, and trust income tax** instead establishes by specific language *imposition* of tax and by specific rates *liability* for the tax imposed and states:

> **57-38-30.3. (Effective for the first two taxable years beginning after December 31, 2010) Individual, estate, and trust income tax.**
> 1. A tax is hereby imposed for each taxable year upon income earned or received in that taxable year by every resident …. The tax for individuals is equal to North Dakota taxable income multiplied by the rates in the applicable rate schedule in subdivisions a through d corresponding to an individual's filing status used for federal income tax purposes….
> …
> **(Effective after the first two taxable years beginning after December 31, 2010) Individual, estate, and trust income tax.**
> 1. A tax is hereby imposed for each taxable year upon income earned or received in that taxable year by every resident …. The tax for individuals is equal to North Dakota taxable income multiplied by the rates in the applicable rate schedule in subdivisions a through d corresponding to an individual's filing status used for federal income tax purposes….
> … [http://law.justia.com/codes/north-dakota/2011/title57/chapter57-38/].

However, **Section 57-38-01 Definitions** refers to the IRC for the *definition* of income that is taxable, actually stating that taxable income means taxable income as computed for *federal* income tax purposes under the US IRC, and states:

> **57-38-01. Definitions.**
> As used in this chapter, unless the context or subject matter otherwise requires:
> …
> 12. "Taxable income" in the case of individuals, estates, trusts, and corporations means the taxable income as computed for an individual, estate, trust, or

corporation for federal income tax purposes under the United States Internal Revenue Code ....
... [http://law.justia.com/codes/north-dakota/2011/title57/chapter57-38/].

Interestingly, moreover, this chapter contains a valuable statement for educational purposes under **Section 57-38-09 Exempt organizations,** which also refers to the IRC for the *definition* of income that is taxable, namely, income of a person exempt from federal income taxation under the provisions of the IRC, and states:

57-38-09. Exempt organizations.
1. A person or organization exempt from federal income taxation under the provisions of the Internal Revenue Code of 1954, as amended, is also exempt from the tax imposed by this chapter in each year such person or organization satisfies the requirements of the Internal Revenue Code of 1954, as amended, for exemption from federal income taxation....
... [http://law.justia.com/codes/north-dakota/2011/title57/chapter57-38/].

This is interesting and valuable because the IRC does not establish liability for federal income tax, so that any person is exempt from federal income taxation, specific exemption from federal income taxation or lack thereof notwithstanding.

So while the Code establishes imposition of individual income tax and liability for the tax imposed, its definition of what is taxable is based on the IRC. In other words, the state legislature has established imposition and liability without also establishing anything on which to impose the liability. (Anything multiplied by nothing is nothing, that is, a percentage of nothing is nothing. Refer to Appendix III and Appendix D for further discussion.)

For corporations, Section 57-38-30 Imposition and rate of tax on corporations also establishes by specific language *imposition* of tax and by specific rates *liability* for the tax imposed and states:

57-38-30. Imposition and rate of tax on corporations.
A tax is hereby imposed upon the taxable income of every domestic and foreign corporation which must be levied, collected, and paid annually as in this chapter provided:
... [http://law.justia.com/codes/north-dakota/2011/title57/chapter57-38/].

However, **Section 57-38-01 Definitions** refers to the IRC for the *definition* of income that is taxable, actually stating that taxable income means taxable income as computed for *federal* income tax purposes under the US IRC, and states:

57-38-01. Definitions.
As used in this chapter, unless the context or subject matter otherwise requires:
...

12. "Taxable income" in the case of individuals, estates, trusts, and corporations means the taxable income as computed for an individual, estate, trust, or corporation for federal income tax purposes under the United States Internal Revenue Code ....
… [http://law.justia.com/codes/north-dakota/2011/title57/chapter57-38/].

Interestingly, moreover, this chapter contains a valuable statement for educational purposes under **Section 57-38-09 Exempt organizations,** which also refers to the IRC for the ***definition*** of income that is taxable, namely, income of an organization exempt from federal income taxation under the provisions of the IRC, and states:

57-38-09. Exempt organizations.

1. A person or organization exempt from federal income taxation under the provisions of the Internal Revenue Code of 1954, as amended, is also exempt from the tax imposed by this chapter in each year such person or organization satisfies the requirements of the Internal Revenue Code of 1954, as amended, for exemption from federal income taxation....
… [http://law.justia.com/codes/north-dakota/2011/title57/chapter57-38/].

This is interesting and valuable because the IRC does not establish liability for federal income tax, so that any organization is exempt from federal income taxation, specific exemption from federal income taxation or lack thereof notwithstanding.

So while the Code establishes imposition of corporate income tax and liability for the tax imposed, its definition of what is taxable is based on the IRC. In other words, the state legislature has established imposition and liability without also establishing anything on which to impose the liability. (Anything multiplied by nothing is nothing, that is, a percentage of nothing is nothing.)

The North Dakota Legislative Assembly has not enacted its own statutes for the definition of income that is taxable for either individual or corporate state income tax. While it has enacted certain statutes that establish imposition of state income tax and liability for the tax imposed, it has relied on the IRC for the definition of what is taxable. So while North Dakota is a ***known*** income-tax state, its legislature does not statutorily require the payment of state income tax.

#35 Ohio, a *Known* Income-Tax State

Federal statute based: Yes
State statute based: Yes
Actual liability: No

"Liable" defined by state statute: No
"Liability" defined by state statute: No

For general state income tax purposes, the Ohio General Assembly relies on both the **Revised Code** and the federal **Internal Revenue Code.**

The **Revised Code** does not define liable or liability for income tax purposes (reference **Title [57] LVII Taxation, Chapter 5701 Definitions, Chapter 5747 Income Tax, Section 5747.01 Income tax definitions**).

For individuals, **Title [57] LVII Taxation, Chapter 5701 Definitions, Chapter 5747 Income Tax, Section 5747.02 Tax rates** instead establishes by specific language *imposition* of tax and by specific rates *liability* for the tax imposed and states:

5747.02 [Effective3/22/2012] Tax rates
(A) For the purpose of providing revenue for the support of schools and local government functions, to provide relief to property taxpayers, to provide revenue for the general revenue fund, and to meet the expenses of administering the tax levied by this chapter, there is hereby levied on every individual, trust, and estate residing in or earning or receiving income in this state, on every individual, trust, and estate earning or receiving lottery winnings, prizes, or awards pursuant to Chapter 3770. of the Revised Code, on every individual, trust, and estate earning or receiving winnings on casino gaming, and on every individual, trust, and estate otherwise having nexus with or in this state under the Constitution of the United States, an annual tax measured in the case of individuals by Ohio adjusted gross income less an exemption for the taxpayer, the taxpayer's spouse, and each dependent as provided in section 5747.025 of the Revised Code; measured in the case of trusts by modified Ohio taxable income under division (D) of this section; and measured in the case of estates by Ohio taxable income. The tax imposed by this section on the balance thus obtained is hereby levied as follows: … [http://codes.ohio.gov/orc/5747.02].

However, **Section 5747.01 Income tax definitions** refers to the IRC for the *definition* of income that is taxable, actually stating that Ohio adjusted gross income means *federal* adjusted gross income as defined in the IRC, and states:

5747.01 Income tax definitions.
…
As used in this chapter:

(A) "Adjusted gross income" or "Ohio adjusted gross income" means federal adjusted gross income, as defined and used in the Internal Revenue Code, adjusted as provided in this section:
… [http://codes.ohio.gov/orc/5747.01].

So while the Code establishes imposition of individual income tax and liability for the tax imposed, its definition of what is taxable is based on the IRC. In other words, the state legislature has established imposition and liability without also establishing anything on which to impose the liability. (Anything multiplied by nothing is nothing, that is, a percentage of nothing is nothing. Refer to Appendix III and Appendix D for further discussion.)

For corporations, it is worth noting that, while **Chapter 5751 Commercial Activity Tax, Sections 5751.02 Commercial activity tax levied on taxable gross receipts** and **5751.03 Commercial activity tax rate - computation** establish *imposition* of tax and a two and six-tenths mills per dollar *liability* for the tax imposed as well as what is taxable, namely, gross receipts from business activities within the State less an exclusion amount.

The Ohio General Assembly has not enacted its own statutes for the definition of income that is taxable for individual state income tax or any statutes for corporate state income tax. While it has enacted a certain statute that establishes imposition of individual state income tax and liability for the tax imposed, it has relied on the IRC for the definition of what is taxable. So while Ohio is a *known* income-tax state, its legislature does not statutorily require the payment of state income tax beyond that relative to less than one percent of gross business receipts.

#36 Oklahoma, a *Known* Income-Tax State

Federal statute based: Yes
State statute based: Yes
Actual liability: No

"Liable" defined by state statute: No
"Liability" defined by state statute: No

For general state income tax purposes, the Oklahoma State Legislature relies on both the **Oklahoma Statutes Citationized** and the federal **Internal Revenue Code.**

The **Oklahoma Statutes Citationized** do not define liable or liability for income tax purposes (reference **Title 68 Revenue and Taxation, Chapter 1 Tax Codes, Article 2 Uniform Tax Procedure, Section 202 Definitions, Article 23 Income Tax, Oklahoma Income Tax Act, Section 2353 Definitions,** and **Article 12 Franchise Tax Code, Section 1217 Definitions**).

Instead, **Title 68 Revenue and Taxation, Chapter 1 Tax Codes, Article 23 Income Tax, Oklahoma Income Tax Act, Section 2355 Tax Imposed - Classes of Taxpayers** establishes by specific language *imposition* of tax and by specific rates *liability* for the tax imposed and states:

> …
> B. Individuals. For all taxable years beginning on or after January 1, 2008, a tax is hereby imposed upon the Oklahoma taxable income of every resident or nonresident individual, which tax shall be computed as follows:
> …
> D. Corporations. For all taxable years beginning after December 31, 1989, a tax is hereby imposed upon the Oklahoma taxable income of every corporation doing business within this state or deriving income from sources within this state in an amount equal to six percent (6%) thereof.
> … [http://www.oscn.net/applications/oscn/DeliverDocument.asp?CiteID=92565].

However, **Section 2353 Definitions** refers to the federal IRC for the ***definitions*** of income that is taxable, actually stating that taxable income means taxable income and any other taxable income as defined in the IRC, adjusted gross income means adjusted gross income as defined in the IRC, Oklahoma taxable income means taxable income as reported to the federal government, and Oklahoma adjusted gross income means adjusted gross income as reported to the federal government, and states:

> For the purpose of and when used in Section 2351 et seq. of this title, unless the context otherwise requires:
> …
> 10. "Taxable income" with respect to any taxpayer means the "taxable income", "life insurance company taxable income", "mutual insurance company taxable

income", "(regulated) investment company taxable income", "real estate investment trust taxable income", and "cooperatives' taxable income" and any other "taxable income" as defined in the Internal Revenue Code as applies to such taxpayer …

11. "Adjusted gross income" means "adjusted gross income" as defined in the Internal Revenue Code;

12. "Oklahoma taxable income" means "taxable income" as reported (or as would have been reported by the taxpayer had a return been filed) to the federal government, and in the event of adjustments thereto by the federal government as finally ascertained under the Internal Revenue Code, adjusted further as hereinafter provided;

13. "Oklahoma adjusted gross income" means "adjusted gross income" as reported to the federal government (or as would have been reported by the taxpayer had a return been filed), or in the event of adjustments thereby by the federal government as finally ascertained under the Internal Revenue Code, adjusted further as hereinafter provided;

… [http://www.oscn.net/applications/oscn/DeliverDocument.asp?CiteID=92563].

So while the Code establishes imposition of and liability for income tax, its definitions of what is taxable are based on the IRC. In other words, the state legislature has established imposition and liability without also establishing anything on which to impose the liability. (Anything multiplied by nothing is nothing, that is, a percentage of nothing is nothing. Refer to Appendix III and Appendix D for further discussion.)

Article 12 Franchise Tax Code, Oklahoma Business Activity Code, Section 1218 Annual Tax - Levy - Applicability also establishes by specific language *imposition* of tax and by a specific rate *liability* for the tax imposed and states:

> …
> B. In addition to the tax levied in subsection A of this section, there shall be levied a tax equal to one percent (1%) of the net revenue derived from business activity that is allocated or apportioned to Oklahoma.
> … [http://www.oscn.net/applications/oscn/DeliverDocument.asp?CiteID=461879].

However, **Section 1217 Definitions** refers to the IRC for the *definitions* of income that is taxable, actually stating that net revenue means total revenue and total revenue means all revenues reportable on the *federal* income tax return, and states:

> As used in the Oklahoma Business Activity Tax Code:
> …
> 6. "Net revenue" means "total revenue" …
> 10. "Total revenue" means all revenues reportable by a person on the federal income tax return filed by such person …
> … [http://www.oscn.net/applications/oscn/DeliverDocument.asp?CiteID=461878].

So while the Code establishes imposition of franchise tax and liability for the tax imposed, its definitions of what is taxable are based on the IRC. In other words, the state legislature has established imposition and liability without also establishing anything on which to impose the liability. (Anything multiplied by nothing is nothing, that is, a percentage of nothing is nothing.)

The Oklahoma State Legislature has not enacted its own statutes for the definition of income that is taxable for either individual or corporate state income or franchise tax. While it has enacted certain statutes that establish imposition of state income and state franchise taxes and liability for the taxes imposed, it has relied on the IRC for the definitions of what is taxable. So while Oklahoma is a *known* income-tax state, its legislature does not statutorily require the payment of state income tax.

#37 Oregon, a *Known* Income-Tax State

Federal statute based: Yes
State statute based: Yes
Actual liability: No

"Liable" defined by state statute: No
"Liability" defined by state statute: No

For general state income tax purposes, the Oregon State Legislature relies on both the **Oregon Revised Statutes** and the federal **Internal Revenue Code.**

The **Oregon Revised Statutes** do not define liable or liability for income tax purposes (reference **Volume 8, Title 29 Revenue and Taxation, Chapter 314 Taxes Imposed Upon or Measured by Net Income, Income Taxation Generally, Revenue and Taxation, General Provisions, Section 314.011 Definitions; conformance with federal income tax law, and Section 314.610 Definitions for ORS 314.605 to 314.675, Chapter 316 Personal Income Tax, Revenue and Taxation, General Provisions, Section 316.022 General definitions, and Chapter 317 Corporation Excise Tax, Revenue and Taxation, General Provisions, Section 317.010 Definitions**).

For individuals, **Volume 8, Title 29 Revenue and Taxation, Chapter 316 Personal Income Tax, Revenue and Taxation, General Provisions, Section 316.037 Imposition and rate of tax** instead establishes by specific language *imposition* of tax and by specific rates *liability* for the tax imposed and states:

> **316.037 Imposition and rate of tax.** (1)(a) A tax is imposed for each taxable year on the entire taxable income of every resident of this state. The amount of the tax shall be determined in accordance with the following table:
> … [http://www.leg.state.or.us/ors/316.html].

However, **Chapter 316 Personal Income Tax, Revenue and Taxation, General Provisions** refers to the IRC for the *definitions* of income that is taxable, actually stating that taxable income means taxable income as defined in the IRC and entire taxable income is *federal* taxable income as defined in US law, and states:

> **316.022 General definitions.** As used in this chapter, unless the context requires otherwise:
> …
> (6) "Taxable income" means the taxable income as defined in subsection (a) or (b), section 63 of the Internal Revenue Code, with such additions, subtractions and adjustments as are prescribed by this chapter.
> … [http://www.leg.state.or.us/ors/316.html].

316.048 Taxable income of resident. The entire taxable income of a resident of this state is the federal taxable income of the resident as defined in the laws of the United States, with the modifications, additions and subtractions provided in this chapter and other laws of this state applicable to personal income taxation [http://www.leg.state.or.us/ors/316.html].

So while the Code establishes imposition of individual income tax and liability for the tax imposed, its definitions of what is taxable are based on the IRC. In other words, the state legislature has established imposition and liability without also establishing anything on which to impose the liability. (Anything multiplied by nothing is nothing, that is, a percentage of nothing is nothing. Refer to Appendix III and Appendix D for further discussion.)

For corporations, **Title 29 Revenue and Taxation** also establishes by specific language *imposition* of tax and by specific rates *liability* for the tax imposed and states:

Chapter 318 Corporation Income Tax, Revenue and Taxation
318.020 Imposition of tax. (1) There hereby is imposed upon every corporation for each taxable year a tax at the rate provided in ORS 317.061 upon its Oregon taxable income derived from sources within this state, ….
… [http://www.leg.state.or.us/ors/318.html].

Chapter 317 Corporation Excise Tax, Revenue and Taxation, General Provisions
317.061 Tax rate. The rate of the tax imposed by and computed under this chapter is:
… [http://www.leg.state.or.us/ors/317.html].

However, **Chapter 317 Corporation Excise Tax, Revenue and Taxation, General Provisions, Section 317.010 Definitions** refers to the IRC for the *definitions* of income that is taxable, actually stating that Oregon taxable income means taxable income and taxable income means the taxable income determined as would be determined under the IRC and any other US law, and states:

317.010 Definitions. As used in this chapter, unless the context requires otherwise:
…
(8) "Oregon taxable income" means taxable income, less the deduction allowed under ORS 317.476, except as otherwise provided with respect to insurers in subsection (11) of this section and ORS 317.650 to 317.665.
…
(10) "Taxable income or loss" means the taxable income or loss determined, or in the case of a corporation for which no federal taxable income or loss is determined, as would be determined, under chapter 1, Subtitle A of the Internal Revenue Code and any other laws of the United States relating to the

determination of taxable income or loss of corporate taxpayers, …
… [http://www.leg.state.or.us/ors/317.html].

So while the Code establishes imposition of corporate income tax and liability for the tax imposed, its definitions of what is taxable are based on the IRC. In other words, the state legislature has established imposition and liability without also establishing anything on which to impose the liability. (Anything multiplied by nothing is nothing, that is, a percentage of nothing is nothing.)

The Oregon State Legislature has not enacted its own statutes for the definition of income that is taxable for either individual or corporate state income tax. While it has enacted certain statutes that establish imposition of state income tax and liability for the tax imposed, it has relied on the IRC for the definitions of what is taxable. So while Oregon is a *known* income-tax state, its legislature does not statutorily require the payment of state income tax.

#38 Pennsylvania, a *Known* Income-Tax State

Federal statute based: No
State statute based: Yes
Actual liability: Yes

"Liable" defined by state statute: No
"Liability" defined by state statute: No

For general state income tax purposes, the Pennsylvania General Assembly relies on both the **Pennsylvania Consolidated Statutes** and the federal **Internal Revenue Code.**

The **Pennsylvania Consolidated Statutes** do not define liable or liability for income tax purposes (reference **Title 72 Taxation and Fiscal Affairs, Chapter 2 Taxes Levied by the State, Income Tax, Article I Short Title and Definitions, Section 3402-2 Definitions,** and **Article III Computation of Tax, Sections 3402-301 Net income** and **3402-303 Gross income**).

For individuals, **Title 72 Taxation and Fiscal Affairs, Chapter 2 Taxes Levied by the State, Income Tax** instead establishes by specific language *imposition* of tax and by specific rates *liability* for the tax imposed as well as the *definition* of income that is taxable and states:

Article II Imposition of Tax
§ 3402-201. Residents and nonresidents

A. A tax is hereby imposed upon every resident taxpayer of this Commonwealth, which tax shall be levied, collected and paid annually, with respect to his entire net income as herein defined, computed at the following rates, after deducting the exemptions provided in this act:

...
[http://weblinks.westlaw.com/result/default.aspx?cite=UUID%28NFC4886D034%2D3A11DA8A989%2DF4EECDB8638%29&db=1000262&findtype=VQ&fn=%5Ft op&pbc=DA010192&rlt=CLID%5FFQRLT443869351635&rp=%2FSearch%2Fdef ault%2Ewl&rs=WEBL12%2E04&service=Find&spa=pac%2D1000&sr=TC&vr=2 %2E0].

Article III Computation of Tax
§ 3402-301. Net income

The term "net income" means the gross income of a taxpayer less the deductions allowed by this article
[http://weblinks.westlaw.com/result/default.aspx?cite=UUID%28NF39CFBB034% 2D3A11DA8A989%2DF4EECDB8638%29&db=1000262&findtype=VQ&fn=%5Ft

op&pbc=DA010192&rlt=CLID%5FFQRLT46238371635&rp=%2FSearch%2Fdefa
ult%2Ewl&rs=WEBL12%2E04&service=Find&spa=pac%2D1000&sr=TC&vr=2%
2E0].

§ 3402-303. Gross income

A. The term "gross income" includes gains, profits and income derived from
salaries, wages or compensation for personal service, of whatever kind and in
whatever form paid, or from professions, vocations, trades, businesses,
commerce, or sales, or dealings in property, whether real or personal, growing
out of the ownership, or use of, or interest in, such property, also from interest,
rent, dividends, securities, or the transaction of any business, carried on for gain
or profit, and all other income derived from any source whatever, including
income derived through estates or trusts by the beneficiaries thereof, whether as
distributed or as distributable shares. The amount of all such items shall be
included in the gross income for the tax year in which received by the taxpayer.

...
[http://weblinks.westlaw.com/result/default.aspx?cite=UUID%28NF2F1EEA034%
2D3A11DA8A989%2DF4EECDB8638%29&db=1000262&findtype=VQ&fn=%5Ft
op&pbc=DA010192&rlt=CLID%5FFQRLT5895926381635&rp=%2FSearch%2Fd
efault%2Ewl&rs=WEBL12%2E04&service=Find&spa=pac%2D1000&sr=TC&vr=
2%2E0].

So, the Code establishes imposition of individual income tax and liability for the tax
imposed as well as the definition of income that is taxable.

**For corporations, Chapter 2 Taxes Levied by the State, Tax on Net Earnings.
Section 2241 Corporations and limited partnerships; manufacturing companies
and cooperative agricultural associations exempt** also establishes by specific
language *imposition* of tax and by specific rates *liability* for the tax imposed as well as
the *definition* of what is taxable and states:

§ 2241. Corporations and limited partnerships; manufacturing companies and cooperative agricultural associations exempt

From and after the passage of this act every incorporated company or limited
partnership whatever, whether the same be incorporated, formed or organized
under the laws of this or any other state or territory, and doing business within
this Commonwealth, and liable to taxation therein, which is not subject to the
taxes imposed by the twenty-first or twenty-fourth sections of this act, except
incorporated banks and savings institutions having capital stock, and foreign
insurance companies, shall annually, upon the fifteenth day of March of each
year, make report to the Department of Revenue setting forth the entire amount
of net earnings or income received by said company or limited partnership from
all sources during the preceding year, and such other information as the

department may require; and upon such net earnings or income, the said company, association or limited partnership, as the case may be, shall pay into the State Treasury, through the Department of Revenue, for the use of the Commonwealth, within the time prescribed by law for the payment of State taxes settled by the Department of Revenue, three per centum upon such annual net earnings or income, in addition to any taxes on personal property to which it may be subject under the first section of this act. The penalty for failure to make such report shall be as provided by [FN1] law: Provided, That this section shall not apply to corporations and limited partnerships chartered or organized for manufacturing purposes, nor to cooperative agricultural associations organized under the laws of this or any other state.

…

[http://weblinks.westlaw.com/result/default.aspx?cite=UUID%28NF56893F034%2D3A11DA8A989%2DF4EECDB8638%29&db=1000262&findtype=VQ&fn=%5Ftop&pbc=DA010192&rlt=CLID%5FFQRLT215242571535&rp=%2FSearch%2Fdefault%2Ewl&rs=WEBL12%2E04&service=Find&spa=pac%2D1000&sr=TC&vr=2%2E0].

It is worth noting that all statutes of the **Chapter 2 Taxes Levied by the State, Tax on Net Earnings, Corporate Net Income Tax** are noted as "Repealed. 1971, March 4, P.L. 86, No. 2, art. IV, § 411"
[http://weblinks.westlaw.com/toc/default.aspx?Abbr=pa%2Dst%2Dweb&Action=ExpandTree&AP=N3459BE350F934F86BEAF1AFB08423243&ItemKey=N3459BE350F934F86BEAF1AFB08423243&RP=%2Ftoc%2Fdefault%2Ewl&Service=TOC&RS=WEBL12.04&VR=2.0&SPa=pac-1000&pbc=DA010192&fragment#N3459BE350F934F86BEAF1AFB08423243] and that all statutes of the **Corporation Income Tax Law** are noted as "Repealed. 1971, March 4, P.L. 88, No. 2, art. V, § 505"
[http://weblinks.westlaw.com/toc/default.aspx?Abbr=pa%2Dst%2Dweb&Action=ExpandTree&AP=N83426E37638F4000B18C96B746D43DDB&ItemKey=N83426E37638F4000B18C96B746D43DDB&RP=%2Ftoc%2Fdefault%2Ewl&Service=TOC&RS=WEBL12.04&VR=2.0&SPa=pac-1000&pbc=DA010192&fragment#N83426E37638F4000B18C96B746D43DDB].

So, the Code establishes imposition of corporate income tax and liability for the tax imposed as well as the definition of income that is taxable.

The Pennsylvania General Assembly statutorily requires the payment of both individual and corporate state income tax. Without any reference to or reliance on the IRC, it has established *all three elements of the essential statutory formula for income tax: imposition of tax, liability for the tax imposed, and the definition of income that is taxable.*

#39 Rhode Island, a *Known* Income-Tax State

Federal statute based: Yes
State statute based: Yes
Actual liability: No

"Liable" defined by state statute: No
"Liability" defined by state statute: No

For general state income tax purposes, the State of Rhode Island General Assembly relies on both the **State of Rhode Island General Laws** and the federal **Internal Revenue Code.**

The **State of Rhode Island General Laws** do not define liable or liability for income tax purposes (reference **Title 44 Taxation, Chapter 44-30 Personal Income Tax, Part 44-30-1 General, Sections 44-30-6 Meaning of terms** and **44-30-2.6 Rhode Island taxable income – Rate of tax,** and **Chapter 44-11 Business Corporation Tax, Section 44-11-1 Definitions**).

For individuals, **Title 44 Taxation, Chapter 44-30 Personal Income Tax, Part 44-30-1 General, Section 44-30-1 Persons subject to tax** instead establishes by specific language *imposition* of tax and states:

> **§ 44-30-1 Persons subject to tax. –** *(a) Imposition of tax.* A Rhode Island personal income tax determined in accordance with the rates set forth in § 44-30-2 is imposed for each taxable year (which shall be the same as the taxable year for federal income tax purposes) on the Rhode Island income of every individual, estate, and trust.
> … [http://www.rilin.state.ri.us/Statutes/TITLE44/44-30/44-30-1.HTM].

However, while **Chapter 44-30 Personal Income Tax** again establishes by specific language *imposition* of tax, it refers to the federal IRC to establish *liability* for the tax imposed and for the *definitions* of income that is taxable and states:

> **Part 44-30-1 General**
> **§ 44-30-2 Rate of tax. –** (a) General.
> (1) A Rhode Island personal income tax is imposed upon the Rhode Island income of residents ….
> …
> (xii) For the period January 1, 2002, and thereafter the rate shall be twenty-five percent (25%) of the taxpayer's federal income tax liability.
> … [http://www.rilin.state.ri.us/Statutes/TITLE44/44-30/44-30-2.HTM].

§ 44-30-2.6 Rhode Island taxable income – Rate of tax. – (a) "Rhode Island taxable income" means federal taxable income as determined under the Internal Revenue Code, 26 U.S.C. § 1 et seq., ...
... [http://www.rilin.state.ri.us/Statutes/TITLE44/44-30/44-30-2.6.HTM].

Part 44-30-11 Residents
§ 44-30-12 Rhode Island income of a resident individual. – *(a) General.* The Rhode Island income of a resident individual means his or her adjusted gross income for federal income tax purposes, with the modifications specified in this section.
... [http://www.rilin.state.ri.us/Statutes/TITLE44/44-30/44-30-12.HTM].

That is, Rhode Island income means adjusted gross income for *federal* income tax purposes, Rhode Island taxable income means *federal* taxable income as determined under the IRC, and liability for the tax imposed is a percentage of *federal* income tax liability.

So while the Code establishes imposition of individual income tax, liability for the tax imposed and the definitions of what is taxable are based on the IRC. In other words, the state legislature has established imposition without also establishing either liability or anything on which to impose a liability. (Anything multiplied by nothing is nothing, that is, a percentage of nothing of nothing is nothing. Refer to Appendix III and Appendix D for further discussion.)

For corporations, **Chapter 44-11 Business Corporation Tax, Section 44-11-2 Imposition of tax** also establishes by specific language *imposition* of tax and by a specific rate *liability* for the tax imposed and states:

§ 44-11-2 Imposition of tax. – (a) Each corporation shall annually pay to the state a tax equal to nine percent (9%) of net income, as defined in § 44-11-11, qualified in § 44-11-12, and apportioned to this state as provided in §§ 44-11-13 – 44-11-15, for the taxable year.
... [http://www.rilin.state.ri.us/Statutes/TITLE44/44-11/44-11-2.HTM].

However, **Section 44-11-11 "Net income" defined** refers to the IRC for the *definition* of income that is taxable, actually stating that net income means taxable income under US law, and states:

§ 44-11-11 "Net income" defined. – (a) "Net income" means, for any taxable year and for any corporate taxpayer, the taxable income of the taxpayer for that taxable year under the laws of the United States, plus:
... [http://www.rilin.state.ri.us/Statutes/TITLE44/44-11/44-11-11.HTM].

So while the Code establishes imposition of corporate income tax and liability for the tax imposed, its definition of what is taxable is based on the IRC. In other words, the state legislature has established imposition and liability without also establishing anything on which to impose the liability. (Anything multiplied by nothing is nothing, that is, a percentage of nothing is nothing.)

The State of Rhode Island General Assembly has not enacted its own statutes for the definition of income that is taxable for either individual or corporate state income tax. While it has enacted certain statutes that establish imposition of state income tax and liability for corporate state income tax, it has relied on the IRC to establish liability for individual state income tax and for the definitions of what is taxable. So while Rhode Island is a *known* income-tax state, its legislature does not statutorily require the payment of state income tax.

#40 South Carolina, a *Known* Income-Tax State

Federal statute based: Yes
State statute based: Yes
Actual liability: No

"Liable" defined by state statute: No
"Liability" defined by state statute: No

For general state income tax purposes, the South Carolina Legislature relies on both the **South Carolina Code of Laws** and the federal **Internal Revenue Code.**

The **South Carolina Code of Laws** does not define liable or liability for income tax purposes (reference **Title 12 Taxation, Chapter 2 General Provisions, Chapter 6 South Carolina Income Tax Act, Article 1, Adoption of Internal Revenue Code-- Definitions, Section 12-6-30 Definitions,** and **Article 5, Tax Rates and Imposition, Section 12-6-530 Corporate income tax, Section 12-6-580 Computation of corporation's gross and taxable income**).

For individuals, **Title 12 Taxation, Chapter 6 South Carolina Income Tax Act, Article 5, Tax Rates and Imposition, Section 12-6-510 Tax rates for individuals, estates, and trusts for taxable years after 1994** instead establishes by specific language *imposition* of tax and by specific rates *liability* for the tax imposed and states:

SECTION 12-6-510. Tax rates for individuals, estates, and trusts for taxable years after 1994.

(A) For taxable years beginning after 1994, a tax is imposed on the South Carolina taxable income of individuals, estates, and trusts and any other entity except those taxed or exempted from taxation under Sections 12-6-530 through 12-6-550 computed at the following rates with the income brackets indexed in accordance with Section 12-6-520:
… [http://www.scstatehouse.gov/code/t12c006.php].

However, **Section 12-6-560 Computation of resident individual's gross, adjusted gross, and taxable income** refers to the federal IRC for the *definitions* of income that is taxable, actually stating that South Carolina gross income, adjusted gross income, and taxable income is computed as determined under the IRC, and states:

SECTION 12-6-560. Computation of resident individual's gross, adjusted gross, and taxable income.

A resident individual's South Carolina gross income, adjusted gross income, and taxable income is computed as determined under the Internal Revenue Code with the modifications provided in Article 9 of this chapter and subject to allocation and apportionment as provided in Article 17 of this chapter [http://www.scstatehouse.gov/code/t12c006.php].

Interestingly, **Chapter 2 General Provisions** contains a valuable statement for educational purposes under **Section 12-2-40 Contracts intended to evade payment of tax or in fraud of tax laws against public policy,** which points out that administration of personal property by contract so as to avoid taxation is not limited, and states:

> **SECTION 12-2-40.** Contracts intended to evade payment of tax or in fraud of tax laws against public policy.
>
> All contracts that are entered into with intent to evade payment of taxes or in fraud of the tax laws of this State are against public policy. The courts of this State may not lend their aid to enforce a contract entered into as a substitute for, or having as its consideration, a previous contract declared to be against public policy. Nothing in this section limits the power of an individual to administer his property by contract or donation so as to manage or avoid the impact of this or other tax laws on his personal property [http://www.scstatehouse.gov/code/t12c002.php].

This is interesting and valuable because this section makes an appropriate distinction between unlawful tax evasion and *lawful tax avoidance,* actually highlighting the fact that advance tax planning by means of contracts lawfully executed and performed is a legitimate means to avoiding or preventing taxation.

So while the Code establishes imposition of individual income tax and liability for the tax imposed, its definitions of what is taxable are based on the IRC. In other words, the state legislature has established imposition and liability without also establishing anything on which to impose the liability. (Anything multiplied by nothing is nothing, that is, a percentage of nothing is nothing. Refer to Appendix III and Appendix D for further discussion.)

For corporations, **Article 5, Tax Rates and Imposition, Section 12-6-530 Corporate income tax** also establishes by specific language *imposition* of tax and by specific rates *liability* for the tax imposed and states:

> **SECTION 12-6-530.** Corporate income tax.
>
> An income tax is imposed annually at the rate of five percent on the South Carolina taxable income of every corporation, other than those described in Sections 12-6-540 and 12-6-550, and any other entity taxed using the rates of a corporation for federal income tax purposes, transacting, conducting, or doing business within this State or having income within this State, regardless of whether these activities are carried on in intrastate, interstate, or foreign commerce. The terms "transacting", "conducting", and "doing business" include

transacting or engaging in any activity for the purpose of financial profit or gain [http://www.scstatehouse.gov/code/t12c006.php].

However, **Section 12-6-580 Computation of corporation's gross and taxable income** refers to the IRC for the *definitions* of income that is taxable, actually stating that South Carolina gross income and taxable income are computed as determined under the IRC, and states:

SECTION 12-6-580. Computation of corporation's gross and taxable income.

A corporation's South Carolina gross income, taxable income, and the unrelated business income of a corporation exempt from taxation under Internal Revenue Code Section 501 et seq., is computed as determined under the Internal Revenue Code with the modifications provided in Article 9 of this chapter and subject to allocation and apportionment as provided in Article 17 of this chapter [http://www.scstatehouse.gov/code/t12c006.php].

So while the Code establishes imposition of corporate income tax and liability for the tax imposed, its definitions of what is taxable are based on the IRC. In other words, the state legislature has established imposition and liability without also establishing anything on which to impose the liability. (Anything multiplied by nothing is nothing, that is, a percentage of nothing is nothing.)

The South Carolina Legislature has not enacted its own statutes for the definition of income that is taxable for either individual or corporate state income tax. While it has enacted certain statutes that establish imposition of state income tax and liability for the tax imposed, it has relied on the IRC for the definitions of what is taxable. So while South Carolina is a *known* income-tax state, its legislature does not statutorily require the payment of state income tax.

#41 South Dakota, a *Known* No-Income-Tax State

Federal statute based: No
State statute based: Yes
Actual liability: No

"Liable" defined by state statute: No
"Liability" defined by state statute: No

For general state income tax purposes, the South Dakota Legislature relies solely on the **South Dakota Codified Laws.**

It is commonly understood—***known***—that South Dakota is a no-income-tax state, that is, The South Dakota Legislature has not enacted any statutes of law that require the payment of individual state income tax. **Title 10** of the **South Dakota Codified Laws** contains various statutes concerning **Taxation** but, with the only exception discussed next, does not establish imposition of tax, liability for tax, or the definition of income that is taxable for either individual or corporate income taxes.

It is worth noting that **Title 10 Taxation, Chapter 10-45D Gross Receipts Tax on Visitor Related Businesses, Section 10-45D-2 Tax on gross receipts of certain visitor-related businesses** establishes *imposition* of tax and a one and one-half percent (one percent effective July 1, 2013) *liability* for the tax imposed as well as the *definition* of income that is taxable, namely, only the gross receipts of certain visitor-related businesses during the taxable period (June through September).

It is also worth noting that **Chapter 10-46A Realty Improvement Contractors' Excise Tax, Section 10-46A-1 Tax imposed on prime contractors' receipts from realty improvement contracts--Rate of tax** establishes *imposition* of tax and a two percent *liability* for the tax imposed as well as the *definition* of income that is taxable, namely, the gross receipts of all prime contractors engaged in realty improvement contracts. (**Chapter 10-46C Contractor's Excise Tax On New Or Expanded Power Production Facilities, Section 10-46C-4 Rate of tax on new or expanded power production facilities** establishes a one percent gross receipts tax relative to new or expanded power production facilities.)

It is also worth noting that **Chapter 10-52A Municipal Gross Receipts Tax, Section 10-52A-2 Additional municipal non-ad valorem tax authorized--Rate--Purpose** establishes *imposition* of tax and a one percent *liability* for the tax imposed as well as the *definition* of income that is taxable, namely, the gross receipts of various businesses.

The South Dakota Legislature does not statutorily require the payment of either individual or corporate state income tax beyond one to two percent of gross business receipts.

South Dakota

#42 Tennessee, a *Known* No-Income-Tax State

Federal statute based: No
State statute based: Yes
Actual liability: No

"Liable" defined by state statute: No
"Liability" defined by state statute: No

For general state income tax purposes, the Tennessee General Assembly relies solely on the **Tennessee Code Unannotated.**

It is commonly understood—***known***—that Tennessee is a no-income-tax state, that is, the Tennessee General Assembly has not enacted any statutes of law that require the payment of individual state income tax. **Title 67** of the **Tennessee Code Unannotated** contains various statutes concerning **Taxes and Licenses** but, with the only exceptions discussed next, does not establish imposition of tax, liability for tax, or the definition of income that is taxable for either individual or corporate income taxes.

It is worth noting that **Title 67 Taxes and Licenses, Chapter 2 Income Taxation, Section 67-2-102 Imposition, rate and collection of tax** establishes *imposition* of tax and a six percent *liability* for the tax imposed as well as the *definition* of income that is taxable, namely, only income derived by way of dividends from stocks or interest on bonds exceeding specific exemption amounts.

It is also worth noting that **Chapter 4 Privilege and Excise Taxes, Part 7 Business Tax, Sections 67-4-709 Tax rates** and **67-4-702 Part definitions** establish *imposition* of tax and between one-fortieth and three-sixteenths of one percent *liability* for the tax imposed as well as the *definitions* of what is taxable, namely, gross business receipts.

It is also worth noting that **Chapter 4 Privilege and Excise Taxes, Part 20 Excise Tax Law of 1999, Section 67-4-2007 Tax imposed** establishes by specific language *imposition* of tax and by a specific rate *liability* for the tax imposed and states:

67-4-2007. Tax imposed.
(a) All persons, except those having not-for-profit status, doing business in Tennessee shall, without exception other than as provided in this part, pay to the commissioner, annually, an excise tax, in addition to all other taxes, equal to six and one half percent (6½%) of the net earnings for the next preceding fiscal year for business done in this state during that fiscal year....
... [http://law.justia.com/codes/tennessee/2010/title-67/chapter-4/part-20/67-4-2007/].

However, **Section 67-4-2006 Net earnings and net loss defined** refers to the IRC for the *definition* of income that is taxable, actually stating that net earnings is defined as *federal* taxable income, and states:

67-4-2006. "Net earnings" and "net loss" defined.
(a) (1) For a corporation or any other taxpayer treated as a corporation for federal tax purposes, ..., except for a corporation electing S corporation status under 26 U.S.C. §§ 1361-1363, and except for a unitary business as is defined in § 67-4-2004, "net earnings" ... is defined as federal taxable income ....
... [http://law.justia.com/codes/tennessee/2010/title-67/chapter-4/part-20/67-4-2006/].

So while the Code establishes imposition of corporate excise tax and liability for the tax imposed, its definition of what is taxable are based on the IRC. In other words, the state legislature has established imposition and liability without also establishing anything on which to impose the liability. (Anything multiplied by nothing is nothing, that is, a percentage of nothing is nothing. Refer to Appendix III and Appendix D for further discussion.)

Quite interestingly, **Chapter 4 Privilege and Excise Taxes** contains a valuable statement for educational purposes under **Part 7 Business Tax Section 67-4-701 Short title -- Nature of tax -- Legislative intent,** which refers to the US Constitution and states:

67-4-701. Short title Nature of tax Legislative intent.
...
(c) It is the legislative intent, within the framework of this part, to recognize that there are limitations upon state taxation imposed by the constitutions of the United States and of this state and not to impose the tax where prohibited by the constitutions; but it is intended to impose that tax to the extent permitted under such constitutions and the words of imposition used in this section [http://law.justia.com/codes/tennessee/2010/title-67/chapter-4/part-7/67-4-701/].

This is quite interesting and valuable because the US Constitution expressly prohibits tax that is not proportional to the census, and the federal IRC accordingly does not establish liability for federal income tax. The US Constitution does not prohibit *state* legislatures from enacting income tax liability statutes or otherwise impose limitations upon state income taxation. Nevertheless, by enacting this statute, the state legislature has demonstrated both its awareness of the US Constitution's express prohibition of *federal* tax that is not proportional to the census and, based on, perhaps, its collective belief that the US Constitution does prohibit or impose limitations upon state income taxation, its general intent not to impose *state* tax where prohibited by the US Constitution (see Appendix II for discussion of limits imposed on the federal government by the US Constitution).

The Tennessee General Assembly does not statutorily require the payment of either individual or corporate state income or excise tax beyond that relative to income derived by way of dividends from stocks or interest on bonds exceeding specific exemption amounts and less than one percent of gross business receipts.

#43 Texas, a *Known* No-Income-Tax State

Federal statute based: No
State statute based: Yes
Actual liability: No

"Liable" defined by state statute: No
"Liability" defined by state statute: No

For general state income tax purposes, the Texas Legislature relies on both the **Texas Statutes** and the federal **Internal Revenue Code.**

It is commonly understood—**known**—that Texas is a no-income-tax state, that is, The Texas Legislature has not enacted any statutes of law that require the payment of individual state income tax. The **Tax Code** of the **Texas Statutes** contains various statutes concerning taxation but does not establish imposition of tax, liability for tax, or the definition of income that is taxable for individual income taxes.

For corporations, it is worth noting that **Tax Code, Title 2 State Taxation, Subtitle F Franchise Tax, Chapter 171 Franchise Tax** establishes by specific language *imposition* of tax and by specific rates *liability* for the tax imposed but refers to the federal IRC for the *definitions* of income that is taxable, actually stating that total revenue is based on the amount reportable as income on an IRS form and an amount reportable as income on an IRS form is the amount entered that complies with federal income tax law, and states:

SUBCHAPTER A. DEFINITIONS; TAX IMPOSED
Sec. 171.001. TAX IMPOSED. (a) A franchise tax is imposed on each taxable entity that does business in this state or that is chartered or organized in this state.
… [http://www.statutes.legis.state.tx.us/Docs/TX/htm/TX.171.htm#171.001].

Sec. 171.002. RATES; COMPUTATION OF TAX. (a) Subject to Sections 171.003 and 171.1016 and except as provided by Subsection (b), the rate of the franchise tax is one percent of taxable margin.
(b) Subject to Sections 171.003 and 171.1016, the rate of the franchise tax is 0.5 percent of taxable margin for those taxable entities primarily engaged in retail or wholesale trade.
… [http://www.statutes.legis.state.tx.us/Docs/TX/htm/TX.171.htm#171.002].

SUBCHAPTER C. DETERMINATION OF TAXABLE MARGIN; ALLOCATION AND APPORTIONMENT
Sec. 171.101. DETERMINATION OF TAXABLE MARGIN. (a) The taxable margin of a taxable entity is computed by:
(1) determining the taxable entity's margin, which is the lesser of:

(A) 70 percent of the taxable entity's total revenue from its entire business, as determined under Section 171.1011; or

(B) an amount computed by:

(i) determining the taxable entity's total revenue from its entire business, under Section 171.1011;

(ii) subtracting, at the election of the taxable entity, either:

(a) cost of goods sold, as determined under Section 171.1012; or

(b) compensation, as determined under Section 171.1013; and

(iii) subtracting, …

… [http://www.statutes.legis.state.tx.us/Docs/TX/htm/TX.171.htm#171.101].

Sec. 171.1011. DETERMINATION OF TOTAL REVENUE FROM ENTIRE BUSINESS. …

(b) In this section, a reference to an amount reportable as income on a line number on an Internal Revenue Service form is the amount entered to the extent the amount entered complies with federal income tax law and includes the corresponding amount entered on a variant of the form, or a subsequent form, with a different line number to the extent the amount entered complies with federal income tax law.

(c) Except as provided by this section, and subject to Section 171.1014, for the purpose of computing its taxable margin under Section 171.101, the total revenue of a taxable entity is:

(1) for a taxable entity treated for federal income tax purposes as a corporation, an amount computed by:

(A) adding:

(i) the amount reportable as income on line 1c, Internal Revenue Service Form 1120;

(ii) the amounts reportable as income on lines 4 through 10, Internal Revenue Service Form 1120; and

… [http://www.statutes.legis.state.tx.us/Docs/TX/htm/TX.171.htm#171.1011].

That is, the taxable margin is the margin, which is based on the total revenue, which is based on the amount reportable as income on IRS Form 1120, which is the amount entered to the extent the amount entered complies with federal income tax law.

So while the Code establishes imposition of corporate franchise tax and liability for the tax imposed, its definitions of what is taxable are based on the IRC. In other words, the state legislature has established imposition and liability without also establishing anything on which to impose the liability. (Anything multiplied by nothing is nothing, that is, a percentage of nothing is nothing. Refer to Appendix III and Appendix D for further discussion.)

The Texas Legislature does not statutorily require the payment of either state income or state franchise tax.

#44 Utah, a *Known* Income-Tax State

Federal statute based: Yes
State statute based: Yes
Actual liability: No

"Liable" defined by state statute: No
"Liability" defined by state statute: No

For general state income tax purposes, the Utah State Legislature relies on both the **Utah Code** and the federal **Internal Revenue Code.**

The **Utah Code** does not define liable or liability for income tax purposes (reference **Title 59 -- Revenue and Taxation, Chapter 01 -- General Taxation Policies, Section 59-1-101 Definitions, Chapter 07 -- Corporate Franchise and Income Taxes, Section 59-7-101 Definitions,** and **Chapter 10 -- Individual Income Tax Act, Sections 59-10-103 Definitions and 59-10-401 Definitions**), although it does identify to what liability refers at **Title 59 - Revenue and Taxation, Chapter 1 -- General Taxation Policies, Section 59-1-1402 Definitions,** which states:

> **59-1-1402. Definitions.**
> As used in this part:
> …
> (5) "Liability" means the following that a person is required to remit to the commission:
> (a) a tax, fee, or charge;
> (b) an addition to a tax, fee, or charge;
> (c) an administrative cost;
> (d) interest that accrues in accordance with Section 59-1-402; or
> (e) a penalty that accrues in accordance with Section 59-1-401.
> … [http://le.utah.gov/~code/TITLE59/htm/59_01_140200.htm].

For individuals, **Chapter 10 -- Individual Income Tax Act, Section 59-10-104 Tax basis -- Tax rate -- Exemption** instead establishes by specific language *imposition* of tax and by specific rates *liability* for the tax imposed and states:

> **59-10-104. Tax basis -- Tax rate -- Exemption.**
> (1) For taxable years beginning on or after January 1, 2008, a tax is imposed on the state taxable income of a resident individual as provided in this section.
> (2) For purposes of Subsection (1), for a taxable year, the tax is an amount equal to the product of:
> (a) the resident individual's state taxable income for that taxable year; and
> (b) 5%.
> … [http://le.utah.gov/~code/TITLE59/htm/59_10_010400.htm].

However, **Section 59-10-103 Definitions** refers to the federal IRC for the ***definitions*** of income that is taxable, actually stating that adjusted gross income is as defined in the IRC, and states:

59-10-103. Definitions.
(1) As used in this chapter:
(a) "Adjusted gross income":
(i) for a resident or nonresident individual, is as defined in Section 62, Internal Revenue Code; or
…
(w) "Taxable income" or "state taxable income":
(i) subject to Section 59-10-1404.5, for a resident individual, means the resident individual's adjusted gross income …
… [http://le.utah.gov/~code/TITLE59/htm/59_10_010300.htm].

That is, state taxable income means adjusted gross income and adjusted gross income is as defined in the IRC.

So while the Code establishes imposition of individual income tax and liability for the tax imposed, its definitions of what is taxable are based on the IRC. In other words, the state legislature has established imposition and liability without also establishing anything on which to impose the liability. (Anything multiplied by nothing is nothing, that is, a percentage of nothing is nothing. Refer to Appendix III and Appendix D for further discussion.)

For corporations, **Chapter 07 -- Corporate Franchise and Income Taxes** also establishes by specific language ***imposition*** of tax and by specific rates ***liability*** for the tax imposed as well as the ***definition*** of income that is taxable and states:

59-7-104. Tax -- Minimum tax.
(1) Each domestic and foreign corporation, except those exempted under Section 59-7-102, shall pay an annual tax to the state based on its Utah taxable income for the taxable year for the privilege of exercising its corporate franchise or for the privilege of doing business in the state.
(2) The tax shall be 5% of a corporation's Utah taxable income.
(3) The minimum tax a corporation shall pay under this chapter is $100 [http://le.utah.gov/~code/TITLE59/htm/59_07_010400.htm].

59-7-201. Tax -- Minimum tax.
(1) There is imposed upon each corporation except those exempt under Section 59-7-102 for each taxable year, a tax upon its Utah taxable income derived from sources within this state other than income for any period which the corporation is required to include in its tax base under Section 59-7-104.
(2) The tax imposed by Subsection (1) shall be 5% of a corporation's Utah taxable income.

(3) In no case shall the tax be less than $100
[http://le.utah.gov/~code/TITLE59/htm/59_07_020100.htm].

59-7-101. Definitions.
As used in this chapter:

...

(34) (a) "Utah taxable income" means Utah taxable income before net loss deduction less Utah net loss deduction.

(b) "Utah taxable income" includes income from tangible or intangible property located or having situs in this state, regardless of whether carried on in intrastate, interstate, or foreign commerce.

(35) "Utah taxable income before net loss deduction" means apportioned income plus nonbusiness income allocable to Utah net of related expenses
[http://le.utah.gov/~code/TITLE59/htm/59_07_010100.htm].

So, the Code establishes imposition of both corporate franchise and corporate income taxes and liability for the taxes imposed as well as the definition of income that is taxable.

The Utah State Legislature has not enacted its own statutes for the definition of income that is taxable for individual state income tax. While it has enacted a certain statute that establishes imposition of individual state income tax and liability for the tax imposed, it has relied on the IRC for the definition of what is taxable. So while Utah is a *known* income-tax state, its legislature does not statutorily require the payment of individual state income tax. However, it does statutorily require the payment of corporate state franchise and income taxes, having—without any reference to or reliance on the IRC— established *all three elements of the essential statutory formula for income tax: imposition of tax, liability for the tax imposed, and the definition of income that is taxable.*

#45 Vermont, a *Known* Income-Tax State

Federal statute based: Yes
State statute based: Yes
Actual liability: No

"Liable" defined by state statute: No
"Liability" defined by state statute: No

For general state income tax purposes, the Vermont State Legislature relies on both the **Vermont Statutes** and the federal **Internal Revenue Code.**

The **Vermont Statutes** do not define liable or liability for income tax purposes (reference **Title 32 Taxation and Finance, Chapter 151 Income Taxes, Sections 5811 Definitions** and **5851 Definitions**).

For individuals, **Title 32 Taxation and Finance, Chapter 151 Income Taxes, Section 5822 Tax on income of individuals, estates, and trusts** instead establishes by specific rates *liability* for the tax imposed and states:

> **§ 5822. Tax on income of individuals, estates, and trusts**
> (a) A tax is imposed for each taxable year upon the taxable income earned or received in that year by every individual, estate, and trust, subject to income taxation under the laws of the United States, in an amount determined by the following tables, and adjusted as required under this section:
> …
> [http://www.leg.state.vt.us/statutes/fullsection.cfm?Title=32&Chapter=151&Section=05822].

Interestingly, this section also contains a valuable statement for educational purposes, as it also refers to the federal IRC to establish *imposition* of tax, actually stating that a tax is imposed upon the taxable income earned or received by every individual subject to income taxation under the laws of the US. This is interesting and valuable because the IRC does not establish liability for federal income tax, so that no individual is subject to income taxation under the laws of the US.

Moreover, **Section 5811 Definitions** refers to the IRC for the *definition* of income that is taxable, actually stating that taxable income means *federal* taxable income, and states:

> **§ 5811. Definitions**
> The following definitions shall apply throughout this chapter unless the context requires otherwise:
> …

(21) "Taxable income" means federal taxable income determined without regard to Section 168(k) of the Internal Revenue Code and:

...

[http://www.leg.state.vt.us/statutes/fullsection.cfm?Title=32&Chapter=151&Section=05811].

So while the Code establishes liability for individual income tax, imposition of the tax and the definition of what is taxable are based on the IRC. In other words, the state legislature has established liability without also establishing either imposition or anything on which to impose the liability. (Anything multiplied by nothing is nothing, that is, a percentage of nothing is nothing. Refer to Appendix III and Appendix D for further discussion.)

For corporations, Section 5832 **Tax on income of corporations** also establishes by specific language **imposition** of tax and by specific rates **liability** for the tax imposed and states:

§ 5832. Tax on income of corporations
A tax is imposed for each calendar year, or fiscal year ending during that calendar year, upon the income earned or received in that taxable year by every taxable corporation, reduced by any Vermont net operating loss allowed under section 5888 of this title, such tax being the greater of
(1) an amount determined in accordance with the following schedule:
Vermont net income of the corporation ...
[http://www.leg.state.vt.us/statutes/fullsection.cfm?Title=32&Chapter=151&Section=05832].

However, **Section 5811 Definitions** refers to the IRC for the **definitions** of income that is taxable, actually stating that Vermont net income means the taxable income under the laws of the US and taxable income means **federal** taxable income, and states:

§ 5811. Definitions
The following definitions shall apply throughout this chapter unless the context requires otherwise:

...

(18) "Vermont net income" means, for any taxable year and for any corporate taxpayer:
(A) the taxable income of the taxpayer for that taxable year under the laws of the United States, without regard to Section 168(k) of the Internal Revenue Code, and excluding income which under the laws of the United States is exempt from taxation by the states:

...

(21) "Taxable income" means federal taxable income determined without regard to Section 168(k) of the Internal Revenue Code and:

...

[http://www.leg.state.vt.us/statutes/fullsection.cfm?Title=32&Chapter=151&Section=05811].

So while the Code establishes imposition of corporate income tax and liability for the tax imposed, its definitions of what is taxable are based on the IRC. In other words, the state legislature has established imposition and liability without also establishing anything on which to impose the liability. (Anything multiplied by nothing is nothing, that is, a percentage of nothing is nothing.)

The Vermont State Legislature has not enacted its own statutes for the definition of income that is taxable for either individual or corporate state income tax. While it has enacted certain statutes that establish imposition of state income tax and liability for the tax imposed, it has relied on the IRC for the definitions of income that is taxable. So while Vermont is a *known* income-tax state, its legislature does not statutorily require the payment of state income tax.

#46 Virginia, a *Known* Income-Tax State

Federal statute based: Yes
State statute based: Yes
Actual liability: No

"Liable" defined by state statute: No
"Liability" defined by state statute: No

For general state income tax purposes, the Virginia General Assembly relies on both the **Code of Virginia** and the federal **Internal Revenue Code.**

The **Code of Virginia** does not define liable or liability for income tax purposes (reference **Title 58.1 Taxation, General Provisions of Title 58.1, Section 58.1-1 Definitions** and **Chapter 3 Income Tax, Section 58.1-302 Definitions**).

For individuals, Title 58.1 Taxation, Chapter 3 Income Tax, Section 58.1-320 **Imposition of tax** instead establishes by specific language *imposition* of tax and by specific rates *liability* for the tax imposed and states:

> **§ 58.1-320. Imposition of tax.**
> A tax is hereby annually imposed on the Virginia taxable income for each taxable year of every individual as follows:
> … [http://leg1.state.va.us/cgi-bin/legp504.exe?000+cod+58.1-320].

However, **Section 58.1-322 Virginia taxable income of residents** refers to the IRC for the *definition* of income that is taxable, actually stating that Virginia taxable income means *federal* adjusted gross income, and states:

> **§ 58.1-322. Virginia taxable income of residents.**
> A. The Virginia taxable income of a resident individual means his federal adjusted gross income for the taxable year, which excludes combat pay for certain members of the Armed Forces of the United States as provided in § 112 of the Internal Revenue Code, as amended, and with the modifications specified in this section.
> … [http://leg1.state.va.us/cgi-bin/legp504.exe?000+cod+58.1-322].

So while the Code establishes imposition of individual income tax and liability for the tax imposed, its definition of what is taxable is based on the IRC. In other words, the state legislature has established imposition and liability without also establishing anything on which to impose the liability. (Anything multiplied by nothing is nothing, that is, a percentage of nothing is nothing. Refer to Appendix III and Appendix D for further discussion.)

For corporations, Section 58.1-400 Imposition of tax also establishes by specific language **imposition** of tax and by a specific rate **liability** for the tax imposed and states:

§ 58.1-400. Imposition of tax.

A tax at the rate of six percent is hereby annually imposed on the Virginia taxable income for each taxable year of every corporation organized under the laws of the Commonwealth and every foreign corporation having income from Virginia sources [http://leg1.state.va.us/cgi-bin/legp504.exe?000+cod+58.1-400].

However, **Section 58.1-402 Virginia taxable income** refers to the IRC for the **definition** of income that is taxable, actually stating that Virginia taxable income means **federal** taxable income and any other income taxable to the corporation under federal law, and states:

§ 58.1-402. Virginia taxable income.

A. For purposes of this article, Virginia taxable income for a taxable year means the federal taxable income and any other income taxable to the corporation under federal law for such year of a corporation adjusted as provided in subsections B, C, D, and E.
… [http://leg1.state.va.us/cgi-bin/legp504.exe?000+cod+58.1-402].

Interestingly, moreover, this is a valuable statement for educational purposes. This is interesting and valuable because the IRC does not establish liability for federal income tax, so that no income is taxable to a corporation under federal law.

So while the Code establishes imposition of corporate income tax and liability for the tax imposed, its definition of what is taxable is based on the IRC. In other words, the state legislature has established imposition and liability without also establishing anything on which to impose the liability. (Anything multiplied by nothing is nothing, that is, a percentage of nothing is nothing.)

The Virginia General Assembly has not enacted its own statutes for the definition of income that is taxable for either individual or corporate state income tax. While it has enacted certain statutes that establish imposition of state income tax and liability for the tax imposed, it has relied on the IRC for the definitions of income that is taxable. So while Virginia is a **known** income-tax state, its legislature does not statutorily require the payment of state income tax.

#47 Washington, a *Known* No-Income-Tax State

Federal statute based: No
State statute based: No
Actual liability: No

"Liable" defined by state statute: No
"Liability" defined by state statute: No

For general state income tax purposes, the Washington State Legislature relies solely on the **Revised Code of Washington.**

It is commonly understood—**known**—that Washington is a no-income-tax state, that is, the Washington State Legislature has not enacted any statutes of law that require the payment of individual state income tax. The **Revised Code of Washington** does not establish imposition of tax, liability for tax, or the definition of income that is taxable for either individual or corporate income taxes.

However, it is worth noting that **Title 82 Excise Taxes, Chapter 82.04 Business and occupation tax, Section 82.04.220 Business and occupation tax imposed** establishes by specific language *imposition* of tax and *liability* for the tax imposed as well as what is taxable and states:

> **RCW 82.04.220**
> **Business and occupation tax imposed.**
>
> (1) There is levied and collected from every person that has a substantial nexus with this state a tax for the act or privilege of engaging in business activities. The tax is measured by the application of rates against value of products, gross proceeds of sales, or gross income of the business, as the case may be. … [http://apps.leg.wa.gov/rcw/supdefault.aspx?cite=82.04.220].

So, the Code establishes imposition of excise tax and liability for the tax imposed on gross receipts from business activities within the State.

The Washington State Legislature does not statutorily require the payment of either individual or corporate state income tax. However, it does statutorily require the payment of business excise tax.

#48 West Virginia, a *Known* Income-Tax State

Federal statute based: No
State statute based: Yes
Actual liability: No

"Liable" defined by state statute: No
"Liability" defined by state statute: No

For general state income tax purposes, the West Virginia Legislature relies on both the **West Virginia Code** and the federal **Internal Revenue Code.**

The **West Virginia Code** does not define liable or liability for income tax purposes (reference **Chapter 11 Taxation, Article 10 West Virginia Tax Procedure and Administration Act, Section 11-10-4 Definitions** and **Article 24 Corporation Net Income Tax, Sections 11-24-3 Meaning of terms; general rule** and **11-24-3a Specific terms defined**).

For individuals, the West Virginia Legislature *has repealed* any statutes of law that require the payment of individual state income tax under **Chapter 11 Taxation, Article 7 Capitation Taxes, Section 11-7-1 Collection of capitation taxes for tax year 1970; effective date; legislative intent,** which states:

> **§11-7-1. Collection of capitation taxes for tax year 1970; effective date; legislative intent.**
> It is hereby declared to be the intent of the Legislature that the provisions of this act whereby the former provisions for collection of capitation taxes are repealed, shall become effective July one, one thousand nine hundred seventy-one, …
> [http://www.legis.state.wv.us/WVCODE/Code.cfm?chap=11&art=7#07].

Interestingly, moreover, this section contains a valuable term for educational purposes: capitation. This is interesting and valuable because the US Constitution uses the same word in its description of authorized federal taxation, namely, tax that is proportional to the census, that is, tax that is the ***exact same dollar amount per person regardless of income or wealth*** (see Appendix II for discussion of limits imposed on the federal government by the US Constitution).

For corporations, **Article 24 Corporation Net Income Tax, Section 11-24-4 Imposition of primary tax and rate thereof; effective and termination dates** establishes by specific language ***imposition*** of tax and by a specific rate ***liability*** for the tax imposed and states:

> **§11-24-4. Imposition of primary tax and rate thereof; effective and termination dates.**
> *Primary tax. --*
> …

(6) In the case of taxable periods beginning on or after the first day of January, two thousand twelve, a tax is hereby imposed for each taxable year on the West Virginia taxable income of every domestic or foreign corporation engaging in business in this state or deriving income from property, activity or other sources in this state, except corporations exempt under section five of this article, at the rate of seven and three-quarters percent: ….
… [http://www.legis.state.wv.us/WVCODE/Code.cfm?chap=11&art=24#24].

However, **Section 11-24-3a Specific terms defined** refers to the IRC for the *definition* of income that is taxable, actually stating that West Virginia taxable income means taxable income as defined in the laws of the US for *federal* income tax purposes, and states:

§11-24-3a. Specific terms defined.
(a) For purposes of this article:

…

(44) *West Virginia taxable income.* -- The term "West Virginia taxable income" means the taxable income of a corporation as defined by the laws of the United States for federal income tax purposes, ….
… [http://www.legis.state.wv.us/WVCODE/Code.cfm?chap=11&art=24#24].

So while the Code establishes imposition of corporate income tax and liability for the tax imposed, its definition of what is taxable is based on the IRC. In other words, the state legislature has established imposition and liability without also establishing anything on which to impose the liability. (Anything multiplied by nothing is nothing, that is, a percentage of nothing is nothing. Refer to Appendix III and Appendix D for further discussion.)

The West Virginia Legislature does not statutorily require the payment of individual state income tax and has not enacted its own statutes for the definition of income that is taxable for corporate state income tax. While it has enacted a certain statute that establishes imposition of corporate state income tax and liability for the tax imposed, it has relied on the IRC for the definition of income that is taxable. So while West Virginia is a *known* income-tax state, its legislature does not statutorily require the payment of state income tax.

#49 Wisconsin, a *Known* Income-Tax State

Federal statute based: Yes
State statute based: Yes
Actual liability: No

"Liable" defined by state statute: No
"Liability" defined by state statute: No

For general state income tax purposes, the Wisconsin State Legislature relies on both the **Wisconsin Statutes & Annotations** and the federal **Internal Revenue Code.**

The **Wisconsin Statutes & Annotations** do not define liable or liability for income tax purposes (reference **Taxation, Chapter 71 Income and franchise taxes for state and local revenues, Subchapter I Taxation of Individuals and Fiduciaries, Section 71.01 Definitions** and **Subchapter IV Taxation of Corporations, Section 71.22 Definitions**).

For individuals, **Taxation, Chapter 71 Income and franchise taxes for state and local revenues, Subchapter I Taxation of Individuals and Fiduciaries** instead establishes by specific language *imposition* of tax and by specific rates *liability* for the tax imposed and states:

71.02 Imposition of tax.
(1) For the purpose of raising revenue for the state and the counties, cities, villages and towns, there shall be assessed, levied, collected and paid a tax on all net incomes of individuals and fiduciaries, ….
… [https://docs.legis.wisconsin.gov/statutes/statutes/71/I/02].

71.06 Rates of taxation.
…
(1p) FIDUCIARIES, SINGLE INDIVIDUALS AND HEADS OF HOUSEHOLDS; AFTER 2000. The tax to be assessed, levied and collected upon the taxable incomes of all fiduciaries, except fiduciaries of nuclear decommissioning trust or reserve funds, and single individuals and heads of households shall be computed at the following rates for taxable years beginning after December 31, 2000:
…
(2) MARRIED PERSONS. The tax to be assessed, levied and collected upon the taxable incomes of all married persons shall be computed at the following rates:
…
(h) For married persons filing separately, for taxable years beginning after December 31, 2000:
… [https://docs.legis.wisconsin.gov/statutes/statutes/71/I/06].

However, **Section 71.01 Definitions** refers to the IRC for the *definitions* of income that is taxable, actually stating that taxable income means Wisconsin taxable income and

Wisconsin taxable income means Wisconsin adjusted gross income and Wisconsin adjusted gross income means *federal* adjusted gross income, and states:

> **71.01 Definitions.** In this chapter in regard to natural persons and fiduciaries, except fiduciaries of nuclear decommissioning trust or reserve funds:
>
> …
>
> **(11)** "Taxable income" when not preceded by the word "federal" means Wisconsin taxable income unless otherwise defined or the context plainly requires otherwise.
>
> …
>
> **(13)** "Wisconsin adjusted gross income" means federal adjusted gross income,
>
> ….
>
> …
>
> **(16)** "Wisconsin taxable income" of natural persons means Wisconsin adjusted gross income ….
> … [https://docs.legis.wisconsin.gov/statutes/statutes/71/I/01].

So while the Code establishes imposition of individual income tax and liability for the tax imposed, its definitions of what is taxable are based on the IRC. In other words, the state legislature has established imposition and liability without also establishing anything on which to impose the liability. (Anything multiplied by nothing is nothing, that is, a percentage of nothing is nothing. Refer to Appendix III and Appendix D for further discussion.)

For corporations, **Subchapter IV Taxation of Corporations** also establishes by specific language *imposition* of tax and by a specific rate *liability* for the tax imposed as well as the *definition* of income that is taxable and states:

> **71.23 Imposition of tax.**
> **(1)** INCOME TAX. For the purpose of raising revenue for the state and the counties, cities, villages and towns, there shall be assessed, levied, collected and paid a tax as provided under this chapter on all Wisconsin net incomes of corporations that are not subject to the franchise tax under sub. (2) and that own property within this state; that derive income from sources within this state or from activities that are attributable to this state; ….
> … [https://docs.legis.wisconsin.gov/statutes/statutes/71/IV/23].
>
> **71.27 Rates of taxation.**
> **(1)** The taxes to be assessed, levied and collected upon Wisconsin net incomes of corporations shall be computed at the rate of 7.9%.
> … [https://docs.legis.wisconsin.gov/statutes/statutes/71/IV/27].
>
> **71.22 Definitions.** In this chapter in regard to corporations and to nuclear decommissioning trust or reserve funds:
> …

(11) Except as provided in s. 71.45 (2), "Wisconsin net income", for corporations engaged in business wholly within this state, means net income and, ... [https://docs.legis.wisconsin.gov/statutes/statutes/71/IV/22].

So, the Code establishes imposition of corporate income tax and liability for the tax imposed as well as the definition of income that is taxable.

The Wisconsin State Legislature has not enacted its own statutes for the definition of income that is taxable for individual state income tax. While it has enacted certain statutes that establish imposition of individual state income tax and liability for the tax imposed, it has relied on the IRC for the definitions of what is taxable. So while Wisconsin is a *known* income-tax state, its legislature does not statutorily require the payment of individual state income tax. However, it does statutorily require the payment of corporate state income tax, having—without any reference to or reliance on the IRC—established *all three elements of the essential statutory formula for income tax: imposition of tax, liability for the tax imposed, and the definition of income that is taxable.*

#50 Wyoming, a *Known* No-Income-Tax State

Federal statute based: No
State statute based: No
Actual liability: No

"Liable" defined by state statute: No
"Liability" defined by state statute: No

For general state income tax purposes, The Legislature of the State of Wyoming relies solely on the **Wyoming Statutes.**

It is commonly understood—***known***—that Wyoming is a no-income-tax state, that is, The Legislature of the State of Wyoming has not enacted *or has repealed* any statutes of law that require the payment of individual state income tax. **Title 39** of the **Wyoming Statutes** contains various statutes concerning **Taxation and Revenue** but does not establish imposition of tax, liability for tax, or the definition of income that is taxable for either individual or corporate income taxes.

It is worth noting that **Title 39 Taxation and Revenue, Chapter 7 Income Taxes, Section 39-7-101,** the only section under this chapter, has been repealed. It is also worth noting that **Chapter 12 Income Tax, Section 39-12-101 Preemption by state,** the only section under this chapter, reserves for the state sole authority to impose and levy income taxes and states:

WY Stat § 39-12-101 (1997 through Reg Sess)
The state of Wyoming does hereby preempt for itself the field of imposing and levying income taxes, earning taxes, or any other form of tax based on wages or other income and no county, city, town or other political subdivision shall have the right to impose, levy or collect such taxes [http://law.justia.com/codes/wyoming/2011/title39/chapter12/section39-12-101/].

The Legislature of the State of Wyoming does not statutorily require the payment of either individual or corporate state income tax.

#51 Washington DC, a *Known* Income-Tax District

Federal statute based: No
State statute based: No
Actual liability: No

"Liable" defined by federal statute: No
"Liability" defined by federal statute: No

For general federal income tax purposes, the US Congress relies solely on the **US Constitution.** (On this basis, the US Congress enacts the statutes which are matriculated into the federal **Internal Revenue Code (IRC).**)

The original **Constitution for the United States of America,** [1st]**Article I The Legislative Branch, Sections 8 Scope of Legislative Power** and **9 Limits on Legislative Power** *specifically and expressly* <u>*prohibit*</u> the laying and collecting of taxes that is not *__uniform and proportional__* and state:

Section. 8.
The Congress shall have Power To lay and collect Taxes, Duties, Imposts and Excises, to pay the Debts and provide for the common Defence and general Welfare of the United States; but all Duties, Imposts and Excises shall be uniform throughout the United States;
… [http://deoxy.org/law/consti.htm#1.8].

Section. 9.
…
No Capitation, or other direct, Tax shall be laid, unless in Proportion to the Census or enumeration herein before directed to be taken.
… [http://deoxy.org/law/consti.htm#1.9].

These sections do not provide for or allow a *flat sales tax* or a *graduated income tax,* the result of either of which is *varied and non-proportional,* that is, each individual pays a different amount of tax and all individuals collectively are not taxed in a manner that is proportional to the census. Instead, these sections authorize *only* capitation and taxation that is *uniform and proportional.*

The New Merriam-Webster Dictionary defines *capitation* as "a direct uniform tax levied on each person," *uniform* as "having always the same form, manner, or degree : not varying" and "of the same form with others : conforming to one rule," and *proportional* as "corresponding in size, degree, or intensity" and "having the same or a constant ratio" [Copyright © 1989 by Merriam-Webster, Inc., Springfield, MA].

This source defines *uniform* as "having *always* the *same* form, manner, or degree, *not varying*" and "of the *same* form with *others,* conforming to *one* rule" rather than *many* rules and *never* having the *same* form with others but *varying* from others according to marital status, number of dependents, income bracket, and nearly-unnumbered other categories of provisions. This source also defines *proportional* as "*corresponding* in size, degree, or intensity" and "having the *same* or a *constant* ratio" rather than *various* ratios and *not corresponding* in size, degree, or intensity.

Similarly, FindLaw.com defines *capitation* this way:

> 1 : a direct uniform tax imposed on each head or person : poll tax [no , or other direct, tax shall be laid "U.S. Constitution art. I"] 2 : a uniform per person payment or fee [http://public.findlaw.com/LCsearch.html?entry=capitation].

USLegal.Com explains further and defines *capitation tax* this way:

> Capitation tax is an assessment levied by the government upon a person at a fixed rate regardless of property, business, or other circumstances. Since it is a tax upon the individual, and not upon merchandise, a capitation tax is frequently labeled as a head tax. A poll tax is a capitation tax.
> In Texas Banking & Ins. Co. v. State, 42 Tex. 636, 639 (Tex. 1874), the court held that the constitutional rule for capitation taxes is that of individuality, without discrimination in respect to its burden [http://definitions.uslegal.com/c/capitation-tax/].

Capitation is a tax that is the <u>exact same dollar amount</u> for each and every person or head. It is a "*uniform* tax imposed on *each head* or *person*" "at a *fixed* rate regardless of property, business, or other circumstances," "a tax upon the *individual, and not* upon merchandise," or *sales* of merchandise, and it does not discriminate "in respect to its burden," that is, its burden—its amount—does not change from one person to the next, whether because of income or property ownership. It is "in proportion to the census" in that it is divided by the number of people in the census to arrive at a specific dollar amount that is *equal* for *each* and *every* individual. In other words, the *formula* for such a tax would be the gross dollar amount of revenue the US Congress wishes to raise divided by the total number of people in the census, which equals the specific dollar amount per individual (regardless of age, employment status, marital status, number of dependents, health, income, or dollar amount of purchases). (Mathematically, this would appear as Gross Tax Revenue / Number of People = Dollar Amount of Tax for Each Person.)

Because of these specific terms and express limitations and prohibitions of the US Constitution, while the US Congress has by specific language established *imposition* of tax on income, it has not established *liability* for the tax imposed or the *definition* of what is taxable (and both the US Supreme Court and the federal IRC itself require that liability for such a tax must exist before anyone actually can be required to pay such a tax), that is, since the 1890's, when the US Supreme Court overturned the last income tax statute(s) as unconstitutional, it has not enacted any statute(s) requiring the payment of federal income tax. (Imposition on nothing is nothing, and imposition without liability is nothing. Refer to Appendix III and Appendix D for further discussion.)

So while Washington DC is a **known** income-tax district, the US Congress does not actually statutorily require the payment of federal income tax in Washington DC or in any other federal district or territory or in any of the fifty States.

These are the reasons that each state legislature that refers to or relies on the federal IRC for the definition of income that is taxable or for the determination of liability for income tax does not actually statutorily require the payment of state income tax.

II: Statistical Summary

	Known income-tax state	Known no-income-tax state	Federal statute based	State statute based	Actual liability	Liable defined	Liability defined	Individual imposition	Individual liability	Individual definition	Essential statutory formula	Refers to or relies on IRC	Corporate imposition	Corporate liability	Corporate definition	Essential statutory formula	Refers to or relies on IRC	Recommended for incorporation	Explanation code*
AL	✓		N	Y	Y	N	N	Y	Y	Y	Y	N	Y	Y	N	N	Y	N	I
AK		✓	N	N	N	N	N	N	N	N	N	N	Y	Y	N	N	Y	N	D
AZ	✓		Y	Y	N	N	N	N	Y	N	N	Y	Y	Y	N	N	Y	N	I
AR	✓		N	Y	Y	N	N	Y	Y	Y	Y	Y	Y	Y	N	N	N	N	D
CA	✓		Y	Y	N	N	N	Y	Y	N	N	Y	Y	Y	N	N	N	N	D
CO	✓		Y	Y	N	N	N	Y	Y	N	N	Y	Y	Y	Y	N	N	N	E
CT	✓		N	Y	Y	N	N	Y	Y	Y	Y	N	Y	Y	N	N	Y	N	I
DE	✓		Y	Y	N	N	N	Y	N	N	N	Y	Y	Y	N	N	Y	N	I
FL		✓	N	Y	N	N	N	N	N	N	N	N	Y	Y	N	N	Y	N	I
GA	✓		Y	Y	N	N	N	Y	Y	N	N	Y	Y	Y	N	N	Y	N	I
HI	✓		Y	Y	N	N	N	Y	Y	N	N	Y	Y	Y	Y	N	N	N	E
ID	✓		Y	Y	N	N	N	Y	Y	N	N	Y	Y	Y	N	N	Y	N	I
IL	✓		Y	Y	N	N	N	Y	Y	N	N	Y	Y	Y	N	N	Y	N	I
IN	✓		Y	Y	N	N	N	Y	Y	N	N	Y	Y	Y	N	N	Y	N	I
IA	✓		Y	Y	N	N	N	Y	Y	N	N	Y	Y	N	N	N	N	N	D
KS	✓		Y	Y	N	N	N	Y	Y	N	N	Y	Y	Y	N	N	Y	N	I
KY	✓		Y	Y	N	N	N	Y	Y	N	N	Y	Y	Y	N	N	Y	N	I
LA	✓		N	Y	Y	N	N	Y	Y	Y	Y	N	Y	Y	N	N	Y	N	I
ME	✓		Y	Y	N	N	N	Y	Y	N	N	Y	Y	Y	N	N	Y	N	I
MD	✓		Y	Y	N	N	N	Y	Y	N	N	Y	Y	Y	N	N	Y	N	I
MA	✓		Y	Y	N	N	N	Y	Y	N	N	Y	Y	Y	N	N	Y	N	I
MI	✓		Y	Y	N	N	N	Y	Y	N	N	Y	Y	Y	N	N	Y	N	I
MN	✓		Y	Y	N	N	N	Y	Y	N	N	Y	Y	Y	N	N	Y	N	I
MS	✓		N	Y	Y	N	N	Y	Y	Y	Y	N	Y	Y	Y	Y	N	N	E
MO	✓		Y	Y	N	N	N	Y	Y	N	N	Y	Y	Y	N	N	Y	N	I
MT	✓		Y	Y	N	N	N	Y	Y	N	N	Y	Y	Y	N	N	Y	N	I
NE	✓		Y	Y	N	N	N	N	N	N	N	Y	Y	Y	N	N	Y	N	I
NV		✓	N	N	N	N	N	N	N	N	N	N	N	N	N	N	N	Y	S
NH		✓	N	N	N	N	N	N	N	N	N	N	Y	Y	N	N	Y	N	I
NJ	✓		N	Y	Y	N	N	Y	Y	Y	Y	N	Y	Y	N	N	Y	N	I
NM	✓		Y	Y	N	N	N	Y	Y	N	N	Y	Y	Y	N	N	Y	N	I
NY	✓		Y	Y	N	N	N	Y	Y	N	N	Y	Y	Y	N	N	N	N	D
NC	✓		Y	Y	N	N	N	Y	Y	N	N	Y	Y	Y	N	N	Y	N	I
ND	✓		Y	Y	N	N	N	Y	Y	N	N	Y	Y	Y	N	N	Y	N	I
OH	✓		Y	Y	N	N	N	Y	Y	N	N	N	N	N	N	N	N	Y	S
OK	✓		Y	Y	N	N	N	Y	Y	N	N	Y	Y	Y	N	N	Y	N	I
OR	✓		Y	Y	N	N	N	Y	Y	N	N	Y	Y	Y	N	N	Y	N	I
PA	✓		N	Y	Y	N	N	Y	Y	Y	Y	N	Y	Y	Y	Y	N	N	E
RI	✓		Y	Y	N	N	N	Y	Y	N	N	Y	Y	Y	N	N	Y	N	I
SC	✓		Y	Y	N	N	N	Y	Y	N	N	Y	Y	Y	N	N	Y	N	I
SD		✓	N	Y	N	N	N	N	N	N	N	N	N	N	N	N	N	Y	G
TN		✓	N	Y	N	N	N	N	N	N	N	N	N	N	N	N	N	N	I
TX		✓	N	Y	N	N	N	N	N	N	N	N	Y	Y	N	N	Y	N	I
UT	✓		Y	Y	N	N	N	Y	Y	N	N	Y	Y	Y	Y	N	N	N	E
VT	✓		Y	Y	N	N	N	Y	Y	N	N	Y	Y	Y	N	N	Y	N	I
VA	✓		Y	Y	N	N	N	Y	Y	N	N	Y	Y	Y	N	N	Y	N	I
WA		✓	N	N	N	N	N	N	N	N	N	N	N	N	N	N	N	Y	S
WV	✓		N	Y	N	N	N	N	N	N	N	Y	Y	Y	N	N	Y	N	I
WI	✓		Y	Y	N	N	N	Y	Y	N	N	Y	Y	Y	Y	Y	N	N	E
WY		✓	N	N	N	N	N	N	N	N	N	N	N	N	N	N	N	Y	S
DC	✓		N	N	N	N	Y	N	N	N	N	N	N	N	N	N	N	--	--
											7	34				6	33	6	

*Explanation codes: D - No definition; E - Essential formula established; I - Relies on IRC; S - No statutory requirement;
    G - Only minimal gross receipts tax

So the **two** states that actually statutorily require the payment of **both individual and corporate income tax** are Mississippi and Pennsylvania, whose legislatures have established the **essential statutory formula for income tax** for both individual and corporate income tax.

Additionally, the **five** states that actually statutorily require the payment of **individual income tax only** are Alabama, Arkansas, Connecticut, Louisiana, and New Jersey, whose legislatures have established the **essential statutory formula for income tax** for individual income tax only.

Additionally, the **four** states that statutorily require the payment of **corporate income tax only** are Colorado, Hawaii, Utah, and Wisconsin, whose legislatures have established the **essential statutory formula for income tax** for corporate income tax only.

So a total of **only eleven** states actually statutorily require the payment of either individual or corporate income tax or both—seven statutorily require the payment of individual income tax, and six statutorily require the payment of corporate income tax.

The remaining **thirty-nine** states that do not statutorily require the payment of either individual or corporate income tax are Alaska, Arizona, California, Delaware, Florida, Georgia, Idaho, Illinois, Indiana, Iowa, Kansas, Kentucky, Maine, Maryland, Massachusetts, Michigan, Minnesota, Missouri, Montana, Nebraska, Nevada, New Hampshire, New Mexico, New York, North Carolina, North Dakota, Ohio, Oklahoma, Oregon, Rhode Island, South Carolina, South Dakota, Tennessee, Texas, Vermont, Virginia, Washington, West Virginia, and Wyoming, whose legislatures have **not** established the **essential statutory formula for income tax** for either individual or corporate income tax (thirty-four of these have referred to or relied on the IRC to some extent). (New Hampshire, South Dakota, Tennessee, and Washington collect tax based on income in specific limited situations.)

III: Reasoning on the Purpose of Legislation (or Lack Thereof)

Considering Taxpayer Attitude

Are legislators voted into their respective offices because of their mental prowess or their superior intelligence? Must they use a certain language that only they can understand? If so, then how can anyone possibly obey their laws? On the other hand, if they use language most people understand, why do many people feel that the laws they enact are too difficult to understand?

There seems to be a general attitude that people are not "smart" enough to understand tax code, that is, it seems that many people believe that they do not have the mental mettle to understand the statutes. On the other hand, could it be that many people simply do not have the **desire to try** to understand the code sections? Do such people truly believe that legislators are rocket scientists and super geniuses with exponentially greater brain power than their "subjects," the "little people" they represent? This book is designed to help those who, perhaps, fit into one of these categories to recognize that the law is not rocket science and that those who legislate it are not necessarily super geniuses or possessed of exponentially greater brain power than the citizens in general.

However, while reading this book, the reader may have begun to suspect that there actually may be **intent** on the part of federal and state legislators to obscure the truth by enacting such an unimaginable quantity of statutes on just the one subject of income taxation, that is, intent to hinder or prevent anyone from learning the facts this book reveals by creating such an almost-incredible amount of information one must assimilate in order to arrive at the correct conclusions. If such intent does exist on the part of legislators, it can certainly be effectively realized in the case of those who for whatever reason do not actually read the statutes or do not read the statutes to a sufficient extent in order to arrive at the correct conclusions. For example, if the reader locates in the IRC **Section 61 Gross income defined, Subsection (a) General definition,** but does not read the entire, short, fifteen-item list thereunder, or locates in the IRC **Part II Items Specifically Included in Gross Income,** but does not read the entire, short, twenty-section list thereunder, the reader will most likely not notice the fact that wages are not listed in either category. So, if there truly is intent to obscure the truth on the part of federal legislators, such intent can be effectively realized if an individual does not read the statutes to a sufficient extent in order to arrive at the correct conclusions and, accordingly, draws **incorrect** conclusions and **voluntarily overpays** the statutory obligation for federal income tax. The same can be said regarding state legislators and state income tax.

In other words, if there is intent on the part of federal and state legislators to overcharge people for income tax by obscuring the truth that federal statutes and the statutes of almost all of the states do not actually require the payment of income tax, the attitude of people in general—their unwillingness to find, read, and properly apply the statutes— can be used against them. Unwillingness to find, save, and use coupons, discounts, and rebates can have the same effect on consumers. If there is intent on the part of commercial advertisers to overcharge people for their products by making it particularly challenging to enjoy reduced prices through coupons, discounts, and rebates, unwillingness—or forgetfulness—on the part of consumers can be used against them.

Determining Legislator Attitude

Why would a state legislature stop short of exercising its authority and power to enact the *essential statutory formula for income tax,* laws that clearly, unambiguously, and actually establish *imposition* of income tax, *liability* for income tax imposed, and *definitions* of terms that identify what income is taxable in order to derive income tax that is required to be paid? Why would it mimic federal legislation that is, due to the specific and express prohibitions of the US Constitution, without force and effect, that neither establishes *liability* for income tax or the *definition* of income that is taxable nor otherwise creates any obligation to pay income tax, and that is thus no more effective for establishing statutory liability for *state* income tax than it is for *federal* income tax? *Are* such state legislatures simply *unaware* of the specific and express prohibitions of the US Constitution and the fact that the US Congress has enacted statutes that are accordingly without force and effect, or *are* they actually *aware* but mimicking the language of the IRC regardless simply because *"it works"* (perhaps only because it is easier and/or more efficient to mimic the language of the IRC than to develop original language)?

Whatever the reason, as mentioned in Chapter I, each sovereign government possesses its own, independent ability to legislate taxation—to enact statutes of law to define terms and to require the payment of taxes—that is, each State has sovereign, unlimited authority and power to tax, whether or not its legislature chooses to act on such authority and power. By contrast, the States have given the *federal* government only *limited* authority and power to tax by means of the US Constitution, which specifically and expressly limits any taxation to a proportional basis (see Appendix II for discussion of limits imposed on the federal government by the US Constitution). As much unimaginable time and effort *federal* legislators have expended to formulate excruciatingly thorough and precise language to legislate their intentions, they have not enacted statutes requiring the payment of *federal* income tax—they have stopped just short, in fact—because they are constitutionally prohibited from doing so.

Interestingly, the following judicial determination regarding the federal legislature contains a valuable statement for education purposes:

> "'[W]here Congress includes particular language in one section of a statute but omits it in another ..., it is generally presumed that Congress acts intentionally and purposely in the disparate inclusion or exclusion.'" Russello v. United States, 464 US 16, 23, 78 L Ed 2d 17, 104 S Ct. 296 (1983) (Quoting United States v. Wong Kim Bo, 472 F. 2nd 720, 722 (CA 1972))

This is interesting and valuable because it highlights the fact that a legislative body *deliberately* includes or excludes language in the statutes it enacts. If *federal*

Reasoning on the Purpose of Legislation (or Lack Thereof)

legislators are so careful and deliberate in choosing their words, is it reasonable that *state* legislators are equally careful and deliberate in choosing *their* words (or *mimicking* the words of *federal* legislators)? Given the nearly immeasurable extent of definitions and explanations contained in the various law codes of the federal and state governments, it *is* reasonable to conclude that, as the Court puts it, federal *and* state legislators act "intentionally and purposely in the disparate *inclusion* or *exclusion*" of specific language in the statutes they enact.

Whether or not any state legislature is prohibited by state constitution from enacting statutes requiring the payment of *state* income tax (Florida's legislature, for example), any state government has various other opportunities for generating revenues through taxation—for just two examples of such opportunities, more than a *third* of the States generate revenues through taxation on gambling and *all* of the States generate revenues through taxation on property. So, it should not be surprising that a number of state legislatures have deliberately *refrained* from legislating income taxation—like any business organization, a particular government may decide not to engage in a certain area of activity, whether because the costs are too high or because the revenue potential is too low or both. It is also possible that a number of state legislatures— whether deliberately or not, though many, in their own legislated words, have indicated *deliberately*—have simply imitated the federal legislature and legislated a *preliminary superstructure* of income tax revenue statutes that lack force and effect without *foundation* statutes that specifically establish *liability* for income tax and the *definition* of income that is taxable—the very *foundation* statutes the *federal* legislature is constitutionally prohibited from enacting.

Many people—perhaps most people—who live in any of the fifty States, especially those who live in *known* income-tax states, tend just to assume that income tax is the norm, a requirement everyone must endure. It may be difficult for those who do not live under this assumption to understand this tendency as much as it may be difficult for those who *do* live under this assumption to understand those who *do not* understand this tendency. Reasonable people, though, may be able to recognize that it is possible for income tax not to exist in the law as much as it is possible for it to exist in the law. Nevertheless, such ones may also be able to recognize that some state legislatures simply choose to generate revenue through taxation opportunities other than income taxation, making income tax other than the norm for such states. (Indeed, having recognized how quick and easy it is to search the state statutes, and having learned how to find what, if anything, any state legislature has to say in its statutes about income tax, the reader should also recognize how quick and easy it is to search for what opportunities other than income taxation any State is pursuing to generate revenues through taxation.)

There is good reason, then, to conclude that, just as the *federal* legislature refrains from *exceeding* its authority and power to enact statutes that establish *liability* for income tax and the *definition* of income that is taxable and does so *deliberately,* any *state* legislature that refrains from *exercising* its authority and power to enact statutes that establish *imposition* of and *liability* for income tax as well as the *definition* of income

Reasoning on the Purpose of Legislation (or Lack Thereof)

that is taxable does so **deliberately.** In any case, whatever their reasoning, whatever their intent (published, legislated, or otherwise), and whatever their state constitutional constraints, state legislatures **deliberately** exercise their authority whether by deliberately **enacting** statutory liability for state income tax or by deliberately **refraining** from enacting statutory liability for state income tax. In other words, the language of the laws they enact, the absence of language of the laws they enact, and the laws they do not enact establish the basis for determining whether or not statutory liability for income tax exists in the state statutes. (There is no suggestion here that any ambiguity exists in any of the statutes of the fifty States—either the law says the payment of state income tax is required or it does not say so—it is the reader's sole responsibility to determine exhaustively whether or not statutory liability for income tax exists in the state statutes.)

Why, though, do both federal and state legislatures define **so many** terms in general but **refrain** from defining certain **basic** terms, namely, those that complete the **essential statutory formula for income tax?** For example, if a particular state legislature defines a term that common sense and customary use of language already define, so that the definition provided by the legislature agrees with the definition according to common sense and customary use of language (i.e., "taxable income" means income that is taxable), why does the state legislature not also define the terms necessary for determining income that is taxable (i.e., income that is taxable is all revenue received in any form derived from all business conducted in this state less the costs of generating such revenue)? While such a definition is typically the apparent, intended goal of legislation, legislatures typically leave out some important component or subcomponent of such a definition. For example, statutes in general typically state that income that is taxable is gross income less adjustments. However, after establishing this element of the formula, such statutes typically make it **impossible*** to identify what income is taxable as (1) they fail to define gross income, and/or (2) they lengthen the definition of income that is taxable with subcomponents of gross income and/or other components necessary for determining income that is taxable but then fail to define one or more of the subcomponents of gross income and/or one or more of the other components, and/or (3) they specifically refer to or rely on the IRC to define such components and subcomponents. By employing one or more of these three methods, state legislatures rely on the definitions according to common sense and customary use of language, or on the definitions provided by federal statutes, or both. However, state legislatures do not statutorily standardize taxation by relying either on what is essentially personal opinion (which can be widely varied) or on federal statutes, which also typically fail to define one or more components and/or subcomponents of income that is taxable and other terms necessary for determining income that is taxable (so that the federal legislature also relies on what is essentially personal opinion, which is to say that the federal legislature does not statutorily standardize taxation).

After considering the brief information presented on each of the fifty States as well as DC and, perhaps, conducting some additional research, after also considering the

---

*Similarly, for example, after designing a highway overpass shortcut, a traffic engineering company makes it **impossible** to traverse the new bridge as (1) it fails to install signs to define the new route, (2) it completes the preliminary superstructure (the steel beams and reinforcements) but fails to complete the concrete road surface and barriers, and (3) it specifically refers to or relies on other routes by means of detour signs.
Reasoning on the Purpose of Legislation (or Lack Thereof)

pattern among federal and state income tax statutes—that is, the pertinent language of the federal and many of the state income tax statutes both is either *identical* or *nearly identical* and does not establish statutory liability (lawful obligation) for income tax— and after also considering the reasonable conclusion that federal and state legislatures *deliberately* include and exclude language and definitions in and from the statutes they enact, the reader may begin to imagine that there is collusion among the numerous federal and state legislators for some purpose (the alignment of strategies and standardization of the use of terms and phrases among the federal and various state legislatures is clear). By creating such a complex code of statutes (the IRC) that does not establish the *essential statutory formula for income tax* but causes particular and great difficulty for any diligent and law abiding individual to gain clear and accurate understanding of the intent, force, and effect of such statutes, federal legislators have— at the very least—perpetuated the collection of federal income tax from the people without violating the specific and express prohibitions of the US Constitution. By so confusing the issue of establishing *imposition* of and *liability* for income tax as well as the *definition* of income that is taxable, and by soliciting, through the US Department of the Treasury - Internal Revenue Service, *voluntary* returns for and payments of federal income tax, federal legislators have made people *believe* that statutory liability for federal income tax has been established and that they are therefore under lawful obligation to pay federal income tax. (Indeed, "Because of what *appears* to be a lawful command on the surface, many Citizens, because of their respect for what *appears* to be law, are cunningly coerced into waiving their rights due to ignorance."—United States Supreme Court, U.S. v. Minker (1950) [emphasis added].) Whether *unaware* of or *unconcerned* about the net effect of federal income tax legislation, by mimicking this practice in spite of their authority and power to enact statutes that *do* establish the *essential statutory formula for income tax,* state legislators demonstrate that they *are* in collusion with federal legislators for some purpose. Accordingly, the reader may begin to believe, or be reinforced in the belief, that there is a general conspiracy of ignorance, that is, that there is an undisclosed agreement (formal or informal, written or unwritten) among the numerous federal and state legislators to keep the greater number of the people uninformed, misinformed, and confused about the facts of federal and state tax law. (Certainly, such legislators do not encourage—at least, they have not *required*—even professionals with top industry certifications to be aware of the facts presented in this book, its Appendix, and its Appendix to the Appendix.)

By mimicking the language of the IRC—if only simply because *"it works"* for procuring *voluntary* returns for and payments of income tax—and so confusing the issue of establishing *imposition* of and *liability* for income tax as well as the *definition* of income that is taxable, state legislators have—at the very least—perpetuated the collection of state income tax from the people, made people *believe* that statutory liability for state income tax has been established and that they are therefore under lawful obligation to pay state income tax, and thereby solicited *voluntary* returns for and payments of state income tax.

Notes on Prerequisite Liability

For each State, this book has shown the reader how to verify that a state legislature does or does not statutorily require the payment of individual and/or corporate income tax or corporate income-based franchise tax: locate the state statutes, locate the relevant category and subcategory(ies) of statutes, locate and read the relevant statutes, and determine whether or not the ***essential statutory formula for income tax*** has been established ((Imposition + Liability) x Definition = Tax). This book has also shown the reader how to locate and read other pertinent statutes in the case of a particular state legislature that has not enacted any income tax statutes. That is, if the reader has duplicated the steps illustrated in Chapter I and any of the sections on the fifty States, the reader has been shown and has ***practiced*** the simple steps for searching, scanning, and reading the statutes.

In certain cases, however, verifying that a state legislature does or does not statutorily require the payment of a certain tax can be a little more complicated. Once again, the States have sovereign authority and power to lay and collect taxes, and their respective legislatures accordingly have authority and power to enact laws for such taxation. However, if certain state constitutions or the pronouncements of certain state supreme courts place certain restrictions on state taxation and, accordingly, if the respective state legislatures abide by such restrictions, legislation or statutes conflicting with such restrictions may not exist or, at the very least, may be subject to judicial review and repeal. Nevertheless, the respective state legislatures may also enact certain statutes that create the ***appearance*** of statutory obligation to pay tax along with other statutes that clearly establish the need for ***liability*** (prerequisite liability) to exist before the payment of tax can be required but not actually enact specific statutes creating such liability or prerequisite liability. In other words, given state constitutional or judicial restrictions on taxation, a particular state legislature may enact ***typical*** statutes that ***seem*** to create the entire statutory obligation for the payment of the subject tax but also enact ***atypical*** statutes that ***modify*** or ***restrict*** the force and effect of the ***typical*** statutes. Existence of liability for income tax would require payment of income tax, so it seems superfluous and redundant to require liability to exist before requiring the payment of tax. Nevertheless, as the next two paragraphs discuss, the US Congress has done this very thing, in ***technical***—or, more accurately, ***disguised*** or ***obscured***—compliance with the express prohibitions of the US Constitution. Given constitutional or judicial restrictions on state income taxation, state legislatures that similarly enact ***atypical*** statutes that require liability or prerequisite liability to exist before the payment of income tax can be required but refrain from enacting ***typical*** liability or prerequisite liability statutes do so in ***technical*** compliance with such state constitutional or judicial restrictions.

As this book has repeatedly mentioned, the US Constitution expressly prohibits any capitation or tax that is not uniform and proportional to the census, specifically, the exact same dollar amount per person regardless of wealth or income (refer to Appendix II for discussion of limits imposed on the federal government by the US Constitution). Since the 1890's, when the US Supreme Court overturned the original income tax

Reasoning on the Purpose of Legislation (or Lack Thereof)

statutes as unconstitutional, the federal legislature, the US Congress, has carefully refrained from enacting statutes that require the payment of federal income tax. The US Congress has enacted nearly countless statutes that **appear** to establish and support the **essential statutory formula for income tax** ((Imposition + Liability) x Definition = Tax) but stopped short of enacting any statute(s) establishing **liability** for the tax imposed or the **definition** of income is taxable. In other words, the US Congress has enacted at least one of the **typical** statutes, establishing the first element of the essential formula, namely, **imposition;** it has also enacted other, **atypical** statutes that require liability, or prerequisite liability, to be established before requiring taxes to be paid; however, it has not enacted any statute(s) establishing such liability or prerequisite liability; and, furthermore, it has carefully refrained from specifically defining nearly all types of income as taxable, particularly by refraining from listing wages as either specifically included in or specifically excluded from gross income that derives taxable income. So, the second and third elements of the essential formula are missing from the federal statutes (the IRC): **liability** for the tax imposed and the **definition** of income that is taxable.

This is appropriate, however, since the US Congress lacks constitutional authority and power to require the payment of federal income tax. This, along with the express prohibitions of the US Constitution, is also the reason, whether or not due to the fact that current federal income tax statutes require both imposition and liability, the US Supreme Court has repeatedly determined that liability (prerequisite liability) for federal income tax must exist before payment of federal income tax can be required. This is also the reason the US Department of the Treasury, through its collection bureau, the IRS, earnestly publishes the fact that payment of federal income tax is **_VOLUNTARY_***— that is, the most the Dept. of the Treasury - IRS lawfully can do is **solicit** (not **require**) **voluntary contributions** of federal income tax. (If not by now, after reading the Appendix the reader should be able to recognize that, if the US Congress **did** enact federal income tax liability statutes, the US Supreme Court would again overturn such statutes for unconstitutionality.)

Given the demonstrated tendency of state legislatures to rely at least partly on the federal IRC and to repeat its language closely or even precisely in at least some of their own statutes, it should not be surprising to discover the same flawed pattern in the statutes of at least some of the states, that is, the pattern of either establishing only **some** (but not **all**) of the elements of the **essential statutory formula for income tax** or establishing typical statutes that establish all of the elements of the essential formula while also establishing atypical statutes that modify or restrict the force and effect of statutes that establish the essential statutory formula for income tax. In the IRC, such atypical statutes are found in the collection statutes under Subtitle F Procedure and Administration (rather than under Subtitle A Income Taxes). However, unlike the federal legislature, the state legislatures are not subject to the express prohibitions of the US Constitution but are authorized and empowered by their respective sovereign states to enact statutes that require the payment of taxes on income. Accordingly, unless they are subject to express income tax prohibitions or limitations by their

*Similarly, for example, after a new toll road is completed, the most the toll authority lawfully can do is **solicit** (not **require**) **voluntary use of the new road,** especially when another route offers similar benefits and no tolls.

Reasoning on the Purpose of Legislation (or Lack Thereof)

respective state constitutions, and unless they are censored by pronouncements of their respective state supreme courts or, possibly, the US Supreme Court, they may exercise their authority and power to choose to enact—or choose not to enact—the typical statutes that establish all the elements of the **essential statutory formula for income tax** without also enacting any atypical statutes that modify or restrict the force and effect of the statutes that establish the essential formula.

IV: Developing Logical and Reasonable Conclusions

Applying This Information

As the Foreword says, it is entirely up to the reader to agree or disagree with the conclusions presented herein. It is appropriate to revisit the Disclaimer, as well. The reader should specifically recognize that none of this book is intended to encourage evasion of any tax the payment of which is actually required by statute. Instead, the reader is encouraged merely to gain accurate knowledge of the actual requirements of applicable tax law, to obey diligently all requirements of such law, and to exercise fully all rights and privileges afforded by such law. (It is the reader's sole responsibility to determine exhaustively whether or not statutory liability for income tax exists in the statutes of the federal or any state government.)

Why should anyone be concerned about paying federal and state income taxes to federal and state governments whose legislatures have not enacted statutes establishing liability—the ***essential statutory formula***—for federal and state income tax? There is a short list of reasons for concern. First, most people don't pay more for their homes and their vehicles than the banks require them to pay. Second, most people seem to feel that they don't have enough disposable income. Third, most people simply don't have the ability to save enough money for retirement. Fourth, excessive income tax costs, insufficient disposable income, and insufficient retirement savings all damage the economy (refer to Appendix X for further discussion). Would not anyone want to reduce his or her federal and state income tax burden as much as legitimately possible, if only to provide better for oneself and one's family, if not also to contribute to the health of the economy?

According to the US Supreme Court, it is certainly appropriate:

> "'***Anyone*** may so arrange his affairs so that his taxes shall be ***as low as possible.*** He is not bound to choose that pattern which best pays the treasury. There is not even a patriotic duty to increase one's taxes.' Over and over again the courts have said that there is nothing sinister in so arraigning affairs as to keep taxes as low as possible, everyone does it, rich and poor alike and all do RIGHT, for ***nobody owes the public duty to pay more than the law demands.***"—Weeks v Sibley; Edwards v. Commissioner; Helvering v. Gregory; and 60 Federal 2nd 809, United States Supreme Court Justice Learned Hand (1872-1961) [emphasis added].

In other words, if the law provides for an individual to arrange his affairs lawfully in a way that reduces his tax obligations as much as possible, such an individual has the blessing of the US Supreme Court to do so.

Considering Fairness and One's Rights and Privileges

There are, at the very least, two perspectives on the matter of income taxation with accurate understanding of federal and state law: the perspective of those who file and pay for income taxes "just like everybody else" and the perspective of those who invoke their rights and privileges under the law and file and pay for taxes only to the extent to which they are lawfully obligated and without regard for what "everybody else" does, that is, whether or not "everybody else" invokes his or her rights and privileges under the law. As the IRS puts it, each taxpayer is responsible for paying "only the correct amount of tax due under the law—no more, no less" [Department of the Treasury - IRS Publication 1, Your Rights as a Taxpayer]. Given that taxpayers in general (which includes both professional tax preparers and non-professional taxpayers) are largely uninformed about federal and state tax law, upon gaining accurate knowledge and understanding of the facts of federal and state tax law, the reader may consider it "fair" to pay about the same amount as all other taxpayers in spite of the general exemption from (or lack of obligation for) income tax under the tax laws of the federal and many of the state governments.

Many IRS agents certainly take this position, that is, their behavior demonstrates that their attitude is that everyone should pay his "fair share" of income tax without regard for what the law says or does not say. Department of the Treasury - IRS Publication 1, Your Rights as a Taxpayer, says of "The IRS Mission": "Provide America's taxpayers top quality service by helping them understand and meet their tax responsibilities and by applying the tax law with integrity and fairness to all." Accordingly, especially since the greater number of people voluntarily file and pay for federal income tax without regard for their rights and privileges under the law, many IRS agents, through the IRS Automated Collection System, demand that *everyone else* also voluntarily file and pay for federal income tax without regard for *their* rights and privileges under the law—that is, since the greater number of people do not invoke their right to pay "no more" than "only the correct amount of tax due under the law" but file federal income tax forms that are based on the presumption of a statutory liability (which demonstrably does not exist) and pay according to the calculations of such income tax forms, many IRS agents, through the IRS Automated Collection System, forego application of the law as well as their duty, as described by the Internal Revenue Manual, to observe the rights of each individual taxpayer and instead engage in a ceaseless battle of wills with the general public to enforce ***"voluntary"*** filing and paying for tax not required by law and expressly prohibited by the US Constitution—certainly, application of the tax law with integrity would result in complete elimination of federal income tax revenues.

On the other hand, given that taxpayers in general make little, if any, effort to gain accurate knowledge and understanding of the facts of federal and state tax law, the reader may consider it "fair" to exercise careful observance of the law and invoke and enjoy all the rights and privileges it affords, particularly in the way of income tax reduction or savings, without regard to whether or not other taxpayers invoke *their* rights and privileges under the law The reader might further reason that this is "fair" since each and every individual has the right to *choose* to invoke or not to invoke his rights and privileges under the law, since the law does not discriminate as to who does and who does not have the right to choose, and since the individual's right to choose to invoke his rights and privileges under the law is not diminished by even a great majority of people who choose not to invoke *their* rights and privileges under the law—that is, since the individual has the IRS-published right to pay "no more" than "only the correct amount of tax due under the law," and since the law does not require the payment of federal income tax, the individual has the right to choose to invoke his rights and privileges under the law—even if nobody else chooses to invoke *his* rights and privileges under the law—and to arrange his affairs so that his taxes are as low as possible.

Perhaps most people would assume that this right applies to state income tax, as well, especially in the case of any state legislature that has deliberately refrained from exercising its authority and power to enact statutes that establish imposition of and liability for income tax as well as the definition of income that is taxable.

The figures on the following chart represent the effective cost of ignorance of the law and no Strategic Tax Planning—**not** arranging one's affairs so that one's taxes are as low as possible—namely, volunteering to pay income taxes not required by law instead of diverting such costs to permanently-tax-free-interest-bearing retirement savings. These figures indicate the results of annual savings of the indicated diverted tax costs and annual interest compounding at the indicated rates: lawfully accumulated tax-free wealth and permanently-tax-free monthly income. These figures are based on specific provisions of the IRC, namely, Sections 72(t) and 101(a), which expressly provide for accumulation of and access to retirement savings on a tax-deferred—and, ultimately, tax-free—basis by means of annuity and life insurance contracts. (There are only two key restrictions: (1) one may not modify payments from an annuity either (a) before the close of the 5-year period beginning with the date of the first payment and after one attains age 59½ or (b) before one attains age 59½, and (2) one may not cancel one's life insurance contract.) Accumulated interest amounts borrowed from one's retirement account(s) are treated as loans or partial withdrawals rather than taxable income.

However, by enacting such a maze of statutes *relative* to federal income tax and yet (in technical compliance with the express prohibitions of the US Constitution) deliberately refraining from exceeding its authority and power to enact statutes that establish liability for income tax and the definition of income that is taxable, and by deliberately refraining from exercising their authority and power to enact statutes that establish imposition of and liability for income tax as well as the definition of income that is taxable, the US Congress and many state legislatures, respectively, have greatly challenged even the staunchly unswerving observer of the law both to comply with the law and to enjoy the rights and privileges the law affords, namely, to pay "no more" than "only the correct amount of tax due under the law" [Dept. of the Treasury - IRS Publication 1, Your Rights as a Taxpayer]. Nevertheless, both complying with the law and enjoying one's rights and privileges under the law is possible by lawfully arranging one's affairs. Primarily, this involves operating through one or more legal persons or entities that have no (and do not incur any) federal or state income tax liability.

Developing Logical and Reasonable Conclusions

Schedule of Lawful Annual Diversion of Income Tax Costs
to Permanently-Tax-Free-Interest-Bearing Retirement Savings*

$1,000.00 Annual Tax Cost Diverted to Annual Savings								
4% Interest			8% Interest			12% Interest		
Yr.	Account Value	Monthly Income	Yr.	Account Value	Monthly Income	Yr.	Account Value	Monthly Income
5	$5,632.98	$18.78	5	$6,335.93	$42.24	5	$7,115.19	$71.15
15	20,824.53	$69.42	15	29,324.28	$195.50	15	41,753.28	$417.53
25	43,311.74	$144.37	25	78,954.42	$526.36	25	149,333.93	$1,493.34
35	76,598.31	$255.33	35	186,102.15	$1,240.68	35	483,463.12	$4,834.63
45	$125,870.57	$419.57	45	$417,426.07	$2,782.84	45	$1,521,217.64	$15,212.18

$2,000.00 Annual Tax Cost Diverted to Annual Savings								
4% Interest			8% Interest			12% Interest		
Yr.	Account Value	Monthly Income	Yr.	Account Value	Monthly Income	Yr.	Account Value	Monthly Income
5	$11,265.95	$37.55	5	$12,671.86	$84.48	5	$14,230.38	$142.30
15	41,649.06	$138.83	15	58,648.57	$390.99	15	83,506.56	$835.07
25	86,623.49	$288.74	25	157,908.83	$1,052.73	25	298,667.87	$2,986.68
35	153,196.63	$510.66	35	372,204.30	$2,481.36	35	966,926.23	$9,669.26
45	$251,741.14	$839.14	45	$834,852.13	$5,565.68	45	$3,042,435.27	$30,424.35

$5,000.00 Annual Tax Cost Diverted to Annual Savings								
4% Interest			8% Interest			12% Interest		
Yr.	Account Value	Monthly Income	Yr.	Account Value	Monthly Income	Yr.	Account Value	Monthly Income
5	$28,164.88	$93.88	5	$31,679.65	$211.20	5	$35,575.95	$355.76
15	104,122.66	$347.08	15	146,621.42	$977.48	15	208,766.40	$2,087.66
25	216,558.72	$721.86	25	394,772.08	$2,631.81	25	746,669.67	$7,466.70
35	382,991.57	$1,276.64	35	930,510.74	$6,203.40	35	2,417,315.58	$24,173.16
45	$629,352.84	$2,097.84	45	$2,087,130.33	$13,914.20	45	$7,606,088.18	$76,060.88

$10,000.00 Annual Tax Cost Diverted to Annual Savings								
4% Interest			8% Interest			12% Interest		
Yr.	Account Value	Monthly Income	Yr.	Account Value	Monthly Income	Yr.	Account Value	Monthly Income
5	$56,329.75	$187.77	5	$63,359.29	$422.40	5	$71,151.89	$711.52
15	208,245.31	$694.15	15	293,242.83	$1,954.95	15	417,532.80	$4,175.33
25	433,117.45	$1,443.72	25	789,544.15	$5,263.63	25	1,493,339.34	$14,933.39
35	765,983.14	$2,553.28	35	1,861,021.48	$12,406.81	35	4,834,631.16	$48,346.31
45	$1,258,705.68	$4,195.69	45	$4,174,260.67	$27,828.40	45	$15,212,176.36	$152,121.76

$20,000.00 Annual Tax Cost Diverted to Annual Savings								
4% Interest			8% Interest			12% Interest		
Yr.	Account Value	Monthly Income	Yr.	Account Value	Monthly Income	Yr.	Account Value	Monthly Income
5	$112,659.51	$375.53	5	$126,718.58	$844.79	5	$142,303.78	$1,423.04
15	416,490.62	$1,388.30	15	586,485.66	$3,909.90	15	835,065.61	$8,350.66
25	866,234.89	$2,887.45	25	1,579,088.30	$10,527.26	25	2,986,678.69	$29,866.79
35	1,531,966.28	$5,106.55	35	3,722,042.96	$24,813.62	35	9,669,262.32	$96,692.62
45	$2,517,411.35	$8,391.37	45	$8,348,521.34	$55,656.81	45	$30,424,352.72	$304,243.53

*E-mail mpllc@ymail.com, Attn: Advance Training, for additional information and recommendations. See a licensed life/annuity agent for implementation.

Developing Logical and Reasonable Conclusions

Such a legal person or entity as the common corporation or partnership, when properly organized and registered in a jurisdiction that does not require either the payment of income tax or the filing of an income tax return (or both), provides the **means** for both complying with the law and also enjoying one's rights and privileges under the law, namely, to pay "no more" than "only the correct amount of tax due under the law." Less expensive to create and maintain than a number of other, more sophisticated organizations such as tax-exempt and non-profit organizations, qualifications for which must first be met and also maintained, the common corporation or partnership is also the typical entity business owners use to establish banking, conduct business, and provide legal separation between business and personal interests.

Contracting for one's services through such a corporation or partnership provides the **method** for both complying with the law and also enjoying one's rights and privileges under the law, namely, to pay "no more" than "only the correct amount of tax due under the law." The individual's constitutional power to contract has been expressly emphasized by the US Supreme Court:

> "The individual may stand upon his **constitutional rights** as a Citizen. He is entitled to carry on his **private business** in his **own way.** His power to contract is **unlimited.**'—United States Supreme Court, *Hale v. Henkle,* 201 US 43 (emphasis added—refer to Appendix II for further discussion).

Accordingly, one may either provide labor via contract (rather than as an employee) or work for oneself. Whereas one's being paid a wage results in heavy taxation one is not required by law to pay, one's providing labor or services by means of constitutional contracts* results in, comparatively, very light taxation, namely, only the taxation one is required by law to pay.

By means of the foregoing audit of the state statutes, this book demonstrates that thirty-nine state legislatures do not statutorily require the payment of either individual or corporate state income tax. By means of the following audit of the federal statutes, the Appendix to this book demonstrates that the federal legislature does not statutorily require the payment of either individual or corporate federal income tax. However, *provisions of law* are not necessarily *provisions of **practice*** (the federal government and most of the States whose respective legislatures have not established the **essential statutory formula for income tax** have the practice of collecting income tax regardless). Accordingly, it is necessary to consider the small number of states whose legislatures specifically do not require the payment of corporate state income tax and whose agents specifically do not have the practice of collecting corporate state income tax.

*Compared to a service-based business, a product-based business typically incurs no sales tax obligation and the scrutiny of sales tax collection agents as well as, possibly, the scrutiny of both state and federal income tax collection agents. For such reasons, the reader might consider a service-based business preferable to a product-based business.

Developing Logical and Reasonable Conclusions

Considering States That Are Recommended

The nine *known* no-income tax states are Alaska, Florida, Nevada, New Hampshire, South Dakota, Tennessee, Texas, Washington, and Wyoming. These are states that generally do not require the payment of *individual* income tax; however, some of these states do statutorily require the payment of *corporate* or *business* income tax in the form of tax based on gross receipts or net income. (Some state legislatures impose on business activities *franchise* taxes instead of *income* taxes. Some of such state legislatures impose a franchise tax that is a flat dollar amount, others impose a franchise tax that is a percentage of taxable income (MN, NJ, NY, and TX), and still another imposes a franchise tax this is both a flat dollar amount *and* a percentage of taxable income (UT). The text of this book considers only the latter two since a franchise tax that is a flat dollar amount is not based on taxable income, that is, the text of this book contains no discussion of tax for state legislatures that impose a franchise tax that is only a flat dollar amount.)

As stated in Chapter II, most of the thirty-nine states that *do not* statutorily require the payment of either individual or corporate income tax nevertheless *do* collect income taxes from individuals and corporations, that is, what occurs in practice is not necessarily what is required by law. Logically, the states that do not have the *practice* of collecting corporate or business income or income-based taxes and whose legislatures clearly do not statutorily require the payment of corporate or business income or income-based taxes are worthy of recommendation, namely, those of the *known* no-income-tax states that also are no-corporate-income-tax states and any other states whose legislatures clearly have not enacted statutes of *intent* to require the payment of corporate or business income or income-based taxes or established *any* of the elements of the *essential statutory formula for income tax* for corporations or businesses.

By contrast, the states who do have the *practice* of collecting corporate or business income or income-based taxes without established statutory liability for such taxes and the states whose legislatures have (a) enacted statutes of *intent* to require the payment of corporate or business income or income-based taxes, (b) enacted statutes establishing *some* or *all* of the elements of the *essential statutory formula for income tax* for corporations or businesses, (c) referred to or relied on the IRC for *liability* for income tax or the *definition(s)* of income that is taxable, or (d) not established any *definition* at all are *not* worthy of recommendation.

Nevada's legislature clearly does not statutorily require the payment of any corporate or business income or income-based taxes and clearly has not enacted statutes of *intent* to require the payment of corporate or business income or income-based taxes or established *any* of the elements of the *essential statutory formula for income tax* for corporations or businesses. Also, the State has no practice of collecting such taxes, does not require income tax returns, has no information sharing agreement with the IRS, and has a confidential (fictitious) address program. State fees are as follows:

Entity	Initial	Annual
Corporations	$400.00	$400.00
Limited liability companies	$400.00	$400.00
Limited liability partnerships	$400.00	$400.00
Limited partnerships	$400.00	$400.00

[https://nvsos.gov/Modules/ShowDocument.aspx?documentid=668,
https://nvsos.gov/Modules/ShowDocument.aspx?documentid=1004,
https://nvsos.gov/Modules/ShowDocument.aspx?documentid=953,
https://nvsos.gov/Modules/ShowDocument.aspx?documentid=980].

Visit the Nevada Secretary of State web site at http://nvsos.gov/ and click on "Start a Business" under the Business Center tab. E-mail mpllc@ymail.com, Attn: Advance Training, for assistance.

Ohio's legislature clearly does not statutorily require the payment of any corporate or business income or income-based taxes for businesses operating outside the State and clearly has not enacted statutes of **intent** to require the payment of corporate or business income or income-based taxes or established **any** of the elements of the **essential statutory formula for income tax** for corporations or businesses. Also, the State has no practice of collecting such taxes and does not require income tax returns for businesses operating outside the State. (Even businesses operating *inside* the State currently enjoy an annual Commercial Activity Tax of either only $150.00 minimum or only 0.26% of gross receipts in excess of $1,000,000. 00.) State fees are as follows:

Entity	Initial	Annual
Corporations	$125.00	$50.00
Limited liability companies	$125.00	(not listed)
Limited liability partnerships	$125.00	$50.00
Limited partnerships	$125.00	(not listed)
Partnerships	$125.00	(not listed)

[http://www.sos.state.oh.us/sos/upload/business/filingformsfeeschedule.aspx?page=251#Domestic].

Visit the Ohio Secretary of State web site at http://www.sos.state.oh.us/ and click on Starting A Business under the Businesses tab. E-mail mpllc@ymail.com, Attn: Advance Training, for assistance.

South Dakota's legislature clearly does not statutorily require the payment of any corporate or business income or income-based taxes, other than one and one-half percent (one percent effective July 1, 2013) gross receipts tax on certain visitor-related businesses during June through September, two percent and one percent contractor excise (gross receipts) taxes, and one percent municipal gross receipts tax on various businesses, and clearly has not enacted statutes of **intent** to require the payment of corporate or business income or income-based taxes or established **any** of the elements of the **essential statutory formula for income tax** for corporations or businesses. Also, the State has no practice of collecting such taxes, other than the specified gross receipts taxes, and does not require income tax returns for businesses operating outside the State. State fees are as follows:

Entity	Initial	Annual
Corporations	$150.00	$50.00
General Partnerships	$125.00	(not listed)
Limited liability companies	$150.00	$50.00
Limited liability partnerships	$125.00	$50.00
Limited partnerships	$125.00	(not listed)

[http://sdsos.gov/content/viewcontent.aspx?cat=corporations&pg=/corporations/corp orations_feeschedule.shtm].

Visit the South Dakota Secretary of State web site at http://sdsos.gov/default.aspx and click on Corporations under the Business Services tab. E-mail mpllc@ymail.com, Attn: Advance Training, for assistance.

Washington's legislature clearly does not statutorily require the payment of any corporate or business income or income-based taxes for businesses operating outside the State and clearly has not enacted statutes of ***intent*** to require the payment of corporate or business income or income-based taxes or established ***any*** of the elements of the ***essential statutory formula for income tax*** for corporations or businesses. Also, the State has no practice of collecting such taxes and does not require income tax returns for businesses operating outside the State. State fees are as follows:

Entity	Initial	Annual
Corporations	$200.00	$69.00
Limited liability companies	$200.00	$69.00
Limited liability partnerships	$180.00	$60.00
Limited partnerships	$180.00	$60.00

["Start a Business" and "Manage a Business"—http://www.sos.wa.gov/corps/].

Visit the Washington Secretary of State web site at http://www.sos.wa.gov/ and click on Start a Business under the Corporations tab. E-mail mpllc@ymail.com, Attn: Advance Training, for assistance.

Wyoming's legislature clearly does not statutorily require the payment of any corporate or business income or income-based taxes and clearly has not enacted statutes of ***intent*** to require the payment of corporate or business income or income-based taxes or established ***any*** of the elements of the ***essential statutory formula for income tax*** for corporations or businesses. Also, the State has no practice of collecting such taxes and does not require income tax returns. State fees are as follows:

Entity	Initial	Annual
Corporations	$100.00	$50.00*
Limited liability companies	$100.00	$50.00*
Limited liability partnerships	$100.00	$50.00*
Limited partnerships	$100.00	$50.00*

*or two-tenths of one mill on the dollar ($.0002) whichever is greater based on the company's assets located and employed in the state of Wyoming [http://soswy.state.wy.us/Business/docs/BusinessFees.pdf].

Visit the Wyoming Secretary of State web site at http://soswy.state.wy.us/ and click on Start a Business under the Business & UCC tab. E-mail mpllc@ymail.com, Attn: Advance Training, for assistance.

Each business entity must have an agent registered with the Secretary of State for initial entity registration and/or licensing, annual renewal, and service of process, at an additional initial and annual cost of, for example, $100.00.

Considering Just One Three-Part Strategy

There are several possible strategies to consider, but this book recommends simply incorporating in one of the recommended States, *not* electing treatment as an "S-corporation" (so that, instead, the corporation will be treated as a "C-corporation"), and strictly *contracting* for one's labor or services through the corporation rather than *working for a wage* for one's labor or services provided to the corporation. Typically, whereas an S-corporation is known as a "pass-through" entity, in that the owner(s) or partners pay federal and state income taxes on the corporate profits, a C-corporation pays federal and state income taxes on its own profits. Accordingly, a C-corporation organized in a State that neither statutorily requires the payment of corporate or business income or income-based taxes nor has the practice of collecting such taxes incurs no state income tax obligation relative to its profits and passes to its owner(s) or partners no state income tax obligation relative to its profits. Furthermore, a C-corporation organized in a State that that does not require income tax returns or that does not require income tax returns for businesses operating outside the State incurs no state income tax return filing obligation and, hence, generates no *"presumptive evidence"** or even the *appearance* of liability for federal income tax. Finally, whereas the IRS publishes a corporate owner's requirement to pay oneself a "reasonable wage," which would result in the payroll withholding tax conundrum discussed in Chapter I, as well as the additional cost of federal and state unemployment taxes, *constitutional contracting* instead lawfully avoids such obligations arising from ignorance of the law.

Considering the Virtues of Strategic Tax Planning

People have often asked, "What if everybody finds out about this?" The question means, "What if everybody discovers that the federal IRC and many of the state tax codes that are *believed* to require the payment of income tax *do not* actually do so?" The concern that people usually express is, "Won't the governments and the economy

*Information—whether accurate or inaccurate, whether obtained or created—which uninformed tax collectors presume to be "evidence" of a liability which such tax collectors presume to exist.
Developing Logical and Reasonable Conclusions

collapse?" The simple answers are (1) most people that find out about this won't act on this information, but (2) if everybody **were** to find out about this **and** act on it, there would be a great **boost** to the economy by their discontinuing overpaying income taxes and by their spending the savings for goods and services in the marketplace, and (3) no, the governments won't collapse but will continue as-is, the federal government printing and electronically depositing more money and hiring more government employees and the state governments collecting sales, property, gambling, and all manner of other taxes, receiving federal government subsidies, and spending what they collect and receive in their respective local economies. The governments do not rely solely on revenues—income tax revenues or otherwise—to remain in operation. The federal government **creates** money, and the state governments are **subsidized** by the federal government, although, comparatively speaking, the state governments do rely heavily on revenues. (The reader is encouraged to research this subject further to verify the accuracy of these last two statements.)

Is there any further recommendation for advantageously using this information? There is. Naturally, it would be imprudent to walk up to a state (or federal) Congressman (or, possibly, a state (or federal) income tax collector) and say, "You haven't legislated state (or federal) income tax, so I'm going to stop paying it." However, if, upon recognizing that, after expending unimaginable time and effort to formulate excruciatingly thorough and precise language to legislate their intentions, the state (or federal) legislators have not enacted statutes requiring the payment of state (or federal) income tax, it would be an entirely prudent, shrewd, wise, lawful, legal, ethical, and moral exercise of one's rights and privileges afforded by law to establish a lawful means of operating so as not to generate any *"presumptive evidence"* or even the **appearance** of liability for state (or federal) income tax. (Most people would likely agree that establishing a lawful means of **avoiding** income tax liability is preferable to **ignoring** any apparent or actual income tax liability and hoping not to get caught not paying income tax.)

Appendix

Strategic Tax Planning:
Auditing the Federal Statutes
(and Other Sources of Authority):
The Truth About Federal Income Tax:
How to Obey the Law and Escape the Unlawful Activities of Others

Appendix I: The Paradox of Legal Extortion

Petty Theft

It is a sad fact of life today that people steal from other people. A person steals from another person when he believes that he will neither be caught nor penalized for the theft or that her rewards will pay handsomely for her efforts and greatly outweigh her risks. A person may steal time at work by taking unauthorized breaks or by simply not working when unsupervised. He might use the company telephone for toll calls without permission or take small items home when leaving the work site for the day. She might use company petty cash funds for personal purposes or obtain a purchase order for a product that she orders delivered not to the company's address but to her own. He might use business credit accounts to purchase fuel or parts for his own car or report personal mileage as business mileage on the company's vehicle. Such petty theft is not only common but also considered by many as appropriate behavior because people just "deserve" these "perks."

Civil Theft

On the other hand, what if someone steals from someone else just because "that's just the way it is," or, "everybody else does it"? Another sad fact of life today, at least in this country, is that *companies* customarily steal from the individuals who work for them (giving rise to the common feeling that the perks listed in the previous paragraph are just, fair, and well deserved). In Florida, "civil theft" is the term sometimes applied to the failure of a business to pay for overtime hours or to render a final paycheck due when the working relationship is terminated. This actually happens quite frequently, although, as is the case with date rape, it often goes unreported and un-prosecuted. The Fair Labor Standards Act requires strict adherence to the "time-and-a-half" pay rule for hours worked in excess of forty hours per week. Some occupations have varied methods for calculating such hours, but the standard rule is one-point-five times the regular rate of pay for overtime hours worked. Some might call not paying overtime "legal theft" since businesses and business owners tend to "get away with it" with impunity. Despite the fact that federal and state laws *heavily favor the employee* in such cases, ironically, very few such cases ever go to court since very few attorneys are willing to spend time on anything but the very largest cases, from which their earnings are naturally substantial. The less-than-highly-paid worker, then, generally gets left in the gutter, bewildered and without either the legal counsel or the personal fortitude necessary to wage the requisite courtroom battle to acquire the paycheck he has earned and rightfully deserves. What a paradox!

Grand Theft Auto By Trade

What, though, if a person steals from other people because of a duty? For example, a person who works for an auto repossession company legally steals vehicles as an occupation. Such a person is required as an agent to locate and retake possession of vehicles for dealerships and banks when the vehicles' drivers default on their loans.

Some might argue principles but might also acquiesce when presented with copies of finance contracts and state and federal statutes that make such repossession both legitimate and lawful.

Routine Criminal Activity

What, though, if *a hundred thousand* people dutifully steal from more than *a hundred million* others as an occupation, *believing* they possess but not *actually* possessing support of the law, and nearly *everyone believes* that "that's just the way it is"? If a common *belief* that there is a common duty to allow such legal extortion to continue is the result of social conditioning and lack of education resulting in ignorance, does this common belief therefore make such legal extortion *actually* legitimate, legal, or lawful? Does the fact that the Mafia is large and in charge make routine felonies and racketeering *lawful* just because everybody *believes* that nothing can be done about it? Does everyone therefore believe that there is a *common duty* to submit to the Mafia? In both of these situations, ignorance of the law perpetuates criminal activity because people believe either that the crimes are not actually crimes at all but lawful activity or that nothing can be done about the situation, or both. What a paradox!

The Difference between Taxpayers and Non-Taxpayers

Based on the just described concept of the continuation of unrelenting crime as a consequence of prevalent ignorance, the underlying theme of this book is now identifiable. There is a recognizable distinction between two groups of people. The first group is the great majority of "taxpayers" who remain ignorant of the law. Accordingly, they continue acting as though they are *actually* taxpayers required by law to pay federal income, capital gains, social security, Medicare, and self-employment taxes and, accordingly, they continue generating presumptive evidence that they are *actually* required by law to pay such taxes. The second group is the relative minority of individuals who make efforts to come to know the law and to practice it continually. Accordingly, they act so as not to create even the *appearance* of being required to pay federal income, capital gains, social security, Medicare, or self-employment taxes and, accordingly, they lawfully pay no such taxes. Due to the momentum of society's prevailing ignorance, some of those of the latter group conscientiously wish not to be simply swept along with the inexorable flow of such ignorance. Such individuals spend extra time and money *securing* the status of "non-taxpayers" in order to prevent any presumptive evidence from ever being generated to the contrary and thus possibly raising a suspicion as to tax liability. They thus eliminate the likelihood—even the remote *possibility*—that they will ever again be victims of the paradox of legal extortion.

The Facts

The simple facts are as follows. First, although the IRS reports 130,423,626 individual income tax returns filed for 2003 [http://www.irs.gov/pub/irs-soi/03in11si.xls—latest statistical table data available], there is no legislated, statutory liability for federal income or capital gains or social security or Medicare or self-employment taxes as these are commonly understood. This means that Congress has passed no law that makes anyone required to pay—voluntarily or otherwise—federal income or capital gains or social security or Medicare or self-employment taxes to the IRS or any US government agency. Second, despite the first fact, due to social conditioning and lack of actual education in the language of the law, nearly everyone believes that everyone must pay federal income, capital gains, social security, Medicare, and self-employment taxes. Accordingly, even after discovering the truth many people feel social pressure to continue paying a "fair share" of taxes they are not lawfully obligated to pay. Third, becoming and remaining lawfully free of federal income, capital gains, social security, Medicare, and self-employment taxes requires the pursuit of either or both of two options. The first option involves terminating any and all voluntary withholding agreements, terminating the generation of presumptive evidence of tax liability where none exists, and operating according to the Constitutional right to contract. The second option involves generating income under a name that by law never pays or generates either liability or presumptive evidence of liability for federal income, capital gains, social security, Medicare, or self-employment taxes for itself or for anyone else and operating according to the Constitutional right to contract.

After reading this book and conducting recommended research, one will begin to understand how not to be a victim of the paradox of legal extortion by recognizing that:

- the Internal Revenue Service has never been authorized either by the Secretary of the Treasury of the US or by the US Congress to force people who have no statutory liability for federal income or capital gains or social security or Medicare or self-employment taxes to pay such taxes by collection at the source of income or by estimated payments or by liens and levies;

- countless statutes and Department of the Treasury, Internal Revenue Service publications discuss *imposition* and *calculation* of federal income and capital gains taxes, but neither the Internal Revenue Code (IRC) nor the Code of Federal Regulations (CFR) actually establishes *liability* for individual federal income or capital gains or social security or Medicare or self-employment taxes; and

- filing a statement or return with the Department of the Treasury, Internal Revenue Service is required by law only for an individual who has a statutory *liability* for federal income or capital gains or self-employment taxes.

What a paradox! If these things are true, why are so many people *paying* federal income, capital gains, social security, Medicare, and self-employment taxes? The reason is legal extortion based on prevalent ignorance of the law—on the part of both perpetrator and victim—"that's just the way it is."

I: The Paradox of Legal Extortion

Appendix II: The US Constitution

The original Constitution for the United States of America outlines and provides the basis for the system of government and law in this country. Knowing what the Constitution actually says helps one enjoy the rights and protections it offers and also prevent others from encroaching on those rights and protections.

The US Government's Power to Tax

The Constitution for the United States of America states at Article I, Section 9:

> No Capitation, or other direct, Tax shall be laid, unless in Proportion to the Census or enumeration herein before directed to be taken. [See the fourth paragraph at http://deoxy.org/law/consti.htm#1.9.]

In other words, the Constitution authorizes no taxation except that which is proportional or *per capita* ("by head," Merriam-Webster). Such a tax would be the same dollar amount per person. Consider an example with a tax of five dollars and a family of five. Each of the parents (working or not) would pay five dollars, the working teen would pay five dollars, the preteen would pay five dollars, and the infant would pay five dollars—no shelters, no deductions, no phase-outs, and no refunds or refundable credits.

Industrialist and lecturer Vivien Kellems (1896-1975) is quoted as writing quite accurately in 1952, "Since a capitation means a tax of the same amount for every person, this provision makes doubly sure that all federal taxes must be at the same uniform rate for everybody. This limitation that direct taxes be levied by the Federal Government must be in proportion to a census and apportioned among the States in accordance with numbers, is the only provision in the Constitution that is stated twice" [http://www.devvy.com/notax.html]. Article I, Section 9, above, is actually the second time this provision is stated. The first is at Article I, Section 8:

> The Congress shall have Power To lay and collect Taxes, Duties, Imposts and Excises, to pay the Debts and provide for the common Defence and general Welfare of the United States; but all Duties, Imposts and Excises shall be uniform throughout the United States. [See the first paragraph at http://deoxy.org/law/consti.htm#1.8.]

The current, graduated-rate (10-35%) federal income tax is neither proportional nor assessed *per capita,* since each person pays a different *amount* of tax. Neither is an income-based "flat tax," for the same reason. Neither is a purchase-based "national sales tax," for the same reason. The only "flat tax" that would be Constitutional would be a tax that is a flat *dollar amount* that is the same for every human, not a flat tax *percentage* that results in *varying dollar amounts* based on income or purchases.

Interestingly, the so-called Income Tax Amendment gave no new power of taxation to the US Government except to disregard the source of *corporate* income:

¹⁶ᵗʰAMENDMENT XVI

Passed by Congress July 2, 1909. Ratified February 3, 1913.
Note: *Article I, section 9, of the Constitution was modified by amendment 16.*
The Congress shall have power to lay and collect taxes on incomes, from whatever source derived, without apportionment among the several States, and without regard to any census or enumeration. [See http://deoxy.org/law/consti.htm#b16.]

An undying debate exists between Bill Benson, who has proved exhaustively and incontrovertibly that this amendment was never *actually* ratified (see http://www.thelawthatneverwas.com/), and those who would profit by the belief that it completely overturned the original Article I, section 9. Whether or not the Sixteenth Amendment was actually ratified, current US law contains no statute that establishes individual *liability* for federal income tax, only *imposition* of such tax.

According to the courts, *a statutory* **liability** *for taxation must be established in* **addition** *to statutory* **imposition** *of such taxation.*

"Taxes should be exacted only from persons upon whom a tax liability is imposed by some statute." The 2ⁿᵈ Circuit in *Botta v. Scanlon* 288 F.2d 504 (1961)

"Liability for taxation must clearly appear from statute imposing tax." *Higley v. Commissioner*, 69 F.2d 160

Without *liability for* federal income tax, one cannot be lawfully compelled to *pay* federal income tax!

"The revenue laws are a code or system in regulation of tax assessment and collection. They relate to taxpayers, and not to nontaxpayers. The latter are without their scope. No procedure is prescribed for nontaxpayers, and no attempt is made to annul any of their rights and remedies in due course of law. With them Congress does not assume to deal, and they are neither of the subject nor of the object of the revenue laws." Economy Plumbing and Heating Co. v. United States, 470 F. 2d 585 (1972)

When there is uncertainty as to the intent of statutes:

"In the interpretation of statutes levying taxes it is the established rule not to extend their provisions, by implication, beyond the clear import of the language used, or to enlarge their operations so as to embrace matters not specifically pointed out. In case of doubt they are construed most strongly against the government, and in favor of the citizen." Supreme Court - Gould v. Gould 245 U.S. 151 (1917); United States v.

Wigglesworth, 2 Story, 369, Fed. Cas. No. 16, 690; American Net & Twine Co. v. Worthington, 141 U.S. 468, 474, 12 S. Sup. Ct. 55; Benziger v. United States, 192 U.S. 38, 55, 24 S. Sup. Ct. 189.

In other words, a requirement that is not specifically stated in statutes of law is not a requirement at all. The advantages of any uncertainty about this fact defaults to the people, the disadvantages to the government.

The People's Right to Contract

While the Constitution does not expressly state a right regarding contracts, numerous courts have repeatedly referred to the Constitutional "right to contract" which cannot be abrogated. The Bill of Rights begins and specifically prevents the denial and disparagement of rights as follows:

> *Congress OF THE United States*
> *begun and held at the City of New-York, on* **Wednesday the Fourth of March, one thousand seven hundred and eighty nine**.
> *THE Conventions of a number of the States having at the time of their adopting the Constitution, expressed a desire, in order to prevent misconstruction or abuse of its powers, that further declaratory and restrictive clauses should be added: And as extending the ground of public confidence in the Government, will best insure the beneficent ends of its institution*
> *RESOLVED by the Senate and House of Representatives of the United States of America, in Congress assembled, two thirds of both Houses concurring, that the following Articles be proposed to the Legislatures of the several States, as Amendments to the Constitution of the United States, all or any of which Articles, when ratified by three fourths of the said Legislatures, to be valid to all intents and purposes, as part of the said Constitution; viz.:*
> *ARTICLES in addition to, and Amendment of the Constitution of the United States of America, proposed by Congress, and ratified by the Legislatures of the several States, pursuant to the* fifth Article *of the original Constitution.*
>
> ...
>
>
> [9th]Amendment IX
> The enumeration in the Constitution, of certain rights, shall not be construed to deny or disparage others retained by the people. [See
> http://deoxy.org/law/consti.htm#bpre and
> http://deoxy.org/law/consti.htm#b9.]

The *right to contract,* neither specifically included in nor specifically excluded from the language of the Constitution, is therefore protected. The *obligation of contracts* is specifically included in the language of the Constitution at Article I, Section 10, which prohibits legislation that would impair this obligation:

> No State shall enter into any Treaty, Alliance, or Confederation; grant Letters of Marque and Reprisal; coin Money; emit Bills of Credit; make any Thing but gold and silver Coin a Tender in Payment of Debts; pass any Bill of Attainder, ex post facto law, or Law impairing the Obligation of Contracts, or grant any Title of Nobility. [See the first paragraph at http://deoxy.org/law/consti.htm#1.10.]

The *power to contract* is specifically included in the language of the US Supreme Court:

> "The individual may stand upon his constitutional rights as a Citizen. He is entitled to carry on his private business in his own way. His power to contract is unlimited.'—United States Supreme Court, *Hale v. Henkle,* 201 US 43.

The US Constitution may be accessed by visiting http://deoxy.org/law/consti.htm.

II: The US Constitution

Appendix III: The Internal Revenue Code

The United States Code (USC) is made up of fifty titles containing the codification of the statutes of law legislated by the US Congress. Title 26, Internal Revenue Code (IRC), is made up of eleven subtitles. The subtitles containing statutes (called "sections" or "§§") discussed in this book are Subtitle A – Income Taxes, Subtitle C – Employment Taxes, Subtitle E – Alcohol, Tobacco, and Certain Other Excise Taxes, and Subtitle F – Procedure and Administration.

Although Title 26 United States Code (Internal Revenue Code), Subtitle A, Chapter 1, Subchapter A is entitled "Determination of Tax Liability," and subsections (a) through (h) of section (§) 1 of that subchapter explain *imposition* of individual income and capital gains taxes, there is *no* IRC section that establishes *liability* for individual income or capital gains taxes (according to IRC, Subtitle F, Chapter 80, Subchapter A, § 7806, the subchapter title "Determination of Tax Liability" has no "legal effect"— http://caselaw.lp.findlaw.com/casecode/uscodes/26/subtitles/f/chapters/80/subchapters/a/sections/section_7806.html). According to the Code of Federal Regulations (CFR), if a person is not a *foreign* taxpayer or a *corporation* and has no *foreign* earned or *possessions* income, the federal income tax is not even *imposed* on that person (see Appendix VI and Appendix E). *According to the courts, statutory liability must exist before a person may be lawfully compelled to pay federal income tax or capital gains tax or social security tax or Medicare tax or self-employment tax:*

> "Liability for taxation must clearly appear from statute imposing tax."
> *Higley v. Commissioner*, 69 F.2d 160

> "Taxes should be exacted only from persons upon whom a tax liability is imposed by some statute." The 2nd Circuit in *Botta v. Scanlon* 288 F.2d 504 (1961)

Income Tax Withholding

However, any person acting as an agent for the government and collecting any tax from another person is liable to the government for the amount of tax so collected. If a person *withholds* a tax from another person, he is made *liable* for such withheld tax:

United States Code
- TITLE 26 - INTERNAL REVENUE CODE
  - SUBTITLE A - INCOME TAXES
    - CHAPTER 3 - WITHHOLDING OF TAX ON NONRESIDENT ALIENS AND FOREIGN CORPORATIONS
      - SUBCHAPTER B - APPLICATION OF WITHHOLDING PROVISIONS

Section 1461. Liability for withheld tax

Every person required to deduct and withhold any tax under this chapter is hereby made *liable* for such tax and is hereby indemnified against the claims and demands of any person for the amount of any payments made in accordance with the provisions of this chapter [emphasis added— http://caselaw.lp.findlaw.com/casecode/uscodes/26/subtitles/a/chapters/3/ subchapters/b/sections/section_1461.html].

Section 1461 is the only case in which liability is established in relation to income tax under Subtitle A – Income Taxes. Liability is established in relation to income tax under Subtitle C – Employment Taxes in Chapter 24 – Collection of Income Tax at Source on Wages for the same reason it is established at § 1461 under Subtitle A:

United States Code
- TITLE 26 - INTERNAL REVENUE CODE
  - SUBTITLE C - EMPLOYMENT TAXES
    - CHAPTER 24 - COLLECTION OF INCOME TAX AT SOURCE ON WAGES

Section 3402. Income tax collected at source

(a) Requirement of withholding
 (1) In general
  Except as otherwise provided in this section, every employer making payment of wages shall deduct and withhold upon such wages a tax determined in accordance with tables or computational procedures prescribed by the Secretary…
[http://caselaw.lp.findlaw.com/casecode/uscodes/26/subtitles/c/chapters/ 24/sections/section_3402.html].

Section 3403. Liability for tax

The employer shall be *liable* for the payment of the tax required to be deducted and withheld under this chapter, and shall not be liable to any person for the amount of any such payment [emphasis added— http://caselaw.lp.findlaw.com/casecode/uscodes/26/subtitles/c/chapters/24 /sections/section_3403.html].

Again, if a person *withholds* a tax from another person—in this case, "employment taxes" or taxes withheld from employment earnings—he is made *liable* for such withheld tax.

It must be noted that *the language of these two statutes does not automatically impose a duty on the employer to withhold such taxes.* Note § 3402(n):

(n) Employees incurring no income tax liability

Notwithstanding any other provision of this section, an employer shall not be required to deduct and withhold any tax under this chapter upon a payment of wages to an employee if there is in effect with respect to such payment a withholding exemption certificate (in such form and containing such other information as the Secretary may prescribe) furnished to the employer by the employee certifying that the employee -

(1) incurred no liability for income tax imposed under subtitle A for his preceding taxable year, and

(2) anticipates that he will incur no liability for income tax imposed under subtitle A for his current taxable year....

Even if the individual has not certified a lack of liability, it is noteworthy that "wages" are neither on the list in Gross Income Defined (IRC § 61) nor on the list in Part II Items Specifically *Included* in Gross Income (IRC §§ 72-90) nor on the list in Part III Items Specifically *Excluded* from Gross Income (IRC §§ 101-140) (see Appendix D). These lists are part of subchapter B:

<u>United States Code</u>
- <u>TITLE 26 - INTERNAL REVENUE CODE</u>
  - <u>SUBTITLE A - INCOME TAXES</u>
    - <u>CHAPTER 1 - NORMAL TAXES AND SURTAXES</u>
      - <u>SUBCHAPTER B - COMPUTATION OF TAXABLE INCOME</u>
        - <u>Part I.</u> Definition Of Gross Income, Adjusted Gross Income, Taxable Income, Etc.
        - <u>Part II.</u> Items Specifically Included In Gross Income
        - <u>Part III.</u> Items Specifically Excluded From Gross Income

[http://caselaw.lp.findlaw.com/casecode/uscodes/26/subtitles/a/chapters/1/subchapters/b/toc.html]

Furthermore, "wages" are generally not subject to income tax withholding since the definition of "employee" encompasses only a certain few individuals:

<u>United States Code</u>
- <u>TITLE 26 - INTERNAL REVENUE CODE</u>
  - <u>SUBTITLE C - EMPLOYMENT TAXES</u>
    - <u>CHAPTER 24 - COLLECTION OF INCOME TAX AT SOURCE ON WAGES</u>

Section 3401. Definitions

(a) Wages
  For purposes of this chapter, the term "wages" means all remuneration (other than fees paid to a public official) for services performed by an employee for his employer, including the cash value of all remuneration (including benefits) paid in any medium other than cash....
(c) Employee
  For purposes of this chapter, the term "employee" includes an officer, employee, or elected official of the United States, a State, or any political subdivision thereof, or the District of Columbia, or any agency or instrumentality of any one or more of the foregoing. The term "employee" also includes an officer of a corporation...
[http://caselaw.lp.findlaw.com/casecode/uscodes/26/subtitles/c/chapters/24/sections/section_3401.html].

Recall from the Definitions at the beginning of the book that "When 'INCLUDE' or 'INCLUDING' is used it expands to take in all of the items stipulated or listed, but is then limited to them" and that "'Including' within statute is interpreted as a word of enlargement or of illustrative application as well as a word of limitation" [Black's Law Dictionary] so that *only what is expressly* listed *as included is included.*

So who is actually "required to deduct and withhold any tax under this chapter"? A withholding requirement is imposed related to the earnings of nonresident aliens:

United States Code
- TITLE 26 - INTERNAL REVENUE CODE
  - SUBTITLE A - INCOME TAXES
    - CHAPTER 3 - WITHHOLDING OF TAX ON NONRESIDENT ALIENS AND FOREIGN CORPORATIONS
      - SUBCHAPTER A - NONRESIDENT ALIENS AND FOREIGN CORPORATIONS

Section 1441. Withholding of tax on nonresident aliens

(a) General rule
  Except as otherwise provided in subsection (c), all persons, in whatever capacity acting (including lessees or mortgagors of real or personal property, fiduciaries, employers, and all officers and employees of the United States) having the control, receipt, custody, disposal, or payment of any of the items of income specified in subsection (b) (to the extent that any of such items constitutes gross income from sources within the United States), of any nonresident alien individual or of any foreign partnership shall (except as otherwise provided in regulations prescribed by the Secretary under section 874) deduct and withhold from such items a tax

equal to 30 percent thereof, except that in the case of any item of income specified in the second sentence of subsection (b), the tax shall be equal to 14 percent of such item.

(b) Income items

The items of income referred to in subsection (a) are interest (other than original issue discount as defined in section 1273), dividends, rent, salaries, wages, premiums, annuities, compensations, remunerations, emoluments, or other fixed or determinable annual or periodical gains, profits, and income, gains described in section 631(b) or (c), amounts subject to tax under section 871(a)(1)(C), gains subject to tax under section 871(a)(1)(D), and gains on transfers described in section 1235 made on or before October 4, 1966. The items of income referred to in subsection (a) from which tax shall be deducted and withheld at the rate of 14 percent are amounts which are received by a nonresident alien individual who is temporarily present in the United States as a nonimmigrant ....

This section appears to require a tax only from nonresident aliens, defined as:

United States Code
- TITLE 26 - INTERNAL REVENUE CODE
  - SUBTITLE F - PROCEDURE AND ADMINISTRATION
    - CHAPTER 79 - DEFINITIONS

Section 7701. Definitions

(b)(1)(B) Nonresident alien
An individual is a nonresident alien if such individual is neither a citizen of the United States nor a resident of the United States ...
[http://caselaw.lp.findlaw.com/casecode/uscodes/26/subtitles/f/chapters/79/sections/section_7701.html].

However, it has been determined that:

The laws of Congress in respect to those matters do not extend into the territorial limits of the states, but have force only in the District of Columbia, and other places that are within the exclusive jurisdiction of the national government. Caha v. United States, 152 U.S. 211, 215, 14 S. Ct. 513 (1894)

Accordingly, the effect of the definition at IRC § 7701(b)(1)(B) is that "An individual is a nonresident alien if such individual is neither [exclusively] a citizen of the United States nor [exclusively] a resident of the United States," that is, neither a citizen nor a resident of any other jurisdiction, such as a state or county or parish or city or township. Furthermore, nonresident aliens living outside "places that are within the exclusive jurisdiction of the national government" (such as Washington D.C.) are not subject to withholding under § 1441.

Income Tax Liability

The CFR lists seventeen specific sources of taxable income in § 1.861-8 (see Appendix VI and Appendix E). Sixteen of these specific sources are foreign and/or corporate in nature. Only one of them is domestic, "effectively connected taxable income," defined as:

> (iv) Effectively connected taxable income. Nonresident alien individuals and foreign corporations engaged in trade or business within the United States … [Appendix VI, page 212, Appendix E, page 298, and http://a257.g.akamaitech.net/7/257/2422/01apr20051500/edocket.access. gpo.gov/cfr_2005/aprqtr/26cfr1.861-8.htm].

By definition of the IRC, "trade or business" does not usually extend beyond the purview of a public office:

Section 7701. Definitions

> (a)(26) Trade or business The term "trade or business" includes [ONLY] the performance of the functions of a public office [http://caselaw.lp.findlaw.com/casecode/uscodes/26/subtitles/f/chapters/79 /sections/section_7701.html].

However, although section 7701 definitions are applicable throughout the title, that is, the entire Internal Revenue Code [paragraph (a)], definition (a)(26) is superseded by § 864 in the case of foreign income, nonresident aliens, and foreign corporations:

United States Code
- TITLE 26 - INTERNAL REVENUE CODE
  - SUBTITLE A - INCOME TAXES
    - CHAPTER 1 - NORMAL TAXES AND SURTAXES
      - SUBCHAPTER N - TAX BASED ON INCOME FROM SOURCES WITHIN OR WITHOUT THE UNITED STATES
        - PART I - SOURCE RULES AND OTHER GENERAL RULES RELATING TO FOREIGN INCOME

Section 864. Definitions and special rules

(a) Produced
   For purposes of this part, the term "produced" includes created, fabricated, manufactured, extracted, processed, cured, or aged.

III: The Internal Revenue Code

(b) Trade or business within the United States

For purposes of this part, part II, and chapter 3, the term "trade or business within the United States" includes the performance of personal services within the United States at any time within the taxable year ....

(c) Effectively connected income, etc.

(1) General rule

For purposes of this title -

(A) In the case of a nonresident alien individual or a foreign corporation engaged in trade or business within the United States during the taxable year, the rules set forth in paragraphs (2), (3), (4), (6), and (7) shall apply in determining the income, gain, or loss which shall be treated as effectively connected with the conduct of a trade or business within the United States.

(B) Except as provided in paragraph (6) or (7) or in section 871(d) or sections 882(d) and (e), in the case of a nonresident alien individual or a foreign corporation not engaged in trade or business within the United States during the taxable year, no income, gain, or loss shall be treated as effectively connected with the conduct of a trade or business within the United States.

(2) Periodical, etc., income from sources within United States - factors

In determining whether income from sources within the United States of the types described in section 871(a)(1), section 871(h), section 881(a), or section 881(c), or whether gain or loss from sources within the United States from the sale or exchange of capital assets, is effectively connected with the conduct of a trade or business within the United States, the factors taken into account shall include whether -

(A) the income, gain, or loss is derived from assets used in or held for use in the conduct of such trade or business, or

(B) the activities of such trade or business were a material factor in the realization of the income, gain, or loss.

In determining whether an asset is used in or held for use in the conduct of such trade or business or whether the activities of such trade or business were a material factor in realizing an item of income, gain, or loss, due regard shall be given to whether or not such asset or such income, gain, or loss was accounted for through such trade or business.

(3) Other income from sources within United States

All income, gain, or loss from sources within the United States (other than income, gain, or loss to which paragraph (2) applies) shall be treated as effectively connected with the conduct of a trade or business within the United States.

(4) Income from sources without United States

(A) Except as provided in subparagraphs (B) and (C), no income, gain, or loss from sources without the United States shall be treated as effectively connected with the conduct of a trade or business within the United States.

III: The Internal Revenue Code

(B) Income, gain, or loss from sources without the United States shall be treated as effectively connected with the conduct of a trade or business within the United States by a nonresident alien individual or a foreign corporation if such person has an office or other fixed place of business within the United States to which such income, gain, or loss is attributable and such income, gain, or loss - (i) consists of rents or royalties for the use of or for the privilege of using intangible property described in section 862(a)(4) derived in the active conduct of such trade or business; (ii) consists of dividends or interest, and either is derived in the active conduct of a banking, financing, or similar business within the United States or is received by a corporation the principal business of which is trading in stocks or securities for its own account; or (iii) is derived from the sale or exchange (outside the United States) through such office or other fixed place of business of personal property described in section 1221(a)(1)…
[http://caselaw.lp.findlaw.com/casecode/uscodes/26/subtitles/a/chapters/1/subchapters/n/parts/i/sections/section_864.html].

The pertinent parts of this extremely lengthy definition are that personal services must be performed within the exclusive jurisdiction of the United States, that income must be from sources within the exclusive jurisdiction of the United States, and that an office must be possessed within the exclusive jurisdiction of the United States to generate income from sources without the exclusive jurisdiction of the United States. The definition expressly states that, if these conditions are not met, "no income, gain, or loss shall be treated as effectively connected with the conduct of a trade or business within the United States" and "no income, gain, or loss from sources without the United States shall be treated as effectively connected with the conduct of a trade or business within the United States." By definition of the CFR, then, the income of nonresident aliens is not taxable income unless it falls within these definitions of IRC § 864.

The IRC specifically states that the income of nonresident aliens does not constitute gross income unless it is derived from "within the exclusive jurisdiction of the national government":

> United States Code
> - TITLE 26 - INTERNAL REVENUE CODE
>   - SUBTITLE A - INCOME TAXES
>   - CHAPTER 1 - NORMAL TAXES AND SURTAXES
>   - SUBCHAPTER N - TAX BASED ON INCOME FROM SOURCES WITHIN OR WITHOUT THE UNITED STATES
>   - PART II - NONRESIDENT ALIENS AND FOREIGN CORPORATIONS
>   - SUBPART A - NONRESIDENT ALIEN INDIVIDUALS

III: The Internal Revenue Code

Section 872. Gross income

(a) General rule
   In the case of a nonresident alien individual, except where the context clearly indicates otherwise, gross income includes only -
   (1) gross income which is derived from sources within the United States and which is not effectively connected with the conduct of a trade or business within the United States, and
   (2) gross income which is effectively connected with the conduct of a trade or business within the United States ...
   [http://caselaw.lp.findlaw.com/casecode/uscodes/26/subtitles/a/chapters/ 1/subchapters/n/parts/ii/subparts/a/sections/section_872.html].

The following letter reveals the parallel thinking of IRS personnel:

> This is in response to your Privacy Act request dated December 12, 1995. The Internal Revenue Code is not positive law, it is special law. It applies to specific persons in the United States who choose to make themselves subject to the requirements of the special laws in the Internal Revenue Code by entering into an employment agreement within the U. S. Government.
>
> The law is that income from sources not effectively connected with the conduct of a trade or business within the U. S. Government is not subject to any tax under subtitle "A" of the Internal Revenue Code.
>
> This concludes our response to your request.
>
> Sincerely yours,
Cynthia J. Mills
Disclosure Officer

[*IRS, Income Tax & The Law: The Fraudulent Fleecing of America* by Dan Shaw on DVD, 2004]

By IRC definition and disclosure officer declaration, then, income that is not derived from the "performance of the functions of a public office" or the "performance of personal services" "within the exclusive jurisdiction of" "the U. S. Government" is not subject to any tax under subtitle "A" [Income Taxes] of the Internal Revenue Code. In other words, unless an individual either holds a US public office or performs personal services within the exclusive jurisdiction of the US Government and does not also have either citizenship or residency in another jurisdiction, he has no income tax *imposition*— but neither the individual who either holds a US public office or performs personal services within the exclusive jurisdiction of the US Government nor the one who does not has a statutory income tax *liability*.

Conclusions on Wages and Non-Employee Compensation

Despite popular belief to the contrary, neither "wages" nor "non-employee compensation" constitutes "gross income" that becomes "taxable income" after "deductions" (see Appendix D). Although Department of the Treasury - Internal Revenue Service Form W-2, Wage and Tax Statement, issued subsequent to the submission of Form W-4, creates the *appearance* of wages and presumptive evidence of taxable income, by definition most so-called "wages" are not actually "wages" that are in fact taxable income. Although Department of the Treasury - Internal Revenue Service Form 1099-MISC, Miscellaneous Income, specifically box 7, Nonemployee compensation, issued subsequent to the submission of Form W-9 or Form I-9, creates the *appearance* of self-employment income and presumptive evidence of taxable income, by one definition (see Appendix VI and Appendix E) such "self-employment income" is not actually "self-employment income" that is in fact "taxable income." Whether or not these items are considered "taxable income," the fact remains that no statutory liability exists requiring anyone to pay federal income, social security, Medicare, or self-employment taxes on these items.

Conclusions on Residents and Nonresident Aliens

The only requirements to withhold income taxes at the source of wages are related to the earnings of certain nonresident aliens who perform either the functions of a public office or personal services within the exclusive jurisdiction of the US government, although nonresident aliens are specifically not required to pay either federal income tax or self-employment tax (see Appendix VI and Appendix E). Residents may be referred to as "nontaxpayers" and as such are likewise never subject to either federal income tax or capital gains tax or self-employment tax. No person is required to pay federal income tax or capital gains tax or self-employment tax without statutory liability. Even nonresident aliens cannot be compelled to pay either of these taxes without statutory liability. Legally speaking, by definition most people that live in the fifty states are actually nonresident aliens since they are neither citizens nor residents exclusively of the United States (Definitions 1, 5 & 6). Whether one considers oneself legally defined as a resident or as a nonresident alien, one is not required by law to pay federal income tax or capital gains tax or social security tax or Medicare tax or self-employment tax (see Appendix D for additional information on nonresident aliens).

Social Security and Medicare Taxes

Based on definitions of "wages" and "employee" that differ from those of § 3401 (see Appendix D), IRC §§ 3101, 3102 and 3509 require "employers" of "employees" to withhold social security and Medicare taxes from "wages" or be penalized for failure to do so. However, § 3503 expressly provides for a refund of erroneous payments for which no liability exists:

> United States Code
> - TITLE 26 - INTERNAL REVENUE CODE
>   - SUBTITLE C - EMPLOYMENT TAXES
>   - CHAPTER 25 - GENERAL PROVISIONS RELATING TO EMPLOYMENT TAXES

Section 3503. Erroneous payments

Any tax paid under chapter 21 or 22 by a taxpayer with respect to any period with respect to which he is not liable to tax under such chapter shall be credited against the tax, if any, imposed by such other chapter upon the taxpayer, and the balance, if any, shall be refunded [http://caselaw.lp.findlaw.com/casecode/uscodes/26/subtitles/c/chapters/25/sections/section_3503.html].

Nevertheless, no procedure exists for requesting and generating a refund of social security or Medicare taxes.

Authority within the Department of the Treasury

The authority of the Secretary of the Department of the Treasury is outlined in § 7801:

United States Code
- TITLE 26 - INTERNAL REVENUE CODE
  - SUBTITLE F - PROCEDURE AND ADMINISTRATION
    - CHAPTER 80 - GENERAL RULES
      - SUBCHAPTER A - APPLICATION OF INTERNAL REVENUE LAWS

Section 7801. Authority of Department of the Treasury

(a) Powers and duties of Secretary
Except as otherwise expressly provided by law, the administration and enforcement of this title shall be performed by or under the supervision of the Secretary of the Treasury… [http://caselaw.lp.findlaw.com/casecode/uscodes/26/subtitles/f/chapters/80/subchapters/a/sections/section_7801.html].

The establishment of the Internal Revenue Service Oversight Board and its general and specific responsibilities are outlined in § 7802:

United States Code
- TITLE 26 - INTERNAL REVENUE CODE
  - SUBTITLE F - PROCEDURE AND ADMINISTRATION
    - CHAPTER 80 - GENERAL RULES
      - SUBCHAPTER A - APPLICATION OF INTERNAL REVENUE LAWS

Section 7802. Internal Revenue Service Oversight Board

(a) Establishment

There is established within the Department of the Treasury the Internal Revenue Service Oversight Board (hereafter in this subchapter referred to as the "Oversight Board").

…

(c) General responsibilities

(1) Oversight

(A) In general

The Oversight Board shall oversee the Internal Revenue Service in its administration, management, conduct, direction, and supervision of the execution and application of the internal revenue laws or related statutes and tax conventions to which the United States is a party.

(B) Mission of IRS

As part of its oversight functions described in subparagraph (A), the Oversight Board shall ensure that the organization and operation of the Internal Revenue Service allows it to carry out its mission.

(C) Confidentiality

The Oversight Board shall ensure that appropriate confidentiality is maintained in the exercise of its duties.

(2) Exceptions

The Oversight Board shall have no responsibilities or authority with respect to -

(A) the development and formulation of Federal tax policy relating to existing or proposed internal revenue laws, related statutes, and tax conventions,

(B) specific law enforcement activities of the Internal Revenue Service, including specific compliance activities such as examinations, collection activities, and criminal investigations,

(C) specific procurement activities of the Internal Revenue Service, or

(D) except as provided in subsection (d)(3), specific personnel actions.

(d) Specific responsibilities

The Oversight Board shall have the following specific responsibilities:

…

(5) Taxpayer protection

To ensure the proper treatment of taxpayers by the employees of the Internal Revenue Service…

[http://caselaw.lp.findlaw.com/casecode/uscodes/26/subtitles/f/chapters/80/subchapters/a/sections/section_7802.html].

Although the Internal Revenue Service itself is not also statutorily established, the Internal Revenue Service Oversight Board is charged with oversight of IRS administration, management, conduct, direction, and supervision of the execution and application of the internal revenue laws or related statutes and tax conventions as well as ensuring that the organization and operation of the IRS allows it to carry out its mission. Although the Oversight Board is not responsible for specific law enforcement or compliance activities such as examinations, collection activities, and criminal investigations, the Board is specifically responsible for ensuring the proper treatment of taxpayers by IRS employees.

The authority of the Commissioner of Internal Revenue, Chief Counsel for the IRS, and Office of the Taxpayer Advocate as well as additional duties of the Treasury Inspector General for Tax Administration are outlined in § 7803:

> United States Code
> - TITLE 26 - INTERNAL REVENUE CODE
>   - SUBTITLE F - PROCEDURE AND ADMINISTRATION
>   - CHAPTER 80 - GENERAL RULES
>   - SUBCHAPTER A - APPLICATION OF INTERNAL REVENUE LAWS

Section 7803. Commissioner of Internal Revenue; other officials

(a) Commissioner of Internal Revenue
  (1) Appointment
  (A) In general
    There shall be in the Department of the Treasury a Commissioner of Internal Revenue who shall be appointed by the President, by and with the advice and consent of the Senate, to a 5-year term. Such appointment shall be made from individuals who, among other qualifications, have a demonstrated ability in management.

  ...
  (2) Duties
    The Commissioner shall have such duties and powers as the Secretary may prescribe, including the power to -
    (A) administer, manage, conduct, direct, and supervise the execution and application of the internal revenue laws or related statutes and tax conventions to which the United States is a party; and
    (B) recommend to the President a candidate for appointment as Chief Counsel for the Internal Revenue Service when a vacancy occurs, and recommend to the President the removal of such Chief Counsel.
If the Secretary determines not to delegate a power specified in subparagraph (A) or (B), such determination may not take effect until 30 days after the Secretary notifies the Committees on Ways and Means, Government Reform and Oversight, and Appropriations of the House of Representatives and the Committees on Finance, Governmental Affairs, and Appropriations of the Senate.

  ...

(b) Chief Counsel for the Internal Revenue Service
(1) Appointment
There shall be in the Department of the Treasury a Chief Counsel for the Internal Revenue Service who shall be appointed by the President, by and with the consent of the Senate.
(2) Duties
The Chief Counsel shall be the chief law officer for the Internal Revenue Service and shall perform such duties as may be prescribed by the Secretary, including the duty -
(A) to be legal advisor to the Commissioner and the Commissioner's officers and employees;
(B) to furnish legal opinions for the preparation and review of rulings and memoranda of technical advice;
(C) to prepare, review, and assist in the preparation of proposed legislation, treaties, regulations, and Executive orders relating to laws which affect the Internal Revenue Service;
(D) to represent the Commissioner in cases before the Tax Court; and
(E) to determine which civil actions should be litigated under the laws relating to the Internal Revenue Service and prepare recommendations for the Department of Justice regarding the commencement of such actions.
If the Secretary determines not to delegate a power specified in subparagraph (A), (B), (C), (D), or (E), such determination may not take effect until 30 days after the Secretary notifies the Committees on Ways and Means, Government Reform and Oversight, and Appropriations of the House of Representatives and the Committees on Finance, Governmental Affairs, and Appropriations of the Senate.
...
(c) Office of the Taxpayer Advocate
(1) Establishment
(A) In general
There is established in the Internal Revenue Service an office to be known as the "Office of the Taxpayer Advocate".
(B) National Taxpayer Advocate
(i) In general
The Office of the Taxpayer Advocate shall be under the supervision and direction of an official to be known as the "National Taxpayer Advocate"....
(ii) Appointment
The National Taxpayer Advocate shall be appointed by the Secretary of the Treasury after consultation with the Commissioner of Internal Revenue and the Oversight Board ....
(iii) Qualifications
An individual appointed under clause (ii) shall have –
(I) a background in customer service as well as tax law; and
(II) experience in representing individual taxpayers.

III: The Internal Revenue Code

(iv) Restriction on employment
   An individual may be appointed as the National Taxpayer Advocate only if such individual was not an officer or employee of the Internal Revenue Service during the 2-year period ending with such appointment and such individual agrees not to accept any employment with the Internal Revenue Service for at least 5 years after ceasing to be the National Taxpayer Advocate. Service as an officer or employee of the Office of the Taxpayer Advocate shall not be taken into account in applying this clause.

(2) Functions of office
 (A) In general
  It shall be the function of the Office of the Taxpayer Advocate to -
  (i) assist taxpayers in resolving problems with the Internal Revenue Service;
  (ii) identify areas in which taxpayers have problems in dealings with the Internal Revenue Service;
  (iii) to the extent possible, propose changes in the administrative practices of the Internal Revenue Service to mitigate problems identified under clause (ii); and
  (iv) identify potential legislative changes which may be appropriate to mitigate such problems.

    ...

(d) Additional duties of the Treasury Inspector General for Tax Administration
  (1) Annual reporting
   The Treasury Inspector General for Tax Administration shall include in one of the semiannual reports under section 5 of the Inspector General Act of 1978 -
   (A) an evaluation of the compliance of the Internal Revenue Service with -

      ...

   (iii) required procedures under section 6320 upon the filing of a notice of a lien;
   (iv) required procedures under subchapter D of chapter 64 for seizure of property for collection of taxes, including required procedures under section 6330 regarding levies;

      ....

  (2) Semiannual reports
   (A) In general. - The Treasury Inspector General for Tax Administration shall include in each semiannual report under section 5 of the Inspector General Act of 1978 -
    (i) the number of taxpayer complaints during the reporting period;
    (ii) the number of employee misconduct and taxpayer abuse allegations received by the Internal Revenue Service or the Inspector General during the period from taxpayers, Internal Revenue Service employees, and other sources;

(iii) a summary of the status of such complaints and allegations; and
(iv) a summary of the disposition of such complaints and allegations, including the outcome of any Department of Justice action and any monies paid as a settlement of such complaints and allegations.
(B) Clauses (iii) and (iv) of subparagraph (A) shall only apply to complaints and allegations of serious employee misconduct.
(3) Other responsibilities
The Treasury Inspector General for Tax Administration shall -
…
(B) establish and maintain a toll-free telephone number for taxpayers to use to confidentially register complaints of misconduct by Internal Revenue Service employees and incorporate the telephone number in the statement required by section 6227 of the Omnibus Taxpayer Bill of Rights (Internal Revenue Service Publication No. 1) [http://caselaw.lp.findlaw.com/casecode/uscodes/26/subtitles/f/chapters/80/subchapters/a/sections/section_7803.html].

Paragraphs (a)(2) and (b)(2) specify that the authority of both the Commissioner of Internal Revenue and Chief Counsel for the IRS is based on *delegation* by the Secretary of the Treasury. The same paragraphs also provide for *not* delegating authority. Subparagraph (c)(2)(A) specifies the function of the Office of the Taxpayer Advocate to assist taxpayers in resolving problems with the IRS. Clauses (iii) and (iv) of subparagraph (d)(1)(A) specify the requirement of inclusion in one of the Treasury Inspector's semiannual reports an evaluation of IRS compliance with procedures required by §§ 6320 and 6330 regarding liens and levies. Clauses (i) through (iv) of subparagraph (d)(2)(A) specify the requirement of inclusion in each of the Treasury Inspector's semiannual reports the number of taxpayer complaints, the number of employee misconduct and taxpayer abuse allegations, and, as regards "serious" employee misconduct, summaries of both the status and the disposition of such complaints and allegations. Subparagraph (d)(3)(B) requires the Treasury Inspector to provide a toll-free number for confidential registration of complaints of IRS employee misconduct (800/366-4484 (800/877-8339 for TTY/TDD)).

The authority of the Commissioner of Internal Revenue to employ and direct persons, who have come to be known collectively as the Internal Revenue Service, is outlined in § 7804:

United States Code
- TITLE 26 - INTERNAL REVENUE CODE
  - SUBTITLE F - PROCEDURE AND ADMINISTRATION
    - CHAPTER 80 - GENERAL RULES
      - SUBCHAPTER A - APPLICATION OF INTERNAL REVENUE LAWS

Section 7804. Other personnel

(a) Appointment and supervision
  Unless otherwise prescribed by the Secretary, the Commissioner of Internal Revenue is authorized to employ such number of persons as the Commissioner deems proper for the administration and enforcement of the internal revenue laws, and the Commissioner shall issue all necessary directions, instructions, orders, and rules applicable to such persons… [http://caselaw.lp.findlaw.com/casecode/uscodes/26/subtitles/f/chapters/80 /subchapters/a/sections/section_7804.html].

The authority of the Secretary of Treasury to prescribe title enforcement rules and regulations is outlined in § 7805:

United States Code
  • TITLE 26 - INTERNAL REVENUE CODE
      • SUBTITLE F - PROCEDURE AND ADMINISTRATION
          • CHAPTER 80 - GENERAL RULES
              • SUBCHAPTER A - APPLICATION OF INTERNAL REVENUE LAWS

Section 7805. Rules and regulations

(a) Authorization
  Except where such authority is expressly given by this title to any person other than an officer or employee of the Treasury Department, the Secretary shall prescribe all needful rules and regulations for the enforcement of this title, including all rules and regulations as may be necessary by reason of any alteration of law in relation to internal revenue.
  …
(c) Preparation and distribution of regulations, forms, stamps, and other matters
  The Secretary shall prepare and distribute all the instructions, regulations, directions, forms, blanks, stamps, and other matters pertaining to the assessment and collection of internal revenue.
  …
[http://caselaw.lp.findlaw.com/casecode/uscodes/26/subtitles/f/chapters/80 /subchapters/a/sections/section_7805.html].

This statute does not require the Secretary to prepare and distribute instructions on determining whether or not an internal revenue tax liability actually *exists,* only on the assessment and collection of internal revenue.

Statutory Enforcement Authority

The IRC gives specific authority to internal revenue *enforcement* officers:

III: The Internal Revenue Code

United States Code
- TITLE 26 - INTERNAL REVENUE CODE
  - SUBTITLE F - PROCEDURE AND ADMINISTRATION
    - CHAPTER 78 - DISCOVERY OF LIABILITY AND ENFORCEMENT OF TITLE
      - SUBCHAPTER A - EXAMINATION AND INSPECTION

Section 7608. Authority of internal revenue enforcement officers

(a) Enforcement of subtitle E and other laws pertaining to liquor, tobacco, and firearms

…

(b) Enforcement of laws relating to internal revenue other than subtitle E

　(1) Any criminal investigator of the Intelligence Division of the Internal Revenue Service whom the Secretary charges with the duty of enforcing any of the criminal provisions of the internal revenue laws, any other criminal provisions of law relating to internal revenue for the enforcement of which the Secretary is responsible, or any other law for which the Secretary has delegated investigatory authority to the Internal Revenue Service, is, in the performance of his duties, authorized to perform the functions described in paragraph (2).

　(2) The functions authorized under this subsection to be performed by an officer referred to in paragraph (1) are -

　(A) to execute and serve search warrants and arrest warrants, and serve subpoenas and summonses issued under authority of the United States;

　(B) to make arrests without warrant for any offense against the United States relating to the internal revenue laws committed in his presence, or for any felony cognizable under such laws if he has reasonable grounds to believe that the person to be arrested has committed or is committing any such felony; and

　(C) to make seizures of property subject to forfeiture under the internal revenue laws…

[http://caselaw.lp.findlaw.com/casecode/uscodes/26/subtitles/f/chapters/78/subchapters/a/sections/section_7608.html].

Paragraph (b)(1) gives authority for enforcing laws related to income taxes *only* to criminal investigators of the Intelligence Division of the IRS and *only* if the Secretary of the Treasury either specifically *charges* them with the duty of enforcing criminal provisions of law or *delegates* investigatory authority to the Internal Revenue Service. However, since the Internal Revenue Service is not statutorily established, it is impossible for the Secretary to delegate investigatory authority to the Internal Revenue Service. As discussed in § 7804, above, unless otherwise prescribed by the Secretary, the Commissioner of Internal Revenue is authorized to employ and direct persons, who have come to be known collectively as the Internal Revenue Service, to administer and enforce the internal revenue laws. According to Irwin Schiff, the Secretary has never delegated authority to the Commissioner of Internal Revenue, which precludes the Commissioner's ability to re-delegate authority to those who the Commissioner employs and directs (see Appendix G).

Paragraph (b)(2) *further* limits such authority to executing and serving search and arrest warrants, serving subpoenas and summonses issued under authority of the US, making arrests without warrant for internal revenue law violations either committed in their presence or believed to be committed, and making forfeitable property seizures. Criminal investigators must *know* that actions committed in their presence are *actually* internal revenue law *violations*. They must also have *reasonable grounds* for believing felonies have been committed. They must also *know* that property is actually subject to forfeiture under internal revenue law. All three of these provisions require the existence of and sufficient knowledge of *statutory basis* before violations can be determined and arrests or seizures made, since "reasonable grounds" does not encompass ignorant presumption. In fact, it is a criminal violation to make baseless, summary presumptions about statutory basis and then try to collect a tax liability that does not exist.

The Crime of Operating under Color of Law

The IRC requires termination of employment as well as fines and/or imprisonment if an IRS agent is convicted of attempting under color of law to extract from a taxpayer more than he lawfully owes:

> <u>United States Code</u>
> - <u>TITLE 26 - INTERNAL REVENUE CODE</u>
>   - <u>SUBTITLE F - PROCEDURE AND ADMINISTRATION</u>
>   - <u>CHAPTER 75 - CRIMES, OTHER OFFENSES, AND FORFEITURES</u>
>   - <u>SUBCHAPTER A - CRIMES</u>
>   - <u>PART I - GENERAL PROVISIONS</u>

Section 7214. Offenses by officers and employees of the United States

(a) Unlawful acts of revenue officers or agents
  Any officer or employee of the United States acting in connection with any revenue law of the United States -
    (1) who is guilty of any extortion or willful oppression under color of law; or
    (2) who knowingly demands other or greater sums than are authorized by law, or receives any fee, compensation, or reward, except as by law prescribed, for the performance of any duty; or
    (3) who with intent to defeat the application of any provision of this title fails to perform any of the duties of his office or employment; or

(4) who conspires or colludes with any other person to defraud the United States; or

(5) who knowingly makes opportunity for any person to defraud the United States; or

(6) who does or omits to do any act with intent to enable any other person to defraud the United States; or

(7) who makes or signs any fraudulent entry in any book, or makes or signs any fraudulent certificate, return, or statement; or

(8) who, having knowledge or information of the violation of any revenue law by any person, or of fraud committed by any person against the United States under any revenue law, fails to report, in writing, such knowledge or information to the Secretary; or

(9) who demands, or accepts, or attempts to collect, directly or indirectly as payment or gift, or otherwise, any sum of money or other thing of value for the compromise, adjustment, or settlement of any charge or complaint for any violation or alleged violation of law, except as expressly authorized by law so to do;

shall be dismissed from office or discharged from employment and, upon conviction thereof, shall be fined not more than $10,000, or imprisoned not more than 5 years, or both. The court may in its discretion award out of the fine so imposed an amount, not in excess of one-half thereof, for the use of the informer, if any, who shall be ascertained by the judgment of the court. The court also shall render judgment against the said officer or employee for the amount of damages sustained in favor of the party injured, to be collected by execution...
[http://caselaw.lp.findlaw.com/casecode/uscodes/26/subtitles/f/chapters/75/subchapters/a/parts/i/sections/section_7214.html].

The Internal Revenue Code can be accessed by visiting either http://caselaw.lp.findlaw.com/casecode/uscodes/26/toc.html or http://www4.law.cornell.edu/uscode/html/uscode26/usc_sup_01_26.html. Other titles of the United States Code can be accessed by visiting http://www4.law.cornell.edu/uscode/. The Strategic Tax Planning mini-seminar demonstrates the lack of statutory liability in the Internal Revenue Code and the Code of Federal Regulations for federal income tax, capital gains tax, social security tax, Medicare tax, and self-employment tax. E-mail mpllc@ymail.com, Attn: Advance Training, for more information.

Appendix IV: The Internal Revenue Manual

Internal Revenue Service Personnel: How to Do Your Jobs

The Internal Revenue Manual (IRM) is the policy manual of the IRS (frequently revised and renumbered). It states:

1.2.1 Policies of the Internal Revenue Service

This IRM contains all existing statements of Service policy. Distribution of the IRM should be to all persons having a need for any of the policy statements.

Each policy statement is printed only once under the Manual Part number to which it has principal application. However, the policy statements apply to all Service personnel involved in the type of program, activity, function, or work process covered by the policy statements [http://www.irs.gov/irm/part1/ch02s01.html].

Acknowledging the applicability of federal tax statutes, it further states:

1.2.1.3.2 (Approved 11-06-1981)
P–2–4
...
2. **Full compliance with tax laws:** Federal agency compliance with the tax laws is required and will be monitored and enforced by Service personnel [http://www.irs.gov/irm/part1/ch02s02.html].

As discussed in Appendix IX, if a taxpayer allows an IRS agent to determine a federal income tax liability where none exists, it's the taxpayer's own fault, from the perspective of the IRS agent. However, the IRM specifically requires that the IRS agent conform strictly to the law in making a determination:

1.2.1.4.5 (Approved 12-23-1960)
P–4–7
1. **Impartial determination of tax liability:** An exaction by the United States Government, which is not based upon law, statutory or otherwise, is a taking of property without due process of law, in violation of the Fifth Amendment to the United States Constitution. Accordingly, a Service representative in his/her conclusions of fact or application of the law, shall hew to the law and the recognized standards of legal construction. It shall be his/her duty to determine the correct amount of the tax, with strict impartiality as between the taxpayer and the Government, and without favoritism or discrimination as between taxpayers [http://www.irs.gov/irm/part1/ch02s02.html].

Furthermore, the IRM publicizes a *commitment* on the part of IRS agents "to educating and assisting taxpayers who make a good faith effort to comply" with the law:

1.2.1.5.1 (Approved 08-18-1994)
P–5–1

1. **Enforcement is a necessary component of a voluntary assessment system:** A tax system based on voluntary assessment would not be viable without enforcement programs to ensure compliance. Accordingly, the Service is responsible for taking all appropriate actions provided by law to compel non-compliant taxpayers to file their returns and pay their taxes.

2. The Service is committed to educating and assisting taxpayers who make a good faith effort to comply. However, enforcement action should be taken promptly, in accordance with Internal Revenue Manual guidelines, against taxpayers who have not shown a good faith effort to comply. These actions include enforcement necessary to move the taxpayer toward compliance.

3. In determining the appropriate enforcement action to take, factors such as the taxpayer's delinquency history should be considered. Promotion of long-term voluntary compliance is a basic goal of the Service, and in reaching this goal, the Service will be cognizant not only of taxpayers' obligations under our system of taxation but also of their rights. However, when a decision to enforce has been made, the Service will have no hesitancy in pursuing the matter to conclusion [http://www.irs.gov/irm/part1/ch02s03.html].

1.2.1.6.1 (Approved 11-04-1977)
P–6–1

1. **Service commitment to Taxpayer Service Program:** The Service is committed to a Taxpayer Service Program which will help taxpayers voluntarily comply with tax laws and assist them in meeting their obligations under the tax laws. The resource requirements needed to fulfill this commitment will be given the same level of consideration as requirements for other major Service Programs [http://www.irs.gov/irm/part1/ch02s04.html].

1.2.1.6.9 (Approved 11-04-1977)
P–6–40

1. **Assistance furnished to taxpayers in the correction of accounts:** Service officials and employees will act objectively and expeditiously to correct errors and discrepancies in taxpayers' accounts. Corrections which will result in a benefit to the taxpayer will be handled as expeditiously as those which will benefit the Government. Service officials and employees dealing with the matter will take every action possible to correct the problem and will assist the taxpayer to the fullest extent possible to understand and to take whatever action is required of him/her [http://www.irs.gov/irm/part1/ch02s04.html].

The IRM requires specific, prompt, responsive replies to taxpayer correspondence:

21.3.3.3.4 (10-01-2004)
Quality and Timely Responses
1. Key terms are defined below:

      A. A quality response is one that is timely, accurate, and professional. Based on information provided, a quality response resolves taxpayer's issues, requests additional information from him/her, or notifies him/her that we have requested information from outside the IRS.

      B. A quality response must be written in language the taxpayers can understand.

      C. Timely means that a final response was initiated within 30 days of IRS received date. However, when possible, you should try to initiate quality responses in less time.

2. For letters addressed to outside sources, reference the date of the incoming letter or inquiry and explain fully the action taken even if it was exactly what addressee requested.

3. Your final or interim response must read … – This is in response to your inquiry of___. If the inquiry is a letter that is not dated, use the postmark date. If that date is unknown, use a date three days prior to IRS-received date.
Exception: If the closing action you take will generate a notice to the taxpayer (for example, CP 210, CP 220, or CP 225, etc.), a final closing letter to the taxpayer is unnecessary.

4. *See IRM 21.3.3.4.2.3* for specific instructions regarding interim letters [http://www.irs.gov/irm/part21/ch03s02.html].

1.2.1.6.4 (Approved 03-14-1991)
P–6–12

1. **Timeliness and Quality of Taxpayer Correspondence:** The Service will issue quality responses to all taxpayer correspondence.

2. Taxpayer correspondence is defined as all written communication from a taxpayer or his/her representative, excluding tax returns, whether solicited or unsolicited. This includes taxpayer requests for information, as well as that which may accompany a tax return; responses to IRS requests for information; and annotated notice responses.

3. A quality response is timely, accurate, professional in tone, responsive to taxpayer needs (i.e., resolves all issues without further contact) [http://www.irs.gov/irm/part1/ch02s04.html].

The IRM specifically states that up-to-date information on tax law and regulations will be made available to all taxpayers:

1.2.1.6.7 (Approved 11-04-1977)
P–6–20

1. **Information provided taxpayers on the application of the tax law:** The Service will develop and conduct effective programs to make available to all taxpayers comprehensive, accurate, and timely information on the requirements of tax law and regulations.

2. Positive efforts will be made to determine taxpayers' needs and to effectively meet these needs. Information will be provided through a variety of means, including telephone and office assistance programs, mass media and taxpayer publications [http://www.irs.gov/irm/part1/ch02s04.html].

The IRM does not require IRS agents to provide taxpayers specific information on what tax law and regulations *do not* require. Furthermore, while information may actually be provided on the application of the tax law, information on statutory liability for internal revenue taxes on income *cannot* be provided since such statutory liability for such taxes does not exist.

The IRM also publicizes the principles to which IRS collection agents must adhere:

> 1.2.1.5.2 (Approved 02-17-2000)
> P–5–2
> 1. **COLLECTING PRINCIPLES:** All our decisions about collecting must be guided by these principles. To the extent that they are, we will succeed in our mission.
> 2. **SERVICE AND ASSISTANCE—All taxpayers are entitled to courteous, responsive, and effective service and assistance in all their dealings with the Service.** We will actively assist taxpayers who try to comply with the law, and work to continually improve the quality of our systems and service to meet the needs of our customes [sic]. All taxpayers, whether delinquent or fully compliant, are entitled to prompt and professional service whenever they deal with Service employees.
> 3. **TAXPAYER RIGHTS—We will observe taxpayers' rights, including their rights to privacy and to fair and courteous treatment.** This affirms our commitment to observe both the spirit as well as the letter of all legal requirements, including the Taxpayer Bill of Rights I and II and the IRS Restructuring and Reform Act of 1998. Taxpayers will be protected from unauthorized disclosure of information...
> [http://www.irs.gov/irm/part1/ch02s03.html—Let's assume that the use of the term "including" and the list that follows in item 3 are not intended to *exclude* the legal requirements of IRC statutes.].

> 1.4.20.13 (01-01-2004)
> **Taxpayer Rights**
> 1. RRA 98, Title 1, Section 1203 was signed into law 7-22-98. There are important sections of the ACT that all IRS employees should thoroughly understand and take very seriously. RRA '98 provides for the mandatory termination of IRS employees under various specific instances of misconduct [see Appendix III]. Consult you [sic] RRA '98 Section 1203 Procedural Handbook for detailed procedures.

2. Managers must be sure that employees know and observe the rights of customers. Taxpayers have the right to prompt, courteous, and impartial treatment. In dealing with taxpayers, ACS employees should:

   A. Assume that each taxpayer wants to comply, unless circumstances of the case indicate otherwise;

   B. Try to put his/her self in the taxpayer's position;

   C. Seek to identify the taxpayer's problem;

   D. Try to resolve the immediate problem and at the same time prevent future problems;

   E. Try to resolve a taxpayer's problem without referring him/her elsewhere;

   F. Allow the taxpayer to appeal to the supervisor if he/she feels the decision is unfair;

   G. Maintain a business like and professional manner [http://www.irs.gov/irm/part1/ch03s15.html].

If a taxpayer asks questions regarding liability and/or procedures, the IRS agent has a duty to cease collection efforts:

   1.2.1.5.3 (Approved 03-01-1984)
   P–5–16
   1. **Forbearance when reasonable doubt exists that assessment is correct:** Whenever a taxpayer raises a question or presents information creating reasonable doubt as to the correctness or validity of an assessment, reasonable forbearance will be exercised with respect to collection provided (1) adjustment of the taxpayer's claim is within control of the Service, and (2) the interests of the Government will not be jeopardized... [http://www.irs.gov/irm/part1/ch02s03.html—also see Appendix A].

Curiously, the IRM has revoked a former policy on returning money wrongfully collected:

   1.2.1.5.9 (Revoked 05-28-1999)
   P–5–36
   1. **Returning money wrongfully collected:** This Policy Statement has been revoked [http://www.irs.gov/irm/part1/ch02s03.html].

However, it is possible for the Taxpayer Advocate to overturn unlawful levies and restore unlawfully collected amounts to individuals who have been unlawfully levied. IRS agents committing such violations must also apologize to the affected taxpayers:

1.2.1.6.2 (Approved 11-26-1979)
P–6–10

1. **The public impact of clarity, consistency, and impartiality in dealing with tax problems must be given high priority:** In dealing with the taxpaying public, Service officials and employees will explain the position of the Service clearly and take action in a way that will enhance voluntary compliance. If a taxpayer problem has been caused by a Service error, the mistake will be acknowledged and an apology given to the taxpayer. Internal Revenue Service officials and employees must bear in mind that the public impact of their official actions can have an effect on respect for tax law and on voluntary compliance far beyond the limits of a particular case or issue [http://www.irs.gov/irm/part1/ch02s04.html].

Tax Payment Deductions

Although the IRC requires "employers" to withhold certain taxes from "wages" (see Appendix III), the IRM, under Part 5, Collecting Process, 5.14.10, <u>Payroll Deduction Agreements and Direct Debit Installment Agreements</u>, states that payroll deduction agreements for IRS installment agreements of "employees" are not required:

5.14.10.1 (09-30-2004)
Overview

1. *This chapter provides procedures for processing Payroll Deduction agreements and Direct Debit installment agreements. Payroll deduction agreements are those agreements where employers deduct payments from taxpayer's wages, and mail them to the Internal Revenue Service. Direct Debit Agreements allow the Service to debit taxpayer's bank accounts. Payroll Deduction agreements and Direct Debit installment agreements benefit the taxpayer by reducing the likelihood of default and lessening taxpayer burden.*

5.14.10.2 (09-30-2004)
Payroll Deduction Agreements

1. The use of Form 2159, Payroll Deduction Agreement, must be strongly encouraged when the taxpayer is a wage earner, particularly if the taxpayer defaulted on a previous installment agreement.
2. Private employers, states, and political subdivisions are ***not required*** to enter into payroll deduction agreements. Taxpayers should determine whether their employers will accept and process executed agreements before agreements are submitted for approval or finalized… [emphasis added— http://www.irs.gov/irm/part5/ch14s10.html].

In other words, curiously, while the *IRC requires* employers to withhold certain taxes for the convenience of "employees" with *current* tax "liabilities," the *IRM excuses* employers from entering into payroll deduction agreements for the convenience of "employees" with *past* tax "liabilities."

Assessment (Form 23C)

With or without evidence of withholding, if IRS agents (incorrectly) believe that a tax liability exists, according to the courts an assessment must be completed via Forms 23C and 4340:

> "It is well established in law that in order to have a valid sale, there must be a valid seizure, and to have a valid seizure, there must be a valid lien …. There must be a signed 23C and a Form 4340 before there is a valid assessment."
> Coplin v. U. S., 952 F.2d 403, Fullmer v. U. S., 93-U.S. Tax Case, P 50, 657, U. S. v. McCallum, 976 F.2d 66, Brewer v. U. S., 746 F. Supp. 309, Geiselman v. U. S., 961 F.2d 1, Tweedy v. U. S., 74 AFTR 2d 5003, Fisher v. U. S., 860 F. Supp. 680

Summarizing this edict, IRC § 6203 and 26 CFR § 301.6203-1, the IRM states, under a curious set of headings and subheadings:

> Part 35. Tax Court Litigation
>
> Chapter 9. Post Opinion Activities
>
> Section 2. Procedures for Assessment of Tax
>
> 35.9.2 Procedures for Assessment of Tax
> …
>
> 35.9.2.1 (08-11-2004)
> **Assessment**
> 1. Assessment is the statutorily required recording of the tax liability. Section 6203. Assessment is made by recording the taxpayer's name, address, and tax liability. The assessment date is the 23C date. The 23C date is the Monday on which the recording of assessment and other adjustments are made in summary manner on Form 23C and signed by a Service Center officer…
> [http://www.irs.gov/irm/part35/ch09s02.html].

The IRM discusses assessments also under Special Topics:

> Part 25. Special Topics
>
> Chapter 6. Statute Of Limitations
>
> Section 5. Assessments
>
> 25.6.5 Assessments

...

25.6.5.1 (10-01-2001)
Assessments Overview

1. This section provides guidelines for assessing tax on Individual Master File (IMF), Business Master File (BMF), Individual Retirement Account (IRAF), and Non Master File (NMF) taxpayer accounts.

25.6.5.2 (10-01-2001)
What are Assessments

1. Assessments are tax increases that post to either IMF, BMF, IRAF and NMF taxpayer accounts. Assessments may be the result of:
   - Original Returns
   - Amended Returns
   - Math errors on returns
   - Claims Received
   - Tax Audits
   - Tax Reconsiderations
   - Substitute For Return Assessments (SFR)

...

25.6.5.4.1 (11-01-2004)
General period

1. The general rule is that the assessment of tax must be made within three years after the return is filed. IRC § 6501(a) [http://www.irs.gov/irm/part25/ch06s05.html].

It is noteworthy that the IRM no longer* expressly directs the use of Form 23C, as it did prior to the edition of 2004, when the IRM was renumbered:

Internal Revenue Manual 3(17)(63)(14).1
Account 6110 Tax Assessments
(2) All tax assessments **must** be recorded on Form 23C Assessment Certificate. The Assessment Certificate must be signed by the Assessment Officer and dated. The Assessment Certificate is the legal document that permits collection activity....

Internal Revenue Manual 3(17)(46)2.3
Certification
(1) All assessments **must** be certified by signature of an authorized official on Form 23-C, Assessment Certificate. A signed Form 23C authorizes issuance of notices and other collection action... [emphasis added—*IRS, Income Tax & The Law: The Fraudulent Fleecing of America* by Dan Shaw on DVD, 2004].

*Internal Revenue Manual 3.17.63.14.4(2) still states: "All principal assessments must be recorded on Summary Record of Assessments (Assessment Certificate). The Assessment Certificate is the legal document that permits collection activity" [http://www.irs.gov/irm/part3/ch10s20.html#d0e541671].

Nevertheless, these procedures must be followed if collections are to be conducted lawfully:

> "However, there is no indication in the record before us that the 'Summary Record of Assessments,' known as Form 23C, was completed and signed by the assessment officer as required by 26 CFR 301.6203-1.3.
> Nor do the Certificates of Assessments and Payments contain 23C dates which would allow us to conclude that a Form 23C form was signed on that date. See United States v. Dixon, 672 F. Supp. 503, 505-506 (M.D. Ala. 1987)
> Thus we find that the plaintiff has raised a factual question concerning whether IRS procedures were followed in making the assessments ...."
> Brewer v. U.S., 764 F. Supp. 309 (S.D.N.Y. 1991)

The current edition of the IRM still requires the signature of an assessment officer, but it also provides an alternative to using Form 23C, namely "IRACS":

> 3.17.63.21.3 (01-01-2007)
> **Summary Record of Assessments ...** (IRACS Report 006)
> ...
> 6. For each Summary Record of Assessment, the audit trail is printed. This includes the Document ID, Document Locator Number or F8166 Recap number in the DLN column and the account date.
>   A. To generate the report, from the Assessment Main Menu Icon, select review, then select the assessment option, followed by the desired assessment type and assessment date.
>   B. The Summary Record of Assessments must be signed by the Assessment Officer on the date the assessment is made as outlined in IRM 3.17.63.19. The certification statement is included in the printed report. At least one person in each campus must be assigned the responsibility of reviewing all certificates for timely entry of the assessment officer's signature and date. The responsible employee will initial the certificate after validation. This practice should be accomplished daily in case statutes are involved.
>   ...
> 8. When IRACS is unavailable, all campuses must use the 23C form, Assessment Certificate, manual assessment (Summary Record of Assessment), under Forms and Publications on the IRWEB. **No other version should be used...**[http://www.irs.gov/irm/part3/ch10s22.html].

The IRM requirement to complete Form 23C only "when IRACS is unavailable" provides IRS agents the opportunity to circumvent the laws requiring the completion of Form 23C as part of a proper assessment. Clearly, the option exists simply to wait until IRACS is available without ever completing Form 23C. However, exercising such an option is in direct violation of the cited court pronouncements (Coplin v. U. S., et al) as well as IRC

§ 6203 and 26 CFR § 301.6203-1. It is also in direct violation of IRM 35.9.2, Procedures for Assessment of Tax, 35.9.2.1 (08-11-2004) Assessment, paragraph 1, which requires that "the recording of assessment and other adjustments are made in summary manner on Form 23C and signed by a Service Center officer" [http://www.irs.gov/irm/part35/ch09s02.html]. In other words, the IRM offers self-contradictory instructions in this regard.

It should be noted here that IRS agents routinely do not respond to requests for Form 23C even though IRC § 6203, 26 CFR § 301.6203-1, the courts, and the IRM require its existence and that copies be provided to requesting taxpayers. IRC § 6203 expressly states: "Upon request of the taxpayer, the Secretary shall furnish the taxpayer a copy of the record of the assessment." The conclusion in Brewer v. U.S. referred to "the 'Summary Record of Assessments,' known as Form 23C."

Letter Rulings Regarding Lawful Tax Avoidance

Although the IRS admits that lawful tax avoidance is permissible (see the Notice to IRS Agents), the IRM expressly states that letter rulings will not be issued in favor of lawful tax avoidance strategies:

> 1.2.1.11.5 (Approved 11-04-1968)
> P–11–32
> 1. **Rulings or determination letters on schemes or devices:** A favorable ruling or determination letter is not issued on the tax consequences of schemes, devices, and plans that have as their principal purpose the avoidance or reduction of Federal taxes [http://www.irs.gov/irm/part1/ch02s04.html].

Furthermore, any letter rulings that are issued are not considered precedent for other cases:

> 1.2.1.11.7 (Approved 06-14-1967)
> P–11–38
> 1. **Unpublished rulings not used as precedents:** Unpublished rulings and technical advice memorandums are not relied on, used, or cited, by any officer or employee of the Service as precedent in the disposition of other cases [http://www.irs.gov/irm/part1/ch02s04.html].

The Internal Revenue Manual may be accessed by visiting http://www.irs.gov/irm/index.html or http://www.irs.gov/ and typing "irm" in the SEARCH box, clicking on SEARCH, and clicking on **Internal Revenue Manual** on the "Search Results" page (use the Advanced Search to search within the IRM). The Strategic Tax Planning mini-seminar highlights the requirements of the Internal Revenue Manual, the Internal Revenue Code, the Code of Federal Regulations, and court pronouncements for Form 23C to be completed and, if requested, provided to the taxpayer. E-mail mpllc@ymail.com, Attn: Advance Training, for more information.

Appendix V: The Internal Revenue Service

"The overwhelming majority of taxpayers appear to be perfectly willing to face serious adverse action without bothering to make any significant effort to learn what the agency knows about them or how they came to be in that situation.
In fact, even subjects of major criminal investigation seldom bother to make such inquiries, apparently being willing to face trial and risk imprisonment without writing a simple letter which could produce information which could literally save their freedom."
Marcus Farbenblum, Chief
Freedom of Information Branch,
National Office of the IRS.

The IRS Mission

Department of the Treasury, Internal Revenue Service, Publication 1, Your Rights as a Taxpayer, states under the heading "The IRS Mission," "Provide America's taxpayers top quality service by helping them understand and meet their tax responsibilities and by applying the tax law with integrity and fairness to all." Very few IRS employees are licensed attorneys, qualified to give legal advice or to answer questions correctly on applying the law. Such few IRS attorneys give legal advice to other IRS employees but generally not to taxpayers (IRC § 7803(b)) [http://www.irs.gov/pub/irs-pdf/p1.pdf and http://caselaw.lp.findlaw.com/casecode/uscodes/26/subtitles/f/chapters/80/subchapters/a/sections/section%5F7803.html—see also Appendix III].

Taxpayer Rights

The same publication states under the headings "Declaration of Taxpayer Rights" and "V. Payment of Only the Correct Amount of Tax," "You are responsible for paying only the correct amount of tax due under the law—no more, no less." This statement both completely ignores and distracts the reader from the fact that the law contains absolutely no statute making anyone *liable* for federal income tax or capital gains tax, which means that *no* tax is due under the law [http://www.irs.gov/pub/irs-pdf/p1.pdf].

The IRS also admits that lawful tax avoidance is permissible:

Department of the Treasury, IRS Handbook for Special Agents, p. 412 on Tax Avoidance Distinguished from Evasion: "Avoidance of taxes is not a criminal offence. Any attempt to reduce, avoid, minimize, or alleviate taxes by legitimate means is permissible" [*IRS, Income Tax & The Law: The Fraudulent Fleecing of America* by Dan Shaw on DVD, 2004].

What Taxpayers Must Report on Form 1040

The Department of the Treasury, Internal Revenue Service 1040 Instructions publication states, under the headings **"Income"** and "Foreign-Source Income," "You **must** report unearned income, such as interest, dividends, and pensions, from sources outside the United States unless exempt by law or a tax treaty. You **must** also report earned income, such as wages and tips, from sources outside the United States" [emphasis added—http://www.irs.gov/pub/irs-pdf/i1040.pdf]. Despite popular beliefs based on social conditioning, according to this publication's own definition only *foreign source* income must be reported, not *domestic* income. According to the law, only foreign source income has a tax *imposition*. Since no income tax *liability* exists, no reporting requirement exists even for foreign source income.

Gross Income Defined

The same publication states, under the headings **"Do You Have To File?"** and **"Chart A—For Most People,"** "Gross income means all income you received in the form of money, goods, property, and services that is not exempt from tax, including any income from sources outside the United States (even if you can exclude part or all of it)" [http://www.irs.gov/pub/irs-pdf/i1040.pdf]. Despite popular beliefs based on social conditioning, according to this publication's own definition only *foreign source* income constitutes gross income, not *domestic* income. According to the law, no income tax or capital gains tax *liability* exists. So whether domestic or foreign in source, according to the law this publication's own definition makes *all* income (from within and without the United States—see Appendix E) *"exempt from tax"* since no statute imposes a tax *liability* on any income or capital gains.

Statutory Filing Requirement

The same publication states, under the heading "Disclosure, Privacy Act, and Paperwork Reduction Act Notice," "Our legal right to ask for information is Internal Revenue Code sections 6001, 6011, and 6012(a), and their regulations. They say that you must file a return or statement with us for any tax you are liable for" [http://www.irs.gov/pub/irs-pdf/i1040.pdf]. Despite popular beliefs based on social conditioning, a tax return is not required without a liability for a tax, so if no liability for a tax exists, no requirement to file a return exists (see Appendix D). Based on this publication's own definition, IRS agents will accept a *statement* in lieu of a return. Properly prepared, such a statement costs the filer no income tax or capital gains tax or social security tax or Medicare tax or self-employment tax since, as it demonstrates, no liability for tax actually exists (which technically precludes the need to file the statement, but some individuals prefer to file *something* with the IRS).

IRS Employee Misconduct, Waste, Fraud, or Abuse

Department of the Treasury, Internal Revenue Service, Publication 1, Your Rights as a Taxpayer, states "If you want to confidentially report misconduct, waste, fraud, or abuse by an IRS employee, you can call 1-800-366-4484 (1-800-877-8339 for TTY/TDD users). You can remain anonymous" [http://www.irs.gov/pub/irs-pdf/p1.pdf].

The Internal Revenue Service may be accessed by visiting http://www.irs.gov/. The Strategic Tax Planning mini-seminar highlights definitions of the Department of the Treasury, Internal Revenue Service, the US Constitution, the Internal Revenue Code, the Code of Federal Regulations, and court pronouncements regarding the distinction between taxpayers who are obligated to file federal income tax returns and pay internal revenue taxes and non-taxpayers who are not. E-mail mpllc@ymail.com, Attn: Advance Training, for more information.

Appendix VI: The Code of Federal Regulations

The Code of Federal Regulations (CFR) is taught in post-secondary curricula as the explanation of the statutes in the United States Code. In other words, *regulations* explain *statutes*. "Title 26 of the Code of Federal Regulations is a compendium of rules created by the Secretary of the Treasury to clarify and implement the Internal Revenue Code" [Joseph R. Banister, CPA, Sunday, October 23, 2005 letter: http://joebanister.blogspot.com/])

Tax Imposition without Tax Liability

The CFR lists seventeen specific sources of income that constitute gross income which, after deductions, constitutes taxable income:

> [Code of Federal Regulations]
> [Title 26, Volume 9]
> [Revised as of April 1, 2002]
> From the U.S. Government Printing Office via GPO Access
> [CITE: 26CFR1.861-8]
>
> [Page 135-162]
>
> TITLE 26--INTERNAL REVENUE
>
> CHAPTER I--INTERNAL REVENUE SERVICE, DEPARTMENT OF THE
> TREASURY
> (CONTINUED)
>
> PART 1--INCOME TAXES--Table of Contents

Sec. 1.861-8 Computation of taxable income from sources within the United States and from other sources and activities.

> (a) In general—(1) Scope.... The rules contained in this section apply in determining taxable income of the taxpayer from specific sources and activities under other sections of the Code, referred to in this section as operative sections....
> (f) Miscellaneous matters—(1) Operative sections. The operative sections of the Code which require the determination of taxable income of the taxpayer from specific sources or activities and which give rise to statutory groupings to which this section is applicable include the sections described below.
> (i) Overall limitation to the foreign tax credit....
> (ii) [Reserved]
> (iii) DISC and FSC taxable income....
> (iv) Effectively connected taxable income....

(v) Foreign base company income....

(vi) Other operative sections. The rules provided in this section also apply in determining—

(A) The amount of foreign source items of tax preference under section 58(g) determined for purposes of the minimum tax;

(B) The amount of foreign mineral income under section 901(e);

(C) [Reserved]

(D) The amount of foreign oil and gas extraction income and the amount of foreign oil related income under section 907;

(E) The tax base for citizens entitled to the benefits of section 931 and the section 936 tax credit of a domestic corporation which has an election in effect under section 936;

(F) The exclusion for income from Puerto Rico for residents of Puerto Rico under section 933;

(G) The limitation under section 934 on the maximum reduction in income tax liability incurred to the Virgin Islands;

(H) The income derived from Guam by an individual who is subject to section 935;

(I) The special deduction granted to China Trade Act corporations under section 941;

(J) The amount of certain U.S. source income excluded from the subpart F income of a controlled foreign corporation under section 952(b);

(K) The amount of income from the insurance of U.S. risks under section 953(b)(5);

(L) The international boycott factor and the specifically attributable taxes and income under section 999; and

(M) The taxable income attributable to the operation of an agreement vessel under section 607 of the Merchant Marine Act of 1936, as mended, and the Capital Construction Fund Regulations thereunder (26 CFR, part 3). See 26 CFR 3.2(b)(3) [http://a257.g.akamaitech.net/7/257/2422/01apr20051500/edocket.access. gpo.gov/cfr_2005/aprqtr/26cfr1.861-8.htm].

The CFR does not list any kind of domestic income or capital gains of *residents* among these specific sources of taxable income, but it does list a certain kind of income of *nonresident aliens:*

26 CFR § 1.861-8(f)(iv)
Effectively connected taxable income [of] nonresident alien individuals and foreign corporations engaged in trade or business within the United States...
[http://a257.g.akamaitech.net/7/257/2422/01apr20051500/edocket.access. gpo.gov/cfr_2005/aprqtr/26cfr1.861-8.htm].

Almost self-contradictorily, however (since imposition does not mean liability), the CFR expressly states that nonresident aliens not engaged in trade or business—performing within the exclusive jurisdiction of the US Government neither the functions of a public office nor personal services—are not subject to federal income tax (for a thorough discussion of the definitions of "engaged in trade or business," see Appendix III and Appendix D):

26 CFR 1.871-7(a)(1) Imposition of tax.

This section applies for purposes of determining the tax of a nonresident alien individual who at no time during the taxable year is engaged in trade or business in the United States…. [A] nonresident alien individual to whom this section applies is not subject to the tax imposed by section 1 [the section that imposes a tax on the taxable income of persons] … [http://a257.g.akamaitech.net/7/257/2422/01apr20051500/edocket.access. gpo.gov/cfr_2005/aprqtr/26cfr1.871-7.htm].

The CFR expressly states also that nonresident aliens are never subject to self-employment tax:

26 CFR § 1.1402(b)-1(d) Nonresident Alien.

A nonresident alien individual never has self-employment income. While a nonresident alien individual who derives income from a trade or business carried on within the United States, Puerto Rico, the Virgin Islands, Guam, or American Samoa … may be subject to the applicable income tax provisions on such income, such nonresident alien individual will not be subject to the tax on self employment income, since any net earnings which he may have from self employment do not constitute self-employment income. For the purpose of the tax on self-employment income, an individual who is not a citizen of the United States but who is a resident of the Commonwealth of Puerto Rico, the Virgin Islands or, for taxable years beginning after 1960, of Guam or American Samoa is not considered to be a nonresident alien individual [http://a257.g.akamaitech.net/7/257/2422/01apr20051500/edocket.access. gpo.gov/cfr_2005/aprqtr/26cfr1.1402(b)-1.htm].

So, neither the domestic income nor the capital gains of either residents or nonresident aliens is subject to federal income tax or capital gains tax. Since no statutory liability exists, the foreign source income, capital gains, and self-employment income of neither residents nor nonresident aliens is subject to federal income tax, capital gains tax, or self-employment tax.

Tax Returns and Statements Contingent on Tax Liability

The CFR specifies the basis and means for filing income tax returns. If a return is required to be made, the appropriate form(s) to be used may be acquired from the IRS:

[Code of Federal Regulations]
[Title 26, Volume 18]
[Revised as of April 1, 2005]
From the U.S. Government Printing Office via GPO Access
[CITE: 26CFR301.6011-1]
[Page 18]

TITLE 26--INTERNAL REVENUE

CHAPTER I--INTERNAL REVENUE SERVICE, DEPARTMENT OF THE
TREASURY
(CONTINUED)

PART 301_PROCEDURE AND ADMINISTRATION--Table of Contents

Information and Returns

Sec. 301.6011-1 General requirement of return, statement or list.

(a) For provisions requiring returns, statements, or lists, see the
regulations relating to the particular tax.
(b) The Internal Revenue Service may prescribe in forms,
instructions, or other appropriate guidance the information or
documentation required to be included with any return or any statement
required to be made or other document required to be furnished under any
provision of the internal revenue laws or regulations.

[T.D. 9040, 68 FR 4921, Jan. 31, 2003]
[http://a257.g.akamaitech.net/7/257/2422/01apr20051500/edocket.access.
gpo.gov/cfr_2005/aprqtr/26cfr301.6011-1.htm]

Almost self-contradictorily, however (since imposition does not mean liability), the CFR
expressly states that returns or statements are required of (only) those persons subject
to any tax under Subtitle A of the Code:

[Code of Federal Regulations]
[Title 26, Volume 13]
[Revised as of April 1, 2005]
From the U.S. Government Printing Office via GPO Access
[CITE: 26CFR1.6011-1]

[Page 58]

TITLE 26--INTERNAL REVENUE

CHAPTER I--INTERNAL REVENUE SERVICE, DEPARTMENT OF THE TREASURY
(CONTINUED)

Returns and Records--Table of Contents

Sec. 1.6011-1 General requirement of return, statement, or list.

(a) General rule. Every person subject to any tax, or required to collect any tax, under Subtitle A of the Code, shall make such returns or statements as are required by the regulations in this chapter. The return or statement shall include therein the information required by the applicable regulations or forms [http://a257.g.akamaitech.net/7/257/2422/01apr20051500/edocket.access. gpo.gov/cfr_2005/aprqtr/26cfr1.6011-1.htm].

In other words, a person not subject to any tax under Subtitle A of the Code is not required to make any return or statement under Subtitle A of the Code, whether or not the IRS provides the otherwise appropriate form(s).

The Code of Federal Regulations may be accessed by visiting http://www.access.gpo.gov/nara/cfr/cfr-table-search.html. To access the portion of the CFR applicable to the Internal Revenue Code, page down and click on the most recent Revision Date next to Title 26, Internal Revenue. The Strategic Tax Planning mini-seminar highlights definitions of the US Constitution, the Internal Revenue Code, the Code of Federal Regulations, court pronouncements, and the Department of the Treasury, Internal Revenue Service regarding the distinction between imposition of and liability for internal revenue taxes, lawful discontinuation of federal income, capital gains, social security, Medicare, and self-employment tax costs, and provisions for accumulating permanently-tax-free-interest on retirement savings. E-mail mpllc@ymail.com, Attn: Advance Training, for more information.

Appendix VII: Reasons IRS Agents Almost Always Win

United States Supreme Court: "Because of what appears to be a lawful command on the surface, many Citizens, because of their respect for what appears to be law, are cunningly coerced into waiving their rights due to ignorance."—U.S. v. Minker (1950)

Collectively, IRS agents are like a big dog with big teeth and a loud bark. As a person begins to understand how IRS agents operate, he begins to recognize that the dog's bark is worse than its bite. As he grows in understanding, he begins to perceive that the bark is more often *imagined* than *heard*. Whether or not the individual has ever had any trouble from an IRS agent, and whether or not he or she has ever heard of any one else having any trouble from an IRS agent, he or she learns to *anticipate* trouble based on social conditioning. Once a person does experience even a little trouble with an IRS agent, he or she expects the worst if ever again confronted by the "big dog." So what he or she actually hears is not the dog's bark but his or her own little voice, the conscience, that constantly offers the reminder, *"Don't provoke the dog!"*

Ignorance and Fear of the Unknown

The question must be asked, "What does it take to provoke the dog?" What must one *do* so as not to agitate the canine and risk getting bitten in the wallet? The questions must then also be asked, "What *negligence* must be avoided?" "How much time is involved in learning offensive and defensive steps to take?" At this point, most people sigh in resignation and turn over their worries to their accountants and tax preparers. They accordingly tend never to learn what deliberate or inadvertent actions actually make the dog bite. They remain in fear of the dog's bite, but since they do not actually *know* what causes the dog to bite, they remain in fear of the *unknown*. (This makes it extremely easy for IRS agents to win arguments with the "you don't know what I don't know" and the "I don't know but I'm not going to admit it because neither do you" tactics discussed in Appendix VIII.)

> "The taxpayer must be liable for the tax. Tax liability is a condition precedent to the demand. Merely demanding payment, even repeatedly, does not cause liability." Booth v. Terry, 713 F.2d 1405, at 1414 (1983)

While it is consistently easiest for IRS agents to mail demanding letters and notices and let the taxpayers pressure *themselves* into compliance out of fear of the unknown, it is still easy for IRS agents to exert pressure in person. Discussion of this reason for the winning record of IRS agents is reserved for Appendix VIII.

"Frivolous" Arguments

So the prevailing ignorance of the masses is the reason IRS agents remain in control and able to exercise almost dictatorial power. The IRS agent is able to tell the taxpayer, "Your argument is frivolous," and expect the taxpayer to acquiesce since he or she does not know how to respond to such an accusation. The US prosecuting attorney is able to insist to the judge and jury, "The defendant's arguments are frivolous," and expect the taxpayer to be found guilty (of so-called "tax evasion" or "failure to file," for example). The reason is that the judge, jury, and attorneys alike don't know tax law and are accordingly unable to argue it properly. None is prepared to argue actual sections of the law that would result in the taxpayer's acquittal. IRS agents are able to publish an endless number of cases that were lost on the principle that taxpayer arguments were frivolous because nobody on the taxpayers' side was able to demonstrate otherwise.

What is *wrong* with this picture?!? Are IRS agents always right? Are all taxpayer arguments frivolous? Do all taxpayer arguments *become* frivolous just because they are *labeled* frivolous? Truthfully, *No!* In fact, labeling as frivolous even legitimate tax arguments is not effective when the taxpayer knows how to overcome this tactic. Naturally, the IRS does not publish cases where taxpayer arguments have been labeled frivolous and yet the taxpayers have overcome the objections of prosecuting attorneys and been acquitted of any false charges. An argument is not automatically frivolous just because someone says it is any more than a child's assertion is automatically untrue just because another child says so. In such a crucial area as tax law, however, one must be especially diligent in researching and *knowing* the language of applicable laws so as to make legitimate arguments that will prevail in spite of any suggestion of frivolity or illegitimacy. No more should an individual presume that the IRS agent is correct in labeling his arguments as frivolous than should he presume that the agent is correct in his determination or in mailing a Notice of Deficiency or a Notice of Lien or Levy.

IRS agents and US prosecuting attorneys are well aware of the many arguments taxpayers have tried to use. Based on the long, successful use of the "frivolous" label and the fact that so many taxpayer arguments have been given this label, it is simply standard procedure to label a familiar argument as frivolous because it has so repeatedly been "proven" frivolous. The fact is, however, that, more often than not, a taxpayer's arguments are "proven" frivolous simply because the taxpayer does not argue properly, if at all, regardless of whether or not his arguments are frivolous. If the prosecuting attorney states that the taxpayer's arguments are frivolous and the taxpayer closes his mouth and the taxpayer's arguments are the same as others that have been declared frivolous, then the judge and jury are going to determine that the taxpayer's arguments are, in fact, frivolous. What is truly frivolous is that a taxpayer raises a legitimate question about the law, and on the premise of that question makes a legitimate argument about the law, and then simply folds his hands, closes his mouth, and says nothing in defense of his own argument while his opponent at law makes a few routine statements and the judge's gavel comes down to punctuate the taxpayer's guilt! Why make a stand at all if unwilling to *continue* standing? Sadly, in this vein IRS agents *are* correct in categorically assuming that all taxpayer arguments are frivolous when so many taxpayers are unwilling to do any more than state what sounds like a good argument without learning the facts beneath the hearsay and learning how to defend themselves based on those facts.

VII: Reasons IRS Agents Almost Always Win

See the document *The Truth About Frivolous Tax Arguments* at
http://www.irs.gov/pub/irs-utl/friv_tax.pdf. Before reading this document, one should
take note that neither the IRS nor the US Treasury nor the US Congress nor the US
government claims authorship. One should also remember that a filing requirement is
contingent on a tax liability, which is contingent on legislation that makes one *liable* for
tax and for filing a corresponding tax return. After reading this book and conducting
recommended research, the reader should be able to recognize that the premises of the
document *The Truth About Frivolous Tax Arguments* are only mildly supported yet
thoroughly refutable and statutorily controvertible. (Cited court pronouncements are
most likely the result of inadequate defense.)

E-mail mpllc@ymail.com, Attn: Advance Training, for more information.

Appendix VIII: Reasons NOT to Appear in Person

The spoken word carries great risk to the speaker. Once spoken in confidence, it cannot be retracted. It leads to success when kept as a bond but to failure when broken. Uttered in haste, it jeopardizes the reputation and security of even the wisest of persons. Cried out under pressure, it measures the limits of one's patience and integrity. Screamed in rage, it betrays one's true colors and beliefs. Thus, the spoken word is sometimes wished by the speaker not to have been uttered at all.

Written Arguments versus Oral Arguments

Conversations are of normally limited duration. Debates, on the other hand, are enduring. Both put all parties to the discussion at risk for a number of reasons. First, people tend to speak spontaneously without giving much forethought as to intent or choice of words. Second, people tend to forget precisely what has been said. Third, people tend to make promises and enter agreements without having any intention of honoring them. Fourth, people tend to make statements and declarations without concern and with little or no confidence in the validity of such assertions. Fifth, and possibly most important, people tend to decide for themselves the true intent behind the utterances of others, to remember according to their own desires what others have actually said, and to enforce contracts they want to believe others have established. Sixth, people tend to insist that their own views are correct despite mountains of irrefutable evidence to the contrary.

A silly example illustrates this reason. One person explains that "Oc**to**ber" is the proper way to pronounce the tenth month on the calendar. His opponent insists that the precise annunciation is "**Oc**tober" and explains that this has to do with the fact that it is two months short of the twelfth. Both have valid reasons even though their conclusions differ, but each believes that since their conclusions differ the other's reasons must be wrong. Even when mincing words, people tend to defend themselves vehemently, in this case even insisting that their way of saying it is correct because they said it even though they said it exactly the way their opponents said it. (As in, I say "Oc**to**ber" and that makes it right because I said it, but when you say "Oc**to**ber" you're wrong because I didn't say it.)

Seventh, and related to the fifth, conversations and debates that are not carefully documented are—not documented. This gives rise to both the second and fifth reasons, that people tend to forget precisely what was said and so tend to remember for themselves what was said and what was *meant* by what was said and who actually agreed to what, and so on. The bottom line, then, is that verbal, unwritten arguments are difficult, if not impossible, to win. Eighth, even if a verbal argument is won, what prevents the loser from retaliating—and with impunity, at that?

A debate that is carried on in writing has intrinsic advantages over one carried on verbally. First, there are almost no time constraints. Without being compromised by schedules and anxious opponents, the points at issue may be written and edited and polished—explained as precisely as possible and presented as thoroughly as necessary—using as much time as necessary. The soundness of arguments can be bolstered before the arguments are presented and preparation can be made for potential counter-arguments. Deliberate, careful consideration can be made as to the appropriateness and sufficiency of responses to counter-arguments as well as to possible counter-responses. There is no need to make statements or responses hastily, without careful forethought. The risk of irrecoverably losing a legal advantage is thereby greatly reduced; the likelihood of prevailing is correspondingly increased. Second, there are no immediate distractions. Opponents may not interrupt or interject counter arguments that allow little or no time for consideration of the validity of the points being presented and that accordingly appear to detract from their value. The lack of such interruptions and interjections prevents inadvertent changes in the direction of the discussion and loss of supporting ideas retained only in memory. Third, there is permanent proof of language used, statutes cited, conclusions reached, and agreements initiated, preventing reliance upon only arbitrary, random, and changing recollections of memory and interpretations of intent. Opponents are accordingly forced either to discuss the issues at hand or to be proven unwilling or unable to do so. Administrative remedies are thus proved exhausted.

Reasons NOT to Meet with an IRS Agent

People tend to defend their jobs as a matter of necessity. People tend to defend their *performance* on their jobs as a matter of pride (whether or not they actually have anything about which to *be* proud), especially those who have had specialized training and therefore possess pertinent information others do not. As a matter of respect, others generally will not voice suspicions about the skills or intelligence of such specially trained persons. Accordingly, few would dare reference the stereotypical association of police officers with doughnut shops while trying to avert a traffic ticket. Few would dare correct a judge about law or procedure. Such a person has generally recognized authority—and for good reason. Due to the specialty of their respective fields, IRS agents have generally recognized authority and understandably retain a measure of professional pride. However, as a matter of course IRS agents presume without ever verifying that their duties consistently harmonize with the language and intent of the Codes of law (see Appendix IV, **TAXPAYER RIGHTS**). They also presume without ever referencing either IRS publications or the Codes of law that every human within reach of the federal government owes a "fair share" of federal income tax, capital gains tax, social security tax, Medicare tax, and self-employment tax.

Mind Games

People love being right and hate being wrong. They *really* hate being *proved* wrong, *especially* in front of other people. People are not stupid, though. Common sense encompasses recognition of predominant attitudes and beliefs among those of a local culture. In other words, people know or at least *think* they know, in general, what other people believe. They also may believe that they know what other people do *not* know.

When arguing, adults often employ childish tactics, such as the "you don't know what I don't know" tactic (or the "I don't know but I'm not going to admit it because neither do you" tactic). An IRS agent might use this tactic in the hope that the taxpayer does not know that *the agent does not know* whether or not the agent is making a correct statement. So the agent might make assertions of knowledge he does not actually possess and hope that the taxpayer does not know at least as much as the agent knows.

Frequently, people play such mind games by making statements that are sufficiently or apparently true but not *entirely* true. For example, the statement, "Traffic lights have green lenses," is sufficiently true for conversation but not *entirely* true since traffic lights also have red and yellow (or amber) lenses. Likewise, the statement, "Everyone is subject to sales tax," is sufficiently true for conversation but not *entirely* true since basic food staples are generally not sales-taxable. Those who survive on welfare and food stamps as well as retirees content to live simple lives pay little, if any, sales tax. A more accurate statement, then, would be, "Everyone who purchases sales-taxable goods and services is subject to sales tax." People in general use an unlimited variety of statements that are sufficiently or *apparently* true but not *entirely* true. Defensive taxpayers, out of ignorance, make statements that are true in general but not *actually* true when all applicable exceptions and provisions are considered—this makes it easy for IRS agents to win arguments that remain in the realm of the rules of IRS publications. The general truth that families with children get the Earned Income Credit (EIC) is not true at all in cases where children are older than the maximum age or where the earned income of the parent(s) is higher than maximum limits. The apparent truth that a married taxpayer can deduct $9,000.00 in mortgage interest is not true at all when close scrutiny reveals that the taxpayer has no other itemized deductions and therefore does not qualify for itemized deductions since his *standard* deduction is $10,000.00 (2005 tax year). IRS agents, likewise, may make statements that are *sufficiently* true but not *entirely* true—sometimes, deliberately—intentionally relying on taxpayer ignorance to prevent the need to verify the reliability of their statements. An IRS agent might quote the IRC and say that section 61 says, "gross income means *all* income." While this is *sufficiently* true—at least from the IRS agent's perspective—it is not *entirely* true when compared with the rest of the same section and related sections of the Code (see Appendix V, **Gross Income Defined,** Appendix D, and Appendix E). The unwise taxpayer may be caught off guard by such an abbreviated citation of law and believe it is entirely true when, in fact, it is not.

> United States Supreme Court: "Because of what appears to be a lawful command on the surface, many Citizens, because of their respect for what appears to be law, are cunningly coerced into waiving their rights due to ignorance."—U.S. v. Minker (1950)

To win a verbal argument, one must keep the other person on the subject being argued. When an IRS agent wants to avoid a particular issue, she will likely dismiss any comments on that issue and raise a different issue as a distraction. When the agent does not know how to respond to a taxpayer's statement or question, she might

VIII: Reasons NOT to Appear in Person

respond inadvertently or even deliberately with information or a question of her own that is completely irrelevant. It is then up to the taxpayer to determine whether the incorrect response was inadvertent or deliberate and then to determine whether to rephrase the statement or question or to insist that the agent respond properly. Even when the agent does understand the language used as well as its meaning and intent, she might deliberately appear either confused or smugly confident that she does understand. She might try to discuss only part of the issue to "clarify" the position of the taxpayer. She might try to refute the choice of words the taxpayer used. She might authoritatively chastise the taxpayer for misapplying established facts, possibly employing the "you don't know what I don't know tactic" and hoping that the taxpayer cannot disprove such an authoritative assertion. Any response the agent makes might be intentionally distracting to prevent the real issue from being resolved. In any case, it is the taxpayer's responsibility to keep the agent on the subject and not allow the agent to discuss irrelevant information.

If the agent simply *refuses* to be proven wrong, he will strenuously avoid the issue or vigorously insist that black is white or just make lame excuses. One who pushes another off a low cliff might argue that he only pushed the other person and that it was gravity's fault that the other person fell down and was injured when he hit the ground. He might also blame the injured person for not grabbing onto something before falling. The fact remains that he pushed the other person, but with his last dying breath he will insist that he is innocent and that someone else is to blame for the person's injuries.

When arguing over a matter of law, the IRS agent may just ignore the law or say that the taxpayer is reading a section out of context or staunchly insist that the statute does not say what it actually says. The agent likely will employ the "you don't know what I don't know" tactic, authoritatively assert what the law really says, and hope the lowly taxpayer has not done his or her homework. The transcripts of meetings between taxpayers and IRS agents are particularly amusing for such reasons. The agents involved clearly and repeatedly demonstrate that they neither want to argue the actual issues at hand nor have sufficient understanding of the subject matter—namely, the Internal Revenue Code—to argue the issues properly. When backed into a corner, they use distraction to shift the direction of the discussion (see an example at http://www.warddeanmd.com/record3.htm).

If the IRS agent absolutely refuses to discuss the issue at hand, no agreement can be reached, regardless of who is right and who is wrong. If a meeting with an IRS agent is ended on this note, the agent will probably continue to act against the taxpayer regardless of the taxpayer's lawful position.

If a meeting with an IRS agent is absolutely unavoidable, full knowledge of the Internal Revenue Code and the Code of Federal Regulations is not prerequisite to prevailing at the meeting. Knowing the language of a few key sections of the Codes as well as a few pertinent court pronouncements is a good start. With that basis, the taxpayer must politely but firmly and persistently ask the agent to display sections of the Codes that make the taxpayer *liable* for federal income tax or capital gains tax or self-employment tax. This is a reliable strategy, since even the knowledgeable and well-prepared agent will be unable to produce such sections of the Codes since they simply do not exist.

Reasons NOT to Go to Court

If properly prepared and either professionally represented or thoroughly self-educated in the rules applicable to courtroom proceedings (known as the rules of civil or criminal procedure), a person might reasonably anticipate a positive outcome from going to court. However, while going to court *might* result in a determination of who did what and what, if any, correction is in order, right and wrong will not necessarily be decided. In the courtroom, it does not matter that the law does not require the payment of federal income taxes or capital gains taxes or social security taxes or Medicare taxes or self-employment taxes. What matters in the courtroom is what people *believe* and how people *behave* (see an example at http://www.paynoincometax.com/). Accordingly, a victim of unlawful activity on the part of an IRS agent should avoid going to court if at all possible. The following are the reasons a victim should try not to go to court. Of course, these reasons are not absolutely, *always* true, but generally:

- The judge believes that everyone has a requirement to pay federal income tax.

- The attorneys believe that everyone has a requirement to pay federal income tax.

- The jurors believe that everyone has a requirement to pay federal income tax.

- The rules of the game of courtroom antics* apply. Courtroom antics are based on the rules of the school playground. The basic rules of the school playground are:

  - If committing improper behavior, don't get caught.

  - If confronted for improper behavior, lie.

  - If witnesses testify regarding improper behavior, distract from the issue by defaming the character of the witnesses—or just change the subject.

- A victim who represents himself but does not know the rules of the game will lose.

*This remark is intended, not to show disrespect for the judicial system, but to identify the fact that those who go to court take the risk that others in the courtroom will act unfairly and even unlawfully, following the maxim, "it's wrong only if you're caught" (or "it's wrong only if your opponent at law objects"). For example, lacking courtroom experience and professional counsel for such a "small" case, a case for $1,965.00 in overtime pay, damages, and administrative and court costs was dismissed without the plaintiff ever being given an opportunity to state the plaintiff's case at the hearing. The defending attorney filed a motion to dismiss after the deadline before the appearance date and then during the hearing asserted that he possessed evidence he did not actually possess. The plaintiff not knowing how to overcome or object to either of these improper actions, with two illegal moves the plaintiff was checkmated.

VIII: Reasons NOT to Appear in Person

- A victim who represents himself and knows the rules but whose opponent cheats without the victim noticing and raising the proper objection will lose.

- If the opposing attorney is better than the victim's attorney, the victim will lose.

- If the victim's attorney is better than his opponent's attorney but his opponent's attorney cheats without the victim's attorney noticing and raising the proper objection, the victim will lose.

- If the opponent or the opponent's attorney cheats and the victim or the victim's attorney notices and raises the proper objection but the judge overrules the objection, the victim will lose.

- If the victim or his attorney allows his opponent or his opponent's attorney to distract the court sufficiently from the real issues and facts of law, the victim will lose.

- If the court sees fit to convict the victim on issues actually unrelated but *apparently* related to the real issues and facts of law, the victim will lose.

- Even if everybody intends to play the game fairly, mistakes on the part of the victim, the victim's attorney, the opponent, the opponent's attorney, the judge, the jury, or even clerks and other personnel of the court could cause the victim to lose.

  - The mistake the victim representing himself *pro se* is most likely to make is related to the language used by attorneys; if the victim does not understand "Legalese," the advantage defaults to the attorneys unless the victim knows the rules of procedure well enough to overcome the language barrier.

  - Being a former attorney, the judge knows this language, and if a mistake of language occurs, since the attorneys and the judge are obligated by law as officers of the court to uphold the supremacy of the court, the advantage defaults to the court.

Even if everybody understands and speaks fluent Legalese and plays the game of courtroom antics fairly, the court has statutory authority to penalize proponents of so-called frivolous arguments:

    United States Code
- TITLE 26 - INTERNAL REVENUE CODE
  - SUBTITLE F - PROCEDURE AND ADMINISTRATION
    - CHAPTER 68 - ADDITIONS TO THE TAX, ADDITIONAL AMOUNTS, AND ASSESSABLE PENALTIES
      - SUBCHAPTER B - ASSESSABLE PENALTIES
        - PART I - GENERAL PROVISIONS

VIII: Reasons NOT to Appear in Person

Section 6673. Sanctions and costs awarded by courts

(a) Tax court proceedings
  (1) Procedures instituted primarily for delay, etc.
    Whenever it appears to the Tax Court that -
      (A) proceedings before it have been instituted or maintained by the taxpayer primarily for delay,
      (B) the taxpayer's position in such proceeding is frivolous or groundless, or
      (C) the taxpayer unreasonably failed to pursue available administrative remedies,
  the Tax Court, in its decision, may require the taxpayer to pay to the United States a penalty not in excess of $25,000.
  (2) Counsel's liability for excessive costs
    Whenever it appears to the Tax Court that any attorney or other person admitted to practice before the Tax Court has multiplied the proceedings in any case unreasonably and vexatiously, the Tax Court may require -
      (A) that such attorney or other person pay personally the excess costs, expenses, and attorneys' fees reasonably incurred because of such conduct, or
      (B) if such attorney is appearing on behalf of the Commissioner of Internal Revenue, that the United States pay such excess costs, expenses, and attorneys' fees in the same manner as such an award by a district court.
(b) Proceedings in other courts
  (1) Claims under section 7433
    Whenever it appears to the court that the taxpayer's position in the proceedings before the court instituted or maintained by such taxpayer under section 7433 is frivolous or groundless, the court may require the taxpayer to pay to the United States a penalty not in excess of $10,000.
  (2) Collection of sanctions and costs
    In any civil proceeding before any court (other than the Tax Court) which is brought by or against the United States in connection with the determination, collection, or refund of any tax, interest, or penalty under this title, any monetary sanctions, penalties, or costs awarded by the court to the United States may be assessed by the Secretary and, upon notice and demand, may be collected in the same manner as a tax.
  (3) Sanctions and costs awarded by a court of appeals
    In connection with any appeal from a proceeding in the Tax Court or a civil proceeding described in paragraph (2), an order of a United States Court of Appeals or the Supreme Court awarding monetary sanctions, penalties or court costs to the United States may be registered in a district court upon filing a certified copy of such order and shall be enforceable as other district court judgments. Any such sanctions, penalties, or costs may be assessed by the Secretary and, upon notice and demand, may be collected in the same manner as a tax

[http://caselaw.lp.findlaw.com/casecode/uscodes/26/subtitles/f/chapters/
68/subchapters/b/parts/i/sections/section_6673.html].

So even in the case of what it believes to be an *appearance* of a deliberate delay, frivolity, or lack of effort at administrative remedy, the Tax Court retains the statutory authority to penalize the taxpayer. Furthermore, even if the taxpayer has a legitimate complaint against an IRS agent for unlawful collection activity (see § 7433, below), in the case of what it believes to be an *appearance* of frivolity the Tax Court retains the statutory authority to penalize the taxpayer. Self-contemptuously, in subsections (b)(2) and (3) the IRC authorizes collection of such a penalty "in the same manner as a tax"!

<u>United States Code</u>
- <u>TITLE 26 - INTERNAL REVENUE CODE</u>
  - <u>SUBTITLE F - PROCEDURE AND ADMINISTRATION</u>
    - <u>CHAPTER 76 - JUDICIAL PROCEEDINGS</u>
      - <u>SUBCHAPTER B - PROCEEDINGS BY TAXPAYERS AND THIRD PARTIES</u>

Section 7433. Civil damages for certain unauthorized collection actions

(a) In general
   If, in connection with any collection of Federal tax with respect to a taxpayer, any officer or employee of the Internal Revenue Service recklessly or intentionally, or by reason of negligence, disregards any provision of this title, or any regulation promulgated under this title, such taxpayer may bring a civil action for damages against the United States in a district court of the United States. Except as provided in section 7432, such civil action shall be the exclusive remedy for recovering damages resulting from such actions.
(b) Damages
   In any action brought under subsection (a) or petition filed under subsection (e), upon a finding of liability on the part of the defendant, the defendant shall be liable to the plaintiff in an amount equal to the lesser of $1,000,000 ($100,000, in the case of negligence) or the sum of -
      (1) actual, direct economic damages sustained by the plaintiff as a proximate result of the reckless or intentional or negligent actions of the officer or employee, and
      (2) the costs of the action
   [http://caselaw.lp.findlaw.com/casecode/uscodes/26/subtitles/f/chapter
   s/76/subchapters/b/sections/section_7433.html]....

How to proceed if going to court is absolutely unavoidable is beyond the scope of this paragraph. However, the taxpayer must be as thoroughly prepared as possible and have either competent professional counsel who is able to argue facts of law (rather than just play the game of courtroom antics) or extreme confidence in himself or herself if appearing *pro se* (alone, not represented by professional counsel). Representing oneself requires an understanding of courtroom procedures and how to work within the guidelines of such procedures in effectively arguing facts of law (see the rules of civil and/or criminal procedure for the respective state of residence and http://www.uscourts.gov/rules/newrules4.html or http://www.law.cornell.edu/rules/frcp/index.html or http://www.law.cornell.edu/rules/frcrmp/). Pursuing administrative procedure and exhausting all available administrative remedies might prevent the need to appear in court but at the very least is a prerequisite to initiating litigation. An IRS agent can prove attempts at administrative remedy with copies of letters and notices mailed to the taxpayer prior to initiating litigation. On the other hand, the taxpayer can prove attempts at administrative remedy with certified mail receipts and copies of certified letters mailed to the IRS agent (see Appendix IX) and *might* prevail simply due to lack of response by the IRS agent (see Appendix IV and Appendix F, #12). E-mail mpllc@ymail.com, Attn: Advance Training, for more information.

Appendix IX: Communicating with IRS Agents

Three Approaches

There are three general approaches to communicating with IRS agents. The first approach is the "cower in fear" method. This approach involves nothing more than dutifully and timely filing Form 1040 every year and paying any amount "due" based on the calculations of the form and then simply obeying the requirements of each and every letter, notice, and demand received from IRS agents. Obeying agent commands—whether they be for payment or for production of books and records or for appearance at an IRS office—usually results in little worse than a little inconvenience, if not extra taxes due in the form of penalties and interest. This approach does not bear the option of complaint or disagreement, only the "Yes, sir, right away, sir" programmed response.

The second approach is the "hire a professional to handle it for you" method. Ironically, despite being the most costly of the three, this method rarely, if ever, guarantees any particular results in proving the IRS agent wrong or reducing taxes, penalties, and interest even if the IRS agent *is* wrong. The greater number of individuals who can afford to do so much prefer to pass the buck and let their accountants and attorneys handle their tax matters as well as their tax problems. The disadvantage created by this approach is that one never needs to learn anything about the lawful obligations of either IRS agents or individual citizens since carrying out the responsibilities of such knowledge is the duty of the professional.

The third approach is the "do it yourself" method. Almost everyone finds this nearly as distasteful as the "cower in fear" method. After all, who has the know-how to defend himself in court without an attorney? Who has the ability to crunch all the numbers and sort them into their proper places but an accountant? Ah, but who *cannot* keep a scrapbook and send a letter now and then? Almost everyone finds the "do it yourself" approach to resolving disputes with IRS agents distasteful because very, *very* few people are even aware that federal tax law, while appearing convoluted and unwieldy, is actually very, very simple when read carefully.

What the Professionals Generally Do Not Know

There is good reason for considering the third approach. Actually, attorneys are not taught what the law says; they are taught *how to read* the law and how to *argue law* in court. Do tax attorneys actually *know* what federal tax law says about liability for federal income or capital gains or social security or Medicare or self-employment taxes? (After reading this book and then asking some simple questions of any number of tax attorneys, one will find that few, if any, actually know since they are not *required* to know.) Any particular tax attorney most assuredly knows *some* federal tax law. Nevertheless, it is up to the taxpayer who hires a tax attorney to determine whether or not the attorney's particular expertise is *applicable* to the taxpayer's situation and therefore beneficial to the taxpayer. The shrewd taxpayer will ascertain whether or not the attorney understands the distinction between taxpayers and nontaxpayers (see Appendix F, #s 1 & 5-7) and first carefully studies the statutes to determine whether or not a tax liability even *exists* before applying the statutes that determine the *amount* of tax liability. The attorney's expertise may not be in determining whether or not a tax liability actually *exists* but only in either determining the *amount* of tax liability based on the *presumption* of statutorily established liability or handling routine abatement requests and offers in compromise in and out of court. In that case, his or her expertise is neither automatically applicable to the taxpayer's situation nor necessarily beneficial to the taxpayer, nor will he or she be able to argue whether or not liability actually *exists* if challenged by an IRS agent or in court by a US prosecuting attorney. A judge would accordingly tend to agree with the prosecutor and find against the taxpayer.

Not surprisingly, certified public accountants in general are as much in the dark about tax law as their professional contemporaries—despite their required, minimal education in *how to read* the law and how to use it to determine tax liability. (Accountants are not required to know what the law says any more than are attorneys, and they are not required to know whether or not statutory tax liability actually *exists*—only how to determine the *amount* of tax liability based on the *presumption* of statutorily established liability.) Academic doctors do not explain to their CPA-wannabe students, "Okay, class, once you determine in *this* part of the law whether or not your client actually *has* a tax liability, if he does go to *that* part of the law to determine *how much* liability." CPA candidates are not taught to distinguish between taxpayers and nontaxpayers or between establishing statutory tax liability and determining the *amount* of tax liability, and less-than-certified accountants are generally just as unable to make these distinctions.

Enrolled agents, experienced and perhaps specially trained though they may be, are equally unable to make these distinctions. Individuals that are uneducated in the language of current federal tax law but that meet minimal qualifications (a background check) and demonstrate by examination minimal proficiency and maintain such minimal qualifications and minimal proficiency through continuing education may become enrolled agents admitted to practice before the IRS.

The fact is that the professionals are too busy with their respective professions to learn more than what society or the law requires of them. Since they are very well paid, none of them recognizes a need (financial, ethical, moral, or otherwise) to verify whether or not the common hearsay among themselves is actually entirely true, lawful, reliable, and ultimately in everyone's best interest.

The Taxpayer's Fault of Presumption

A significant lack on the part of competing tax services resulted in a corresponding initial boon to the author's tax practice. In the author's experience, other people providing tax services tend not to ask their clients enough questions, if any. The client is treated as though he already knows everything he needs to know about available tax breaks and what he does and does not have to report. The educational system hardly does any more than that to help anyone recognize that there is a distinction to be made about taxpayers and Form 1040. A taxpayer is a taxpayer if he pays taxes but not necessarily because a law *requires* him to pay those taxes. At the same time, a person completes Form 1040 to determine the amount of his tax liability but not necessarily because a law *requires* him to file. Form 1040 *presumes* a tax liability just as people *presume* that they are liable for tax and many of those operating tax services *presume* that a person knows what information and documents to bring to his tax preparer. The law requires a person to file a federal income tax return to determine the *amount* of tax liability only after that person has determined that he *actually has* a tax liability and, hence, a filing requirement. If he determines* no tax liability, the law does not require him to file a tax return or to pay any tax.

A parent who has taught her child not to touch the hot stove says, "It's your own fault," when her child burns his little fingers on the hot stove anyway (since he should have known better). From a legal standpoint, the IRS agent can make the disclaimer, "It's your own fault," when a taxpayer presumes to file Form 1040 and endures the resulting pain even though the law does not require her to do so (since she should have known better). After all, tax reform acts proclaimed for simplification of tax laws and instructions are also proclaimed for making things so easy that anybody can figure out tax laws and tax forms for himself or herself. So if a taxpayer makes a mistake or makes a *presumption,* it's her own fault, from the perspective of the IRS agent.

If a taxpayer makes the presumption that the IRS agent is correct in his or her determination and thereby suffers inconvenience and unnecessary cost, it's his own fault, from the perspective of the IRS agent. If he pays additional tax, interest, and penalties based on the *presumption* that the IRS agent is correct in issuing a Notice of Deficiency, it's his own fault, from the perspective of the IRS agent. If his paycheck and bank account are levied based on the *presumption* that the IRS agent is correct in issuing a Notice of Levy, it's his own fault, from the perspective of the IRS agent. If a lien is placed on his home based on the *presumption* that the IRS agent is correct in issuing a Notice of Lien, it's his own fault, from the perspective of the IRS agent.

Definitions of Terminology

As illustrated in Appendix I, IRS agents tend to presume that their occupational duties in tax collection are thoroughly, unequivocally based on US law. Taxpayers likewise presume that all IRS agents have complete, absolute, lawful authority to carry out their respective duties. In addition to ignorance of the law, a key reason IRS agents and taxpayers alike make these presumptions is ignorance or presumption of the definitions of terminology used in the law. For example, most individuals make the false presumption that they are earning "wages," even though their "employers" make the related false presumption that they are *paying* "wages" and accordingly give each of

*"Voluntary self-assessment" means not only determining for oneself the *amount* of liability but also *first* determining for oneself whether or not a liability actually *exists*. It also means that well over a hundred million taxpayers are just too many among whom any one organization could try to enforce an unpopular tax. Visit http://www.freedomabovefortune.com/ and click on DOWNLOAD REPORT to read further explanation from Joseph R. Banister, CPA, on the meaning and purpose of IRS use of the term "voluntary."

IX: Communicating with IRS Agents

their "employees" a Department of the Treasury - Internal Revenue Service Form W-2, Wage and Tax Statement with his or her name on it each year. As Black's Law Dictionary states (see Definition #4), "When 'INCLUDE' or 'INCLUDING' is used it expands to take in all of the items stipulated or listed, but is then limited to them." Accordingly, a statute that uses the word "include" or "including" limits the items that are included to only what is expressly listed (usually following the word "include" or "including"). As Appendix III explained (pages 181 & 182), the term "'wages' means all remuneration … for services performed by an employee." The term "'employee' includes an officer, employee, or elected official of the United States, a State, or any political subdivision thereof, or the District of Columbia, or any agency or instrumentality of any one or more of the foregoing. The term 'employee' also includes an officer of a corporation." Extremely few people, then, are "employees" that earn "wages" according to the definitions of the IRC, since only "an officer, employee, or elected official of the United States, a State, or any political subdivision thereof, or the District of Columbia, or any agency or instrumentality of any one or more of the foregoing" or "an officer of a corporation" is an "employee."

Additionally, most individuals residing in the fifty states make the false presumption that they are (exclusively) US citizens and are thereby automatically subject to internal revenue taxes by virtue of their US citizenship. "In general, all citizens of the United States, wherever resident, and all resident alien individuals are liable to the income taxes imposed by the Code whether the income is received from sources within or without the United States"—whatever "liable *to*" means—if people were lawfully required to pay the income taxes imposed by the Code, they would be "liable *for*" such taxes. However, according to the very same statute, only "Every person born or naturalized in the United States and subject to its [exclusive] jurisdiction is a citizen" [26 CFR § 1.1-1(b) & (c) and Appendix E, page E-289]. (The term "exclusive" is inserted into the latter CFR definition based on the court's pronouncement in *Caha:* "The laws of Congress in respect to those matters do not extend into the territorial limits of the states, but have force only in the District of Columbia, and other places that are within the exclusive jurisdiction of the national government" [Caha v. United States, 152 U.S. 211, 215, 14 S. Ct. 513 (1894)].) Extremely few people, then, are actually *exclusively* US citizens, since only "Every person born or naturalized in the United States and subject to its [exclusive] jurisdiction is a citizen"—those who were born and raised and *still* live in the District of Columbia or one of the many other federal territories, zones or installations (Puerto Rico, Guam, and military stations, for example). These people are exclusively citizens of the US, since they are not *also* citizens of states, counties, and (sometimes) cities and/or townships, as are the rest of us.

This book makes it easy for one to verify the lawful definitions of gross income and taxable income to determine whether or not one actually has gross income and taxable income (Appendix D, pages D-259-D-275, and Appendix E, pages E-290-E-309 & E-318-E-325). It also highlights the distinction that must be made between *imposition of* and *liability for* internal revenue taxes (Appendix D, pages D-276-D-284, and Appendix F, #s 1-4, 6 & 7) as well as the language of the law that expressly relieves nonresident alien individuals from federal income tax and self-employment tax (Appendix VI, page 214, and Appendix D, pages D-267-D-272).

The Taxpayer's Obligations

The taxpayer must verify the *validity* of the lien or levy or deficiency or determination before accepting the opinion of the IRS agent as lawfully reliable. Without such verification or contest, the IRS agent will continue to act against the taxpayer to the extent his (usually less-than-informed) understanding of the law allows. If the agent has made a determination or calculated a deficiency or issued a lien or levy, the taxpayer must verify the validity of the determination based on the source and accuracy of the information the agent used in the determination. Naturally, however, saying, "No, that's not true," will not result in immediate termination of the agent's collection efforts. More effort is required.

Department of the Treasury, Internal Revenue Service, Publication 1, Your Rights as a Taxpayer, states as The IRS Mission, "Provide America's taxpayers top quality service by helping them understand and meet their tax responsibilities and by applying the tax law with integrity and fairness to all." Under Declaration of Taxpayer Rights, V. Payment of Only the Correct Amount of Tax, it also states, "You are responsible for paying only the correct amount of tax due under the law—no more, no less." This language describes one's *duty* to determine what the law says—and especially what it *does not* say—in regard to one's liability for any tax. The taxpayer is obligated to pay no less than what the law says she must pay, but she is also *not* obligated to pay *more* than what the law says she must pay. Since IRS agents have been conditioned, "educated," and trained to believe that the law requires *everyone* to pay federal income tax, IRS agents automatically determine a federal income tax liability for everyone. It is the individual taxpayer's responsibility to determine otherwise—"the *correct* amount of tax due under the law"—by applying the statutes of law about which IRS agents generally know nothing. Once making this determination, it is necessary only to prevent other people from determining a federal income tax liability where none exists. However, if the taxpayer instead *allows* another person (such as an IRS agent or a tax preparer) to determine a federal income tax liability where none exists, it's his own fault, from the perspective of the IRS agent.

Carefully reading and replying to correspondence from IRS agents is *key* to preventing improper determinations of federal income tax liability where none exists and subsequent, unlawful collection activity. If a taxpayer fails to read and reply to correspondence from an IRS agent and thereby prevent collection efforts, and if collection efforts are carried out due to her lack of reply, it's her own fault, from the perspective of the IRS agent. If she assigns another person the task of reading and replying to correspondence from an IRS agent and the other person makes the wrong determination, it's her own fault, from the perspective of the IRS agent.

Sample IRS Agent Letters

A common authoritative letter IRS agents send taxpayers contains the following text:

> Federal tax laws are passed by Congress and signed by the President.
> The Internal Revenue Service is responsible for administering federal tax
> laws fairly and ensuring that taxpayers comply with the laws. We do not
> have authority to change the laws.
>
> The Internal Revenue Service strives to collect the proper amount of
> revenues at the least cost to the public, and in a manner that warrants the
> highest degree of public confidence in our integrity, efficiency, and
> fairness. In accomplishing this, we continually strive to help taxpayers
> resolve legitimate account problems as effectively as possible. While tax
> collection is not a popular function of government, it clearly is a necessary
> one. Without it all other functions would eventually cease.

The truth of these statements gives the letter a strong appearance of legitimacy.
However, this is a standard reply to taxpayer letters containing specific questions on
statutes of law. In spite of the language of the IRS mission, neither the first two
paragraphs, above, nor the remaining paragraphs of the letter, below, actually provide
any help in understanding the law.

> There are people who encourage others to deliberately violate our nation's
> tax laws. It would be unfortunate if you were to rely on their opinions.
> These persons take legal statements out of context and claim that they
> are not subject to tax laws. Many offer advice that is false and misleading,
> hoping to encourage others to join them. Generally, their advice isn't free.
> Taxpayers who purchase this kind of information often wind up paying
> more in taxes, interest, and penalties that they would have paid simply by
> filing correct tax returns. Some may subject themselves to criminal
> penalties, including fines and possible imprisonment.
>
> Federal courts have consistently ruled against the arguments you have
> made. Therefore, we will not respond to future correspondence
> concerning these issues
> [Letter 3175 (SC) (Rev. 2-1999) Cat. No. 26859J].

The truth of these statements maintains the appearance of legitimacy, but such
statements neither answer specific questions on statutes of law nor specifically cite any
sections of the Codes or even IRS publications that answer the questions. The
taxpayer that receives this letter and takes no note of the fact that it does not specifically
answer his questions is likely to conclude—incorrectly—that the law supports the IRS
agent and that there is nothing he can do. Other letters IRS agents commonly use
contain references to sections of the IRC or the CFR, but it is up to the taxpayer to *read*
these sections of the Codes and determine whether or not they actually apply to him. If

he is unable or unwilling to find and read these sections, he is likely to conclude—incorrectly—that the law supports the IRS agent and that there is nothing he can do.

When writing the IRS Taxpayer Advocate with specific questions on tax law, the taxpayer is likely to receive the following standard response:

> Your inquiry does not meet Taxpayer Advocate Service criteria. The Taxpayer Advocate Service is an independent office within the Internal Revenue Service (IRS) that addresses taxpayer's concerns that have not been resolved through regular contacts. Although advocates cannot change the tax laws, we work to protect individual taxpayer rights and reduce taxpayer burden. We represent your interests and concerns with the IRS to ensure a fair and equitable resolution to your issues.
>
> It is the policy of the Taxpayer Advocate Service not to respond on a point-by-point basis to questions such as those raised in your correspondence. This type of letter reflects personal opinions and frustrations with the tax system, of which the Taxpayer Advocate Service is unable to address.
>
> The IRS is responsible for administering and enforcing the Federal tax laws enacted by Congress. Individuals who do not file correct returns and/or pay correct taxes to the IRS will be subject to applicable penalties and interest in addition to their tax liability until such time as the tax laws are changed. I have forwarded your inquiry to the Examination Division. You may contact them at telephone number 1-866-899-9083. This is a toll-free number.
>
> The Taxpayer Advocate Service does not address your types of issues and will not respond to any future correspondence regarding these same issues [no citation available since this letter bears no OMB number or other reference].

Obviously, this response provides neither encouragement nor motive to continue asking questions or trying to resolve disputes.

Taxpayers are frequently advised of discrepancies via Notice of Deficiency letters:

> We have determined that you owe additional tax or other amounts, or both, for the tax year(s) identified above. This letter is your NOTICE OF DEFICIENCY, as required by law. The enclosed statement shows how we figured the deficiency.
>
> If you want to contest this determination in court before making any payment, you have 90 days from the date of this letter (150 days if this letter is addressed to you outside of the United States) to file a petition

with the United States Tax Court for a redetermination of the deficiency. You can get a copy of the rules for filing a petition and a petition form you can use by writing to the address below.

United States Tax Court, 400 Second Street, NW, Washington, DC 20217

The Tax Court has a simplified procedure for small tax cases when the amount in dispute for each tax year is $50,000 or less. If you intend to file a petition for multiple tax years and the amount in dispute for any one or more of the tax years exceeds $50,000, this simplified procedure is not available to you. If you use this simplified procedure, you cannot appeal the Tax Court's decision. You can get information pertaining to the simplified procedure for small cases from the Tax Court by writing to the court at the above address or from the court's internet site at www.ustaxcourt.gov.

Send the completed petition form, a copy of this letter, and copies of all statements and/or schedules you received with this letter to the Tax Court at the above address. The Court cannot consider your case if the petition is filed late. The petition is considered timely if the postmark date falls within the prescribed 90 or 150 day period and the envelope containing the petition is properly addressed with the correct postage.

The time you have to file a petition with the court is set by law and cannot be extended or suspended. Thus, contacting the Internal Revenue Service (IRS) for more information, or receiving other correspondence from the IRS won't change the allowable period for filing a petition with the Tax Court.

As required by law, separate notices are sent to husbands and wives. If this letter is addressed to both husband and wife, and both want to petition the Tax Court, both must sign and file the petition or each must file a separate, signed petition. If more than one tax year is shown above, you may file one petition form showing all of the years you are contesting.

You may represent yourself before the Tax Court, or you may be represented by anyone admitted to practice before the Tax Court.

If you decide not to file a petition with the Tax Court, please sign the enclosed waiver form and return it to us at the IRS address on the top of the first page of this letter. This will permit us to assess the deficiency quickly and can help limit the accumulation of interest.

If you decide not to sign and return the waiver, and you do not file a petition with the Tax Court within the time limit, the law requires us to assess and bill you for the deficiency after 90 days from the date of this

IX: Communicating with IRS Agents

letter (150 days if this letter is addressed to you outside the United States).

NOTE: If you are a C-corporation, section 6621(c) of the Internal Revenue Code requires that we charge an interest rate two percent higher than the normal rate on corporate underpayments in excess of $100,000.

If you have questions about this letter, you may write to or call the contact person whose name, telephone number, and IRS address are shown on the front of this letter. If you write, please include your telephone number, the best time for us to call you if we need more information, and a copy of this letter to help us identify your account. Keep the original letter for your records. If you prefer to call and the telephone number is outside your local calling area, there will be a long distance charge to you.

The contact person can access your tax information and help you get answers. You also have the right to contact the office of the Taxpayer Advocate. Taxpayer Advocate assistance is not a substitute for established IRS procedures such as the formal appeals process. The Taxpayer Advocate is not able to reverse legally correct tax determinations, nor extend the time fixed by law that you have to file a petition in the U.S. Tax Court. The Taxpayer Advocate can, however, see that a tax matter that may not have been resolved through normal channels gets prompt and proper handling. If you want Taxpayer Advocate assistance, please contact the Taxpayer Advocate for the IRS office that issued this notice of deficiency. See the enclosed Notice 1214, *Helpful Contacts for Your "Notice of Deficiency"*, for Taxpayer Advocate telephone numbers and addresses.

Thank you for your cooperation
[Letter 531 (DO) (Rev. 6-2003) Catalog Number 40322A].

This bold looking letter gives the impression that a problem exists with such sizeable proportions that it deserves the attention of the US Tax Court. In fact, this is a routine notice that the IRS agent has determined some discrepancy either with a tax computation or an unpaid balance due. However, while this notice seems to be alerting the taxpayer that the case will be presented to the US Tax Court in ninety days, it is merely inviting the taxpayer to petition the court to contest the determination *in court,* if so desired. This invitation does not preclude the taxpayer's right to contest the determination with the IRS agent, either in writing or by some other method. Neither does it actually cause the taxpayer's case automatically to be referred to the tax court at the end of ninety days, whether or not the taxpayer files a petition.

Both Letter 3175 and Letter 531 contain statements of fact that serve to distract the recipient from the truth of the recipient's rights and protections under the law. A response to an inquiry on statutes of law with "We do not have authority to change the laws" is as empty as a response to a request for tax rules on residency in Guam with "I live in Florida"—as if to say, "I can't help you" or "I don't want to help you." Even *suggesting* contest of a determination in Tax Court before notifying the recipient of the option to contact the IRS agent whose name, address and phone appear on the front of the letter is as good as suggesting that the individual *cannot* contact an IRS agent to try to understand and correct the situation. (As discussed on page 232, however, if a taxpayer fails to read and reply to correspondence from an IRS agent and thereby prevent collection efforts, and if collection efforts are carried out due to her lack of reply, it's her own fault, from the perspective of the IRS agent.) Not until the very last paragraph does Letter 531 admit that "The contact person can access your tax information and help you get answers." (This admission might be much more helpful if used to open the *first* paragraph instead of the last.) Suggesting that making either this contact or contact with the Taxpayer Advocate is futile, the last paragraph also states that "The Taxpayer Advocate is not able to reverse legally correct tax determinations," suggesting further that the determination which is the subject of the letter is *already* legally correct and *should not* be contested with an IRS agent or in the Tax Court or with the Taxpayer Advocate (although the criteria letter on page 235 identifies unwillingness to help on the part of the Taxpayer Advocate).

IRS agents frequently use such form letters to give the *appearance* of legitimacy to tax liabilities wholly contrived and with absolutely no basis in fact or in law for determining the amounts listed as tax liabilities. Without such factual or lawful basis, IRS agents routinely simply review taxpayer records from previous tax years and *extrapolate* (or just plain guess) amounts for current year tax liabilities.

It may be, however, that an agent has not simply extrapolated or just guessed at a nontaxpayer's "liability" since the Secretary may periodically direct efforts to locate potential taxpayers:

> United States Code
> - TITLE 26 - INTERNAL REVENUE CODE
>   - SUBTITLE F - PROCEDURE AND ADMINISTRATION
>   - CHAPTER 78 - DISCOVERY OF LIABILITY AND ENFORCEMENT OF TITLE
>   - SUBCHAPTER A - EXAMINATION AND INSPECTION

Section 7601. Canvass of districts for taxable persons and objects

(a) General rule
   The Secretary shall, to the extent he deems it practicable, cause officers or employees of the Treasury Department to proceed, from time to time, through each internal revenue district and inquire after and concerning all persons therein who may be liable to pay any internal revenue tax, and all persons owning or having the care and management of any objects with respect to which any tax is imposed.

(b) Penalties

For penalties applicable to forcible obstruction or hindrance of Treasury officers or employees in the performance of their duties, see section 7212 [http://caselaw.lp.findlaw.com/casecode/uscodes/26/subtitles/f/chapters/78/subchapters/a/sections/section_7601.html].

It remains the nontaxpayer's responsibility to protect his rights and communicate properly with the IRS agent making an inquiry under such direction.

What to Write and What to Expect

One should be aware of the departmentalized structure of the IRS when trying to communicate with agents. In simple terms, IRS offices are organized according to taxpayer geographic regions, tax types, and tax periods. When trying to communicate with agents, one should not be anxious about IRS office locations.

The IRM requires specific, prompt, responsive replies to taxpayer correspondence:

21.3.3.3.4 (10-01-2004)
Quality and Timely Responses
...
3. Your final or interim response must read ... – This is in response to your inquiry of___. If the inquiry is a letter that is not dated, use the postmark date. If that date is unknown, use a date three days prior to IRS-received date... [http://www.irs.gov/irm/part21/ch03s02.html].

1.2.1.6.4 (Approved 03-14-1991)
P–6–12
1. **Timeliness and Quality of Taxpayer Correspondence:** The Service will issue quality responses to all taxpayer correspondence.
...
3. A quality response is timely, accurate, professional in tone, responsive to taxpayer needs (i.e., resolves all issues without further contact) [http://www.irs.gov/irm/part1/ch02s04.html].

However, the responsible person should be prepared for inconsistencies between these requirements and actual letters generated by IRS agents. As illustrated in the previous section, IRS agents are notoriously, routinely evasive about specific questions and declarations based on law. Furthermore, responses or original inquiries may be generated from more than one IRS office location. The fact that the IRS uses a computerized system is no guarantee that agents at each location possess all of the same information or are as up-to-date on specific taxpayer issues as are agents at other locations.

When responding to an IRS inquiry or request, the individual may simply use the address provided on the letter received (and should not be concerned if the address contains no street address, i.e., Internal Revenue Service Center, Atlanta, GA 39901-0002). She must make specific responses to the specific points in the letter received and may ask any appropriate, specific questions of her own, asserting herself and making appropriate declarations as necessary. Many IRS inquiries and requests are actually standard, straightforward, and simple, which makes it relatively easy to respond to them. Even without expertise, the one who carefully *reads* the letter can easily spot incorrect information and simply reply. For example, if an IRS agent issues a letter requesting a corporate tax return from an individual who does not own and never has owned a corporation, she might reply in this manner:

(Taxpayer's Street Address)
(Taxpayer's City, State and ZIP)
(Today's Date)

(Name of Agent, If Any)
Internal Revenue Service Center
Atlanta, GA 39901-0002

RE: Letter Dated (00/00/00)   Tax Type: 1120   Tax Years: 2000, 2001

Dear Sir or Madam (or Name of Agent):

I am responding to the above referenced letter requesting a corporate tax return for 2000 and 2001.

Please update your records to reflect the fact that I do not own a corporation, did not own a corporation during the specified tax years, and had no corporate activity during the specified tax years. Further, I have not filed Department of the Treasury, Internal Revenue Service Form SS-4 Application for Employer Identification Number for a corporation for the specified tax years.

Thank you for your assistance and anticipated response.

Sincerely,

Jane Doe

Note that this sample letter specifies the information requested from the IRS agent (whose name may or may not appear on the original letter) and specifically responds to that request without discussing anything beyond the scope of the original letter. Other letters might discuss statutes of law and IRM procedures that require certain efforts on the part of the IRS agent before the agent may elicit a response from the individual.

Knowing the law, the astute individual can draft his own response to an inquiry or request. Even if the information contained in the inquiry or request is accurate, he still may request verification from the IRS agent (even if the agent's name is not listed on the inquiry or request) as to the agent's authority and the lawful basis for the inquiry or request. The law provides for requesting a copy of Form 23C Certificate of Assessment (or Summary Record of Assessments—IRC § 6203 and 26 CFR § 301.6203-1) and Form 17 Notice and Demand (IRC §§ 6303(a) & 6321 and CFR § 301.6303-1(a)). Both of these forms, as well as others, must be completed prior to collection activity, so the taxpayer may choose to advise the IRS agent of this fact (citing the related statutes) with a fair warning about proceeding with collection efforts without first having complied with applicable law (see Appendix III). As a part of administrative procedure, diligently reminding IRS agents of their obligations under the law reduces the likelihood that they will proceed with unlawful collection activities.

Since the IRM requires responses to taxpayer communications (see Appendix IV), the individual who responds to inquiries and requests with questions and declarations may enjoy a time lapse while an IRS agent prepares a response (or creates a further delay by passing the individual's letter to IRS attorneys). In some cases, the individual may never receive a further response (a desirable outcome).

Keeping Records

Care should be taken to ensure that IRS agents receive all written communication and that IRS agents respond to all written communication:

> "Silence can be equated with fraud where there is a legal or moral duty to speak, or where an inquiry left unanswered would be intentionally misleading …. We cannot condone this shocking behavior by the IRS. Our revenue system is based on the good faith of the taxpayer and the taxpayer should be able to expect the same from the government in its enforcement and collection activities."
> U. S. v. Tweel, 550 F. 2d 297, 299. See also U. S. v. Prudden, 424 F.2d, 1021, 1032; Carmine v. Bowen, 64 A. 932.

Using certified mail with return receipt is a consistently effective method of being able to prove, if necessary, that an individual has in fact sent written communication to an IRS agent and that the IRS agent has in fact received the written communication from the individual. Attaching the signed (or stamped), returned certified mail return receipt to an extra copy of the written communication and keeping it in permanent records is a good rule to follow.

E-mail mpllc@ymail.com, Attn: Advance Training, for more information.

Appendix X: How Strategic Tax Planning Benefits the Economy

"What if *everybody* finds out about this?"

People frequently ask, "If *everybody* finds out about this, won't the economy collapse?" The answer is, "If everybody suddenly had an extra, say, $5,000 or $10,000 of disposable income every year—wouldn't the economy *boom* from the extra money being spent?" More employees would be needed at groceries and shopping centers to keep up with the increased demand for more food and household items. Insurance and investment companies would need to hire more people to keep up with the increased demand for retirement savings. Even auto dealers would need more salesmen to keep up with the increased demand for cars and trucks. With more disposable income, people would *spend* more money, increasing the need for more people to supply their needs. Since spending money puts other people to work, unemployment and associated government spending for benefits would disappear. If we can recognize that the government's job is to keep the economy going, we can also recognize that Strategic Tax Planning actually *helps* the government do its job!

Why the Economy Does Not Fail

A large part of managing the economy is managing commerce and exchange. Although the government operates at a perpetual budget deficit due to ever-increasing spending* unmatched by "internal revenues," the economy does not fail since the government simply creates money wherever and whenever it is needed to make up for the difference. (For thorough details on banking and the Federal Reserve System, see http://www.wealth4freedom.com/creature.htm on *The Creature from Jekyll Island* by G. Edward Griffin and http://members.aol.com/rmckin6412/liberty/tom.htm on *America's Hope To Cancel Bank Loans Without Going To Court* by Tom Schauf, CPA (retired). Mr. Schauf also explains the reasons for economic failure in the past, i.e., 1929.)

Explanation of the technical facts and truths of the money system is beyond the scope of this book. However, technically, when one pays the IRS for "internal revenue" taxes, resulting in a decrease in one's bank account or legal tender or available credit card balance, there is no corresponding *increase* in the IRS bank account or in the US Treasury bank account. The only thing that actually happens, then, is that one loses the spending power represented by that amount of money or credit. Accordingly, over a hundred million people paying the IRS or the US Treasury for "internal revenue" taxes they are not lawfully obligated to pay makes over a hundred million people individually poorer than they would be otherwise. Even if it is considered that everybody is still thereby on the same playing field, all of them being correspondingly poorer, this condition is actually *negatively stimulating* to the economy since people are less able to spend money and put other people to work. Once again, the decrease in the collective bank accounts of over a hundred million people has no corresponding *increase* in the IRS bank account or in the US Treasury bank account. Accordingly, "internal revenue" taxes "paid" to the IRS or the US Treasury do not actually *pay* for even *some* of government spending! Technically, since the government already owns all the money

*See "Where do your 'income' tax dollars go?" at http://www.devvy.com/notax.html and "Where Your Income Tax Money Really Goes" at http://www.warresisters.org/piechart.htm.

anyway, "internal revenues" are not actually "revenues" at all, so the government effectively finances its own activities without actually generating any "internal revenues" and will continue to do so* whether or not it *ever* generates any "internal revenues."

Personal Economic Benefits of Strategic Tax Planning

Astutely recognizing the truth of these statements as well as the validity and general benefits of Strategic Tax Planning, one will strive to improve one's personal economy and also that of one's neighbors as well as the economy in general by implementing appropriate strategies that provide for, not unnecessary *decrease,* but *increase* in one's bank and retirement accounts—yes, concurrent *increase* in both short-term and long-term savings. Such an increase is accomplished by implementing Strategic Tax Planning and then earning "tax-deferred" interest on the savings realized.

In simple terms, "tax-deferred" is the type of income that is generally not taxed until after retirement. Account administrators are not required to report such "qualified" tax-deferred interest earnings as income unless withdrawn in a manner inconsistent with the earnings' tax-deferred nature. For example, interest is not taxed if earned on retirement savings associated with a life insurance contract and either borrowed from policy values or paid as a death benefit to beneficiaries. Accordingly, tax-deferred interest generally is not considered taxable or reportable even if the one earning the interest is filing Form 1040 annually (IRC § 101 and 26 CFR § 1.101-1(a)).

Federal income tax brackets currently range from ten to thirty-five percent (10-35%). Knowing one's current and future internal revenue tax costs, one can determine mathematically how Strategic Tax Planning can benefit one's personal economy. Since tax-free income makes it easier for one to fund a retirement plan (since one's paycheck is bigger when taxes are no longer withheld), some or all of the savings in internal revenue tax costs each year can be used to fund a qualified, tax-deferred retirement plan that accumulates each year with contributions and compounded interest. Strategic Tax Planning provides for lawfully paying no federal income tax or penalties on early withdrawal of funds, such as with an IRA, or on early or late withdrawal of funds, such as with a 401-K plan, or on surrender of policy values and accumulated interest, such as with a life insurance policy. The tax effects on tax-deferred retirement plans *without* Strategic Tax Planning are shown on the next page (not all qualified plans are shown).

Without Strategic Tax Planning, one faces the never-ending challenge of saving enough for retirement after paying current internal revenue tax costs during the working years, having enough left over for retirement after paying future internal revenue tax costs during the retirement years, risking paying penalties for excess retirement contributions, such as with an IRA or a life insurance policy, and risking paying penalties of ten to fifty percent (10-50%) on withdrawals that are inconsistent with the nature of tax-deferred retirement accounts. Comparatively, Strategic Tax Planning provides for tax savings that in turn provides for greater amounts of retirement savings, provides no limitations on contributions of such greater amounts, and provides for the accumulation and growth of retirement savings by a significantly greater rate and to a significantly greater extent.

*Since "internal revenues" are demonstrably *not* "internal revenues," perhaps such continuing activity should be known as "imaginary derivatives."

Tax-Deferred Retirement Plan:	IRA	Roth IRA	401-K	Life Ins.
Tax-deferred contributions:	Yes	No	Yes	No
Tax-deferred interest:	Yes	Yes	Yes	Yes
Withdrawal penalty prior to age 59½:	10%	None*	10%	None*
Withdrawal penalty after age 70½:	None	None	50%	None*
Taxation for normal withdrawal:	10-35%	None	10-35%	None*
Total possible taxation:	20-45%	None*	20-85%	None*

No Planning vs. Strategic Tax Planning

The following illustrates the difference between a couple who employs no tax or retirement planning and a couple who employs Strategic Tax Planning:

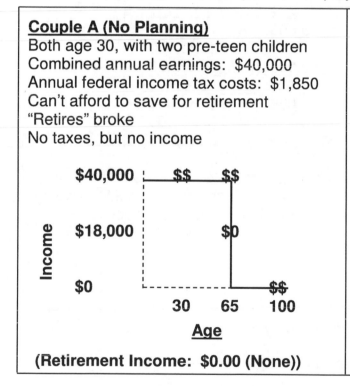

Couple A (No Planning)
Both age 30, with two pre-teen children
Combined annual earnings: $40,000
Annual federal income tax costs: $1,850
Can't afford to save for retirement
"Retires" broke
No taxes, but no income

(Retirement Income: $0.00 (None))

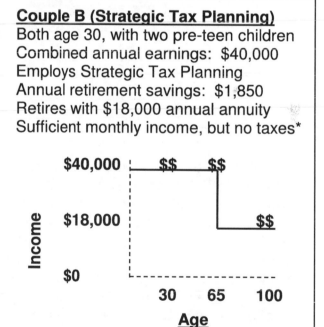

Couple B (Strategic Tax Planning)
Both age 30, with two pre-teen children
Combined annual earnings: $40,000
Employs Strategic Tax Planning
Annual retirement savings: $1,850
Retires with $18,000 annual annuity
Sufficient monthly income, but no taxes*

(Retirement income: $1,500/month)

*Withdrawing from a Roth IRA or either withdrawing from or annuitizing an annuity contract before age 59½ results in withdrawn or annuitized interest earnings reported as taxable income (and ordinarily penalized at 10% and taxed at 10-35%). Surrendering a life insurance contract results in *all* interest earnings reported as taxable income (and ordinarily taxed at 10-35%), making it wiser to keep the policy in force *for life, borrowing* one's own contributions and interest earnings rather than *surrendering* the policy and receiving all values in a lump sum. In any event, Strategic Tax Planning lawfully *prevents* penalties and taxation on all interest earnings.
            X: How Strategic Tax Planning Benefits the Economy

This illustration assumes that both couples have paid off all debts by age 65. Even with no debts, however, Couple A must struggle to survive with no retirement savings. On the other hand, Couple B receives a monthly variable annuity payment and has money *left over* each month, even though total monthly income is lower than it was during the working years when expenses were higher and debts were being eliminated. This illustration also assumes that both couples have already contributed to the social security system on a full-time basis for forty quarters (ten years) so that both couples qualify for full social security "retirement" benefits at age 65. Nevertheless, such benefits are not enough for subsistence for Couple A. However, for Couple B, such benefits are decorative icing on a carefully baked, rich layer cake!

The Rule of 72

Understanding the Rule of 72 is an important part of saving money for any purpose. In simple terms, 72 divided by the rate of interest earned equals the number of years it takes for one's initial savings to double with interest. For example, $10,000 saved once at 4% interest will take eighteen years to double to $20,000 (72 / 4% = 18 years). At 6%, it will take the same $10,000 only twelve years to double (72 / 6% = 12 years), and at 12%, only six years (72 / 12% = 6 years). To illustrate:

	4%	6%	12%
Age 30	$10,000	$10,000	$10,000
Age 36			$20,000
Age 42		$20,000	$40,000
Age 48	$20,000		$80,000
Age 54		$40,000	$160,000
Age 60			$320,000
Age 66	$40,000	$80,000	**$640,000!!!**

In this illustration, $10,000 saved once at 12% interest grows to $640,000 in thirty-six years—*a $630,000 interest increase!* A 10% return on this accumulated balance would provide annual retirement income of $64,000, a 12% return, $76,800! If such a retirement account were attached to a life insurance contract, annual or monthly loans from the interest earnings would be tax-deferred even if the owner of the policy were filing Form 1040. Strategic Tax Planning provides for such a retirement account to be *completely tax-free* regardless of its structure and regardless of whether it is "qualified" or "non-qualified."* Once again, this is beneficial to one's personal economy and also to that of one's neighbors as well as to the economy in general.

General Economic Benefits of Strategic Tax Planning

Improving one's personal economy automatically improves the rest of the economy since one has more disposable income to spend and thereby can put other people to work. Whether saving for retirement all tax savings realized through Strategic Tax Planning or choosing to save for retirement *less* than all tax savings realized, one puts more people to work locally, which drives the local economy. The shrewd one's

*"Non-qualified" plans are not tax-deferred, so interest earnings are reported annually as income, creating presumptive evidence of a tax liability (discussed in Appendices I and XI).
X: How Strategic Tax Planning Benefits the Economy

exemplary behavior in the community is imitated by other shrewd ones in the community, thereby improving their collective personal economy as well as the economy around them.

As suggested in the opening paragraph of this chapter, unemployment and associated government spending for benefits would disappear if everyone employed Strategic Tax Planning. Concerns about the failure of the social security system would likewise disappear, young people could be taught in high school how to plan for retirement, and associated government spending for benefits would disappear. The government could reallocate the savings from such unneeded unemployment and retirement benefits for whatever programs it deems appropriate and put former IRS personnel* to work administering such programs. The economy in general would accordingly be improved.

The Wise Course of Action

As discussed in Appendix III, based on delegation by the Secretary of the Treasury, statutory authority exists for the IRS Commissioner to carry out statutory directives as they relate to internal revenue taxes (pages 190, 193 & 194). At the very least, an organization as large as the Internal Revenue Service, with roughly 100,000 employees, intrinsically contributes to the economy both in the form of providing the means to earn a living for such droves of individuals and in the form of the money such droves of individuals spend in their respective communities (one person hiring another person by buying something from him churns the economy). It is appropriate, therefore, to be cautious about developing and fueling feelings of frustration with such an unpopular organization as the IRS. (Besides, it does little good to fume about something about which probably nothing can be done, anyway.) One's efforts are productively and profitably directed at becoming informed on how to spend one's hard earned dollars most wisely and prevent oneself from being defrauded, particularly through the unlawful tax collection activities of individuals who believe they are just doing their jobs.

Please e-mail mpllc@ymail.com, Attn: Advance Training, for a Strategic Tax Planning contract for review and/or a free consultation and/or to schedule a 120-minute Strategic Tax Planning mini-seminar without cost or obligation (must have Internet access for optional video-supported teleconference).

*Hypothetically speaking, of course, some might conclude that those making up the IRS would be suddenly unemployed if *everyone* employed Strategic Tax Planning. However, while the ranks of the IRS could be reasonably thinned in such a scenario, IRS personnel still serve a function since income taxes are not the only source of "internal revenues."
                        X: How Strategic Tax Planning Benefits the Economy

Appendix XI: How to Proceed Lawfully

Two Steps and Two Options

Basically, there are only two steps to becoming and remaining lawfully free from federal income, capital gains, social security, Medicare, and self-employment taxes. The first step is *learning,* recognizing that the law provides for such freedom and distinguishing between the two groups of people discussed in Appendix I. The second step is *doing,* pursuing either or both of two options, as discussed in Appendix I. The first option involves terminating any and all voluntary withholding agreements, terminating the generation of presumptive evidence of tax liability where none exists, and operating according to the Constitutional right to contract. The second option involves generating income under a name that by law never pays or generates either liability or presumptive evidence of liability for federal income, capital gains, social security, Medicare, or self-employment taxes for itself or for anyone else and operating according to the Constitutional right to contract.

Step One: *Learning*
Nobody Owes a "Fair Share" of Such Internal Revenue Taxes

Since no law makes anyone responsible for knowing the entire Internal Revenue Code, professionals and non-professionals alike perpetuate the idea that everyone owes a "fair share" of such internal revenue taxes. Such social conditioning leads people in general to believe that everyone must file a federal income tax return and pay federal income, capital gains, social security, and Medicare taxes (the latter two comprising self-employment tax for the sole proprietor). Amazingly, however, Congress has never legislated statutes making *anyone* liable for these taxes, whether or not they are based on one's income. Certain that it's in there somewhere, tax preparers and scholastic doctors alike hide behind the mountain of statutes that make up the IRC without bothering ever to search for the elusive would-be statute establishing liability for tax. He who makes the excuse, "I can't put my finger on it," should first use his fingers to open the Code and *try* to put his finger on it rather than summarily dismiss without verifying any suggestion that it simply does not exist.

Step One: *Learning*
Sixteenth Amendment to the US Constitution

Endless arguments exist about the legitimacy of the internal revenue tax laws. One of them relates to the ratification of the 16th Amendment. Bill Benson has exhaustively proved that the 16th Amendment was not properly ratified by Congress (http://www.thelawthatneverwas.com/). Others argue that the purpose of the 16th Amendment was solely to provide relief from determining the source of *corporate* income. Still others argue that the 16th Amendment neither created new tax legislation nor changed existing tax legislation. Whether or not the 16th Constitutional Amendment actually expanded congressional taxation authority beyond the original Constitutional limitations, current law and court pronouncements clearly indicate that, without statutory liability, no one is required to pay internal revenue taxes.

Step One: *Learning*
Authority of the Internal Revenue Commissioner

Other arguments exist about the legitimacy of the IRS. One of them relates to authority. Irwin Schiff makes an exhaustive argument that the IRS has neither Congressional nor Secretarial (Department of the Treasury) authority to assess and collect taxes (see http://www.paynoincometax.com/ and Appendix G). Others argue that the IRS was never established by law or that the IRS has no statutory authority. Actually, the IRC establishes authority for the Internal Revenue *Commissioner* to administer US tax laws (see Appendix III). Regardless, current law and court pronouncements clearly indicate that, without statutory liability, no one is required to pay internal revenue taxes to either the Internal Revenue Service or the US Department of Treasury.

Step One: *Learning*
Distinction between Taxpayers and Nontaxpayers

Recognizing that the law provides for freedom from federal income, capital gains, social security, Medicare, and self-employment taxes is based on recognizing the distinction between the two groups of people discussed in Appendix I. The first group is the great majority of "taxpayers" who remain ignorant of the law and continue paying taxes they are not lawfully obligated to pay. The second group is the relative minority of "nontaxpayers" who make efforts to come to know the law and to practice it continually, lawfully paying no taxes for which they have no statutory liability (see Appendix F, #s 1-7). Of course, recognizing this distinction is based on gaining sufficient knowledge and understanding of pertinent statutes of tax law and portions of the IRM and IRS publications. Maintaining familiarity with these and keeping abreast of developments are necessary to *remaining* free from taxes for which no statutory liability exists (many no-cost and some one-time cost options available).

Step Two: *Doing*
Option One

The first option for becoming and remaining lawfully free from federal income, capital gains, social security, Medicare, and self-employment taxes requires establishing a lawful basis for terminating tax withholdings and generation of presumptive evidence of tax liability where none exists. This involves completing and submitting documents to all persons with whom one has an income generating working relationship or contract. Contemptuously, IRS agents have actually instructed some not to file Form 1040 for years when no such presumptive evidence has been generated (i.e., Forms W-2 or 1099-MISC), demonstrating the occasional tendency of IRS agents to ignore individuals against whom no such presumptive evidence has been generated.

Department of the Treasury, Internal Revenue Service Form W-4, Employee's Withholding Allowance Certificate, is used by an employer to determine the amount of federal income tax to withhold from the employee's paycheck. No statutory requirement exists for a worker to submit this form or for an employer to demand this form as a condition of employment (visit http://www.irs.faithweb.com/ and page down to the heading **Form W-4 Not Required By Law**). However, IRC § 3402(n)(1) & (2) specifically provides for the use of Form W-4 to certify a lack of "liability for income tax imposed under subtitle A." Anyone who is already under a Form W-4 withholding agreement may either revoke Form W-4 (see Appendix B) or submit a new Form W-4 with the word "EXEMPT" in the blank for number of allowances to terminate federal income tax withholding from "gross pay." Since submitting such a new Form W-4 does not prevent continued withholding of social security and Medicare taxes but does generate presumptive evidence of a tax liability where none exists, *revoking* Form W-4 is recommended (see Appendix B—no cost involved).

The first option also requires investigation of and administrative rebuttal to the contents of the computerized IRS Individual Master File (IMF), known as "IMF decoding." The purpose of "decoding" is to eliminate the effects of pre-existing presumptive evidence of tax liability in computerized IRS records and, hence, to reduce the likelihood that IRS agents will attempt unlawful actions in the future. "IMF decoding" demonstrates due diligence to understand one's obligations under the law and to correct any discrepancies existing in computerized IRS records and also demonstrates lack of statutory liability for federal income, capital gains, social security, Medicare, and self-employment taxes. Decoded files and supporting documentation are required to be entered as permanent records in the IRS system.

Department of the Treasury, Internal Revenue Service Form 1040, U.S. Individual Income Tax Return, is used by people who believe they have statutory liability for federal income, capital gains, and/or self-employment tax to determine the exact amount of tax due. No statutory requirement exists for anyone who does not have a statutory liability for these taxes to file this form with the Department of the Treasury, Internal Revenue Service (visit http://www.givemeliberty.org/RTPLawsuit/Update2005-05-21.htm to read the article **"Hard Evidence That Form 1040 Has <u>NO</u> Legal Basis In Law"** and the subheading **"The Hard Evidence That Form 1040 Has No Legal Authority"**). Anyone who is already filing Form 1040 annually may reason on filing an annual IRS Filing Statement in Affidavit Form *instead* of Form 1040 (which complies with IRS requirements—see Appendix V, **Statutory Filing Requirement** and Appendix D) or discontinuing filing entirely since the statutory filing requirement states that "you must file a return or statement with us [only] for any tax you are liable for." Since filing Form 1040 generates presumptive evidence of a tax liability where none exists, discontinuing filing entirely or filing an annual statement instead of Form 1040 might seem reasonable, but filing Form 1040 each year is more effective for preventing liens and levies of unsecured earnings and bank accounts.

The first option also requires Constitutional contracting. At least for income generating purposes, one must discontinue disclosing Privacy Act protected information such as one's social security number and discontinue submitting withholding allowance certificates (Forms W-4) and entering into payroll deduction agreements, especially since even the IRS does not require such agreements (IRM 5.14.10.2 (09-30-2004) and Appendix IV, page 203). Using a written contract for exchange of assets for each working relationship is a responsible way to demonstrate that the relationship is a Constitutional contract rather than an employment agreement that could be misconstrued by IRS agents as presumptive evidence of a tax liability where none exists.

Naturally, one must decide for oneself how important it is to become and remain lawfully free from federal income, capital gains, social security, Medicare, and self-employment taxes and therefore to move diligently toward Constitutional contracting, motivated by the goal of earning permanently-tax-free interest on the tax savings realized from one's efforts. Since most people already work as "employees" for other people and companies, Constitutional contracting may, at first, appear unnecessarily inconvenient. Since people and companies routinely insist on submission of Forms W-4 or W-9 (for non-employee contractors) as a prerequisite to any kind of working agreement or contract, some may find it unreasonably challenging to convert existing working relationships to Constitutional contracts or to find work using the Constitutional contracting method. In combination with using a written contract for exchange of assets, taking steps to legally prevent or stop withholding by all persons with whom one hopes to establish or maintain an income generating working relationship or contract is conducive to establishing Constitutional contracts (see Appendix B). The purpose of these steps is to prevent such persons from withholding taxes from earnings under such Constitutional contracts and/or generating presumptive evidence of a tax liability where none exists (no cost involved).

Step Two: *Doing*
Option Two

The second option for becoming and remaining lawfully free of federal income, capital gains, social security, Medicare, and self-employment taxes requires creating a legal person that by law neither pays nor generates either liability or presumptive evidence of liability for these taxes for anyone. Exercising the second option eliminates not only these taxes but also state income and federal estate taxes. One may begin operating an existing business organization and/or a commercial activity under the new legal person and accordingly discontinue creating the appearance of being required to pay taxes based on the profits of such operations. This is particularly important for a member of a partnership or an owner or part-owner of an S-corporation, since the annual partnership or S-corporation income tax return generates presumptive evidence of tax liability in the form of Schedule K-1 for each partner or owner (intrinsic to such "flow-through" entities). Exercising the second option provides for freedom from income, capital gains, social security, Medicare, and self-employment taxes *during* and estate taxes *beyond* one's lifetime, thereby making it possible to amass particular wealth and leave one's entire fortune available for the use of heirs and beneficiaries (i.e., family heirlooms and businesses, income producing properties and investments—

initial and renewal costs involved—e-mail mpllc@ymail.com, Attn: Advance Training, for more information and referral).

The second option also requires Constitutional contracting. One must establish private, written contracts for all business relationships with the newly created legal person. A private business contract may be a contract for exchange of assets or another appropriate contract. Establishing such contracts prevents the generation of presumptive evidence of a tax liability where none exists.

A legal person should use a properly prepared personnel leasing agreement or a non-covered employee contracting firm to meet its personnel needs without creating the appearance of being required to pay taxes based on the personnel activities related to its business operations. The legal person may thus prevent the generation of presumptive evidence of a tax liability where none exists and also avoid the marginal tax costs of "payroll," usually an extra ten to fifteen percent of "gross pay."

Strategic Tax Planning and Constitutional contracting together allow one to provide for oneself and one's family and to refrain from paying taxes not required by law and from allowing the creation of presumptive evidence of internal revenue tax liability without infringing on the rights and freedoms of others. In fact, as Appendix X discussed, such is beneficial not only to one's personal economy but also to that of one's neighbors as well as to the economy in general.

Step Two: *Doing*
Vigilance and Security

Pursuit of either option in the second step requires vigilance since the continued, unlawful activities of others present a risk to the nontaxpayer. Such vigilance requires preparing for the contingency that, based on previously generated presumptive evidence in the form of wage and miscellaneous income statements (Forms W-2 and 1099-MISC), Schedules K-1, and Form 1040 filings, IRS agents might unlawfully attempt to collect taxes for which no statutory liability exists (see Appendix IX). This is particularly important, especially if one allows presumptive evidence continually to be generated. It is necessary, therefore, to maintain familiarity with pertinent statutes of tax law and portions of the IRM and IRS publications and to keep abreast of developments so as to communicate successfully with and to provide security from IRS agents that might unlawfully attempt to collect taxes for which no statutory liability exists.

Step Two: *Doing*
Which Approach to Use

Appendix IX discussed three approaches to communicating with IRS agents: the "cower in fear" method, the "hire a professional to handle it for me" method, and the "do it yourself" method. Although the chapter suggests that the second option is the most expensive and yet offers no guarantee of success, and that the last of the three is the least expensive, even after becoming somewhat educated in tax law, people tend to choose the second method anyway and "pass the buck" to a professional. So the recommendation of this book is a combination of the second and third methods: the nontaxpayer should become sufficiently familiar with tax law and administrative procedure so as to be able to supervise a professional assigned to act on behalf of the nontaxpayer. This frees the nontaxpayer from the burden of all of the homework involved in necessarily fastidious administration yet allows him or her to be reasonably confident in the methods and progress of the hired professional.

If a nontaxpayer employs Strategic Tax Planning and an IRS agent subsequently proceeds to contact the nontaxpayer with requests for information, tax returns, and/or tax payments, it is necessary to respond proficiently so as to inform the IRS agent of his or her obligations under the law, to help the IRS agent preserve the rights of the nontaxpayer (see Appendix IV), and to prevent the IRS agent from carrying out unlawful activity against the nontaxpayer (periodic rebuttal costs involved).

Just Plain Tax Planning

If it's tax time (January through March) and there is anxiety about filing *something* with the IRS while decisions are being made about possibly implementing Strategic Tax Planning, filing a request for an automatic extension of time to file is recommended. If decisions are being made to employ Strategic Tax Planning, one might reason on immediately terminating tax withholding and estimated payments so as to save as much as possible right away (no internal revenue tax payments will be refunded without Form 1040 and a calculated overpayment). (E-mail mpllc@ymail.com, Attn: Advance Training, for assistance.)

If it's the second quarter (April through June), one should decide whether or not one desires to pay another six to nine months before deciding to discontinue paying internal revenue taxes not required by law. If not, one might reason on immediately terminating tax withholding and estimated payments so as to save as much as possible right away (no internal revenue tax payments will be refunded without Form 1040 and a calculated overpayment). (E-mail mpllc@ymail.com, Attn: Advance Training, for assistance.)

If it's the third quarter (July through September), one should decide whether or not additional payments of internal revenue taxes would generate a refund of an amount greater than total additional payments for the current tax year. It may be projected that paying additional taxes and filing Form 1040 would generate a refund. If not, one might reason on immediately terminating tax withholding and estimated payments so as to save as much as possible right away (no internal revenue tax payments will be refunded without Form 1040 and a calculated overpayment). (E-mail mpllc@ymail.com, Attn: Advance Training, for assistance.)

If it's the fourth quarter (October through December), one should decide whether or not total payments of internal revenue taxes to date are sufficient to generate a refund if Form 1040 is filed for that purpose. If not, one should decide whether or not additional payments of internal revenue taxes would generate a refund of an amount greater than total additional payments for the current tax year. It may be projected that paying additional taxes and filing Form 1040 would generate a refund. If not, one might reason on immediately terminating tax withholding and estimated payments so as to save as much as possible right away (no internal revenue tax payments will be refunded without Form 1040 and a calculated overpayment). (E-mail mpllc@ymail.com, Attn: Advance Training, for assistance.)

What to Do Next

This book helps one recognize important distinctions between the truth of the law and the beliefs of the ignorant masses (the educated, the uneducated, and almost everyone in between). It also helps one make informed decisions about how best to comply with applicable laws, lawfully minimize income related yet statutorily baseless internal revenue tax costs, and start accumulating permanently-tax-free-interest-bearing savings for retirement. It also helps one weigh the costs against the personal and general economic benefits of Strategic Tax Planning.

This book recommends either a lawfully-income-tax-free business structure or a semi-private corporation. This strategy provides education and lawful minimization of all income related yet statutorily baseless internal revenue tax costs.

Please e-mail mpllc@ymail.com, Attn: Advance Training, for a Strategic Tax Planning contract for review and/or a free consultation and/or to schedule a 120-minute Strategic Tax Planning mini-seminar without cost or obligation (must have Internet access for optional video-supported teleconference).

Appendix to the Appendix
Appendix A: Lawful Tax Liens and Levies

Several things must be accomplished for a tax lien or levy to be intiated lawfully:

1. Statutory **liability** for the tax must exist (Appendix F, #s 2 - 4).

2. An assessment recorded on Forms* 23C and 4340 must be accomplished (IRC § 6203 and 26 CFR § 301.6203-1 and Appendix F, #10).

3. Form* 23C, Assessment Certificate must be made available to the taxpayer, if requested (IRC § 6203 and 26 CFR § 301.6203-1).

4. Notice of deficiency must be sent to the taxpayer (IRC § 6212(a) and IRM 25.6.5.7.2 1.).

5. Form* 17, Notice and Demand must be sent to the taxpayer (IRC §§ 6303(a) & 6321 and CFR § 301.6303-1(a)).

6. The Secretary of the Treasury, via the IRS Commissioner or the IRS Chief Counsel, must authorize civil action for the recovery of taxes and request the Attorney General to direct a civil action in the appropriate US district court for enforcement of a lien [prerequisite to a levy] and so the Court may appoint a receiver to enforce the lien (IRC §§ 7401 through 7403 and CFR §§ 301.7401-1(a) & 301.7403-1(a)—also see Appendix III).

7. Notice of lien or levy and right to hearing must be sent to the taxpayer who must first be **liable** for a tax. This notice must be sent prior to instituting lien or levy action (IRC §§ 6320, 6321, 6330, & 6331 and IRM 1.2.1.5.13 3.a.: http://www.irs.gov/irm/part1/ch02s03.html).

8. Collections efforts must be suspended if the taxpayer requests a collections due process hearing, which is held by the IRS Appeals Office (IRC §§ 6320 & 6330).

IRS agents routinely ignore the fact that, before a tax lien can be filed with a courthouse, a tax liability must first be established and tax assessed against the individual who is liable. Thereafter, a tax lien may be entered in public records as an encumbrance against property owned by such individual. For an individual to be subject to a lien for internal revenue taxes, a liability for such taxes must first be statutorily established (IRC § 6321). If—and *only* if—such a liability exists, a tax return must be filed (IRC §§ 6001 and 6011) and tax assessed within three years after the tax return is filed (IRC § 6501(a)). If the individual fails to file a tax return, the tax may be assessed at any time (IRC § 6501(c)(3)). If payments corresponding to the amount of the assessment are insufficient (IRC § 6211(a)), notice of the deficiency must be sent to the individual (IRC § 6212(a)). If payments continue to be insufficient, a civil action may (but is not required to) be directed to the US Tax Court before a tax lien is initiated

---

*Due to periodic procedural updates, the IRS will argue that revisions and replacements apply.

against the individual (CFR § 301.7401-1(a)). The individual must be provided notice before a tax lien is filed (IRM 5.12.2.3 1. (05-20-2005)), although the individual need not be notified of the actual filing of a tax lien until within five days *after* the tax lien is actually filed (IRC § 6320(a)).

If a tax lien is not updated (re-filed) within ten years and thirty days of the original assessment date, the original tax lien automatically expires (IRC §§ 6322 and 6323(g)(3)). The original tax lien also expires if it is otherwise legally unenforceable (i.e., if the tax lien is not supported by any underlying tax liability), however it will not be dropped from public records unless either ten years has expired or either a court order or some other legal documentation overturns it.

Whether the tax lien is legally unenforceable or the statute of limitations has expired, the individual may request a certificate of release (Form 668-Z), which the IRM requires to be issued within thirty days of satisfaction of the liability (IRM 5.12.6.5.1 1., 7. & 8. (10-01-2003)), and Notice 48, Release of Federal Tax Lien, which the IRM requires to be issued within five days of the taxpayer's request (IRM 5.12.6.5.1.3 2. & 7. (03-15-2005)).

In the case of a levy, the IRM states:

5.11.1.2.1 (07-01-2004)
Required Notices
1. Before property can be levied, the taxpayer must be given a
   - Notice and demand
   - Notice of intention to levy, and
   - Notice of a right to a Collection Due Process (CDP) hearing [http://www.irs.gov/irm/part5/ch11s01.html]

5.10.1.5 (12-13-2005)
Pre-Seizure Taxpayer Notifications

1. Letter 1058 (L–1058), Notice of Intent to Levy and Notice of Your Right to a Hearing, or ACS LT 11 must have been provided to the taxpayer at least 30 days before the seizure for each tax period and each assessment that will be identified on the Form 668–B.

Caution:

The CP 504 issued when a case enters status 58 does not include the required due process notification. Do not include any assessments on Form 668—B for which the L-1058 has not been issued.

2. The following information must be included with the L–1058:

- Publication 594 (Understanding the Collection Process)

- Publication 1660 (Collection Appeal Rights)

- Form 12153 (Request for a Collection Due Process Hearing)

- Copy of the letter

- Envelope

3. Taxpayers should receive only one pre-levy notice regarding their rights to a collection due process hearing for each tax assessment. If the required notice for a module has already been sent and additional tax is assessed, a new notice offering a due process hearing must be sent before the additional assessment may be included on Form 668–B. See IRM 5.10.1.5.1, Supplemental Pre-Seizure Taxpayer Notification, for information on the timeliness of this notice [http://www.irs.gov/irm/part5/ch10s01.html#d0e139179].

Once again, IRS agents routinely ignore the fact that, before a tax levy can be initiated, a tax liability must first be established and tax assessed against the individual who is liable. Thereafter, a tax levy may be initiated against property owned by such individual. For an individual to be subject to a levy for internal revenue taxes, a liability for such taxes must first be statutorily established (IRC § 6331). The language of procedures and statutes related to tax liens discussed above is similar to that related to tax levies. The individual must be provided notice at least thirty days before a tax levy is initiated (IRC § 6330(a)(2)), although the individual need not be notified at all of the actual initiation of the tax levy. The tax levy may continue until it is released (IRC § 6331(h)). The finite list of "property subject to forfeiture under the internal revenue laws" (see Appendix III) notwithstanding, IRS agents typically levy whatever property to which they can gain access. Bank and employer personnel typically believe IRS agents have the authority to make such seizures and rarely, if ever, resist their attempts.

Appendix B: Instructions on How to Legally Stop Withholding

Go to http://www.irs.faithweb.com/ and click on

<u>Stopping Tax Withholding</u>

in the right column of the page (page down once or twice).

Simply read and follow the brief instructions that appear.

E-mail mpllc@ymail.com, Attn: Advance Training, for assistance.

Appendix C: How Sections of the Codes Are Arranged

Laws are legislated by Congress as statutes or sections of the fifty Titles of the United States Code, the system of federal laws. Similar to a topical outline, the Code arranges statutes or sections into chapters, sub-chapters, parts, subparts, and so on, but without renumbering sections as "A" or "a" or "1" or "i" with each new sub-chapter and sub-part. Topical outlines generally look like the following:

I.   Introduction
II.   Problems
    A.   Problem
    B.   Problem
        i.   Sub-Problem
        ii.   Sub-Problem
        iii.   Sub-Problem
    C.   Problem
        i.   Sub-Problem
        ii.   Sub-Problem
III.   Discussion
    A.   Sub-Discussion
    B.   Sub-Discussion
IV.   Solutions
    A.   Solution
        i.   Sub-Solution
        ii.   Sub-Solution
        iii.   Sub-Solution
        iv.   Sub-Solution
    B.   Solution
        i.   Sub-Solution
        ii.   Sub-Solution
        iii.   Sub-Solution
        iv.   Sub-Solution
    C.   Solution
        i.   Sub-Solution
        ii.   Sub-Solution
        iii.   Sub-Solution
        iv.   Sub-Solution
    D.   Solution
        i.   Sub-Solution
        ii.   Sub-Solution
        iii.   Sub-Solution
        iv.   Sub-Solution
V.   Conclusion
    A.   Sub-Conclusion
    B.   Sub-Conclusion
    C.   Sub-Conclusion

Laws contained in the United States Code appear as sections (abbreviated "§§") that are never renumbered as "A" or "a" or "1" or "i" with each new sub-part and sub-chapter. Notice how the section (§) numbers increase regardless of the location in the Code:

Title 26 Internal Revenue Code
    Subtitle A—Income Taxes
        CHAPTER 1—NORMAL TAXES AND SURCHARGES
            Subchapter A—Determination of Tax Liability
                PART I—TAX ON INDIVIDUALS
                    § 1. Tax imposed
                    § 2. Definitions and special rules
                    § 3. Tax tables for individuals
                    § 4. Repealed
                    § 5. Cross references relating to tax on individuals
                PART II—TAX ON CORPORATIONS
                    § 11. Tax imposed
                    § 12. Cross references relating to tax on corporations
                PART III—CHANGES IN RATES DURING A TAXABLE YEAR
                    § 15. Effect of changes

        ...

            Subchapter B—Computation of Taxable Income
                PART I—DEFINITION OF GROSS INCOME, ADJUSTED GROSS INCOME, TAXABLE INCOME, ETC.
                    § 61. Gross income defined
                    § 62. Adjusted gross income defined
                    § 63. Taxable income defined
                    § 64. Ordinary income defined
                    § 65. Ordinary loss defined

      ...
    Subtitle B—Estate and Gift Taxes
        CHAPTER 11—ESTATE TAX
            Subchapter A—Estates of Citizens or Residents
                PART I—TAX IMPOSED
                    § 2001. Imposition and rate of tax
                    § 2002. Liability for payment
                PART II—CREDITS AGAINST TAX
                    § 2010. Unified credit against estate tax
                    § 2011. Credit for State death taxes
                    § 2012. Credit for gift tax

     ...

Numbers of corresponding sections of the Code of Federal Regulations are also sequential and begin with a number followed by a decimal and then the number of the section. (See http://www.access.gpo.gov/nara/cfr/cfr-table-search.html, http://www4.law.cornell.edu/uscode/ and Appendix E.)

Appendix C: How Sections of the Codes Are Arranged

Appendix D: The Internal Revenue Code

Gross Income

IRS Publication 1 Your Rights as a Taxpayer, Article V. Payment of Only the Correct Amount of Tax (Rev. May 2005), states:

> You are responsible for paying only the correct amount of tax due under the law—no more, no less.

See 1.1-1, CFR 1
Paragraphs (a) through (e) of United States Code, Title 26 Internal Revenue Code, Subtitle A Income Taxes, Chapter 1 Normal Taxes and Surcharges, Subchapter A Determination of Tax Liability, Part I Tax on Individuals, **Section 1 Tax imposed** (abbreviated 26 USC §1 or 26 IRC §1, with or without the section "§" symbol) begin with the words, "There is hereby imposed on the **taxable income** of." These five paragraphs are in reference to "Married individuals filing joint returns and surviving spouses," "Heads of households," "Unmarried individuals (other than surviving spouses and heads of households)," "Married individuals filing separate returns," and "Estates and trusts."

Section 2 Definitions and special rules states:

> (e) Cross reference For definition of **taxable income**, see section 63.

Subchapter B Computation of Taxable Income, Part I Definition of Gross Income, Adjusted Gross Income, Taxable Income, Etc., **Section 63 Taxable income defined** (26 IRC 63) states:

> (a) In general Except as provided in subsection (b), for purposes of this subtitle, the term "**taxable income**" means **gross income** minus the deductions allowed by this chapter....

See 1.61-2, 1.61-3, CFR 4, 5
Section 61 Gross income defined states:

> (a) General definition Except as otherwise provided in this subtitle, **gross income** means all income from whatever source derived, including (but not limited to) the following items:
> (1) Compensation for services, including fees, commissions, fringe benefits, and similar items;
> (2) Gross income derived from business;
> (3) Gains derived from dealings in property;
> (4) Interest;
> (5) Rents;
> (6) Royalties;
> (7) Dividends;
> (8) Alimony and separate maintenance payments;
> (9) Annuities;
> (10) Income from life insurance and endowment contracts;

(11) Pensions;

(12) Income from discharge of indebtedness;

(13) Distributive share of partnership gross income;

(14) Income in respect of a decedent; and

(15) Income from an interest in an estate or trust.

(b) Cross references For items specifically included in gross income, see part II (sec. 71 and following). For items specifically excluded from gross income, see part III (sec. 101 and following).

Section 64 Ordinary income defined provides this extraneous definition:

For purposes of this subtitle, the term "ordinary income" includes any gain from the sale or exchange of property which is neither a capital asset nor property described in section 1231 (b). Any gain from the sale or exchange of property which is treated or considered, under other provisions of this subtitle, as "ordinary income" shall be treated as gain from the sale or exchange of property which is neither a capital asset nor property described in section 1231 (b).

Part II **Items Specifically Included in Gross Income** lists the following items:

See 1.861-8, CFR 12, Courts 6, 8, Definition 4

§ 71 Alimony and separate maintenance payments

§ 72 Annuities; certain proceeds of endowment and life insurance contracts

§ 73 Services of child

§ 74 Prizes and awards

§ 75 Dealers in tax-exempt securities

§ 76 [Repealed]

§ 77 Commodity credit loans

§ 78 Dividends received from certain foreign corporations by domestic corporations choosing foreign tax credit

See Part II, Sec. 871, 3121, IRC 3, 9, 14, 1.1402(b)-1, CFR 38

§ 79 Group-term life insurance purchased for employees

§ 80 Restoration of value of certain securities

§ 81 [Repealed]

§ 82 Reimbursement for expenses of moving

§ 83 Property transferred in connection with performance of services

§ 84 Transfer of appreciated property to political organization

§ 85 Unemployment compensation

§ 86 Social security and tier 1 railroad retirement benefits

§ 87 Alcohol fuel credit

§ 88 Certain amounts with respect to nuclear decommissioning costs

§ 89 [Repealed]

§ 90 Illegal Federal irrigation subsidies

Sections 71 through 74, 79, 82, 85 through 88, and 90 contain language that expressly refers to the respective type of income or a calculated portion thereof as included in gross income. Section 75 discusses the methods tax-exempt securities dealers use in computing gross income and make no indication as to what is included in gross income. Section 77 states that the taxpayer *may elect* to include amounts received as loans in gross income. Sections 78 and 80 pertain to corporations and make no indication as to what is included in gross income of the taxpayer. Section 83 states that the excess of the fair market value of property transferred in connection with the performance of services to any person other than the person for whom the services are performed over any amount paid for such property shall be included in the gross income of the person who performed such services. It further states that any person who performs services in connection with which property is transferred to any person *may elect* to include such excess in gross income. It makes no indication that property or any amount paid for property is included in gross income. Section 84 pertains to the transfer of property to political organizations and makes no indication as to what is included in gross income of the taxpayer. **Sections 71 through 90 make no indication that exchanges of assets or wages or contract payments or remuneration for labor or services rendered are included in gross income.**

See Sec.
3121, 871,
IRC 9, 14,
1.1402(b)-1,
CFR 38

Part III **Items Specifically Excluded from Gross Income** lists the following items:

§ 101 Certain death benefits
§ 102 Gifts and inheritances
§ 103 Interest on State and local bonds
§ 103A [Repealed]
§ 104 Compensation for injuries or sickness
§ 105 Amounts received under accident and health plans
§ 106 Contributions by employer to accident and health plans
§ 107 Rental value of parsonages
§ 108 Income from discharge of indebtedness
§ 109 Improvements by lessee on lessor's property
§ 110 Qualified lessee construction allowances for short-term leases
§ 111 Recovery of tax benefit items
§ 112 Certain combat zone compensation of members of the Armed Forces
§ 113 [Repealed]
§ 114 Extraterritorial income
§ 115 Income of States, municipalities, etc.
§ 116 [Repealed]
§ 117 Qualified scholarships
§ 118 Contributions to the capital of a corporation
§ 119 Meals or lodging furnished for the convenience of the employer
§ 120 Amounts received under qualified group legal services plans
§ 121 Exclusion of gain from sale of principal residence
§ 122 Certain reduced uniformed services retirement pay
§ 123 Amounts received under insurance contracts for certain living expenses
§ 124 [Repealed]

§ 125 Cafeteria plans
§ 126 Certain cost-sharing payments
§ 127 Educational assistance programs
§ 128 [Repealed]
§ 129 Dependent care assistance programs
§ 130 Certain personal injury liability assignments
§ 131 Certain foster care payments
§ 132 Certain fringe benefits
§ 133 [Repealed]
§ 134 Certain military benefits
§ 135 Income from United States savings bonds used to pay higher education tuition and fees
§ 136 Energy conservation subsidies provided by public utilities
§ 137 Adoption assistance programs
§ 138 Medicare+Choice MSA
§ 139 Disaster relief payments
§ 140 Cross references to other Acts

See Part II,
Sec. 871,
3121, IRC
3, 9, 14,
1.1402(b)-1
CFR 38

Sections 101 through 140 make no indication that exchanges of assets or wages or contract payments or remuneration for labor or services rendered are excluded from gross income.

Subchapter N Tax Based on Income From Sources Within or Without the United States, Part I Source Rules and Other General Rules Relating to Foreign Income, **Section 861 Income from sources within the United States** enumerates the items of gross income treated as income from sources within the United States:

See
1.861-1,
1.861-4,
1.861-5,
1.861-8,
CFR 6,
8, 11,
12,
Courts 7

(a) Gross income from sources within United States The following items of gross income shall be treated as income from sources within the United States:
(1) Interest
Interest from the United States or the District of Columbia, and interest on bonds, notes, or other interest-bearing obligations of noncorporate residents or domestic corporations ....
(2) Dividends
The amount received as dividends ....
(3) Personal services
Compensation for labor or personal services performed in the United States; except that compensation for labor or services performed in the United States shall not be deemed to be income from sources within the United States if—
(A) the labor or services are performed by a nonresident alien individual temporarily present in the United States for a period or periods not exceeding a total of 90 days during the taxable year,

(B) such compensation does not exceed $3,000 in the aggregate, and

(C) the compensation is for labor or services performed as an employee of or under a contract with—

(i) a nonresident alien, foreign partnership, or foreign corporation, not engaged in trade or business within the United States, or

(ii) an individual who is a citizen or resident of the United States, a domestic partnership, or a domestic corporation, if such labor or services are performed for an office or place of business maintained in a foreign country or in a possession of the United States by such individual, partnership, or corporation.

In addition, compensation for labor or services performed in the United States shall not be deemed to be income from sources within the United States if the labor or services are performed by a nonresident alien individual in connection with the individual's temporary presence in the United States as a regular member of the crew of a foreign vessel engaged in transportation between the United States and a foreign country or a possession of the United States.

(4) Rentals and royalties

Rentals or royalties from property located in the United States or from any interest in such property, including rentals or royalties for the use of or for the privilege of using in the United States patents, copyrights, secret processes and formulas, good will, trade-marks, trade brands, franchises, and other like property.

(5) Disposition of United States real property interest

Gains, profits, and income from the disposition of a United States real property interest (as defined in section 897 (c)).

(6) Sale or exchange of inventory property

Gains, profits, and income derived from the purchase of inventory property (within the meaning of section 865 (i)(1)) without the United States (other than within a possession of the United States) and its sale or exchange within the United States.

(7) Amounts received as underwriting income (as defined in section 832 (b)(3)) derived from the issuing (or reinsuring) of any insurance or annuity contract ....

(8) Social security benefits

Any social security benefit (as defined in section 86 (d)).

(b) Taxable income from sources within United States From the items of gross income specified in subsection (a) as being income from sources within the United States there shall be deducted the expenses, losses, and other deductions properly apportioned or allocated thereto and a ratable part of any expenses, losses, or other deductions which cannot definitely be allocated to some item or class of gross income. The remainder, if any, shall be included in full as taxable income from sources within the United States. In the case of an individual who does not itemize deductions, an amount equal to the standard deduction shall be considered a deduction which cannot definitely be allocated to some item or class of gross income.

Section 862 Income from sources without the United States enumerates the items of gross income treated as income from sources without the United States:

See 1.862-1, CFR 15, 16

(a) Gross income from sources without United States The following items of gross income shall be treated as income from sources without the United States:

(1) interest other than that derived from sources within the United States as provided in section 861 (a)(1);

(2) dividends other than those derived from sources within the United States as provided in section 861 (a)(2);

See Part II, Sec. 871, 3121, IRC 3, 9, 14, 1.1402(b)-1, CFR 38

(3) compensation for labor or personal services performed without the United States;

(4) rentals or royalties from property located without the United States or from any interest in such property, including rentals or royalties for the use of or for the privilege of using without the United States patents, copyrights, secret processes and formulas, good will, trade-marks, trade brands, franchises, and other like properties;

(5) gains, profits, and income from the sale or exchange of real property located without the United States;

(6) gains, profits, and income derived from the purchase of inventory property (within the meaning of section 865 (i)(1)) within the United States and its sale or exchange without the United States;

(7) underwriting income other than that derived from sources within the United States as provided in section 861 (a)(7); and

(8) gains, profits, and income from the disposition of a United States real property interest (as defined in section 897 (c)) when the real property is located in the Virgin Islands.

(b) Taxable income from sources without United States From the items of gross income specified in subsection (a) there shall be deducted the expenses, losses, and other deductions properly apportioned or allocated thereto, and a ratable part of any expenses, losses, or other deductions which cannot definitely be allocated to some item or class of gross income. The remainder, if any, shall be treated in full as taxable income from sources without the United States. In the case of an individual who does not itemize deductions, an amount equal to the standard deduction shall be considered a deduction which cannot definitely be allocated to some item or class of gross income.

Definitions

Section 864 Definitions and special rules makes the following definitions applicable to Sections 861 and 862:

Supersedes 7701 (26) "Trade or business" as indicated [in brackets]

See 1.872-2, CFR 34, Courts 7, Definition 4

(b) Trade or business within the United States For purposes of this part [Source Rules And Other General Rules Relating To Foreign Income], part II [Nonresident Aliens And Foreign Corporations], and chapter 3 [Withholding Of Tax On Nonresident Aliens And Foreign Corporations], the term "trade or business within the United States" includes the performance of personal services within the United States at any time within the taxable year, but does not include—

(1) Performance of personal services for foreign employer
The performance of personal services—

(A) for a nonresident alien individual, foreign partnership, or foreign corporation, not engaged in trade or business within the United States, or

(B) for an office or place of business maintained in a foreign country or in a possession of the United States by an individual who is a citizen or resident of the United States or by a domestic partnership or a domestic corporation,

by a nonresident alien individual temporarily present in the United States for a period or periods not exceeding a total of 90 days during the taxable year and whose compensation for such services does not exceed in the aggregate $3,000....

(c) Effectively connected income, etc.

(1) General rule

For purposes of this title—

See 1.864-5, 1.872-2, CFR 17-23, 34, Courts 7, Definition 5

(A) In the case of a nonresident alien individual or a foreign corporation engaged in trade or business within the United States during the taxable year, the rules set forth in paragraphs (2), (3), (4), (6), and (7) shall apply in determining the income, gain, or loss which shall be treated as effectively connected with the conduct of a trade or business within the United States.

(B) Except as provided in paragraph (6) or (7) or in section 871 (d) or sections 882 (d) and (e), in the case of a nonresident alien individual or a foreign corporation not engaged in trade or business within the United States during the taxable year, no income, gain, or loss shall be treated as effectively connected with the conduct of a trade or business within the United States.

See Courts 7

(2) Periodical, etc., income from sources within United States—factors

In determining whether income from sources within the United States of the types described in section 871 (a)(1), section 871(h), section 881 (a), or section 881 (c), or whether gain or loss from sources within the United States from the sale or exchange of capital assets, is effectively connected with the conduct of a trade or business within the United States, the factors taken into account shall include whether—

(A) the income, gain, or loss is derived from assets used in or held for use in the conduct of such trade or business, or

(B) the activities of such trade or business were a material factor in the realization of the income, gain, or loss.

In determining whether an asset is used in or held for use in the conduct of such trade or business or whether the activities of such trade or business were a material factor in realizing an item of income, gain, or loss, due regard shall be given to whether or not such asset or such income, gain, or loss was accounted for through such trade or business.

See Courts 7

(3) Other income from sources within United States

All income, gain, or loss from sources within the United States (other than income, gain, or loss to which paragraph (2) applies) **shall be treated as effectively connected with the conduct of a trade or business within the United States.**

(4) Income from sources without United States

See 1.862-1, 1.872-2, CFR 16, 34

(A) Except as provided in subparagraphs (B) and (C), no income, gain, or loss from sources without the United States shall be treated as effectively connected with the conduct of a trade or business within the United States.

(B) Income, gain, or loss from sources without the United States shall be treated as effectively connected with the conduct of a trade or business within the United

See Courts 7, Definition 5

States by a nonresident alien individual or a foreign corporation if such person has an office or other fixed place of business within the United States to which such income, gain, or loss is attributable and such income, gain, or loss—

(i) consists of rents or royalties for the use of or for the privilege of using intangible property described in section 862 (a)(4) derived in the active conduct of such trade or business;

(ii) consists of dividends or interest, and either is derived in the active conduct of a banking, financing, or similar business within the United States or is received by a corporation the principal business of which is trading in stocks or securities for its own account; or

(iii) is derived from the sale or exchange (outside the United States) through such office or other fixed place of business **of personal property** described in section 1221 (a)(1), except that this clause shall not apply if the property is sold or exchanged for use, consumption, or disposition outside the United States and an office or other fixed place of business of the taxpayer in a foreign country participated materially in such sale.

(C) In the case of a foreign corporation taxable under part I or part II of subchapter L, any income from sources without the United States which is attributable to its United States business shall be treated as effectively connected with the conduct of a trade or business within the United States....

Part II Nonresident Aliens and Foreign Corporations, Subpart A Nonresident Alien Individuals, **Section 871 Tax on Nonresident Alien Individuals** states:

(a) Income not connected with United States business - 30 percent tax

(1) Income other than capital gains

See 1.861-8, 1.871-7, 1.872-1, 1.872-2, CFR 12, 24, 32, 33, 34, Courts 7, Definition 5

Except as provided in subsection (h), **there is hereby imposed for each taxable year a tax of 30 percent of the amount received from sources within the United States by a nonresident alien individual** as -

See Part II, Sec 3121, IRC 3, 14, 1.1402(b)-1, CFR 38

(A) interest (other than original issue discount as defined in section 1273), **dividends, rents, salaries, wages, premiums, annuities, compensations, remunerations, emoluments, and other fixed or determinable annual or periodical gains, profits, and income,**

(B) gains described in section 631(b) or (c), and gains on transfers described in section 1235 made on or before October 4, 1966,

(C) in the case of -

(i) a sale or exchange of an original issue discount obligation, the amount of the original issue discount accruing while such obligation was held by the nonresident alien individual (to the extent such discount was not theretofore taken into account under clause (ii)), and

(ii) a payment on an original issue discount obligation, an amount equal to the original issue discount accruing while such obligation was held by the nonresident alien individual (except that such original issue discount shall be taken into account under this clause only to the extent such discount was not theretofore taken into account under this clause and only to the extent that the tax thereon does not exceed the payment less the tax imposed by subparagraph (A) thereon), and

(D) gains from the sale or exchange after October 4, 1966, of patents, copyrights, secret processes and formulas, good will, trademarks, trade brands, franchises, and other like property, or of any interest in any such property, to the extent such gains are from payments which are contingent on the productivity, use, or disposition of the property or interest sold or exchanged,

but only to the extent the amount so received is not effectively connected with the conduct of a trade or business within the United States.

(2) Capital gains of aliens present in the United States 183 days or more

In the case of a nonresident alien individual present in the United States for a period or periods aggregating 183 days or more during the taxable year, there is hereby imposed for such year a tax of 30 percent of the amount by which his gains, derived from sources within the United States, from the sale or exchange at any time during such year of capital assets exceed his losses, allocable to sources within the United States, from the sale or exchange at any time during such year of capital assets. For purposes of this paragraph, gains and losses shall be taken into account only if, and to the extent that, they would be recognized and taken into account if such gains and losses were effectively connected with the conduct of a trade or business within the United States, except that such gains and losses shall be determined without regard to section 1202 and such losses shall be determined without the benefits of the capital loss carryover provided in section 1212. Any gain or loss which is taken into account in determining the tax under paragraph (1) or subsection (b) shall not be taken into account in determining the tax under this paragraph. For purposes of the 183-day requirement of this paragraph, a nonresident alien individual not engaged in trade or business within the United States who has not established a taxable year for any prior period shall be treated as having a taxable year which is the calendar year.

(3) Taxation of social security benefits

For purposes of this section and section 1441 -

(A) 85 percent of any social security benefit (as defined in section 86(d)) shall be included in gross income (notwithstanding section 207 of the Social Security Act), and

(B) section 86 shall not apply.

For treatment of certain citizens of possessions of the United States, see section 932(c). (FOOTNOTE 1)

(FOOTNOTE 1) See References in Text note below.

(b) Income connected with United States business - graduated rate of tax

(1) Imposition of tax

See Courts 7, Definition 5

A nonresident alien individual engaged in trade or business within the United States during the taxable year shall be taxable as provided in section 1 or 55 on his taxable income which is effectively connected with the conduct of a trade or business within the United States.

(2) Determination of taxable income

See Courts 7

In determining taxable income for purposes of paragraph (1), gross income includes only gross income which is effectively connected with the conduct of a trade or business within the United States.

...

Section 872 Gross Income states:

(a) General rule

See 1.871-7, 1.872-2, 1.1402(b)-1, CFR 24, 34, 39, Courts 7, Definition 5

In the case of a nonresident alien individual, except where the context clearly indicates otherwise, **gross income includes only -**
(1) gross income which is derived from sources within the United States and which is not effectively connected with the conduct of a trade or business within the United States, and
(2) gross income which is effectively connected with the conduct of a trade or business within the United States.

Section 877 discusses the expatriation of a nonresident alien individual to avoid tax.

Subpart B Foreign Corporations, Section 882 discusses tax on income of foreign corporations connected with United States business.

Subtitle F Procedure and Administration, Chapter 79 Definitions, **Section 7701 Definitions** provides the following definitions:

(a) When used in this title, where not otherwise distinctly expressed or manifestly incompatible with the intent thereof—

...

(3) Corporation
The term "corporation" includes associations, joint-stock companies, and insurance companies.
(4) Domestic
The term "domestic" when applied to a corporation or partnership means created or organized in the United States or under the law of the United States or of any State unless, in the case of a partnership, the Secretary provides otherwise by regulations.
(5) Foreign

The term "foreign" when applied to a corporation or partnership means a corporation or partnership which is not domestic....

(9) United States

See Sec. 3121, 3306, 4612, IRC 16, 17, 1.911-2, CFR 35

The term "United States" when used in a geographical sense includes only the States and the District of Columbia.

(10) State

The term "State" shall be construed to include the District of Columbia, where such construction is necessary to carry out provisions of this title....

(14) Taxpayer

The term "taxpayer" means any person subject to any internal revenue tax....

(16) Withholding agent

The term "withholding agent" means any person required to deduct and withhold any tax under the provisions of section 1441, 1442, 1443, or 1461....

(20) Employee

For the purpose of applying the provisions of section 79 with respect to group-term life insurance purchased for employees, for the purpose of applying the provisions of sections 104, 105, and 106 with respect to accident and health insurance or accident and health plans, and for the purpose of applying the provisions of subtitle A with respect to contributions to or under a stock bonus, pension, profit-sharing, or annuity plan, and with respect to distributions under such a plan, or by a trust forming part of such a plan, and for purposes of applying section 125 with respect to cafeteria plans, the term "employee" shall include a full-time life insurance salesman who is considered an employee for the purpose of chapter 21, or in the case of services performed before January 1, 1951, who would be considered an employee if his services were performed during 1951....

(26) Trade or business

The term "trade or business" includes the performance of the functions of a public office.... [Superseded by Section 864 for Foreign Income, Nonresident Aliens, and Foreign Corporations.]

(28) Other terms

Any term used in this subtitle with respect to the application of, or in connection with, the provisions of any other subtitle of this title shall have the same meaning as in such provisions.

See Definition 5

(b) Definition of resident alien and nonresident alien

(1) In general

For purposes of this title (other than subtitle B)—

> **(A) Resident alien An alien individual shall be treated as a resident of the United States with respect to any calendar year if (and only if) such individual meets the requirements of clause (i), (ii), or (iii):**

(i) Lawfully admitted for permanent residence
Such individual is a lawful permanent resident of the United States at any time during such calendar year.
(ii) Substantial presence test Such individual meets the substantial presence test of paragraph (3).
(iii) First year election Such individual makes the election provided in paragraph (4).
(B) Nonresident alien An individual is a nonresident alien if such individual is neither a citizen of the United States nor a resident of the United States (within the meaning of subparagraph (A))....
(3) Substantial presence test
(A) In general
Except as otherwise provided in this paragraph, an individual meets the substantial presence test of this paragraph with respect to any calendar year (hereinafter in this subsection referred to as the "current year") **if –**
(i) such individual was present in the United States on at least 31 days during the calendar year, and
(ii) the sum of the number of days on which such individual was present in the United States during the current year and the 2 preceding calendar years (when multiplied by the applicable multiplier determined under the following table) equals or exceeds 183 days:

In the case of days in:	The applicable multiplier is:
Current year	1
1st preceding year	1/3
2nd preceding year	1/6

...

(6) Lawful permanent resident
For purposes of this subsection, an individual is a lawful permanent resident of the United States at any time if—
(A) such individual has the status of having been lawfully accorded the privilege of residing permanently in the United States as an immigrant in accordance with the immigration laws, and
(B) such status has not been revoked (and has not been administratively or judicially determined to have been abandoned).
(7) Presence in the United States
For purposes of this subsection—
(A) In general Except as provided in subparagraph (B), (C), or (D), an individual shall be treated as present in

the United States on any day if such individual is physically present in the United States at any time during such day.

(B) Commuters from Canada or Mexico If an individual regularly commutes to employment (or self-employment) in the United States from a place of residence in Canada or Mexico, such individual shall not be treated as present in the United States on any day during which he so commutes.

(C) Transit between 2 foreign points If an individual, who is in transit between 2 points outside the United States, is physically present in the United States for less than 24 hours, such individual shall not be treated as present in the United States on any day during such transit.

(D) Crew members temporarily present An individual who is temporarily present in the United States on any day as a regular member of the crew of a foreign vessel engaged in transportation between the United States and a foreign country or a possession of the United States shall not be treated as present in the United States on such day unless such individual otherwise engages in any trade or business in the United States on such day....

(c) Includes and including The terms "includes" and "including" when used in a definition contained in this title shall not be deemed to exclude other things otherwise within the meaning of the term defined.

Subtitle C Employment Taxes, Chapter 21 Federal Insurance Contributions Act, Subchapter C General Provisions, **Section 3121 Definitions** provides the following definitions related to withholding social security and Medicare taxes:

See Part II, Sec. 871, IRC 3, 9, 1.1402(b)-1, CFR 38

(a) Wages
For purposes of this chapter, the term "wages" means all remuneration for employment, including the cash value of all remuneration (including benefits) paid in any medium other than cash; ....

(b) Employment
For purposes of this chapter, the term "employment" means any service, of whatever nature, performed (A) by an employee for the person employing him, irrespective of the citizenship or residence of either, (i) within the United States, or (ii) on or in connection with an American vessel or American aircraft under a contract of service which is entered into within the United States or during the performance of which and while the employee is employed on the vessel or aircraft it touches at a port in the United States, if the employee is employed on and in connection with such vessel or aircraft when outside the United States, **or (B) outside the United States by a citizen or resident of the United**

States as an employee for an American employer (as defined in subsection (h)), or (C) if it is service, regardless of where or by whom performed, which is designated as employment or recognized as equivalent to employment under an agreement entered into under section 233 of the Social Security Act; ….

(c) Included and excluded service

For purposes of this chapter, if the services performed during one-half or more of any pay period by an employee for the person employing him constitute employment, all the services of such employee for such period shall be deemed to be employment; but if the services performed during more than one-half of any such pay period by an employee for the person employing him do not constitute employment, then none of the services of such employee for such period shall be deemed to be employment. As used in this subsection, the term "pay period" means a period (of not more than 31 consecutive days) for which a payment of remuneration is ordinarily made to the employee by the person employing him. This subsection shall not be applicable with respect to services performed in a pay period by an employee for the person employing him, where any of such service is excepted by subsection (b)(9).

(d) Employee

For purposes of this chapter, the term "employee" means -

    (1) any officer of a corporation; or

    (2) any individual who, under the usual common law rules applicable in determining the employer-employee relationship, has the status of an employee; or

    (3) any individual (other than an individual who is an employee under paragraph (1) or (2)) who performs services for remuneration for any person -

        (A) as an agent-driver or commission-driver engaged in distributing meat products, vegetable products, fruit products, bakery products, beverages (other than milk), or laundry or dry-cleaning services, for his principal;

        (B) as a full-time life insurance salesman;

        (C) as a home worker performing work, according to specifications furnished by the person for whom the services are performed, on materials or goods furnished by such person which are required to be returned to such person or a person designated by him; or

        (D) as a traveling or city salesman, other than as an agent-driver or commission-driver, engaged upon a full-time basis in the solicitation on behalf of, and the transmission to, his principal (except for side-line sales activities on behalf of some other person) of orders from wholesalers, retailers, contractors, or operators of hotels, restaurants, or other similar establishments for merchandise for resale or supplies for use in their business operations; if the contract of service contemplates that substantially all of such services are to be performed personally by such individual; except that an individual shall not be included in the term "employee" under the provisions of this paragraph if such individual has a substantial investment in facilities used in connection with the performance of such services (other than in facilities for transportation), or if the services are in the nature of a single transaction not part of a continuing relationship with the person for whom the services are performed; or

(4) any individual who performs services that are included under an agreement entered into pursuant to section 218 of the Social Security Act.

See Sec. 7701, 3306, 4612, IRC 11, 12, 16, 17, 1.911-2, CFR 35

(e) State, United States, and citizen
For purposes of this chapter -
   (1) State
   The term "State" includes the District of Columbia, the Commonwealth of Puerto Rico, the Virgin Islands, Guam, and American Samoa.
   (2) United States
   The term "United States" when used in a geographical sense includes the Commonwealth of Puerto Rico, the Virgin Islands, Guam, and American Samoa.
An individual who is a citizen of the Commonwealth of Puerto Rico (but not otherwise a citizen of the United States) shall be considered, for purposes of this section, as a citizen of the United States.

Chapter 22 Railroad Retirement Tax Act, Subchapter D General Provisions, **Section 3231 Definitions** pertains to terms used for purposes of Chapter 22.

Chapter 23 Federal Unemployment Tax Act, **Section 3306 Definitions** provides the following definition:

(j) State, United States, and American employer
For purposes of this chapter -
   (1) State
   The term "State" includes the District of Columbia, the Commonwealth of Puerto Rico, and the Virgin Islands.

See Sec. 7701, 3121, 4612, IRC 11, 12, 16, 17, 1.911-2, CFR 35

   (2) United States
   The term "United States" when used in a geographical sense includes the States, the District of Columbia, the Commonwealth of Puerto Rico, and the Virgin Islands.
   (3) American employer
   The term "American employer" means a person who is -
      (A) an individual who is a resident of the United States,

(B) a partnership, if two-thirds or more of the partners are residents of the United States,

(C) a trust, if all of the trustees are residents of the United States, or

(D) a corporation organized under the laws of the United States or of any State.

An individual who is a citizen of the Commonwealth of Puerto Rico or the Virgin Islands (but not otherwise a citizen of the United States) shall be considered, for purposes of this section, as a citizen of the United States.

Subtitle D Miscellaneous Excise Taxes, Chapter 38 Environmental Taxes, Subchapter A Tax on Petroleum, **Section 4612 Definitions and Special Rules** provides the following definition:

(a) Definitions

For purposes of this subchapter -

…

See Sec. 7701, 3121, 3306, IRC 11, 12, 16, 1.911-2, CFR 35

(4) United States

(A) In general

The term "United States" means the 50 States, the District of Columbia, the Commonwealth of Puerto Rico, any possession of the United States, the Commonwealth of the Northern Mariana Islands, and the Trust Territory of the Pacific Islands.

Liability

Subtitle A Income Taxes, Chapter 3 Withholding of Tax on Nonresident Aliens and Foreign Corporations, Subchapter B Application of Withholding Provisions, **Section 1461 Liability for Withheld Tax** states:

> Every person required to deduct and withhold any tax under this chapter is hereby made liable for such tax and is hereby indemnified against the claims and demands of any person for the amount of any payments made in accordance with the provisions of this chapter.

Subtitle F, Chapter 61 Information and Returns, Subchapter A Returns and Records, Part I Records, Statements, and Special Returns, **Section 6001 Notice or regulations requiring records, statements, and special returns** states:

See
Courts
2-5

Every person liable for any tax imposed by this title, or for the collection thereof, shall keep such records, render such statements, make such returns, and comply with such rules and regulations as the Secretary may from time to time prescribe. Whenever in the judgment of the Secretary it is necessary, he may require any person, by notice served upon such person or by regulations, to make such returns, render such statements, or keep such records, as the Secretary deems sufficient to show whether or not such person is liable for tax under this title. The only records which an employer shall be required to keep under this section in connection with charged tips shall be charge receipts, records necessary to comply with section 6053 (c), and copies of statements furnished by employees under section 6053 (a).

Part II Tax Returns or Statements, Subpart A General Requirement, **Section 6011 General requirement of return, statement, or list** states:

See
Courts
2-5

(a) General rule When required by regulations prescribed by the Secretary any person made liable for any tax imposed by this title, or with respect to the collection thereof, shall make a return or statement according to the forms and regulations prescribed by the Secretary. Every person required to make a return or statement shall include therein the information required by such forms or regulations.

Subpart B Income Tax Returns, **Section 6012 Persons required to make returns of income** states:

(a) General rule Returns with respect to income taxes under subtitle A shall be made by the following:
  (1)

(A) Every individual having for the taxable year gross income which equals or exceeds the exemption amount, except that a return shall not be required of an individual—

> (i) who is not married (determined by applying section 7703), is not a surviving spouse (as defined in section 2 (a)), is not a head of a household (as defined in section 2 (b)), and for the taxable year has gross income of less than the sum of the exemption amount plus the basic standard deduction applicable to such an individual,
>
> (ii) who is a head of a household (as so defined) and for the taxable year has gross income of less than the sum of the exemption amount plus the basic standard deduction applicable to such an individual,
>
> (iii) who is a surviving spouse (as so defined) and for the taxable year has gross income of less than the sum of the exemption amount plus the basic standard deduction applicable to such an individual, or
>
> (iv) who is entitled to make a joint return and whose gross income, when combined with the gross income of his spouse, is, for the taxable year, less than the sum of twice the exemption amount plus the basic standard deduction applicable to a joint return, but only if such individual and his spouse, at the close of the taxable year, had the same household as their home.

Clause (iv) shall not apply if for the taxable year such spouse makes a separate return or any other taxpayer is entitled to an exemption for such spouse under section 151 (c).

(B) The amount specified in clause (i), (ii), or (iii) of subparagraph (A) shall be increased by the amount of 1 additional standard deduction (within the meaning of section 63 (c)(3)) in the case of an individual entitled to such deduction by reason of section 63 (f)(1)(A) (relating to individuals age 65 or more), and the amount specified in clause (iv) of subparagraph (A) shall be increased by the amount of the additional standard deduction for each additional standard deduction to which the individual or his spouse is entitled by reason of section 63 (f)(1).

(C) The exception under subparagraph (A) shall not apply to any individual—

> (i) who is described in section 63 (c)(5) and who has—

> > (I) income (other than earned income) in excess of the sum of the amount in effect under section 63 (c)(5)(A) plus the additional

standard deduction (if any) to which the individual is entitled, or
(II) total gross income in excess of the standard deduction, or
(ii) for whom the standard deduction is zero under section 63 (c)(6).
(D) For purposes of this subsection—
(i) The terms "standard deduction", "basic standard deduction" and "additional standard deduction" have the respective meanings given such terms by section 63 (c).
(ii) The term "exemption amount" has the meaning given such term by section 151 (d). In the case of an individual described in section 151 (d)(2), the exemption amount shall be zero.
(2) Every corporation subject to taxation under subtitle A;
(3) Every estate the gross income of which for the taxable year is $600 or more;
(4) Every trust having for the taxable year any taxable income, or having gross income of $600 or over, regardless of the amount of taxable income;
(5) Every estate or trust of which any beneficiary is a nonresident alien;
(6) Every political organization (within the meaning of section 527 (e)(1)), and every fund treated under section 527 (g) as if it constituted a political organization, which has political organization taxable income (within the meaning of section 527 (c)(1)) for the taxable year; and [1]
(7) Every homeowners association (within the meaning of section 528 (c)(1)) which has homeowners association taxable income (within the meaning of section 528 (d)) for the taxable year.[1]
(8) Every individual who receives payments during the calendar year in which the taxable year begins under section 3507 (relating to advance payment of earned income credit).[1]
(9) Every estate of an individual under chapter 7 or 11 of title 11 of the United States Code (relating to bankruptcy) the gross income of which for the taxable year is not less than the sum of the exemption amount plus the basic standard deduction under section 63 (c)(2)(D).[1]
except that subject to such conditions, limitations, and exceptions and under such regulations as may be prescribed by the Secretary, nonresident alien individuals subject to the tax imposed by section 871 and foreign corporations subject to the tax imposed by section 881 may be exempted from the requirement of making returns under this section.

Chapter 63 Assessment, Subchapter A In General, **Section 6203 Method of assessment** states:

See
Courts
2-5

The assessment shall be made by recording the liability of the taxpayer in the office of the Secretary in accordance with rules or regulations prescribed by the Secretary. Upon request of the taxpayer, the Secretary shall furnish the taxpayer a copy of the record of the assessment.

Chapter 64 Collection, Subchapter A General Provisions, **Section 6303 Notice and demand for tax** states:

See
Courts
2-5

(a) General rule Where it is not otherwise provided by this title, the Secretary shall, as soon as practicable, and within 60 days, after the making of an assessment of a tax pursuant to section 6203, give notice to each person liable for the unpaid tax, stating the amount and demanding payment thereof. Such notice shall be left at the dwelling or usual place of business of such person, or shall be sent by mail to such person's last known address.

Subchapter C Lien for Taxes, Part II Liens, **Section 6321 Lien for Taxes** states:

See
Courts
2-5

If any person liable to pay any tax neglects or refuses to pay the same after demand, the amount (including any interest, additional amount, addition to tax, or assessable penalty, together with any costs that may accrue in addition thereto) shall be a lien in favor of the United States upon all property and rights to property, whether real or personal, belonging to such person.

Section 6322 Period of lien states:

Unless another date is specifically fixed by law, **the lien imposed by section 6321 shall arise at the time the assessment is made** and shall continue until the liability for the amount so assessed (or a judgment against the taxpayer arising out of such liability) is satisfied or becomes unenforceable by reason of lapse of time.

Section 6325 Release of lien or discharge of property states:

(a) Release of lien Subject to such regulations as the Secretary may prescribe, the Secretary shall issue a certificate of release of any lien imposed with respect to any internal revenue tax not later than 30 days after the day on which—
    (1) Liability satisfied or unenforceable

The Secretary finds that the liability for the amount assessed, together with all interest in respect thereof, has been fully satisfied or has become legally unenforceable

Section 6326 Administrative appeal of liens states:

(a) In general In such form and at such time as the Secretary shall prescribe by regulations, any person shall be allowed to appeal to the Secretary after the filing of a notice of a lien under this subchapter on the property or the rights to property of such person for a release of such lien alleging an error in the filing of the notice of such lien.
(b) Certificate of release If the Secretary determines that the filing of the notice of any lien was erroneous, the Secretary shall expeditiously (and, to the extent practicable, within 14 days after such determination) issue a certificate of release of such lien and shall include in such certificate a statement that such filing was erroneous.

Subchapter D Seizure of Property for Collection of Taxes, Part II Levy, **Section 6331 Levy and distraint** states:

See
Courts
2-5
(a) Authority of Secretary If any person liable to pay any tax neglects or refuses to pay the same within 10 days after notice and demand, it shall be lawful for the Secretary to collect such tax (and such further sum as shall be sufficient to cover the expenses of the levy) by levy upon all property and rights to property (except such property as is exempt under section 6334) belonging to such person or on which there is a lien provided in this chapter for the payment of such tax. Levy may be made upon the accrued salary or wages of any officer, employee, or elected official, of the United States, the District of Columbia, or any agency or instrumentality of the United States or the District of Columbia, by serving a notice of levy on the employer (as defined in section 3401(d)) of such officer, employee, or elected official. If the Secretary makes a finding that the collection of such tax is in jeopardy, notice and demand for immediate payment of such tax may be made by the Secretary and, upon failure or refusal to pay such tax, collection thereof by levy shall be lawful without regard to the 10-day period provided in this section.

Section 6343 Authority to release levy and return property states:

(a) Release of levy and notice of release
(1) In general
Under regulations prescribed by the Secretary, the Secretary shall release the levy upon all, or part of, the property or rights to property levied upon and shall promptly notify the person upon

whom such levy was made (if any) that such levy has been released if—

(A) the liability for which such levy was made is satisfied or becomes unenforceable by reason of lapse of time,

(B) release of such levy will facilitate the collection of such liability,

(C) the taxpayer has entered into an agreement under section 6159 to satisfy such liability by means of installment payments, unless such agreement provides otherwise,

(D) the Secretary has determined that such levy is creating an economic hardship due to the financial condition of the taxpayer, or

(E) the fair market value of the property exceeds such liability and release of the levy on a part of such property could be made without hindering the collection of such liability.

For purposes of subparagraph (C), the Secretary is not required to release such levy if such release would jeopardize the secured creditor status of the Secretary.

(2) Expedited determination on certain business property

In the case of any tangible personal property essential in carrying on the trade or business of the taxpayer, the Secretary shall provide for an expedited determination under paragraph (1) if levy on such tangible personal property would prevent the taxpayer from carrying on such trade or business.

(3) Subsequent levy

The release of levy on any property under paragraph (1) shall not prevent any subsequent levy on such property.

(b) Return of property If the Secretary determines that property has been wrongfully levied upon, it shall be lawful for the Secretary to return—

(1) the specific property levied upon,

(2) an amount of money equal to the amount of money levied upon, or

(3) an amount of money equal to the amount of money received by the United States from a sale of such property.

Property may be returned at any time. An amount equal to the amount of money levied upon or received from such sale may be returned at any time before the expiration of 9 months from the date of such levy. For purposes of paragraph (3), if property is declared purchased by the United States at a sale pursuant to section 6335 (e) (relating to manner and conditions of sale), the United States shall be treated as having received an amount of money equal to the minimum price determined pursuant to such section or (if larger) the amount received by the United States from the resale of such property.

(c) Interest Interest shall be allowed and paid at the overpayment rate established under section 6621—

(1) in a case described in subsection (b)(2), from the date the Secretary receives the money to a date (to be determined by the Secretary) preceding the date of return by not more than 30 days, or

(2) in a case described in subsection (b)(3), from the date of the sale of the property to a date (to be determined by the Secretary) preceding the date of return by not more than 30 days.

(d) Return of property in certain cases If—

(1) any property has been levied upon, and

(2) the Secretary determines that—

(A) the levy on such property was premature or otherwise not in accordance with administrative procedures of the Secretary,

(B) the taxpayer has entered into an agreement under section 6159 to satisfy the tax liability for which the levy was imposed by means of installment payments, unless such agreement provides otherwise,

(C) the return of such property will facilitate the collection of the tax liability, or

(D) with the consent of the taxpayer or the National Taxpayer Advocate, the return of such property would be in the best interests of the taxpayer (as determined by the National Taxpayer Advocate) and the United States,

the provisions of subsection (b) shall apply in the same manner as if such property had been wrongly levied upon, except that no interest shall be allowed under subsection (c).

(e) Release of levy upon agreement that amount is not collectible In the case of a levy on the salary or wages payable to or received by the taxpayer, upon agreement with the taxpayer that the tax is not collectible, the Secretary shall release such levy as soon as practicable.

Chapter 65 Abatements, Credits, and Refunds, Subchapter A Procedure in General, **Section 6402 Authority to make credits or refunds** states:

(a) General rule In the case of any overpayment, the Secretary, within the applicable period of limitations, may credit the amount of such overpayment, including any interest allowed thereon, against any liability in respect of an internal revenue tax on the part of the person who made the overpayment and shall, subject to subsections (c), (d), and (e) refund any balance to such person.

Chapter 66 Limitations, Subchapter A Limitations on Assessment and Collection, **Section 6501 Limitations on assessment and collection** states:

(a) General rule Except as otherwise provided in this section, **the amount of any tax imposed by this title shall be assessed within 3 years after**

the return was filed (whether or not such return was filed on or after the date prescribed) or, if the tax is payable by stamp, at any time after such tax became due and before the expiration of 3 years after the date on which any part of such tax was paid, and no proceeding in court without assessment for the collection of such tax shall be begun after the expiration of such period. For purposes of this chapter, the term "return" means the return required to be filed by the taxpayer (and does not include a return of any person from whom the taxpayer has received an item of income, gain, loss, deduction, or credit)....

(c) Exceptions

    (1) False return

In the case of a false or fraudulent return with the intent to evade tax, the tax may be assessed, or a proceeding in court for collection of such tax may be begun without assessment, at any time.

    (2) Willful attempt to evade tax

In case of a willful attempt in any manner to defeat or evade tax imposed by this title (other than tax imposed by subtitle A or B), the tax may be assessed, or a proceeding in court for the collection of such tax may be begun without assessment, at any time.

    (3) No return

In the case of failure to file a return, the tax may be assessed, or a proceeding in court for the collection of such tax may be begun without assessment, at any time.

Section 6502 Collection after assessment states:

(a) Length of period Where the assessment of any tax imposed by this title has been made within the period of limitation properly applicable thereto, such tax may be collected by levy or by a proceeding in court, but only if the levy is made or the proceeding begun—

    (1) within 10 years after the assessment of the tax, or

    (2) if—

        (A) there is an installment agreement between the taxpayer and the Secretary, prior to the date which is 90 days after the expiration of any period for collection agreed upon in writing by the Secretary and the taxpayer at the time the installment agreement was entered into; or

        (B) there is a release of levy under section 6343 after such 10-year period, prior to the expiration of any period for collection agreed upon in writing by the Secretary and the taxpayer before such release.

If a timely proceeding in court for the collection of a tax is commenced, the period during which such tax may be collected by levy shall be extended and shall not expire until the liability for the tax (or a judgment against the taxpayer arising from such liability) is satisfied or becomes unenforceable.

(b) Date when levy is considered made The date on which a levy on property or rights to property is made shall be the date on which the notice of seizure provided in section 6335 (a) is given.

Chapter 66 Limitations, Subchapter B Limitations on Credit or Refund, **Section 6511 Limitations on credit or refund** states:

(a) Period of limitation on filing claim Claim for credit or refund of an overpayment of any tax imposed by this title in respect of which tax the taxpayer is required to file a return shall be filed by the taxpayer within 3 years from the time the return was filed or 2 years from the time the tax was paid, whichever of such periods expires the later, or if no return was filed by the taxpayer, within 2 years from the time the tax was paid. Claim for credit or refund of an overpayment of any tax imposed by this title which is required to be paid by means of a stamp shall be filed by the taxpayer within 3 years from the time the tax was paid.

Appendix

The Appendix to the Internal Revenue Code provides an outline for United States Tax Court procedures applicable to disputing IRS lien and levy activity:

TITLE 26 App. > TITLE I. > Rule 1
Rule 1. Scope of Rules and Construction

Release date: 2005-08-31

(a) Scope: These Rules govern the practice and procedure in all cases and proceedings in the United States Tax Court. Where in any instance there is no applicable rule of procedure, the Court or the Judge before whom the matter is pending may prescribe the procedure, giving particular weight to the Federal Rules of Civil Procedure to the extent that they are suitably adaptable to govern the matter at hand.
(b) Construction: These Rules shall be construed to secure the just, speedy, and inexpensive determination of every case
[http://www4.law.cornell.edu/uscode/html/uscode26a/usc_sec_26a_00000 001----000-.html].

It states the rules and jurisdiction for lien and levy actions:

TITLE 26 App. > TITLE XXXII. > Rule 330
Rule 330. General

Release date: 2005-08-31

(a) Applicability: The Rules of this Title XXXII set forth the provisions that apply to lien and levy actions under Code sections 6320 (c) and 6330 (d). Except as otherwise provided in this Title, the other Rules of Practice and Procedure of the Court, to the extent pertinent, are applicable to such actions.
(b) Jurisdiction: The Court shall have jurisdiction of a lien or levy action under this Title when the conditions of Code section 6320 (c) or 6330 (d), as applicable, have been satisfied
[http://www4.law.cornell.edu/uscode/html/uscode26a/usc_sec_26a_00000 330----000-.html].

It states particularly that the Tax Court must be petitioned for lien and levy actions:

TITLE 26 App. > TITLE XXXII. > Rule 331
Rule 331. Commencement of Lien and Levy Action

Release date: 2005-08-31

(a) Commencement of Action: A lien and levy action under Code sections 6320 (c) and 6330 (d) shall be commenced by filing a petition with the Court. See Rule 20, relating to commencement of case; Rule 22, relating to the place and manner of filing the petition; and Rule 32, regarding the form of pleadings.

(b) Content of Petition: A petition filed pursuant to this Rule shall be entitled "Petition for Lien or Levy Action Under Code Section 6320 (c) or 6330 (d)", as applicable, and shall contain the following:

(1) In the case of a petitioner other than a corporation, the petitioner's name and legal residence; in the case of a corporate petitioner, the petitioner's name and principal place of business or principal office or agency; and, in all cases, the petitioner's mailing address and taxpayer identification number (e.g., Social Security number or employer identification number). The mailing address, legal residence, and principal place of business, or principal office or agency, shall be stated as of the date that the petition is filed.

(2) The date of the notice of determination concerning collection action(s) under Code section 6320 and/or 6330 by the Internal Revenue Service Office of Appeals (hereinafter the "notice of determination"), and the city and State of the Office which made such determination.

(3) The amount or amounts and type of underlying tax liability, and the year or years or other periods to which the notice of determination relates.

(4) Clear and concise assignments of each and every error which the petitioner alleges to have been committed in the notice of determination. Any issue not raised in the assignments of error shall be deemed to be conceded. Each assignment of error shall be separately lettered.

(5) Clear and concise lettered statements of the facts on which the petitioner bases each assignment of error.

(6) A prayer setting forth the relief sought by the petitioner.

(7) The signature, mailing address, and telephone number of each petitioner or each petitioner's counsel, as well as counsel's Tax Court bar number.

(8) As an attachment, a copy of the notice of determination.

A claim for reasonable litigation or administrative costs shall not be included in the petition in a lien and levy action. For the requirements as to claims for reasonable litigation or administrative costs, see Rule 231.

(c) Small Tax Case Under Code Section 7463 (f)(2): For provisions regarding the content of a petition in a small tax case under Code section 7463 (f)(2), see Rules 170 through 175.

(d) Filing Fee: The fee for filing a petition for a lien and levy action shall be $60, payable at the time of filing [http://www4.law.cornell.edu/uscode/html/uscode26a/usc_sec_26a_00000 331----000-.html].

Appendix E: The Code of Federal Regulations

[Code of Federal Regulations]
[Title 26, Volume 1]
[Revised as of April 1, 2003]
From the U.S. Government Printing Office via GPO Access
[CITE: 26CFR1.1-1]

[Page 9-10]

TITLE 26--INTERNAL REVENUE

CHAPTER I--INTERNAL REVENUE SERVICE, DEPARTMENT OF THE TREASURY

PART 1--INCOME TAXES--Table of Contents

Sec. 1.1-1 Income tax on individuals.

See Secs. 871, 872, 877, IRC 9-11, Sec. 7701, IRC 11-14, 1.864-5, CFR 17

See Part II, Sec. 3121, IRC 3, 14, 1.1402(b)-1, CFR 38

(a) General rule. (1) Section 1 of the Code imposes an income tax on the income of every individual who is a citizen or resident of the United States and, to the extent provided by section 871(b) or 877(b), on the income of a nonresident alien individual. For optional tax in the case of taxpayers with adjusted gross income of less than $10,000 (less than $5,000 for taxable years beginning before January 1, 1970) see section 3. The tax imposed is upon taxable income (determined by subtracting the allowable deductions from gross income). The tax is determined in accordance with the table contained in section 1. See subparagraph (2) of this paragraph for reference guides to the appropriate table for taxable years beginning on or after January 1, 1964, and before January 1, 1965, taxable years beginning after December 31, 1964, and before January 1, 1971, and taxable years beginning after December 31, 1970. In certain cases credits are allowed against the amount of the tax. See part IV (section 31 and following), subchapter A, chapter 1 of the Code. In general, the tax is payable upon the basis of returns rendered by persons liable therefor (subchapter A (sections 6001 and following), chapter 61 of the Code) or at the source of the income by withholding. For the computation of tax in the case of a joint return of a husband and wife, or a return of a surviving spouse, for taxable years beginning before January 1, 1971, see section 2. The computation of tax in such a case for taxable years beginning after December 31, 1970, is determined in accordance with the table contained in section 1(a) as amended by the Tax Reform Act of 1969. For other rates of tax on individuals, see section 5(a). For the imposition of an additional tax for the calendar years 1968, 1969, and 1970, see section 51(a).

(2)(i) For taxable years beginning on or after January 1, 1964, the tax imposed upon a single individual, a head of a household, a married individual filing a separate return, and estates and trusts is the tax imposed by section 1 determined in accordance with the appropriate table contained in the following subsection of section 1:

	Taxable years beginning in 1964	Taxable years beginning after 1964 but before 1971	Taxable years beginning after Dec. 31, 1970 (references in this column are to the Code as amended by the Tax Reform Act of 1969)
Single individual	Sec. 1(a)(1)	Sec. 1(a)(2)	Sec. 1(c).
Head of a household	Sec. 1(b)(1)	Sec. 1(b)(2)	Sec. 1(b).
Married individual filing a separate return.	Sec. 1(a)(1)	Sec. 1(a)(2)	Sec. 1(d).
Estates and trusts	Sec. 1(a)(1)	Sec. 1(a)(2)	Sec. 1(d).

(ii) For taxable years beginning after December 31, 1970, the tax imposed by section 1(d), as amended by the Tax Reform Act of 1969, shall apply to the income effectively connected with the conduct of a trade or business in the United States by a married alien individual who is a nonresident of the United States for all or part of the taxable year or by a foreign estate or trust. For such years the tax imposed by section 1(c), as amended by such Act, shall apply to the income effectively connected with the conduct of a trade or business in the United States by an unmarried alien individual (other than a surviving spouse) who is a nonresident of the United States for all or part of the taxable year. See paragraph (b)(2) of Sec. 1.871-8.

(3) The income tax imposed by section 1 upon any amount of taxable income is computed by adding to the income tax for the bracket in which that amount falls in the appropriate table in section 1 the income tax upon the excess of that amount over the bottom of the bracket at the rate indicated in such table.

(4) The provisions of section 1 of the Code, as amended by the Tax Reform Act of 1969, and of this paragraph may be illustrated by the following examples:

Example 1. A, an unmarried individual, had taxable income for the calendar year 1964 of $15,750. Accordingly, the tax upon such taxable income would be $4,507.50, computed as follows from the table in section 1(a)(1):

Tax on $14,000 (from table) $3,790.00
Tax on $1,750 (at 41 percent as determined from the table).............717.50

Total tax on $15,750 ....4,507.50

Example 2. Assume the same facts as in example (1), except the figures are for the calendar year 1965. The tax upon such taxable income would be $4,232.50, computed as follows from the table in section 1(a)(2):

Tax on $14,000 (from table) $3,550.00
Tax on $1,750 (at 39 percent as determined from the table).............682.50

Total tax on $15,750 ....4,232.50

Example 3. Assume the same facts as in example (1), except the figures are for the calendar year 1971. The tax upon such taxable income would be $3,752.50, computed as follows from the table in section 1(c), as amended:

Tax on $14,000 (from table) $3,210.00
Tax on $1,750 (at 31 percent as determined from the table).............542.50

Total tax on $15,750 ....3,752.50

See Part II,
Sec. 871,
3121, IRC
3, 9, 14,
1.1402(b)-1,
CFR 38

(b) Citizens or residents of the United States liable to tax. In general, all citizens of the United States, wherever resident, and all resident alien individuals are liable to the income taxes imposed by the Code whether the income is received from sources within or without the United States. Pursuant to section 876, a nonresident alien individual who is a bona fide resident of Puerto Rico during the entire taxable year is, except as provided in section 933 with respect to Puerto Rican source income, subject to taxation in the same manner as a resident alien individual. As to tax on nonresident alien individuals, see sections 871 and 877.

See Courts 7

(c) Who is a citizen. Every person born or naturalized in the United States and subject to its jurisdiction is a citizen. For other rules governing the acquisition of citizenship, see chapters 1 and 2 of title III of the Immigration and Nationality Act (8 U.S.C. 1401-1459). For rules governing loss of citizenship, see sections 349 to 357, inclusive, of such Act (8 U.S.C. 1481-1489), Schneider v. Rusk, (1964) 377 U.S. 163, and Rev. Rul. 70-506, C.B. 1970-2, 1. For rules pertaining to persons who are nationals but not citizens at birth, e.g., a person born in American Samoa, see section 308 of such Act (8 U.S.C. 1408). For special rules applicable to certain expatriates who have lost citizenship with a principal purpose of avoiding certain taxes, see section 877. A foreigner who has filed his declaration of intention of becoming a citizen but who has not yet been admitted to citizenship by a final order of a naturalization court is an alien.

[T.D. 6500, 25 FR 11402, Nov. 26, 1960, as amended by T.D. 7332, 39 FR 44216, Dec. 23, 1974]

[Code of Federal Regulations]
[Title 26, Volume 2]
[Revised as of April 1, 2004]
From the U.S. Government Printing Office via GPO Access
[CITE: 26CFR1.61-2]

[Page 11-14]

TITLE 26--INTERNAL REVENUE

CHAPTER I--INTERNAL REVENUE SERVICE, DEPARTMENT OF THE TREASURY (CONTINUED)

PART 1_INCOME TAXES--Table of Contents

See Sec. 61, IRC 1

Sec. 1.61-2 Compensation for services, including fees, commissions, and similar items.

See Part II, Sec. 871, 3121, IRC 3, 9, 14, 1.1402(b)- 1, CFR 38

(a) In general. (1) Wages, salaries, commissions paid salesmen, compensation for services on the basis of a percentage of profits, commissions on insurance premiums, tips, bonuses (including Christmas bonuses), termination or severance pay, rewards, jury fees, marriage fees and other contributions received by a clergyman for services, pay of persons in the military or naval forces of the United States, retired pay of employees, pensions, and retirement allowances **are income to the recipients unless excluded by law.** Several special rules apply to members of the Armed Forces, National Oceanic and Atmospheric Administration, and Public Health Service of the United

[Code of Federal Regulations]
[Title 26, Volume 2]
[Revised as of April 1, 2004]
From the U.S. Government Printing Office via GPO Access
[CITE: 26CFR1.61-3]

[Page 35]

TITLE 26--INTERNAL REVENUE

CHAPTER I--INTERNAL REVENUE SERVICE, DEPARTMENT OF THE
TREASURY (CONTINUED)

PART 1_INCOME TAXES--Table of Contents

See Sec. 61,
IRC 1

Sec. 1.61-3 Gross income derived from business.

(a) In general. In a manufacturing, merchandising, or mining business, "gross income" means the total sales, less the cost of goods sold, plus any income from investments and from incidental or outside operations or sources. Gross income is determined without subtraction of depletion allowances based on a percentage of income to the extent that it exceeds cost depletion which may be required to be included in the amount of inventoriable costs as provided in Sec. 1.471-11 and without subtraction of selling expenses, losses or other items not ordinarily used in computing costs of goods sold or amounts which are of a type for which a deduction would be disallowed under section 162 (c), (f), or (g) in the case of a business expense. The cost of goods sold should be determined in accordance with the method of accounting consistently used by the taxpayer. Thus, for example, an amount cannot be taken into account in the computation of cost of goods sold any earlier than the taxable year in which economic performance occurs with respect to the amount (see Sec. 1.446-1(c)(1)(ii)).

(b) State contracts. The profit from a contract with a State or political subdivision thereof must be included in gross income. If warrants are issued by a city, town, or other political subdivision of a State, and are accepted by the contractor in payment for public work done, the fair market value of such warrants should be returned as income. If, upon conversion of the warrants into cash, the contractor does not receive and cannot recover the full value of the warrants so returned, he may deduct any loss sustained from his gross income for the year in which the warrants are so converted. If, however, he realizes more than the value of the warrants so returned, he must include the excess in his gross income for the year in which realized.

[T.D. 6500, 25 FR 11402, Nov. 26, 1960; 25 FR 14021, Dec. 31, 1960, as amended by T.D. 7207, 37 FR 20767, Oct. 5, 1972; T.D. 7285, 38 FR 26184, Sept. 19, 1973; T.D. 8408, 57 FR 12419, Apr. 10, 1992]

[Code of Federal Regulations]
[Title 26, Volume 9]
[Revised as of April 1, 2004]
From the U.S. Government Printing Office via GPO Access
[CITE: 26CFR1.861-1]

[Page 122-123]

TITLE 26--INTERNAL REVENUE

CHAPTER I--INTERNAL REVENUE SERVICE, DEPARTMENT OF THE TREASURY (CONTINUED)

PART 1_INCOME TAXES--Table of Contents

See Sec. 861, IRC 4

See Part II, Sec. 871, 3121, IRC 3, 9, 14, 1.1402(b)-1, CFR 38

Sec. 1.861-1 Income from sources within the United States.

(a) Categories of income. Part I (section 861 and following), subchapter N, chapter 1 of the Code, and the regulations thereunder determine the sources of income for purposes of the income tax. These sections explicitly allocate certain important sources of income to the United States or to areas outside the United States, as the case may be; and, with respect to the remaining income (particularly that derived partly from sources within and partly from sources without the United States), authorize the Secretary or his delegate to determine the income derived from sources within the United States, either by rules of separate allocation or by processes or formulas of general apportionment. The statute provides for the following three categories of income:

(1) Within the United States. The gross income from sources within the United States, consisting of the items of gross income specified in section 861(a) plus the items of gross income allocated or apportioned to such sources in accordance with section 863(a). See Sec. Sec. 1.861-2 to 1.861-7, inclusive, and Sec. 1.863-1. The taxable income from sources within the United States, in the case of such income, shall be determined by deducting therefrom, in accordance with sections 861(b) and 863(a), the expenses, losses, and other deductions properly apportioned or allocated thereto and a ratable part of any other expenses, losses, or deductions which cannot definitely be allocated to some item or class of gross income. See Sec. Sec. 1.861-8 and 1.863-1.

(2) Without the United States. The gross income from sources without the United States, consisting of the items of gross income specified in section 862(a) plus the items of gross income allocated or apportioned to such sources in accordance with section 863(a). See Sec. Sec. 1.862- 1 and 1.863-1. The taxable income from sources without the United States, in the case of such income, shall be determined by deducting therefrom, in accordance with sections 862(b) and 863(a), the expenses, losses, and other deductions properly apportioned or allocated thereto and a ratable part of any other expenses, losses, or deductions which cannot definitely be allocated to some item or class of gross income. See Sec. Sec. 1.862-1 and 1.863-1.

(3) Partly within and partly without the United States. The gross income derived from sources partly within and partly without the United States, consisting of the items specified in section 863(b) (1), (2), and (3). The taxable income allocated or apportioned to sources within the United States, in the case of such income, shall be determined in accordance with section 863 (a) or (b). See Sec. Sec. 1.863-2 to 1.863- 5, inclusive.

(4) Exceptions. An owner of certain aircraft or vessels first leased on or before December 28, 1980, may elect to treat income in respect of these aircraft or vessels as income from sources within the United States for purposes of sections 861(a) and 862(a). See Sec. 1.861-9. An owner of certain aircraft, vessels, or spacecraft first leased after December 28, 1980, must treat income in respect of these craft as income from sources within the United States for purposes of sections 861(a) and 862(a). See Sec. 1.861-9A.

(b) Taxable income from sources within the United States. The taxable income from sources within the United States shall consist of the taxable income described in paragraph (a)(1) of this section plus the taxable income allocated or apportioned to such sources, as indicated in paragraph (a)(3) of this section.

(c) Computation of income. If a taxpayer has gross income from sources within or without the United States, together with gross income derived partly from sources within and partly from sources without the United States, the amounts thereof, together with the expenses and investment applicable thereto, shall be segregated; and the taxable income from sources within the United States shall be separately computed therefrom.

[T.D. 6500, 25 FR 11910, Nov. 26, 1960, as amended by T.D. 7928, 48 FR 55845, Dec. 16, 1983]

[Code of Federal Regulations]
[Title 26, Volume 9]
[Revised as of April 1, 2004]
From the U.S. Government Printing Office via GPO Access
[CITE: 26CFR1.861-4]

[Page 135-137]

TITLE 26--INTERNAL REVENUE

CHAPTER I--INTERNAL REVENUE SERVICE, DEPARTMENT OF THE
TREASURY (CONTINUED)

PART 1_INCOME TAXES--Table of Contents

See Sec.
861, IRC
4

See Part
II, Sec.
871, 3121,
IRC 3, 9,
14,
1.1402(b)-
1, CFR 38

Sec. 1.861-4 Compensation for labor or personal services.

(a) In general. (1) Gross income from sources within the United States includes compensation for labor or personal services performed in the United States irrespective of the residence of the payer, the place in which the contract for service was made, or the place or time of payment; except that such compensation shall be deemed not to be income from sources within the United States, if—

(i) The labor or services are performed by a nonresident alien individual temporarily present in the United States for a period or periods not exceeding a total of 90 days during his taxable year,

(ii) The compensation for such labor or services does not exceed in the aggregate a gross amount of $3,000, and

(iii) The compensation is for labor or services performed as an employee of, or under any form of contract with--

(a) A nonresident alien individual, foreign partnership, or foreign corporation, not engaged in trade or business within the United States, or

(b) An individual who is a citizen or resident of the United States, a domestic partnership, or a domestic corporation, if such labor or services are performed for an office or place of business maintained in a foreign country or in a possession of the United States by such individual, partnership, or corporation.

(2) As a general rule, the term "day", as used in subparagraph (1)(i) of this paragraph, means a calendar day during any portion of which the nonresident alien individual is physically present in the United States.

(3) Solely for purposes of applying this paragraph, the nonresident alien individual, foreign partnership, or foreign corporation for which the nonresident alien individual is performing personal services in the United States shall not be considered to be engaged in trade or business in the United States by reason of the performance of such services by such individual.

(4) In determining for purposes of subparagraph (1)(ii) of this paragraph whether compensation received by the nonresident alien individual exceeds in the aggregate a gross amount of $3,000, any amounts received by the individual from an employer as advances or reimbursements for travel expenses incurred on behalf of the employer shall be omitted from the compensation received by the individual, to the extent of expenses incurred, where he was required to account and did account to his employer for such expenses and has met the tests for such accounting provided in Sec. 1.162-17 and paragraph (e)(4) of Sec. 1.274-5. If advances or reimbursements exceed such expenses, the amount of the excess shall be included as compensation for personal services for purposes of such subparagraph. Pensions and retirement pay attributable to labor or personal services performed in the United States are not to be taken into account for purposes of subparagraph (1)(ii) of this paragraph.
(5) For definition of the term "United States", when used in a geographical sense, see sections 638 and 7701(a)(9).
(b) Amount includible in gross income--(1) Taxable years beginning after December 31, 1975. (i) If a specific amount is paid for labor or personal services performed in the United States, that amount (if income from sources within the United States) shall be included in the gross income. If no accurate allocation or segregation of compensation for labor or personal services performed in the United States can be made, or when such labor or service is performed partly within and partly without the United States, the amount to be included in the gross income shall be determined on the basis that most correctly reflects the proper source of income under the facts and circumstances of the particular case. In many cases the facts and circumstances will be such that an apportionment on the time basis will be acceptable, that is, the amount to be included in gross income will be that amount which bears the same relation to the total compensation as the number of days of performance of the labor or services within the United States bears to the total number of days of performance of labor or services for which the payment is made. In other cases, the facts and circumstances will be such that another method of apportionment will be acceptable.
(ii) The application of this subparagraph may be illustrated by the following examples:

Example 1. B, a nonresident alien individual, was employed by M from March 1, 1976, to June 12, 1976, a total of 104 days, for which he received compensation in the amount of $12,240. During that period B was present in the United States 59 days. Under his contract B was subject to call at all times by his employer and was in a payment status on a 7-day week basis. There was no specific agreement as to the amount of pay for services performed within the United States; moreover, he received his stipulated salary payments regardless of the number of days per week he actually performed services. Under these circumstances the amount of compensation to be included in gross income as income from sources within the United States will be $6,943.85 ($12,240x59/104). Example 2. C, a citizen of the United States, was a resident of a foreign country during his entire taxable year. He is employed by N, a domestic corporation, and paid a salary of $17,600 per annum. Under his contract C is required to work only on a 5-day week basis, [[Page 137]] Monday through Friday. During 1976 he was in the United States for 6 weeks, performing services therein for N for 30 work days. During the year he worked 240 days for N for which payment was made, determined by eliminating his vacation period for which no payment was made. Under these circumstances the amount of compensation for personal services performed in the United States is $2,200 ($17,600x30/240).

(2) Taxable years beginning before January 1, 1976. If a specific amount is paid for labor or personal services performed in the United States, that amount (if income from sources within the United States) shall be included in the gross income. If no accurate allocation or segregation of compensation for labor or personal services performed in the United States can be made, or when such labor or service is performed partly within and partly without the United States, the amount to be included in the gross income shall be determined by an apportionment on the time basis; that is, there shall be included in the gross income an amount which bears the same relation to the total compensation as the number of days of performance of the labor or services within the United States bears to the total number of days of performance of labor or services for which the payment is made.

(c) Coastwise travel. Except as to income excluded by paragraph (a) of this section, wages received for services rendered inside the territorial limits of the United States and wages of an alien seaman earned on a coastwise vessel are to be regarded as from sources within the United States.

(d) Effective date. This section applies with respect to taxable years beginning after December 31, 1966. For corresponding rules applicable to taxable years beginning before January 1, 1967, see 26 CFR 1.861-4 (Revised as of January 1, 1972).

[T.D. 6500, 25 FR 11910, Nov. 26, 1960; 25 FR 14021, Dec. 31, 1960, as amended by T.D. 7378, 40 FR 45433, Oct. 2, 1975; 40 FR 48508, Oct. 16, 1975]

[Code of Federal Regulations]
[Title 26, Volume 9]
[Revised as of April 1, 2004]
From the U.S. Government Printing Office via GPO Access
[CITE: 26CFR1.861-5]

[Page 137]

TITLE 26--INTERNAL REVENUE

CHAPTER I--INTERNAL REVENUE SERVICE, DEPARTMENT OF THE
TREASURY (CONTINUED)

PART 1_INCOME TAXES--Table of Contents

See Sec.
861, IRC 5

Sec. 1.861-5 Rentals and royalties.

Gross income from sources within the United States includes rentals or
royalties from property located in the United States or from any interest in
such property, including rentals or royalties for the use of, or for the
privilege of using, in the United States, patents, copyrights, secret
processes and formulas, good will, trademarks, trade brands, franchises,
and other like property. The income arising from the rental of property,
whether tangible or intangible, located within the United States, or from
the use of property, whether tangible or intangible, within the United
States, is from sources within the United States. For taxable years
beginning after December 31, 1966, gains described in section
871(a)(1)(D) and section 881(a)(4) from the sale or exchange after
October 4, 1966, of patents, copyrights, and other like property shall be
treated, as provided in section 871(e)(2), as rentals or royalties for the use
of, or privilege of using, property or an interest in property. See paragraph
(e) of Sec. 1.871-11.

[T.D. 7378, 40 FR 45434, Oct. 2, 1975]

[Code of Federal Regulations]
[Title 26, Volume 9]
[Revised as of April 1, 2005]
From the U.S. Government Printing Office via GPO Access
[CITE: 26CFR1.861-8]

[Page 138-164]

TITLE 26--INTERNAL REVENUE

CHAPTER I--INTERNAL REVENUE SERVICE, DEPARTMENT OF THE TREASURY (CONTINUED)

PART 1_INCOME TAXES--Table of Contents

See Sec. 861, IRC 4-6

Sec. 1.861-8 Computation of taxable income from sources within the United States and from other sources and activities.

...

See Part II, Sec. 871, 3121, IRC 3, 9, 14, 1.1402(b)-1, CFR 38

(f) Miscellaneous matters--(1) Operative sections. The operative sections of the Code which require the determination of taxable income of the taxpayer from specific sources or activities and which give rise to statutory groupings to which this section is applicable include the sections described below.

(i) Overall limitation to the foreign tax credit. Under the overall limitation to the foreign tax credit, as provided in section 904(a)(2) (as in effect before enactment of the Tax Reform Act of 1976, or section 904(a) after such enactment) the amount of the foreign tax credit may not exceed the tentative U.S. tax (i.e., the U.S. tax before application of the foreign tax credit) multiplied by a fraction, the numerator of which is the taxable income from sources without the United States and the denominator of which is the entire taxable income. Accordingly, in this case, the statutory grouping is foreign source income (including, for example, interest received from a domestic corporation which meets the tests of section 861(a)(1)(B), dividends received from a domestic corporation which has an election in effect under section 936, and other types of income specified in section 862). Pursuant to sections 862(b) and 863(a) and Sec. Sec. 1.862-1 and 1.863-1, this section provides rules for identifying the deductions to be taken into account in determining taxable income from sources without the United States. See section 904(d) (as in effect after enactment of the Tax Reform Act of 1976) and the regulations thereunder which require separate treatment of certain types of income. See example 3 of paragraph (g) of this section for one example of the application of this section to the overall limitation.

(ii) [Reserved]

(iii) DISC and FSC taxable income. Sections 925 and 994 provide rules for determining the taxable income of a FSC and DISC, respectively, with respect to qualified sales and leases of export property and qualified services. The combined taxable income method available for determining a DISC's taxable income provides, without consideration of export promotion expenses, that the taxable income of the DISC shall be 50 percent of the combined taxable income of the DISC and the related supplier derived from sales and leases of export property and from services. In the FSC context, the taxable income of the FSC equals 23 percent of the combined taxable income of the FSC and the related supplier. Pursuant to regulations under section 925 and 994, this section provides rules for determining the deductions to be taken into account in determining combined taxable income, except to the extent modified by the marginal costing rules set forth in the regulations under sections 925(b)(2) and 994(b)(2) if used by the taxpayer. See Examples (22) and (23) of paragraph (g) of this section. In addition, the computation of combined taxable income is necessary to determine the applicability of the section 925(d) limitation and the "no loss" rules of the regulations under sections 925 and 994.

(iv) Effectively connected taxable income. Nonresident alien individuals and foreign corporations engaged in trade or business within the United States, under sections 871(b)(1) and 882(a)(1), on taxable income which is effectively connected with the conduct of a trade or business within the United States. Such taxable income is determined in most instances by initially determining, under section 864(c), the amount of gross income which is effectively connected with the conduct of a trade or business within the United States. Pursuant to sections 873 and 882(c), this section is applicable for purposes of determining the deductions from such gross income (other than the deduction for interest expense allowed to foreign corporations (see Sec. 1.882-5)) which are to be taken into account in determining taxable income. See example 21 of paragraph (g) of this section.

(v) Foreign base company income. Section 954 defines the term "foreign base company income" with respect to controlled foreign corporations. Section 954(b)(5) provides that in determining foreign base company income the gross income shall be reduced by the deductions of the controlled foreign corporation "properly allocable to such income". This section provides rules for identifying which deductions are properly allocable to foreign base company income.

(vi) Other operative sections. The rules provided in this section also apply in determining—

(A) The amount of foreign source items of tax preference under section 58(g) determined for purposes of the minimum tax;

(B) The amount of foreign mineral income under section 901(e);

(C) [Reserved]

(D) The amount of foreign oil and gas extraction income and the amount of foreign oil related income under section 907;

(E) The tax base for citizens entitled to the benefits of section 931 and the section 936 tax credit of a domestic corporation which has an election in effect under section 936;

(F) The exclusion for income from Puerto Rico for residents of Puerto Rico under section 933;

(G) The limitation under section 934 on the maximum reduction in income tax liability incurred to the Virgin Islands;

(H) The income derived from Guam by an individual who is subject to section 935;

(I) The special deduction granted to China Trade Act corporations under section 941;

(J) The amount of certain U.S. source income excluded from the subpart F income of a controlled foreign corporation under section 952(b);

(K) The amount of income from the insurance of U.S. risks under section 953(b)(5);

(L) The international boycott factor and the specifically attributable taxes and income under section 999; and

(M) The taxable income attributable to the operation of an agreement vessel under section 607 of the Merchant Marine Act of 1936, as amended, and the Capital Construction Fund Regulations thereunder (26 CFR, part 3). See 26 CFR 3.2(b)(3)....

[Code of Federal Regulations]
[Title 26, Volume 9]
[Revised as of April 1, 2005]
From the U.S. Government Printing Office via GPO Access
[CITE: 26CFR1.862-1]

[Page 266-267]

TITLE 26--INTERNAL REVENUE

CHAPTER I--INTERNAL REVENUE SERVICE, DEPARTMENT OF THE
TREASURY (CONTINUED)

PART 1_INCOME TAXES--Table of Contents

See Sec. 862, IRC 6

Sec. 1.862-1 Income specifically from sources without the United States.

See Part II, IRC 2, 3, Part III, IRC 3, 4

See Sec. 871, 3121, IRC 9, 14, 1.1402(b)-1, CFR 38

(a) Gross income. (1) The following items of gross income shall be treated as income from sources without the United States:
(i) Interest other than that specified in section 861(a)(1) and Sec. 1.861-2 as being derived from sources within the United States;
(ii) Dividends other than those derived from sources within the United States as provided in section 861(a)(2) and Sec. 1.861-3;
(iii) Compensation for labor or personal services performed without the United States;
(iv) Rentals or royalties from property located without the United States or from any interest in such property, including rentals or royalties for the use of, or for the privilege of using, without the United States, patents, copyrights, secret processes and formulas, goodwill, trademarks, trade brands, franchises, and other like property;
(v) Gains, profits, and income from the sale of real property located without the United States; and
(vi) Gains, profits, and income derived from the purchase of personal property within the United States and its sale without the United States.

(2) In applying subparagraph (1)(iv) of this paragraph for taxable years beginning after December 31, 1966, gains described in section 871(a)(1)(D) and section 881(a)(4) from the sale or exchange after October 4, 1966, of patents, copyrights, and other like property shall be treated, as provided in section 871(e)(2), as rentals or royalties for the use of, or privilege of using, property or an interest in property. See paragraph (e) of Sec. 1.871-11.

(3) For determining the time and place of sale of personal property for purposes of subparagraph (1)(vi) of this paragraph, see paragraph (c) of Sec. 1.861-7.

(4) Income derived from the purchase of personal property within the United States and its sale within a possession of the United States shall be treated as derived entirely from within that possession.

(5) If interest is paid on an obligation of a nonresident of the United States by a resident of the United States acting in the resident's capacity as a guarantor of the obligation of the nonresident, the interest will be treated as income from sources without the United States.

(6) For rules treating certain interest as income from sources without the United States, see paragraph (b) of Sec. 1.861-2.

(7) For the treatment of compensation for labor or personal services performed partly within the United States and partly without the United States, see paragraph (b) of Sec. 1.861-4.

See Sec. 864, IRC 8

(b) Taxable income. The taxable income from sources without the United States, in the case of the items of gross income specified in paragraph (a) of this section, shall be determined on the same basis as that used in Sec. 1.861-8 for determining the taxable income from sources within the United States.

(c) Income from certain property. For provisions permitting a taxpayer to elect to treat amounts of gross income attributable to certain aircraft or vessels first leased on or before December 28, 1980, as income from sources within the United States which would otherwise be treated as income from sources without the United States under paragraph (a) of this section, see Sec. 1.861-9. For provisions requiring amounts of gross income attributable to certain aircraft, vessels, or spacecraft first leased by the taxpayer after December 28, 1980, to be treated as income from sources within the United States which would otherwise be treated as income from sources without the United States under paragraph (a) of this section, see Sec. 1.861-9A.

[T.D. 6500, 25 FR 11910, Nov. 26, 1960; 25 FR 14021, Dec. 31, 1960, as amended by T.D. 7378, 40 FR 45434, Oct. 2, 1975; 40 FR 48508, Oct. 16, 1975; T.D. 7928, 48 FR 55847, Dec. 16, 1983]

[Code of Federal Regulations]
[Title 26, Volume 9]
[Revised as of April 1, 2005]
From the U.S. Government Printing Office via GPO Access
[CITE: 26CFR1.864-5]

[Page 304-307]

TITLE 26--INTERNAL REVENUE

CHAPTER I--INTERNAL REVENUE SERVICE, DEPARTMENT OF THE
TREASURY (CONTINUED)

PART 1_INCOME TAXES--Table of Contents

**Sec. 1.864-5 Foreign source income effectively connected with U.S.
business.**

See Sec.
864,
IRC 7, 8

**(a) In general. This section applies only to a nonresident alien
individual or a foreign corporation that is engaged in a trade or
business in the United States at some time during a taxable year
beginning after December 31, 1966, and to the income, gain, or loss
of such person from sources without the United States.** The income,
gain, or loss of such person for the taxable year from sources without the
United States which is specified in paragraph (b) of this section shall be
treated as effectively connected for the taxable year with the conduct of a
trade or business in the United States, only if he also has in the United
States at some time during the taxable year, but not necessarily at the
time the income, gain, or loss is realized, an office or other fixed place of
business, as defined in Sec. 1.864-7, to which such income, gain, or loss
is attributable in accordance with Sec. 1.864-6. The income of such
person for the taxable year from sources without the United States which
is specified in paragraph (c) of this section shall be treated as effectively
connected for the taxable year with the conduct of a trade or business in
the United States when derived by a foreign corporation carrying on a life
insurance business in the United States. Except as provided in
paragraphs (b) and (c) of this section, no income, gain, or loss of a
nonresident alien individual or a foreign corporation for the taxable year
from sources without the United States shall be treated as effectively
connected for the taxable year with the conduct of a trade or business in
the United States by that person. Any income, gain, or loss described in
paragraph (b) or (c) of this section which, if it were derived by the taxpayer
from sources within the United States for the taxable year, would not be
treated under Sec. 1.864-4 as effectively connected for the taxable year
with the conduct of a trade or business in the United States shall not be

treated under this section as effectively connected for the taxable year with the conduct of a trade or business in the United States.

(b) Income other than income attributable to U.S. life insurance business. Income, gain, or loss from sources without the United States other than income described in paragraph (c) of this section shall be taken into account pursuant to paragraph (a) of this section in applying Sec. Sec. 1.864-6 and 1.864-7 only if it consists of--

(1) Rents, royalties, or gains on sales of intangible property. (i) Rents or royalties for the use of, or for the privilege of using, intangible personal property located outside the United States or from any interest in such property, including rents or royalties for the use, or for the privilege of using, outside the United States, patents, copyrights, secret processes and formulas, good will, trademarks, trade brands, franchises, and other like properties, if such rents or royalties are derived in the active conduct of the trade or business in the United States.

(ii) Gains or losses on the sale or exchange of intangible personal property located outside the United States or from any interest in such property, including gains or losses on the sale or exchange of the privilege of using, outside the United States, patents, copyrights, secret processes and formulas, good will, trademarks, trade brands, franchises, and other like properties, if such gains or losses are derived in the active conduct of the trade or business in the United States.

(iii) Whether or not such an item of income, gain, or loss is derived in the active conduct of a trade or business in the United States shall be determined from the facts and circumstances of each case. The frequency with which a nonresident alien individual or a foreign corporation enters into transactions of the type from which the income, gain, or loss is derived shall not of itself determine that the income, gain, or loss is derived in the active conduct of a trade or business.

(iv) This subparagraph shall not apply to rents or royalties for the use of, or for the privilege of using, real property or tangible personal property, or to gain or loss from the sale or exchange of such property.

(2) Dividends or interest, or gains or loss from sales of stocks or securities--(i) In general. Dividends or interests from any transaction, or gains or losses on the sale or exchange of stocks or securities, realized by (a) a nonresident alien individual or a foreign corporation in the active conduct of a banking, financing, or similar business in the United States or (b) a foreign corporation engaged in business in the United States whose principal business is trading in stocks or securities for its own account. Whether the taxpayer is engaged in the active conduct of a banking, financing, or similar business in the United States for purposes of this subparagraph shall be determined in accordance with the principles of paragraph (c)(5)(i) of Sec. 1.864-4.

(ii) Substitute payments. For purposes of this paragraph (b)92) [sic], a substitute interest payment (as defined in Sec. 1.861-2(a)(7)) received by a foreign person subject to tax under this paragraph (b) pursuant to a securities lending transaction or a sale-repurchase transaction (as defined in Sec. 1.861-2(a)(7)) with respect to a security (as defined in Sec. 1.864-6(b)(2)(ii)(c)) shall have the same character as interest income paid or accrued with respect to the terms of the transferred security. Similarly, for purposes of this paragraph (b)(2), a substitute dividend payment (as defined in Sec. 1.861-3(a)(6)) received by a foreign person pursuant to a securities lending transaction or a sale-repurchase transaction (as defined in Sec. 1.861-3(a)(6)) with respect to a stock shall have the same character as a distribution with respect to the transferred security. This paragraph (b)(2)(ii) is applicable to payments made after November 13, 1997.

(iii) Incidental investment activity. This subparagraph shall not apply to income, gain, or loss realized by a nonresident alien individual or foreign corporation on stocks or securities held, sold, or exchanged in connection with incidental investment activities carried on by that person. Thus, a foreign corporation which is primarily a holding company owning significant percentages of the stocks or securities issued by other corporations shall not be treated under this subparagraph as a corporation the principal business of which is trading in stocks or securities for its own account, solely because it engages in sporadic purchases or sales of stocks or securities to adjust its portfolio. The application of this subdivision may be illustrated by the following example:

Example. F, a foreign corporation, owns voting stock in foreign corporations M, N, and P, its holdings in such corporations constituting 15, 20, and 100 percent, respectively, of all classes of their outstanding voting stock. Each of such stock holdings by F represents approximately 20 percent of its total assets. The remaining 40 percent of F's assets consist of other investments, 20 percent being invested in securities issued by foreign governments and in stocks and bonds issued by other corporations in which F does not own a significant percentage of their outstanding voting stock, and 20 percent being invested in bonds issued by N. None of the assets of F are held primarily for sale; but if the officers of that corporation were to decide that other investments would be preferable to its holding of such assets, F would sell the stocks and securities and reinvest the proceeds therefrom in other holdings. Any income, gain, or loss which F may derive from this investment activity is not considered to be realized by a foreign corporation described in subdivision (i) of this subparagraph.

(3) Sale of goods or merchandise through U.S. office. (i) Income, gain, or loss from the sale of inventory items or of property held primarily for sale to customers in the ordinary course of business, as described in section 1221(1), where the sale is outside the United States but through the office or other fixed place of business which the nonresident alien or

foreign corporation has in the United States, irrespective of the destination to which such property is sent for use, consumption, or disposition.

(ii) This subparagraph shall not apply to income, gain, or loss resulting from a sales contract entered into on or before February 24, 1966. See section 102(e)(1) of the Foreign Investors Tax Act of 1966 (80 Stat. 1547). Thus, for example, the sales office in the United States of a foreign corporation enters into negotiations for the sale of 500,000 industrial bearings which the corporation produces in a foreign country for consumption in the Western Hemisphere. These negotiations culminate in a binding agreement entered into on January 1, 1966. By its terms delivery under the contract is to be made over a period of 3 years beginning in March of 1966. Payment is due upon delivery. The income from sources without the United States resulting from this sale negotiated by the U.S. sales office of the foreign corporation shall not be taken into account under this subparagraph for any taxable year.

(iii) This subparagraph shall not apply to gains or losses on the sale or exchange of intangible personal property to which subparagraph (1) of this paragraph applies or of stocks or securities to which subparagraph (2) of this paragraph applies.

(c) Income attributable to U.S. life insurance business. (1) All of the income for the taxable year of a foreign corporation described in subparagraph (2) of this paragraph from sources without the United States, which is attributable to its U.S. life insurance business, shall be treated as effectively connected for the taxable year with the conduct of a trade or business in the United States by that corporation. Thus, in determining its life insurance company taxable income from its U.S. business for purposes of section 802, the foreign corporation shall include all of its items of income from sources without the United States which would appropriately be taken into account in determining the life insurance company taxable income of a domestic corporation. The income to which this subparagraph applies shall be taken into account for purposes of paragraph (a) of this section without reference to Sec. Sec. 1.864-6 and 1.864-7.

(2) A foreign corporation to which subparagraph (1) of this paragraph applies is a foreign corporation carrying on an insurance business in the United States during the taxable year which--

(i) Without taking into account its income not effectively connected for that year with the conduct of any trade or business in the United States, would qualify as a life insurance company under part I (section 801 and following) of subchapter L, chapter 1 of the Code, if it were a domestic corporation, and

(ii) By reason of section 842 is taxable under that part on its income which is effectively connected for that year with its conduct of any trade or business in the United States.

(d) Excluded foreign source income. Notwithstanding paragraphs (b) and (c) of this section, no income from sources without the United

States shall be treated as effectively connected for any taxable year with the conduct of a trade or business in the United States by a nonresident alien individual or a foreign corporation if the income consists of--

(1) Dividends, interest, or royalties paid by a related foreign corporation. Dividends, interest, or royalties paid by a foreign corporation in which the nonresident alien individual or the foreign corporation described in paragraph (a) of this section owns, within the meaning of section 958(a), or is considered as owning, by applying the ownership rules of section 958(b), at the time such items are paid more than 50 percent of the total combined voting power of all classes of stock entitled to vote.

(2) Subpart F income of a controlled foreign corporation. Any income of the foreign corporation described in paragraph (a) of this section which is subpart F income for the taxable year, as determined under section 952(a), even though part of the income is attributable to amounts which, if distributed by the foreign corporation, would be distributed with respect to its stock which is owned by shareholders who are not U.S. shareholders within the meaning of section 951(b). This subparagraph shall not apply to any income of the foreign corporation which is excluded in determining its subpart F income for the taxable year for purposes of section 952(a). Thus, for example, this subparagraph shall not apply to--

(i) Foreign base company shipping income which is excluded under section 954(b)(2),

(ii) Foreign base company income amounting to less than 10 percent (30 percent in the case of taxable years of foreign corporations ending before January 1, 1976) of gross income which by reason of section 954(b)(3)(A) does not become subpart F income for the taxable year,

(iii) Any income excluded from foreign base company income under section 954(b)(4), relating to exception for foreign corporations not availed of to reduce taxes,

(iv) Any income derived in the active conduct of a trade or business which is excluded under section 954(c)(3), or

(v) Any income received from related persons which is excluded under section 954(c)(4).

This subparagraph shall apply to the foreign corporation's entire subpart F income for the taxable year determined under section 952(a), even though no amount is included in the gross income of a U.S. shareholder under section 951(a) with respect to that subpart F income because of the minimum distribution provisions of section 963(a) or because of the reduction under section 970(a) with respect to an export trade corporation. This subparagraph shall apply only to a foreign corporation which is a controlled foreign corporation within the meaning of section 957 and the regulations thereunder. The application of this subparagraph may be illustrated by the following examples:

Example 1. Controlled foreign corporation M, incorporated under the laws of foreign country X, is engaged in the business of purchasing and selling merchandise manufactured in foreign country Y by an unrelated person. M negotiates sales, through its sales office in the United States, of its merchandise for use outside of country X. These sales are made outside the United States, and the merchandise is sold for use outside the United States. No office maintained by M outside the United States participates materially in the sales made through its U.S. sales office. These activities constitute the only activities of M. During the taxable year M derives $100,000 income from these sales made through its U.S. sales office, and all of such income is foreign base company sales income by reason of section 954(d)(2) and paragraph (b) of Sec. 1.954-3. The entire $100,000 is also subpart F income, determined under section 952(a). In addition, all of this income would, without reference to section 864(c)(4)(D)(ii) and this subparagraph, be treated as effectively connected for the taxable year with the conduct of a trade or business in the United States by M. Through its entire taxable year 60 percent of the one class of stock of M is owned within the meaning of section 958(a) by U.S. shareholders, as defined in section 951(b), and 40 percent of its one class of stock is owned within the meaning of section 958(a) by persons who are not U.S. shareholders, as defined in section 951(b). Although only $60,000 of the subpart F income of M for the taxable year is includible in the income of the U.S. shareholders under section 951(a), the entire subpart F income of $100,000 constitutes income which, by reason of section 864(c)(4)(D)(ii) and this subparagraph, is not effectively connected for the taxable year with the conduct of a trade or business in the United States by M.

Example 2. The facts are the same as in example 1 except that the foreign base company sales income amounts to $150,000 determined in accordance with paragraph (d)(3)(i) of Sec. 1.954-1, and that M also has gross income from sources without the United States of $50,000 from sales, through its sales office in the United States, of merchandise for use in country X. These sales are made outside the United States. All of this income would, without reference to section 864(c)(4)(D)(ii) and this subparagraph, be treated as effectively connected for the taxable year with the conduct of a trade or business in the United States by M. Since the foreign base company income of $150,000 amounts to 75 percent of the entire gross income of $200,000, determined as provided in paragraph (d)(3)(ii) of Sec. 1.954-1, the entire $200,000 constitutes foreign base company income under section 954(b)(3)(B). Assuming that M has no amounts to be taken into account under paragraphs (1), (2), (4), and (5) of section 954(b), the $200,000 is also subpart F income, determined under section 952(a). This subpart F income of $200,000 constitutes income which, by reason of section 864(c)(4)(D)(ii) and this subparagraph, is not effectively connected for the taxable year with the conduct of a trade or business in the United States by M.

(3) Interest on certain deposits. Interest which, by reason of section 861(a)(1)(A) (relating to interest on deposits with banks, savings and loan associations, and insurance companies paid or credited before January 1, 1976) and paragraph (c) of Sec. 1.864-4, is determined to be income from sources without the United States because it is not effectively connected for the taxable year with the conduct of a trade or business in the United States by the nonresident alien individual or foreign corporation.

[T.D. 7216, 37 FR 23429, Nov. 3, 1972, as amended by T.D. 7893, 48 FR 22507, May 19, 1983; T.D. 8735, 62 FR 53501, Oct. 14, 1997]

[Code of Federal Regulations]
[Title 26, Volume 9]
[Revised as of April 1, 2005]
From the U.S. Government Printing Office via GPO Access
[CITE: 26CFR1.871-7]

[Page 334-339]

TITLE 26--INTERNAL REVENUE

CHAPTER I--INTERNAL REVENUE SERVICE, DEPARTMENT OF THE
TREASURY (CONTINUED)

PART 1_INCOME TAXES--Table of Contents

Sec. 1.871-7 Taxation of nonresident alien individuals not engaged in U.S. business.

See Sec.
871, IRC
9,
Definition
5

(a) Imposition of tax. (1) This section applies for purposes of determining the tax of a nonresident alien individual who at no time during the taxable year is engaged in trade or business in the United States. However, see also Sec. 1.871-8 where such individual is a student or trainee deemed to be engaged in trade or business in the United States or where he has an election in effect for the taxable year in respect to real property income. Except as otherwise provided in Sec. 1.871-12, **a nonresident alien individual to whom this section applies is not subject to the tax imposed by section 1** or section 1201(b) but, pursuant to the provision of section 871(a), is liable to a flat tax of 30 percent upon the aggregate of the amounts determined under paragraphs (b), (c), and (d) of this section which are received during the taxable year from sources within the United States. Except as specifically provided in such paragraphs, such amounts do not include gains from the sale or exchange of property. To determine the source of such amounts, see sections 861 through 863, and the regulations thereunder.

See Sec.
872,
IRC 11,
1.872-2,
CFR 34

(2) The tax of 30 percent is imposed by section 871(a) upon an amount only to the extent the amount constitutes gross income. Thus, for example, the amount of an annuity which is subject to such tax shall be determined in accordance with section 72.

(3) Deductions shall not be allowed in determining the amount subject to tax under this section except that losses from sales or exchanges of capital assets shall be allowed to the extent provided in section 871(a)(2) and paragraph (d) of this section.

(4) Except as provided in Sec. Sec. 1.871-9 and 1.871-10, a nonresident alien individual not engaged in trade or business in the United States during the taxable year has no income, gain, or loss for the taxable year which is effectively connected for the taxable year with the conduct of

a trade or business in the United States. See section 864(c)(1)(B) and Sec. 1.864-3.

(5) Gains and losses which, by reason of section 871(d) and Sec. 1.871-10, are treated as gains or losses which are effectively connected for the taxable year with the conduct of a trade or business in the United States by the nonresident alien individual shall not be taken into account in determining the tax under this section. See, for example, paragraph (c)(2) of Sec. 1.871-10.

(6) For special rules applicable in determining the tax of certain nonresident alien individuals, see paragraph (b) of Sec. 1.871-1.

(b) Fixed or determinable annual or periodical income--(1) General rule. **The tax of 30 percent imposed by section 871(a)(1) applies to the gross amount received from sources within the United States as fixed or determinable annual or periodical gains, profits, or income. Specific items of fixed or determinable annual or periodical income are enumerated in section 871(a)(1)(A) as interest, dividends, rents, salaries, wages, premiums, annuities, compensations, remunerations, and emoluments,** but other items of fixed or determinable annual or periodical gains, profits, or income are also subject to the tax, as, for instance, royalties, including royalties for the use of patents, copyrights, secret processes and formulas, and other like property. As to the determination of fixed or determinable annual or periodical income see Sec. 1.1441-2(b). For special rules treating gain on the disposition of section 306 stock as fixed or determinable annual or periodical income for purposes of section 871(a), see section 306(f) and paragraph (h) of Sec. 1.306-3.

See Sec. 871, IRC 9, Courts 7

See Part II, Sec. 3121, IRC 3, 14, 1.1402(b)-1, CFR 38

(2) Substitute payments. For purposes of this section, a substitute interest payment (as defined in Sec. 1.861-2(a)(7)) received by a foreign person pursuant to a securities lending transaction or a sale-repurchase transaction (as defined in Sec. 1.861-2(a)(7)) shall have the same character as interest income paid or accrued with respect to the terms of the transferred security. Similarly, for purposes of this section, a substitute dividend payment (as defined in Sec. 1.861- 3(a)(6)) received by a foreign person pursuant to a securities lending transaction or a sale-repurchase transaction (as defined in Sec. 1.861- 3(a)(6)) shall have the same character as a distribution received with respect to the transferred security. Where, pursuant to a securities lending transaction or a sale-repurchase transaction, a foreign person transfers to another person a security the interest on which would qualify as portfolio interest under section 871(h) in the hands of the lender, substitute interest payments made with respect to the transferred security will be treated as portfolio interest, provided that in the case of interest on an obligation in registered form (as defined in Sec. 1.871-14(c)(1)(i)), the transferor complies with the documentation requirement described in Sec. 1.871-14(c)(1)(ii)(C) with respect to the payment of the substitute interest and none of the

exceptions to the portfolio interest exemption in sections 871(h) (3) and (4) apply. See also Sec. Sec. 1.861-2(b)(2) and 1.894-1(c).

(c) Other income and gains--(1) Items subject to tax. The tax of 30 percent imposed by section 871(a)(1) also applies to the following gains received during the taxable year from sources within the United States:

(i) Gains described in section 402(a)(2), relating to the treatment of total distributions from certain employees' trusts; section 403(a)(2), relating to treatment of certain payments under certain employee annuity plans; and section 631 (b) or (c), relating to treatment of gain on the disposal of timber, coal, or iron ore with a retained economic interest;

(ii) [Reserved]

(iii) Gains on transfers described in section 1235, relating to certain transfers of patent rights, made on or before October 4, 1966; and

(iv) Gains from the sale or exchange after October 4, 1966, of patents, copyrights, secret processes and formulas, good will, trademarks, trade brands, franchises, or other like property, or of any interest in any such property, to the extent the gains are from payments (whether in a lump sum or in installments) which are contingent on the productivity, use or disposition of the property or interest sold or exchanged, or from payments which are treated under section 871(e) and Sec. 1.871-11 as being so contingent.

(2) Nonapplication of 183-day rule. The provisions of section 871(a)(2), relating to gains from the sale or exchange of capital assets, and paragraph (d)(2) of this section do not apply to the gains described in this paragraph; as a consequence, the taxpayer receiving gains described in subparagraph (1) of this paragraph during a taxable year is subject to the tax of 30 percent thereon without regard to the 183-day rule contained in such provisions.

(3) Determination of amount of gain. The tax of 30 percent imposed upon the gains described in subparagraph (1) of this paragraph applies to the full amount of the gains and is determined (i) without regard to the alternative tax imposed by section 1201(b) upon the excess of the net long-term capital gain over the net short-term capital loss; (ii) without regard to the deduction allowed by section 1202 in respect of capital gains; (iii) without regard to section 1231, relating to property used in the trade or business and involuntary conversions; and (iv), except in the case of gains described in subparagraph (1)(ii) of this paragraph, whether or not the gains are considered to be gains from the sale or exchange of property which is a capital asset.

(d) Gains from sale or exchange of capital assets--(1) Gains subject to tax. The tax of 30 percent imposed by section 871(a)(2) applies to the excess of gains derived from sources within the United States over losses allocable to sources within the United States, which are derived from the sale or exchange of capital assets, determined in accordance with the provisions of subparagraphs (2) through (4) of this paragraph.

(2) Presence in the United States 183 days or more. (i) If the nonresident alien individual has been present in the United States for a period or periods aggregating 183 days or more during the taxable year, he is liable to a tax of 30 percent upon the amount by which his gains, derived from sources within the United States, from sales or exchanges of capital assets effected at any time during the year exceed his losses, allocable to sources within the United States, from sales or exchanges of capital assets effected at any time during that year. Gains and losses from sales or exchanges effected at any time during such taxable year are to be taken into account for this purpose even though the nonresident alien individual is not present in the United States at the time the sales or exchanges are effected. In addition, if the nonresident alien individual has been present in the United States for a period or periods aggregating 183 days or more during the taxable year, gains and losses for such taxable year from sales or exchanges of capital assets effected during a previous taxable year beginning after December 31, 1966, are to be taken into account, but only if he was also present in the United States during such previous taxable year for a period or periods aggregating 183 days or more.

(ii) If the nonresident alien individual has not been present in the United States during the taxable year, or if he has been present in the United States for a period or periods aggregating less than 183 days during the taxable year, gains and losses from sales or exchanges of capital assets effected during the year are not to be taken into account, except as required by paragraph (c) of this section, in determining the tax of such individual even though the sales or exchanges are effected during his presence in the United States. Moreover, gains and losses for such taxable year from sales or exchanges of capital assets effected during a previous taxable year beginning after December 31, 1966, are not to be taken into account, even though the nonresident alien individual was present in the United States during such previous year for a period or periods aggregating 183 days or more.

(iii) For purposes of this subparagraph, a nonresident alien individual is not considered to be present in the United States by reason of the presence in the United States of a person who is an agent or partner of such individual or who is a fiduciary of an estate or trust of which such individual is a beneficiary or a grantor-owner to whom section 671 applies.

(iv) The application of this subparagraph may be illustrated by the following examples:

Example 1. B, a nonresident alien individual not engaged in trade or business in the United States and using the calendar year as the taxable year, is present in the United States from May 1, 1971, to November 15, 1971, a period of more than 182 days. While present in the United States, B effects for his own account on various dates a number of transactions in stocks and securities on the stock exchange, as a result of which he has recognized capital gains of $10,000. During the period from January 1, 1971, to April 30, 1971, he carries out similar transactions through an agent in the United States, as a result of which B has recognized capital gains of $5,000. On December 15, 1971, through an agent in the United States B sells a capital asset on the installment plan, no payments being made by the purchaser in 1971. During 1972, B receives installment payments of $50,000 on the installment sale made in 1971, and the capital gain from sources within the United States for 1972 attributable to such payments is $12,500. In addition, during the period from January 1, 1972, to May 31, 1972, B effects for his own account, through an agent in the United States, a number of transactions in stocks and securities on the stock exchange, as a result of which B has recognized capital gains of $20,000. At no time during 1972 is B present in the United States or engaged in trade or business in the United States. Accordingly, for 1971, B is subject to tax under section 871(a)(2) on his capital gains of $15,000 from the transactions in that year on the stock exchange. For 1972, B is not subject to tax on the capital gain of $12,500 from the installment sale in 1971 or on the capital gains of $20,000 from the transactions in 1972 on the stock exchange.

Example 2. The facts are the same as in example 1 except that B is present in the United States from June 15, 1972, to December 31, 1972, a period of more than 182 days. Accordingly, B is subject to tax under section 871(a)(2) for 1971 on his capital gains of $15,000 from the transactions in that year on the stock exchange. He is also subject to tax under section 871(a)(2) for 1972 on his capital gains of $32,500 ($12,500 from the installment sale in 1971 plus $20,000 from the transactions in 1972 on the stock exchange).

Example 3. D, a nonresident alien individual not engaged in trade or business in the United States and using the calendar year as the taxable year, is present in the United States from April 1, 1971, to August 31, 1971, a period of less than 183 days. While present in the United States, D effects for his own account on various dates a number of transactions in stocks and securities on the stock exchange, as a result of which he has recognized capital gains of $15,000. During the period from January 1, 1971, to March 31, 1971, he carries out similar transactions through an agent in the United States, as a result of which D has recognized capital gains of $8,000. On December 20, 1971, through an agent in the United States D sells a capital asset on the installment plan, no payments being made by the purchaser in 1971. During 1972, D receives installment payments of $200,000 on the installment sale made in 1971, and the capital gain from sources within the United States for 1972 attributable to such payments is $50,000. In addition, during the period from February 1, 1972, to August 15, 1972, a period of more than 182 days. D effects for his own account, through an agent in the United States, a number of transactions in stocks and securities on the stock exchange, as a result of which D has recognized capital gains of $25,000.

At no time during 1972 is D present in the United States or engaged in trade or business in the United States. Accordingly, D is not subject to tax for 1971 or 1972 on any of his recognized capital gains.

Example 4. The facts are the same as in example 3 except that D is present in the United States from February 1, 1972, to August 15, 1972, a period of more than 182 days. Accordingly, D is not subject to tax for 1971 on his capital gains of $23,000 from the transactions in that year on the stock exchange. For 1972 he is subject to tax under section 871(a)(2) on his capital gains of $25,000 from the transactions in that year on the stock exchange, but he is not subject to the tax on the capital gain of $50,000 from the installment sale in 1971.

(3) Determination of 183-day period--(i) In general. In determining the total period of presence in the United States for a taxable year for purposes of subparagraph (2) of this paragraph, all separate periods of presence in the United States during the taxable year are to be aggregated. If the nonresident alien individual has not previously established a taxable year, as defined in section 441(b), he shall be treated as having a taxable year which is the calendar year, as defined in section 441(d). Subsequent adoption by such individual of a fiscal year as the taxable year will be treated as a change in the taxpayer's annual accounting period to which section 442 applies, and the change must be authorized under this part (Income Tax Regulations) or prior approval must be obtained by filing an application on Form 1128 in accordance with paragraph (b) of Sec. 1.442-1. If in the course of his taxable year the nonresident alien individual changes his status from that of a citizen or resident of the United States to that of a nonresident alien individual, or vice versa, the determination of whether the individual has been present in the United States for 183 days or more during the taxable year shall be made by taking into account the entire taxable year, and not just that part of the taxable year during which he has the status of a nonresident alien individual.

(ii) Definition of "day". The term "day", as used in subparagraph (2) of this paragraph, means a calendar day during any portion of which the nonresident alien individual is physically present in the United States (within the meaning of sections 7701(a)(9) and 638) except that, in the case of an individual who is a resident of Canada or Mexico and, in the normal course of his employment in transportation service touching points within both Canada or Mexico and the United States, performs personal services in both the foreign country and the United States, the following rules shall apply:

(a) The performance of labor or personal services during 8 hours or more in any 1 day within the United States shall be considered as 1 day in the United States, except that if a period of more or less than 8 hours is considered a full workday in the transportation job involved, such period shall be considered as 1 day within the United States.

(b) The performance of labor or personal services during less than 8 hours in any day in the United States shall, except as provided in (a) of this subdivision, be considered as a fractional part of a day in the United States. The total number of hours during which such services are performed in the United States during the taxable year, when divided by eight, shall be the number of days during which such individual shall be considered present in the United States during the taxable year.

(c) The aggregate number of days determined under (a) and (b) of this subdivision shall be considered the total number of days during which such individual is present in the United States during the taxable year.

(4) Determination of amount of excess gains--(i) In general. For the purpose of determining the excess of gains over losses subject to tax under this paragraph, gains and losses shall be taken into account only if, and to the extent that, they would be recognized and taken into account if the nonresident alien individual were engaged in trade or business in the United States during the taxable year and such gains and losses were effectively connected for such year with the conduct of a trade or business in the United States by such individual. However, in determining such excess of gains over losses no deduction may be taken under section 1202, relating to the deduction for capital gains, or section 1212, relating to the capital loss carryover. Thus, for example, in determining such excess gains all amounts considered under chapter 1 of the Code as gains or losses from the sale or exchange of capital assets shall be taken into account, except those gains which are described in section 871(a)(1) (B) or (D) and taken into account under paragraph (c) of this section and are considered to be gains from the sale or exchange of capital assets. Also, for example, a loss described in section 631 (b) or (c) which is considered to be a loss from the sale of a capital asset shall be taken into account in determining the excess gains which are subject to tax under this paragraph. In further illustration, in determining such excess gains no deduction shall be allowed, pursuant to the provisions of section 267, for losses from sales or exchanges of property between related taxpayers. Any gains which are taken into account under section 871(a)(1) and paragraph (c) of this section shall not be taken into account in applying section 1231 for purposes of this paragraph. Gains and losses are to be taken into account under this paragraph whether they are short-term or long-term capital gains or losses within the meaning of section 1222.

(ii) Gains not included. The provisions of this paragraph do not apply to any gains described in section 871(a)(1) (B) or (D), and in subdivision (i), (iii), or (iv) of paragraph (c)(1) of this section, which are considered to be gains from the sale or exchange of capital assets.

(iii) Allowance of losses. In determining the excess of gains over losses subject to tax under this paragraph losses shall be allowed only to the extent provided by section 165(c). Losses from sales or exchanges of capital assets in excess of gains from sales or exchanges of capital assets shall not be taken into account.

(e) Credits against tax. The credits allowed by section 31 (relating to tax withheld on wages), by section 32 (relating to tax withheld at source on nonresident aliens), by section 39 (relating to certain uses of gasoline and lubricating oil), and by section 6402 (relating to overpayments of tax) shall be allowed against the tax of a nonresident alien individual determined in accordance with this section.

(f) Effective date. Except as otherwise provided in this paragraph, this section shall apply for taxable years beginning after December 31, 1966. Paragraph (b)(2) of this section is applicable to payments made after November 13, 1997. For corresponding rules applicable to taxable years beginning before January 1, 1967, see 26 CFR 1.871-7 (b) and (c) (Revised as of January 1, 1971).

[T.D. 7332, 39 FR 44219, Dec. 23, 1974, as amended by T.D. 8734, 62 FR 53416, Oct. 14, 1997; T.D. 8735, 62 FR 53501, Oct. 14, 1997]

[Code of Federal Regulations]
[Title 26, Volume 9]
[Revised as of April 1, 2004]
From the U.S. Government Printing Office via GPO Access
[CITE: 26CFR1.872-1]

[Page 360-361]

TITLE 26--INTERNAL REVENUE

CHAPTER I--INTERNAL REVENUE SERVICE, DEPARTMENT OF THE
TREASURY (CONTINUED)

PART 1_INCOME TAXES--Table of Contents

Sec. 1.872-1 Gross income of nonresident alien individuals.

See Sec. 864, IRC 7, 8, Definition 5

(a) In general--(1) Inclusions. The gross income of a nonresident alien individual for any taxable year includes only (i) the gross income which is derived from sources within the United States and which is not effectively connected for the taxable year with the conduct of a trade or business in the United States by that individual and (ii) the gross income, irrespective of whether such income is derived from sources within or without the United States, which is effectively connected for the taxable year with the conduct of a trade or business in the United States by that individual. For the determination of the sources of income, see sections 861 through 863 and the regulations thereunder. For the determination of whether income from sources within or without the United States is effectively connected for the taxable year with the conduct of a trade or business in the United States, see sections 864(c) and 871 (c) and (d), Sec. Sec. 1.864-3 through 1.864-7, and Sec. Sec. 1.871-9 and 1.871-10. For special rules for determining the income of an alien individual who changes his residence during the taxable year, see Sec. 1.871-13.

(2) Exchange transactions. Even though a nonresident alien individual who effects certain transactions in the United States in stocks, securities, or commodities during the taxable year may not, by reason of section 864(b)(2) and paragraph (c) or (d) of Sec. 1.864-2, be engaged in trade or business in the United States during the taxable year through the effecting of such transactions, nevertheless he shall be required to include in gross income for the taxable year the gains and profits from those transactions to the extent required by Sec. 1.871-7 or Sec. 1.871-8.

(3) Exclusions. For exclusions from gross income, see Sec. 1.872-2.

(b) Individuals not engaged in U.S. business. In the case of a nonresident alien individual who at no time during the taxable year is

See Sec.
871, IRC 9-
11, Courts
7,
Definition 5

engaged in trade or business in the United States, the gross income shall include only (1) the gross income from sources within the United States which is described in section 871(a) and paragraphs (b), (c), and (d) of Sec. 1.871-7, and (2) the gross income from sources within the United States which, by reason of section 871 (c) or (d) and Sec. 1.871-9 or Sec. 1.871-10, is treated as effectively connected for the taxable year with the conduct of a trade or business in the United States by that individual.

(c) Individuals engaged in U.S. business. In the case of a nonresident alien individual who is engaged in trade or business in the United States at any time during the taxable year, the gross

See Sec.
864, IRC 7,
8,
Definition 5

income shall include (1) the gross income from sources within and without the United States which is effectively connected for the taxable year with the conduct of a trade or business in the United States by that individual, (2) the gross income from sources within the United States which, by reason of the election provided in section 871(d) and Sec. 1.871-10, is treated as effectively connected for the taxable year with the conduct of a trade or business in the United States by that individual, and (3) the gross income from sources within the United States which is described in section 871(a) and paragraphs (b), (c), and (d) of Sec. 1.871-7 and is not effectively connected for the taxable year with the conduct of a trade or business in the United States by that individual.

(d) Special rules applicable to certain expatriates. For special rules for determining the gross income of a nonresident alien individual who has lost U.S. citizenship with a principal purpose of avoiding certain taxes, see section 877(b)(1).

(e) Alien resident of Puerto Rico. This section shall not apply in the case of a nonresident alien individual who is a bona fide resident of Puerto Rico during the entire taxable year. See section 876 and Sec. 1.876-1.

(f) Effective date. This section shall apply for taxable years beginning after December 31, 1966. For corresponding rules applicable to taxable years beginning before January 1, 1967, see 26 CFR 1.872-1 (Revised as of January 1, 1971).

[T.D. 6500, 25 FR 11910, Nov. 26, 1960, as amended by T.D. 7332, 39 FR 44228, Dec. 23, 1974]

[Code of Federal Regulations]
[Title 26, Volume 9]
[Revised as of April 1, 2004]
From the U.S. Government Printing Office via GPO Access
[CITE: 26CFR1.872-2]

[Page 361-363]

TITLE 26--INTERNAL REVENUE

CHAPTER I--INTERNAL REVENUE SERVICE, DEPARTMENT OF THE
TREASURY (CONTINUED)

PART 1_INCOME TAXES--Table of Contents

Sec. 1.872-2 Exclusions from gross income of nonresident alien individuals.

...

See Sec. 864, 871, IRC 7-9

See Part II, Sec. 3121, IRC 3, 14, 1.1402(b)-1, CFR 38, Definition 5

(f) Other exclusions. **Income which is from sources without the United States, as determined under the provisions of sections 861 through 863, and the regulations thereunder, is not included in the gross income of a nonresident alien individual unless such income is effectively connected for the taxable year with the conduct of a trade or business in the United States by that individual.** To determine specific exclusions in the case of other items which are from sources within the United States, see the applicable sections of the Code. For special rules under a tax convention for determining the sources of income and for excluding, from gross income, income from sources without the United States which is effectively connected with the conduct of a trade or business in the United States, see the applicable tax convention. For determining which income from sources without the United States is effectively connected with the conduct of a trade or business in the United States, see section 864(c)(4) and Sec. 1.864-5....

[Code of Federal Regulations]
[Title 26, Volume 10]
[Revised as of April 1, 2005]
From the U.S. Government Printing Office via GPO Access
[CITE: 26CFR1.911-2]

[Page 9-12]

TITLE 26--INTERNAL REVENUE

CHAPTER I--INTERNAL REVENUE SERVICE, DEPARTMENT OF THE
TREASURY (CONTINUED)

PART 1_INCOME TAXES--Table of Contents

Sec. 1.911-2 Qualified individuals*.

...

See
Sec.
7701,
3121,
3306,
4612,
IRC 11,
12, 16,
17

**(g) United States. The term "United States" when used in a
geographical sense includes any territory under the sovereignty of
the United States. It includes the states, the District of Columbia, the
possessions and territories of the United States,** the territorial waters
of the United States, the air space over the United States, and the seabed
and subsoil of those submarine areas which are adjacent to the territorial
waters of the United States and over which the United States has
exclusive rights, in accordance with international law, with respect to the
exploration and exploitation of natural resources.

[*Pertains to individuals qualified by bona fide foreign country tax home in
conjunction with U. S. citizenship and/or residency to elect to exclude the
individual's foreign earned income and the housing cost amount from the
individual's gross income for the taxable year.]

[Code of Federal Regulations]
[Title 26, Volume 12]
[Revised as of April 1, 2005]
From the U.S. Government Printing Office via GPO Access
[CITE: 26CFR1.1402(b)-1]

[Page 28-30]

TITLE 26--INTERNAL REVENUE

CHAPTER I--INTERNAL REVENUE SERVICE, DEPARTMENT OF THE TREASURY (CONTINUED)

PART 1_INCOME TAXES--Table of Contents

Sec. 1.1402(b)-1 Self-employment income.

(a) In general. Except for the exclusions in paragraphs (b) and (c) of this section and the exception in paragraph (d) of this section, the term "self-employment income" means the net earnings from self-employment derived by an individual during a taxable year.

(b) Maximum self-employment income--(1) General rule. Subject to the special rules described in subparagraph (2) of this paragraph, the maximum self-employment income of an individual for a taxable year (whether a period of 12 months or less) is:

(i) For any taxable year beginning in a calendar year after 1974, an amount equal to the contribution and benefit base (as determined under section 230 of the Social Security Act) which is effective for such calendar year; and

(ii) For any taxable year:

Ending before 1955	$3,600
Ending after 1954 and before 1959	4,200
Ending after 1958 and before 1966	4,800
Ending after 1965 and before 1968	6,600
Ending after 1967 and beginning before 1972	7,800
Beginning after 1971 and before 1973	9,000
Beginning after 1972 and before 1974	10,800
Beginning after 1973 and before 1975	13,200

(2) Special rules. (i) If an individual is paid wages as defined in subparagraph (3) of this paragraph in a taxable year, the maximum self-employment income for such taxable year is computed as provided in subdivision (ii) or (iii) of this subparagraph.

(ii) If an individual is paid wages as defined in subparagraph (3) (i) or (ii) of this paragraph in a taxable year, the maximum self-employment income of such individual for such taxable year is the excess of the amounts indicated in subparagraph (1) of this paragraph over the amount of the wages, as defined in subparagraph (3) (i) and (ii) of this paragraph, paid to him during the taxable year. For example, if for his taxable year beginning in 1974, an individual has $15,000 of net earnings from self-employment and during such taxable year is paid $1,000 of wages as defined in section 3121(a) (see subparagraph (3)(i) of this paragraph), he has $12,200 ($13,200 -$1,000) of self-employment income for the taxable year.

(iii) For taxable years ending on or after December 31, 1968, wages, as defined in subparagraph (3)(iii) of this paragraph, are taken into account in determining the maximum self-employment income of an individual for purposes of the tax imposed under section 1401(b) (hospital insurance), but not for purposes of the tax imposed under section 1401(a) (old-age survivors, and disability insurance). If an individual is paid wages as defined in subparagraph (3)(iii) of this paragraph in a taxable year, his maximum self-employment income for such taxable year for purposes of the tax imposed under section 1401(a) is computed under subparagraph (1) of this paragraph or subdivision (ii) of this subparagraph (whichever is applicable), and his maximum self-employment income for such taxable year for purposes of the tax imposed under section 1401(b) is the excess of his section 1401(a) maximum self-employment income over the amount of wages, as defined in subparagraph (3)(iii) of this paragraph, paid to him during the taxable year. For purposes of this subdivision, wages as defined in subparagraph (3)(iii) of this paragraph are deemed paid to an individual in the period with respect to which the payment is made, that is, the period in which the compensation was earned or deemed earned within the meaning of section 3231(e). For an explanation of the term "compensation" and for provisions relating to when compensation is earned, see the regulations under section 3231(e) in part 31 of this chapter (Employment Tax Regulations). The application of the rules set forth in this subdivision may be illustrated by the following example:

Example. M, a calendar-year taxpayer, has $15,000 of net earnings from self-employment for 1974 and during the taxable year is paid $1,000 of wages as defined in section 3121(a) (see subparagraph (3)(i) of this paragraph) and $1,600 of compensation subject to tax under section 3201 (see subparagraph (3)(iii) of this paragraph). Of the $1,600 of taxable compensation, $1,200 represents compensation for services rendered in 1974 and the balance ($400) represents compensation which pursuant to the provisions of section 3231(e) is earned or deemed earned in 1973. M's maximum self-employment income for 1974 for purposes of the tax imposed under section 1401(a), computed as provided in subdivision (ii) of this subparagraph, is $12,200 ($13,200-$1,000), and for purposes of the tax imposed under section 1401(b) is $11,000 ($12,200-$1,200). However, M may recompute his maximum self-employment income for 1973 for purposes of the tax imposed under section 1401(b) by taking into account the $400 of compensation which is deemed paid in 1973.

See Sec. 3121, IRC 14

(3) Meaning of term "wages". For the purpose of the computation described in subparagraph (2) of this paragraph, the term "wages" includes:

(i) Wages as defined in section 3121(a);

(ii) Such remuneration paid to an employee for services covered by:

(a) An agreement entered into pursuant to section 218 of the Social Security Act (42 U.S.C. 418), which section provides for extension of the Federal old-age, survivors and disability insurance system to State and local government employees under voluntary agreements between the States and the Secretary of Health, Education, and Welfare (Federal Security Administrator before April 11, 1953), or

(b) An agreement entered into pursuant to the provisions of section 3121(1), relating to coverage of citizens of the United States who are employees of foreign subsidiaries of domestic corporations, as would be wages under section 3121(a) if such services constituted employment under section 3121(b). For an explanation of the term "wages", see the regulations under section 3121(a) in part 31 of this chapter (Employment Tax Regulations); and

(iii) Compensation, as defined in section 3231(e), which is subject to the employee tax imposed by section 3201 or the employee representative tax imposed by section 3211.

(c) Minimum net earnings from self-employment. Self-employment income does not include the net earnings from self-employment of an individual when the amount of such earnings for the taxable year is less than $400. Thus, an individual having only $300 of net earnings from self-employment for the taxable year would not have any self-employment income. However, an individual having net earnings from self-employment of $400 or more for the taxable year may, by application of paragraph (b)(2) of this section, have less than $400 of self-employment income for purposes of the tax imposed under section 1401(a) and the tax imposed under section 1401(b) or may have self-employment income of $400 or more for purposes of the tax imposed under section 1401(a) and of less than $400 for purposes of the tax imposed under section 1401(b). This could occur in a case in which the amount of the individual's net earnings from self-employment is $400 or more for a taxable year and the amount of such net earnings from self-employment plus the amount of wages, as defined in paragraph (b)(3) of this section, paid to him during the taxable year exceed the maximum self-employment income, as set forth in paragraph (b)(1) of this section, for the taxable year. However, the result occurs only if such maximum self-employment income exceeds the amount of such wages. The application of this paragraph may be illustrated by the following example:

Example. For 1974 M, a calendar-year taxpayer, has net earnings from self-employment of $2,000 and wages (as defined in paragraph (b)(3) (i) and (ii) of this section) of $12,500. Since M's net earnings from self-employment plus his wages exceed the maximum self-employment income for 1974 ($13,200), his self-employment income for 1974 is $700 ($13,200-$12,500). If M also had wages, as defined in paragraph (b)(3)(iii) of this section, of $200, his self-employment income would be $700 for purposes of the tax imposed under section 1401(a) and $500 ($13,200-$12,700 ($12,500+$200)) for purposes of the tax imposed under section 1401(b).

For provisions relating to when wages as defined in paragraph (b)(3)(iii) of this section are treated as paid, see paragraph (b)(2)(iii) of this section.

See Sec. 872, IRC 11, Definition 5

(d) Nonresident aliens. A nonresident alien individual never has self-employment income. While a nonresident alien individual who derives income from a trade or business carried on within the United States, Puerto Rico, the Virgin Islands, Guam, or American Samoa (whether by agents or employees, or by a partnership of which he is a member) may be subject to the applicable income tax provisions on such income, such nonresident alien individual will not be subject to the tax on self-employment income, since any net earnings which he may have from self-employment do not constitute self-employment income. For the purpose of the tax on self-employment income, an individual who is not a citizen of the United States but who is a resident of the Commonwealth of Puerto Rico, the Virgin Islands, or, for taxable years beginning after 1960, of Guam or American Samoa is not considered to be a nonresident alien individual.

[T.D. 6691, 28 FR 12796, Dec. 3, 1963, as amended by T.D. 7333, 39 FR 44447, Dec. 24, 1974]

[Code of Federal Regulations]
[Title 26, Volume 18]
[Revised as of April 1, 2004]
From the U.S. Government Printing Office via GPO Access
[CITE: 26CFR301.6203-1]

[Page 155]

TITLE 26--INTERNAL REVENUE

CHAPTER I--INTERNAL REVENUE SERVICE, DEPARTMENT OF THE TREASURY (CONTINUED)

PART 301_PROCEDURE AND ADMINISTRATION--Table of Contents

Assessment

Sec. 301.6203-1 Method of assessment.

The district director and the director of the regional service center shall appoint one or more assessment officers. The district director shall also appoint assessment officers in a Service Center servicing his district. **The assessment shall be made by an assessment officer signing the summary record of assessment.** The summary record, through supporting records, shall provide identification of the taxpayer, the character of the liability assessed, the taxable period, if applicable, and the amount of the assessment. The amount of the assessment shall, in the case of tax shown on a return by the taxpayer, be the amount so shown, and in all other cases the amount of the assessment shall be the amount shown on the supporting list or record. The date of the assessment is the date the summary record is signed by an assessment officer. **If the taxpayer requests a copy of the record of assessment, he shall be furnished a copy of the pertinent parts of the assessment which set forth the name of the taxpayer, the date of assessment, the character of the liability assessed, the taxable period, if applicable, and the amounts assessed.**

Appendix F: The Courts

1. "The revenue laws are a code or system in regulation of tax assessment and collection. They relate to taxpayers, and not to nontaxpayers. The latter are without their scope. No procedure is prescribed for nontaxpayers, and no attempt is made to annul any of their rights and remedies in due course of law. With them Congress does not assume to deal, and they are neither of the subject nor of the object of the revenue laws."
Economy Plumbing and Heating Co. v. United States, 470 F. 2d 585 (1972)

2. "Liability for taxation must clearly appear from statute imposing tax."
Higley v. Commissioner, 69 F.2d 160

3. "The taxpayer must be liable for the tax. Tax liability is a condition precedent to the demand. Merely demanding payment, even repeatedly, does not cause liability."
Booth v. Terry, 713 F.2d 1405, at 1414 (1983)

4. "Taxes should be exacted only from persons upon whom a tax liability is imposed by some statute."
The 2nd Circuit in *Botta v. Scanlon* 288 F.2d 504 (1961)

5. "'Anyone may so arrange his affairs so that his taxes shall be as low as possible. He is not bound to choose that pattern which best pays the treasury. There is not even a patriotic duty to increase one's taxes.' Over and over again the courts have said that there is nothing sinister in so arraigning affairs as to keep taxes as low as possible, everyone does it, rich and poor alike and all do RIGHT, for nobody owes the public duty to pay more than the law demands."—Weeks v Sibley; Edwards v. Commissioner; Helvering v. Gregory; and 60 Federal 2nd 809, United States Supreme Court Justice Learned Hand (1872-1961).

6. "In the interpretation of statutes levying taxes it is the established rule not to extend their provisions, by implication, beyond the clear import of the language used, or to enlarge their operations so as to embrace matters not specifically pointed out. In case of doubt they are construed most strongly against the government, and in favor of the citizen." Supreme Court - Gould v. Gould 245 U.S. 151 (1917); United States v. Wigglesworth, 2 Story, 369, Fed. Cas. No. 16, 690; American Net & Twine Co. v. Worthington, 141 U.S. 468, 474, 12 S. Sup. Ct. 55; Benziger v. United States, 192 U.S. 38, 55, 24 S. Sup. Ct. 189.

7. "The laws of Congress in respect to those matters do not extend into the territorial limits of the states, but have force only in the District of Columbia, and other places that are within the exclusive jurisdiction of the national government."
Caha v. United States, 152 U.S. 211, 215, 14 S. Ct. 513 (1894)

8. "Includes is a term of limitation....is a term to indicate restriction rather than enlargement." Powers ex re. Covon v. Charron R.I., 135 A. 2nd 829, 832.

9. "The IRS is to comply strictly to the conditions imposed by statute in the seizure and levy process." Goodwin v. United States, 935 F.2d 1061, (9th Cir. 1991)

10. "It is well established in law that in order to have a valid sale, there must be a valid seizure, and to have a valid seizure, there must be a valid lien …. There must be a signed 23C and a Form 4340 before there is a valid assessment."
Coplin v. U. S., 952 F.2d 403, Fullmer v. U. S., 93-U.S. Tax Case, P 50, 657, U. S. v. McCallum, 976 F.2d 66, Brewer v. U. S., 746 F. Supp. 309, Geiselman v. U. S., 961 F.2d 1, Tweedy v. U. S., 74 AFTR 2d 5003, Fisher v. U. S., 860 F. Supp. 680

11. "However, there is no indication in the record before us that the 'Summary Record of Assessments,' known as Form 23C, was completed and signed by the assessment officer as required by 26 CFR 301.6203-1.3.
Nor do the Certificates of Assessments and Payments contain 23C dates which would allow us to conclude that a Form 23C form was signed on that date. See United States v. Dixon, 672 F. Supp. 503, 505-506 (M.D. Ala. 1987)
Thus we find that the plaintiff has raised a factual question concerning whether IRS procedures were followed in making the assessments …."
Brewer v. U.S., 764 F. Supp. 309 (S.D.N.Y. 1991)

12. "Silence can be equated with fraud where there is a legal or moral duty to speak, or where an inquiry left unanswered would be intentionally misleading …. We cannot condone this shocking behavior by the IRS. Our revenue system is based on the good faith of the taxpayer and the taxpayer should be able to expect the same from the government in its enforcement and collection activities."
U. S. v. Tweel, 550 F. 2d 297, 299. See also U. S. v. Prudden, 424 F.2d, 1021, 1032; Carmine v. Bowen, 64 A. 932.

13. "The IRS cannot sue anyone and they are not a branch of the federal government."
U. S. v. Sylvester A. Ziebarth & Rusel J. Jagim, CR 90-50040

14. "The United States of America, through undersigned counsel, hereby responds to the numbered paragraphs of plaintiff's complaint as follows:
…
4. Denies that the Internal Revenue Service is an agency of the United States Government but admits that the United States of America would be a proper party to the action."—Diversified Metal Products, Inc. v. T-Bow Company Trust, Internal Revenue Service, and Steve Morgan, Civil No. 93-105-E-EJL

15. "Only the rare taxpayer would be likely to know that he could refuse to produce his records to the IRS agents…. Who would believe the ironic truth that the cooperative taxpayer fares far worse than the individual who relies upon his constitutional rights."
US v. Dickerson, 413 F.2d 1111, (1969)

16. "In numerous cases where the IRS has sought enforcement of its summons pursuant to statute, courts have held that a taxpayer may refuse production of personal books and records by assertion of his privilege against self-incrimination." Hill v. Philpott, 445 F.2d 144, 146

17. "Because of what appears to be a lawful command on the surface, many Citizens, because of their respect for what appears to be law, are cunningly coerced into waiving their rights due to ignorance."—United States Supreme Court, U.S. v. Minker (1950)

18. "Fraud destroys the validity of everything into which it enters," *Nudd v. Burrows,* 91 U.S. 426.

19. "Fraud vitiates everything," *Boyce v. Grundy,* 3 Pet. 210.

20. "Fraud vitiates the most solemn contracts, documents and even judgments," *U.S. v. Throckmorton,* 98 U.S. 61.

21. "The individual may stand upon his constitutional rights as a Citizen. He is entitled to carry on his private business in his own way. His power to contract is unlimited."—United States Supreme Court, *Hale v. Henkle,* 201 US 43.

Appendix G: Lack of Authority Delegation

The following summarizes Irwin Schiff's arguments of fraud and lack of jurisdiction:

1. The IRS is not mentioned[1] in Subtitle A of the IRC.
2. The Secretary of the Treasury has never delegated authority to the Commissioner of Internal Revenue to assess or forcibly collect income taxes, and the government lacks proof of any such delegation. The IRS has never been given any statutory authority to ascertain, compute, assess, or collect income taxes—such functions have never been given to the IRS by any law. The IRC gives the Secretary of the Treasury sole authority[2] to assess and forcibly collect internal revenue taxes.
   a. The Secretary must in turn delegate authority to the Commissioner of Internal Revenue who must in turn delegate authority to lower-level IRS employees before any such employee may assess and forcibly collect internal revenue taxes. Since the Secretary of the Treasury has never delegated authority to the Commissioner of Internal Revenue to assess or forcibly collect income taxes, lawful authority has never be delegated to lower-level IRS employees.
   b. Such delegation of authority by the Secretary to the Commissioner must be in the form of a Delegation Order that must be published in the Federal Register. Such delegation has never been published in the Federal Register, and the government lacks proof of any such publication.
   c. Delegation of authority by the Commissioner of Internal Revenue to lower-level IRS employees must be in the form of (1) a "delegation order," (2) Treasury Department regulations (which also support and confirm delegation orders), (3) job descriptions, and (4) pocket commissions. No IRS special agent or revenue officer has ever been given any authority by any (1) Treasury Department regulation, (2) job description, or (3) pocket commission allowing the enforcement of the payment of income taxes by levy, and the government lacks refuting documentation.
3. Furthermore, the IRC, at Chapter 63, Subchapter A, Section 6201, states:
   Section 6201. Assessment authority
     (a) Authority of Secretary
        The Secretary is authorized and required to make the inquiries, determinations, and assessments of all taxes (including interest, additional amounts, additions to the tax, and assessable penalties) imposed by this title, or accruing under any former internal revenue law, which have not been duly paid by stamp at the time and in the manner provided by law....
   Statutorily, then, the Secretary of the Treasury is solely authorized to assess those federal taxes that "have not been duly paid by stamp," not federal income taxes[3] since such are not paid by stamp.

[1] The IRC first mentions the IRS at §6404 (Subtitle F).
[2] The Commissioner of Internal Revenue had such directly conferred authority before Congress aligned the Code of 1954 with the Constitution and early Supreme Court decisions.
[3] Schiff points out that "Since the Code 'knows' that the income tax is not imposed pursuant to any of Congress' constitutional powers to 'lay and collect taxes' … the Code, understandably, denied conferring any power to the Secretary to assess a tax which is not imposed pursuant to those constitutional powers. This is why the Code does not contain any provision making anyone 'liable' for income taxes or requiring anyone 'to pay' such an alleged tax." [See http://www.paynoincometax.com/ for full details.]

4. Furthermore, implementing regulations for § 6201 and others are found only in 27 CFR (relating to alcohol, tobacco and firearms), not in 26 CFR, which prevents the Secretary from delegating authority to the IRS to assess income taxes. Accordingly, since the Secretary has never been given statutory authority to assess income taxes, all IRS income tax assessments against Schiff have been illegal and unauthorized by law. The "notice and demand" for payment, required by IRC §§ 6303, 6321 and 6331, which must be sent out "within 60 days, after the making of an assessment" can never legally be sent out with respect to income taxes since such a demand[1] can be made only by following a lawful assessment.

   a. Schiff says that "Since no 'notice and demand' for the payment of income taxes can lawfully be made, no IRS agent can lawfully seize property in payment of income taxes, since Section 6331 makes all tax seizures dependant on: (1) the existence of a tax 'liability,' and (2) a failure to pay the tax 'within 10 days after notice and demand.' Based on all of the above, it is clear that all of the income tax assessments (and penalties) which were made against Defendant for the years 1979 - 1985 were made illegally."

   b. Schiff says that "In addition, since Defendant was never sent the statutory 'notice and demand' for payment of any taxes allegedly due for the years 1979 - 1985 (as identified in Treasury Decision 1995), he could not have sought to 'evade and defeat' such taxes as alleged in count 17 because (1) they were never lawfully assessed; and (2) they were never lawfully 'demanded.'"

   c. Schiff says, furthermore, that "both I.R.S. special agents and revenue officers must fall into subsection (a) of Code Section 7608. (Magistrate-Judge Leavitt **already agrees** … that special agents fall into 7608(a))…. [A]s such, if they have any enforcement authority at all, it can only apply for the 'Enforcement of subtitle E and other laws pertaining to liquor, tobacco, and firearms'—but not to income taxes. And revenue officers must also fall into this subsection, so they **too** can only be authorized to enforce subtitle E taxes and 'other laws pertaining to liquor, tobacco, and firearms'—but not to income taxes."

5. The US District Court has no subject matter jurisdiction to hear the case since § 7402(f) provides for civil jurisdiction, not criminal. Title 8 § 1329 specifically provides for both criminal and civil jurisdiction in connection with that Title, so Congress knows how to do the same if it intended federal courts to have both kinds of jurisdiction in connection with Title 26. Additionally, expressio unius exclusio alterius (The express mention of one thing implies the exclusion of others).

Despite mountains of evidence in favor of Mr. Schiff, U.S. District Court Judge Kent Dawson completely railroaded Mr. Schiff recently (Dawson's activity highlighted at http://www.givemeliberty.org/RTPLawsuit/Misc/SCHIFF-Criminal-Dawson.pdf). To view the rest of the filings related to Mr. Schiff's case, click on the listed links at http://www.givemeliberty.org/RTPLawsuit/Update2005-10-31.htm#links.

---

[1]Schiff points out that "Since the income tax 'laws' themselves are lawfully written … a 'notice and demand' for payment is **never** sent out. Why would the 'law' allow the government to 'demand' payment of a tax that the 'law' itself: (1) does not allow to be assessed; (2) makes no one 'liable' to pay; and (3) makes impossible to derive from 'income' it makes sure no one can ever receive? As identified in Treasury Decision 1995, the statutory notice and demand for payment is IRS Form 17—and that form is never sent out by the IRS. Since Treasury Decision 1995 has never been revoked or replaced, IRS Form 17 still remains the statutory 'notice and demand' for payment called for by such statutes as 6303, 6321, and 6332. However, the IRS never sends out the statutory 'notice and demand' for payment—for reasons already explained." [See http://www.paynoincometax.com/ for full details.]

Appendix H: Resources

Banister, Joseph R., CPA
> http://www.freedomabovefortune.com/
> http://joebanister.blogspot.com/

Benson, Bill
> http://www.thelawthatneverwas.com/

Code of Federal Regulations
> http://www.access.gpo.gov/nara/cfr/cfr-table-search.html

Great IRS Hoax: Why We Don't Owe Income Tax [an *exhaustive* report]
> http://famguardian.org/Publications/GreatIRSHoax/GreatIRSHoax.htm

Griffin, G. Edward: *The Creature from Jekyll Island*
> http://www.wealth4freedom.com/creature.htm

Info Please: Internal Revenue Service Statistics
> http://www.infoplease.com/ipa/A0005923.html

Internal Revenue Code
> http://caselaw.lp.findlaw.com/casecode/uscodes/26/toc.html
> http://www4.law.cornell.edu/uscode/html/uscode26/usc_sup_01_26.html

Internal Revenue Manual
> http://www.irs.gov/irm/index.html

Internal Revenue Service
> http://www.irs.gov
> http://www.irs.gov/pub/irs-soi/03in11si.xls

Kidd, Devy: *Why an Income Tax is Not Necessary to Fund the U.S. Government*
> http://www.devvy.com/notax.html

Schauf, Tom, CPA (retired):
> *America's Hope To Cancel Bank Loans Without Going To Court*
> http://members.aol.com/rmckin6412/liberty/tom.htm

Schiff, Irwin
> http://www.paynoincometax.com/
> http://www.givemeliberty.org/RTPLawsuit/Update2005-10-31.htm#links

Treasury Inspector General for Tax Administration
> Call for confidential, anonymous registration of complaints of IRS employee
> misconduct, waste, fraud, or abuse: 800/366-4484 (800/877-8339 for TTY/TDD)

Truth About Frivolous Tax Arguments, The
       http://www.givemeliberty.org/RTPLawsuit/Documents/IRSfriv_tax.pdf
          http://www.irs.gov/pub/irs-utl/friv_tax.pdf US Code
     http://www4.law.cornell.edu/uscode/

US Constitution
     http://deoxy.org/law/consti.htm

War Resisters League: *The United States Federal Budget for Fiscal Year 2006:*
                    Where Your Income Tax Money Really Goes
     http://www.warresisters.org/piechart.htm

We The People Foundation
     http://www.givemeliberty.org/

Xtra information can be found at:
     http://famguardian.org/Subjects/Taxes/taxes.htm
     http://www.irs.faithweb.com/

Appendix H: Strategic Tax Planning Checklist

1. To verify the information* in this book visit **http://www.irs.faithweb.com/** and also these sites:

- **http://www.access.gpo.gov/uscode/uscmain.html** or **http://www.access.gpo.gov/nara/cfr/cfr-table-search.html** Page down and click on Title 26, then click on Subtitle A and Chapter 1 and Subchapter A and Part I and Sec. 1 to begin your search—also click on Chapter 1 Subchapter N and Part I and Sec. 861 as well as Subtitle E and Chapter 51 and Subchapter A and Part I and Subpart A and Secs. 5001 and 5005 and Subtitle E and Chapter 52 and Subchapter A and Secs. 5701 and 5703. **Code sections make up the law.**

- **http://www.gpoaccess.gov/ecfr/** Click the drop-down list arrow under Browse, click on Title 26, and click on the "Go" button. From the list, click on 1.851-1.907 and §1.861-8 to read the explanatory regulation of the associated code Section 861. **Regulations explain code sections.**

- **http://www.house.gov/Constitution/Constitution.html** This web page contains The Constitution for the United States of America. Page down to Article I, Section 8, Clause 1, and Section 9, Clause 4.

- **http://www.irs.gov/pub/irs-pdf/i1040.pdf** Page down to the page you wish to verify. You may also obtain a free copy of 2007 1040 Instructions by visiting your local library or post office or by requesting it directly from the IRS: 800/829-3676.

*Some of the information on this list may change periodically. If you experience any difficulty obtaining information, please e-mail mpllc@ymail.com, Attn: Checklist Update for an update.

- **http://www.usdoj.gov/04foia/privstat.htm** This web page displays the Privacy Act of 1974.

2. E-mail mpllc@ymail.com, Attn: Advance Training, for a Strategic Tax Planning contract for review and/or a free consultation and/or to schedule a 120-minute Strategic Tax Planning mini-seminar without cost or obligation (must have Internet access for optional video-supported teleconference).

3. Contribute your former tax costs to your existing retirement account. Contribute your former tax costs to a variable, variable universal, or index universal life insurance policy or annuity to generate permanently-tax-free interest that is never reported as taxable income unless the policy or annuity contract is cancelled. (Distribution of life insurance policy proceeds in the event of the death of the insured is as a death benefit and not as a surrender.) Borrow your interest and retire.